PROFESSIONAL COCOA® APPLICATION SECUR...

PROFESSIONAL

Cocoa® Application Security

PROFESSIONAL

Cocoa® Application Security

Graham J. Lee

Wiley Publishing, Inc.

Professional Cocoa® Application Security

Published by
Wiley Publishing, Inc.
10475 Crosspoint Boulevard
Indianapolis, IN 46256
www.wiley.com

ISBN: 978-0-470-52595-1

ISBN: 978-0-470-88704-2 (ebk)

ISBN: 978-0-470-88706-6 (ebk)

Manufactured in the United States of America

10 9 8 7 6 5 4 3 2 1

Library of Congress Control Number: 2010926599

ABOUT THE AUTHOR

GRAHAM J. LEE is an independent Mac, iPhone and iPad contract developer. He lives in Oxford, England with his girl friend and an ever-growing collection of vegetables. Graham maintains a security column for the Mac Developer Network, and discusses Cocoa security issues on the network's podcast, "The MDN Show."

He has spoken to conferences and university courses on security matters. He is also studying for a postgraduate qualification in software security from Oxford University. In his spare time, Graham tries to find out where all his spare time went.

ABOUT THE TECHNICAL EDITOR

JAMES LYNE is a security and technology strategist who grew up with technology (his first computer was a Mac!). Working with some of the world's largest and most paranoid enterprises to form security strategy, James has seen it all go wrong in detail. Coming from a background of mathematics and cryptography, he has a range of experience from detailed implementation to broad strategy. He holds a collection of qualifications and industry awards from a variety of institutes and also contributes heavily to education, presenting at open public forums on security challenges for the coming years.

CREDITS

ACQUISITIONS EDITOR
Scott Meyers

PROJECT EDITOR
William Bridges

TECHNICAL EDITOR
James Lyne

PRODUCTION EDITOR
Daniel Scribner

COPY EDITOR
Sadie Kleinman

EDITORIAL DIRECTOR
Robyn B. Siesky

EDITORIAL MANAGER
Mary Beth Wakefield

MARKETING MANAGER
David Mayhew

PRODUCTION MANAGER
Tim Tate

VICE PRESIDENT AND EXECUTIVE GROUP PUBLISHER
Richard Swadley

VICE PRESIDENT AND EXECUTIVE PUBLISHER
Barry Pruett

ASSOCIATE PUBLISHER
Jim Minatel

PROJECT COORDINATOR, COVER
Lynsey Stanford

COMPOSITOR
Craig Woods, Happenstance-Type-O-Rama

PROOFREADER
Nancy Bell

INDEXER
Robert Swanson

COVER DESIGN
Michael E. Trent

COVER IMAGE
© Duncan Walker/istockphoto

ACKNOWLEDGMENTS

THE MOST IMPORTANT CONTRIBUTION to this book, I must acknowledge, is from the Mac developer community. Thanks, everyone, for showing me that application security does need a champion, and for all your suggestions of topics to cover here and in the Mac Developer Network. Special mention and gratitude must go to Steve "Scotty" Scott for accepting that in lieu of a better option, I could be that champion.

Scott originally suggested that I write a book and James, Sadie and Bill all did a great job of beating my drafts into a publishable state: I'm very grateful to all of them. Of course, I assume full responsibility for any errors that snuck through. Finally, a developer is only as good as the caffeine that fuels him, so particular thanks are due to Freya for her fine supply of coffee and moral support.

CONTENTS

INTRODUCTION

THE WORLD IN WHICH WE USE TODAY'S IMACS AND MACBOOKS has little in common with the world of the first Macintosh computer Steve Jobs unveiled in 1984. The idea that everybody would be using a computer at home and at work — and indeed on the road — with permanent connections to the rest of the world via the Internet would have been thought out of the question back then. Forget completely the idea that people could carry full-featured computer/telephone/music player/camera devices in their jeans pockets. Or that you would be able to use your laptop or even your mobile phone to organize your finances with your bank, buy the latest movies, and get on with your work while away from the office. Taken to the extreme now, such technology is actually starting to provide dynamic connections between the digital and physical world — for example allowing you to photograph a physical object and associate it with online content such as a shop store or reviews. This is undoubtedly convenient, but it also brings new risks that were unheard of when the computers, their operating systems, and many of their applications were designed.

The organization Fight Identity Theft (`http://www.fightidentitytheft.com`) claims that identity theft cost 8.4 million Americans a total of $49.3 billion in 2008. The impact on any individual victim can be ruinous. As a result, this and other "cybercrimes" receive a lot of coverage in the media. It's reported frequently that a company or government department has leaked thousands of personal records; the hit the organization's reputation takes can easily be worse than the direct liability for the loss, such as government fines. Therefore, the total cost of the crime is unknown — businesses prefer not to disclose details unless obliged to, so we don't find exact figures for corporate identity theft. However, it is evident just from visible cases that the impact of such misconduct can be vast, and since the commercial world is increasingly underpinned by data as a key asset, security is high on the agenda of business risks.

Traditionally viruses, worms, and Trojan horses (collectively, "malware") have been seen by Mac users as Windows-only phenomena; they've quickly forgotten the Autostart problems of the 1990s and dismissed modern OS X malware as proof-of-concept or otherwise something that "real" Mac users need not worry about. Presumably the Mac malware infects only those machines owned by fake Mac owners, whoever they are. The reality is, of course, somewhat different from this simplistic picture. It's true that much less malicious software is known to target the Mac. But the way this software is sent to the victim's computer, the way the user is tricked into installing it, and the actions it takes once installed are the same on both platforms. Many attacks now involve a web server's detecting whether the user has a Mac or PC, and sending the appropriate malware in each case, as described in `http://blog.trendmicro.com/more-mac-malware-in-the-wild/`.

A successful attack does not need to start with the user's downloading a malicious application such as a Trojan horse. A whole class of "data-driven" attacks relies on being able to subvert a legitimate application to the attacker's ends by feeding it data that it cannot handle properly. A well-publicized example is one of the early "jail-breaking" tools for the iPhone, which used an error in the way Mobile Safari loaded TIFF images to cause Mobile Safari to run the jail-breaking code.

Then there are the more personal security compromises, which don't generate as many headlines or column inches as the big cybercrimes but nonetheless cause the victims to question their choice of applications and vendors. Finding that someone else has posted to the victim's Twitter account, or that his or her partner has been reading private e-mails or online banking statements, are examples of this form of attack.

Despite all these problems, there is no need to paint a picture of doom. If mitigating risk in software were a futile effort, there would be no need for the rest of this book. In Mac OS X and the iPhone OS, Apple has made a number of significant enhancements to the traditional UNIX platform design in order to improve its relevance in the 21st century. You, as a software developer working on those platforms, can easily spend some small amount of time on security considerations when designing your applications, which results in a big return for your users who receive a more secure product. You can identify the risks that will be present when the application is deployed to your users, and work to reduce the impact of those risks. The risks you deal with will be those that are relevant to the modern environment, with its modern threats; you don't need to (and indeed no longer can) rely on application conventions from the 1980s. You can develop your applications with an eye on security, so that they cannot be hijacked as they help their users communicate with people across the world. You can also communicate with your users in an open and honest manner, so that they understand the risks you're helping them to avoid, those risks you aren't, and the users' part in reducing all of them.

In Mac OS X and the iPhone OS, Apple has provided a number of APIs and security features that you can take advantage of in your applications to improve the security of those applications. Integrating with these features is as much a part of the overall user experience as is integration with "headline" features such as Spotlight or Automator. By providing a security experience consistent with those of the built-in and third-party applications, you make it easier for your users to understand how to get their work done in your applications with little risk. This reduces the mental effort they must spend on using the application, and makes it less likely that they will make mistakes in using or configuring it — just as developing with an eye on usability and accessibility helps to provide an easier user experience. Users enjoy being pleasantly surprised by the ease of using your application; they do not enjoy being surprised to find that it's sharing their information with the world when they thought it was not.

The purpose of this book is twofold. First, I hope to show how we developers of Mac and iPhone applications can reason about the security requirements of our users and the risks to which our applications are exposed. Then you can examine the security features and APIs available on the Mac and iPhone platforms in the context of that fresh understanding of your apps, to see how to reduce risks and provide your customers with a secure experience.

WHO SHOULD READ THIS BOOK

This book is for Cocoa and Cocoa Touch developers who are interested in ensuring that their applications provide a secure experience. You do not need any experience or familiarity with security principles or secure application development. I do assume that you are comfortable with the C and Objective-C languages, and familiar enough with the APIs that the discussions of code samples can focus on the aspect directly relevant to the matter at hand.

Perhaps you're reading this thinking, "But my app is so small, and doesn't have anything of value, so why would hackers target me"? First, disabuse yourself of the idea that all security risks come from pimply teenagers "hacking" their way into important computers from their parents' basements. The attacker could easily be an otherwise legitimate user of your app who has found a way to subvert it for his or her own needs, whether to craft a fake high-score entry for an online game or to read documents to which the user should not have access. The attack could even be entirely accidental: a user who mistakenly deletes critical data from an application has unintentionally exploited a weakness in that application. These possibilities will be explored throughout the rest of the book.

Nonetheless, consider the accuracy of the traditional view of the hacker. Is this person trying to compromise your app specifically? Maybe, if the purpose is to show that some competitor's app is a better choice. The attacker could have some other target in mind, for which your application provides a convenient stepping stone. Perhaps the idea is to get a document from a user who also has your application installed. Maybe your app uses some web service such as a social networking site, and it's that site the hacker is targeting. Maybe the hacker just wants to show that a Mac (or iPhone) can be compromised, and any application is fair game in proving that point. In January 2007, a project known as the "Month of Apple Bugs" (`http://projects.info-pull.com/moab/`) was launched, with the aim of publicizing security problems on the Mac platform. A large fraction of the vulnerabilities reported in that month did not affect Mac OS X itself, or even Apple's software, but third-party applications that run on the Mac platform. You have to agree with Michael Howard and David LeBlanc, who in their book *Writing Secure Code* said, "The defender must defend all points; the attacker can choose the weakest point." The security profile of a user's system depends on the concerted efforts of all the developers who write all the apps the user relies on.

WHAT ARE WE TRYING TO SECURE, AND FROM WHAT?

The first chapter of this book provides an overview of the security considerations to take into account when designing an application. Its message can easily be distilled into one sentence: know your app and its users. There, that's it; you can stop reading now (though I still recommend you buy the whole book because the wordy version is more interesting, I promise you that much). Without an understanding of what your users are trying to get done, whom they're communicating with to get it done, and how they're communicating, you cannot possibly know which security techniques are relevant to your application. Time you spend on adding irrelevant security countermeasures is time (and money) wasted with no valuable return — imagine building the Great Wall today to protect China from an enemy armed with cruise missiles.

In fact you can even do worse than build irrelevant countermeasures — you can build ones that stop your users from getting their work done. Increasingly, modern applications experience the challenge of flexibility vs. security. As we interact in a more connected world, the balance of these two objectives is being stressed more each day. There's a cliché in the security world that the most secure computer is one that is disconnected from the power supply, encased in a concrete block, and sunk to the bottom of an ocean. That's great, but how do I check my mail on it? If the reason I want a computer is to check my mail, and I can't, then the so-called security is actively working against me. I'll choose a different computer that doesn't have that "protection," and the person who poured the concrete has lost a sale.

The point of this story is that there is no such thing as a "most secure" or "perfectly secure" system or application. Many are *appropriately* secure, and even more could be made appropriately secure with very little effort correctly applied. This book is intended to help you decide what is appropriately secure for your users, and then how to use the tools at your disposal to achieve that security. Appropriate security means that you provide a reasonably risk-free user experience; you do not stop the user at every turn with a password prompt to keep the bad guys out. While this book will help you reason about the security model of your application, it cannot possibly be a substitute for performing that reasoning yourself. Turning to the last code sample now and typing the example source into your app will not add security pixie dust to the app; unfortunately, the security pixies do not exist (though I expect one of the anti-virus vendors might use them in its marketing someday).

By knowing what the users (and, of course, the attackers) want to do, you can easily identify the most important risks to the application. You can then work to mitigate just those risks — a wise and fruitful investment in your application's development. Some of the risks you find may be reduced by a different application design. Others may be mitigated by your taking advantage of Mac OS X or iPhone OS security features; this is the focus of Chapters 2 through 8. Still others may require careful coding to avoid buffer overruns or the mishandling of incoming data, which is addressed in Chapter 9.

Of course you will want to choose a point where sufficient, but not excessive, energy and time have been spent on the application and it is ready to ship. Security is no different from features, graphics, or bug fixes in this regard: put in too much time and the returns will decrease, all the while giving your competitors more time to ship their apps. Chapter 10 describes the security implications of shipping software, including security documentation, and handling any security issues that arise in the field.

Finally, Chapter 11 takes a brief tour through the world of Mac OS X kernel extensions. Kernel code operates in a significantly different environment from application code; it is important to understand this environment to produce secure kernel extensions.

ABOUT THE EXAMPLES

I hope you can tell that I believe the security considerations of app developers are highly dependent on the applications they are writing, and the environments and contexts within which their users operate. With that in mind, please take the code samples in this book in the spirit in which they are intended — as examples of using a particular API to achieve certain goals, rather than recipes to be pasted verbatim into other applications.

It may be that the risk addressed by one of the code samples is not one your application faces, so the effect of integrating the example would be to spend time and effort without any meaningful result. Worse, indiscriminately applying sample code to your application could increase some risks. For example, if you require authorization to enable some security feature (see Chapter 6 on performing privileged tasks), then it is harder for non-administrator users to enable that feature. Conversely, providing access to the feature to all comers might lead to a *privilege escalation* vulnerability — a problem discussed in Chapter 1. The only way to resolve the conflict is to weigh the importance of each risk — something that depends strongly on the specifics of your application. Of course, should you decide that the threat countered in the sample is one you need to address, feel free to use the code and techniques in the examples in your own application.

CONVENTIONS USED IN THIS BOOK

To help you get the most from the text and keep track of what's happening, we've used some conventions throughout the book. Typical examples follow:

Notes, tips, hints, tricks, and asides to the current discussion are offset and placed in italics like this.

A warning tells you that something terrible will happen should a particular event occur. For example, if you perform a task incorrectly, you might see data loss.

As for styles in the text:

- We *italicize* new terms and important words when we introduce them.
- We show keyboard strokes like this: Ctrl+A.
- We show filenames, URLs, and code within the text like so: `persistence.properties`.
- We present code in the following way:

```
We use a monofont type with no highlighting for most code examples.
```

SOURCE CODE

As you work through the examples in this book, you may choose either to type in all the code manually, or to use the source code files that accompany the book. All the source code used in this book is available for download at `http://www.wrox.com`. When at the site, simply locate the book's title (use the Search box or one of the title lists) and click the Download Code link on the book's detail page to obtain all the source code for the book. Code that is included on the web site is highlighted by the following icon:

Listings include the filename in the title. If it is just a code snippet, you'll find the filename in a code note such as this:

Code snippet filename

Because many books have similar titles, you may find it easiest to search by ISBN; this book's ISBN is 978-0-470-52595-1.

Once you download the code, just decompress it with your favorite compression tool. Alternately, you can go to the main Wrox code download page at `http://www.wrox.com/dynamic/books/download.aspx` to see the code available for this book and all other Wrox books.

ERRATA

We make every effort to ensure that there are no errors in the text or in the code. However, no one is perfect, and mistakes do occur. If you find an error in one of our books, like a spelling mistake or faulty piece of code, we would be very grateful for your feedback. By sending in errata you may save another reader hours of frustration and at the same time you will be helping us provide even higher quality information.

To find the errata page for this book, go to `http://www.wrox.com` and locate the title using the Search box or one of the title lists. Then, on the Book Search Results page, click the Errata link. On this page you can view all errata that has been submitted for this book and posted by Wrox editors.

A complete book list including links to each book's errata is also available at `www.wrox.com/misc-pages/booklist.shtml`.

If you don't spot "your" error on the Errata page, click the Errata Form link and complete the form to send us the error you have found. We'll check the information and, if appropriate, post a message to the book's errata page and fix the problem in subsequent editions of the book.

P2P.WROX.COM

For author and peer discussion, join the P2P forums at `p2p.wrox.com`. The forums are a Web-based system for you to post messages relating to Wrox books and related technologies and interact with other readers and technology users. The forums offer a subscription feature to e-mail you topics of interest of your choosing when new posts are made to the forums. Wrox authors, editors, other industry experts, and your fellow readers are present on these forums.

At `http://p2p.wrox.com` you will find a number of different forums that will help you not only as you read this book, but also as you develop your own applications. To join the forums, just follow these steps:

1. Go to `p2p.wrox.com` and click the Register link.
2. Read the terms of use and click Agree.

3. Complete the required information to join as well as any optional information you wish to provide, and click Submit.
4. You will receive an e-mail with information describing how to verify your account and complete the joining process.

You can read messages in the forums without joining P2P but in order to post your own messages, you must join.

Once you join, you can post new messages and respond to messages other users post. You can read messages at any time on the Web. If you would like to have new messages from a particular forum e-mailed to you, click the Subscribe to This Forum icon by the forum name in the forum listing.

For more information about how to use the Wrox P2P, be sure to read the P2P FAQs for answers to questions about how the forum software works as well as many common questions specific to P2P and Wrox books. To read the FAQs, click the FAQ link on any P2P page.

1

Secure by Design

WHAT'S IN THIS CHAPTER?

- Understanding your application's security needs
- Discovering the threats to your users
- Identifying potential vulnerabilities

As with any other class of bug, addressing a security issue becomes more expensive the longer you wait to fix it. If there's a problem in the design of the application, trying to fix it in a bugfix release will be very costly because you'll need to change multiple classes. You'll also need to understand and account for the myriad uses and configurations your customers have in place, and be ready to support migration of all these to the new, fixed version of the application. Addressing the issue the first time around means not only spending less time on the issue, but also avoiding the additional (direct and indirect) costs of a security vulnerability out in the field and coordinating a fix release. I once worked on a project for which we spent about three weeks addressing an issue that had been caused by a bad choice of file system path in the planning phase, some years earlier.

Of course it's not going to be possible or even desirable to identify and fix every single vulnerability before writing any code. That's a recipe for spending a great deal of money and taking a very long time to get to market, by which time your competitors will have gotten their apps to the customers. There is a principle software engineers have borrowed from economics called the Pareto Principle, also known as the "80/20 rule." The principle says that 80 percent of the observable effects in any situation are often the result of only 20 percent of the causes. It's a good idea to follow the 80/20 rule in software design — addressing only the most important issues so that the product is of a high enough quality to ship. Which of course leads us to the question, "Which are the important issues?"

ABOUT COCOA SECURITY

Users of your application do not think about what technology was used to create it — whether it was written in Cocoa, Carbon, or Java. What they care about is using the app on their iPhones or their Macs to get their work done. Similarly, their concerns regarding security come not from Cocoa-specific features or issues, but from how the application's security helps or hinders them in doing their work (or, in the case of a game, in having their fun). Your model of the important security considerations in your app will therefore be largely technology-agnostic, although there are vulnerabilities specific to Objective-C and Cocoa, as discussed in Chapter 9, "Writing Secure Application Code."

The particular capabilities and APIs available in Cocoa and Cocoa Touch applications become more relevant when you determine how some of the threats you identify might be exploited by an attacker. Cocoa applications on the Mac are part of a multi-user system, as explained in Chapter 2, "Managing Multiple Users," so understanding how the different users can interact through inter-process communication or by sharing files on the file system will help you decide whether particular interactions could lead to one user's threatening the security of another. Prioritizing security issues will always be based on an understanding of what your users are trying to do and how that fits in with their processes and with the environment.

You must also have Cocoa-specific features and technology in mind when deciding how to mitigate the threats that attackers may be posing to your application and its users. Users will expect your app to behave in the same way as others on the Mac or iPhone platform, which can be easily achieved if you adopt the frameworks Apple provides for the purpose. As an example, if your application stores a user's password, he will expect it to use the keychain to do so, because then he can change the settings for that password in the same way as for all his other applications. Keychain Services are described in Chapter 5, "Storing Confidential Information with the Keychain."

We must now leave Cocoa behind temporarily for the rest of this chapter, as we discuss the principles of application security and discover the threats your users will face as they use your application. These are threats that will be present however you choose to write the app.

PROFILING YOUR APPLICATION'S SECURITY RISKS

To understand an application's security profile is to understand what risks exist in using that application. That means understanding what your users want to do, what obstacles they might face in getting it done, and the likelihood and severity of those obstacles. Obstacles could come in the form of people attacking the system in some way to extract something of value; honest people could also make mistakes interacting with the application. Either way, a risk is posed only if the application presents the opportunity for the obstacle to upset the user's work. Figure 1-1 shows how these components go together to form a vulnerability: a possibility that users can't get their work done safely in the application.

By extension, secure application development is meant to mitigate either the likelihood or impact of those obstacles; you want to reduce to an acceptable level the risk involved in using your app. You can mitigate risk by preventing an attack from occurring, limiting an attack's impact, or detecting and responding to an attack that is already in progress or complete.

Risk can also be passed on to other entities, usually through insurance policies or service-level agreements (SLAs), but the assumption for now is that this is not an acceptable option, and that you are taking responsibility for the security of your application.

So what presents the greatest risk to your customers? Answering that question is the focus of the rest of this chapter.

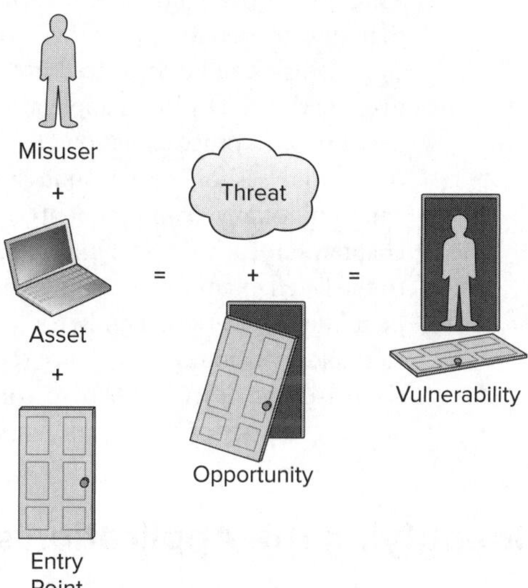

FIGURE 1-1: Anatomy of a vulnerability

Remember that while the discussion is about planning, design, and implementation as if they were separate phases, it's very useful to treat security as an iterative process. Rather than writing a nice security document while designing your app and leaving it to gather metaphorical dust on the hard drive, reevaluate the security model whenever you do a bugfix release or add a new feature. Verify that the issues you prioritized the last time around are still relevant as customers find new uses for your application, or as new classes of vulnerability are discovered and reported by the security community. Have another look whenever a competitor releases a security fix — did you already address that issue, or is your application vulnerable? Automated tests, discussed further in Chapter 9, can be applied just as readily to security practices as to functional testing. You can encapsulate your security assumptions in unit tests or regression tests and discover whether the assumptions continue to hold as the application evolves. Your understanding of the security issues your app faces is therefore critical if you are to have any confidence in the security of your application. This chapter will discuss the creation of a *threat model*, a description of the hostile aspects of the environment your app is in, and of how well the app can protect itself and its users. Maintaining this threat model in electronic form is a must to make it easy to update, and it's a good idea to keep it in the same version control system as your source code so that the state of any version or branch of the application is easy to find. Consider using a database application such as Bento so that the different attackers, threats, and vulnerabilities can be indexed and cross-referenced.

DEFINING THE SECURITY ENVIRONMENT

In order to start protecting your application against vulnerabilities, you need to know what the threats to the application are and which are the most important. Before you can even list the threats your application will face, you need to know something about the world the application finds itself in. We can define the application's world in terms of users (both legitimate and otherwise), objects of value that the application holds or accesses, and ways data gets in, around, and out of the application. These are the most important aspects of the threat model, because without a good understanding of the way the app will be used (and misused) there is no way to be sure that the vulnerabilities you invest time in protecting are important or even present in the app. There is no benefit in protecting against SQL injection attacks, for example, if the application does not communicate with a database.

THREAT MODEL: THYTUNES MUSIC APPLICATION

Throughout this section we'll look at the example of ThyTunes, a free Mac application that allows users to import their own music as well as to buy music from an online store. Music can be organized in the application's library into playlists and synchronized with the ThyTunes application on an iPhone. Music can also be shared over the network with other copies of ThyTunes. And of course the music can be played. None of the analyses for the ThyTunes application shown here will be complete, so see if you can think of any examples of attackers, assets, or threats that are not covered in this chapter. For each new example you think of, consider how important it is in relation to the listed examples; i.e., how important an attack using your new example would be to the application. Think, too, about whether any of the examples here or any examples you come up with are relevant to your own applications, and about applying the reasoning described here to your own app.

Identifying the Application's Users

You should already have some idea of who will be using your app, since you have a customer for your application in mind and have been designing the user interaction for the benefit of that customer. So who is the user? Think about whether you have different classes of users in mind. If so, which is the most important? What will the users mainly be doing with your application? It is important to understand the users' expectations and needs so that you can think realistically about how they will prioritize different risks, how they will react to security issues, and how well they understand the security implications of working with your app. Knowing how your users are working with your application also leads to a better understanding of the risks they could potentially expose themselves to. Which features of the application will they turn on? Will they leave the preferences window alone, or play with every control available? The answers to these questions will help you concentrate your effort on securing the default and most likely configurations of your app.

It is important that the "out-of-the-box" configuration of your app be secure, because that is the one configuration to which all your users will be exposed. Many may never change it, so enabling lightly used features and options means more work to secure the default state of the app. This leads to a higher chance of vulnerabilities being present in a fresh install of the application — vulnerabilities that affect all your users.

You should also think about how technically competent your user is, in relation both to the use cases of your application and to computers (and networks, if relevant) in general. How much information is it appropriate to give the user about what your application is doing, and how much can be treated as "magic" that happens behind the scenes? Should a decision need to be made about a security-related question, is it appropriate to make the decision on the user's behalf or ask that user about it? Or should the decision be made automatically based on a configurable default? If the application does it automatically, should the user be notified or can it be hidden? Users will appreciate an application that does not ask them any more questions than it needs to, and will be frustrated by one that asks them questions they do not understand. It is not acceptable to wash your hands of security concerns by saying, "I asked the user what to do, and he chose the insecure option." Aim to provide a great user experience by taking responsibility for the security decisions — after all, you're the one who has read this book (and if your competitors haven't, then you get the jump on them).

Closely related to this collection of questions is the question of how likely you think your target user is to make mistakes while using your application. Will this user carefully consider the meaning of any question you might ask, or just hit whichever button is farthest to the right of the dialog? This depends quite strongly on the environment in which your application is used. If your users sit at desks in offices and rely on the application to do their day jobs, then it's quite likely that they'll concentrate on what's going on in the application and pay attention to everything that happens. On the other hand, if you're writing an iPhone utility, the user may be in a noisy, distracting environment when using the application. If the users are outside in bright sunlight you can't even rely on their being able to see the display well, let alone concentrate on it. Their interaction may be limited to launching the app and clicking a couple of buttons before putting the device away again, without worrying about the details.

In that environment users may unwittingly expose themselves to risks by failing to understand or consider at all the consequences of their interaction with the application. In such cases you should be designing the workflow to reduce exposure to risk by minimizing the number of decisions users have to make regarding security, and by making it easier to choose the lower-risk paths through the app than those paths with higher risk.

INVESTING THE USER'S MENTAL EFFORT

An example of where *mental investment* by users in security matters becomes important is in dealing with the Internet-based attack called *phishing*. In phishing, the attacker tricks a user into visiting a web site that looks as if it offers some useful service but that is actually under the attacker's control, such as a site that looks like the user's online banking service. The user enters account and identification information into the web site — information which is actually sent to the attacker, who can now use it to access the user's bank account. Users are told to be vigilant, not to click a link without first checking the URL, and not to enter personal information into any web site they're not sure of. But how reasonable is it to assume that users will do any of these things when they're using mobile browsers on their phones?

The users of the application may also turn out to be *misusers* — people who can access the application to perform unintended tasks. There is the possibility that a user could accidentally cause a security incident; is there also the chance of a user's going rogue and deliberately attacking other users? An often-cited example is that of an employee who, dissatisfied with the behavior of the company, uses its internal applications to cause it, or specific employees, damage. Such inside attacks can be more damaging than external hacker attacks, as the user already (legitimately) has greater access to the company's facilities and assets. For each of the users you have listed, you need to think about whether this user could become a misuser, and if appropriate to list him or her among the misusers, as described in the following section.

To represent the information you have gathered about your users in a useful and succinct form, create a description of each type you identify. A common technique in user experience and marketing circles, which can help you think about who these users are, is to create a profile of a typical individual in each class of user. These profiles are known as *personae*; for each persona choose a name and even find a photo to put a face to that name. Assign them brief biographies and quotes about why they are using your application and what security concerns they have. Provide each persona with a one- or two-sentence answer to each of the questions asked earlier in this section (along with any others you think could be important for your app). This will help you to reason out the needs and wants of the users by letting you put yourself in their shoes. If you are using a database to prepare your threat model, then each of these descriptions would be a single row in a table. See the following example, "ThyTunes: User List," for two sample personae relating to the ThyTunes application described earlier.

THYTUNES: USER LIST

This example discusses two ThyTunes users, Susan and Roger.

APPLICATION USER: SUSAN

A typical user of ThyTunes is Susan, a student at a West Coast liberal arts university in the United States. She is not particularly computer-literate, let alone familiar with the workings of computer music or security — she cannot be expected to look after the security configuration of the app herself, and neither does she have an IT administrator looking after her computer to do it. Susan does not even particularly want to spend much time with the application — she just wants to get her tunes playing and then carry on with something else, such as preparing an essay. Therefore, any time she has to stop and think of an answer to a question about working with the application — particularly a technical question requiring special knowledge — will be a time when she considers whether she really needs to be using ThyTunes at all.

Susan has heard of identity theft but believes this happens "to people who visit the wrong web sites on the net, you know the kind I mean — the kind with pictures." This makes the ThyTunes developers think that she will be likely to ignore any potential confidentiality concerns when using ThyTunes and its music store. It is likely that she could accidentally allow misuse of her credit card information or purchased music unless the application guides her away from risky actions.

MUSIC INDUSTRY EXECUTIVE: ROGER

A second class of user is important enough to the success of ThyTunes to require serious consideration. This class is personified by Roger, the director of partner relations at Balony Music Group, one of the largest record labels. He doesn't actually use the ThyTunes application but is in charge of deciding whether Balony's music can appear on the ThyTunes music store and of determining what to charge the ThyTunes developers for listing that music. He's very concerned that the whole digital music scene makes it much too easy for people to share music without paying the rights holders. If ThyTunes isn't doing enough to stop piracy he'll take the songs off the catalogue. Being able to sell Balony music is a key competitive advantage for ThyTunes, so the developers must treat vulnerabilities that exploit the store or sharing features of the app to pirate music as business-critical bugs.

Identifying the Application's Misusers

Understanding who your users are has helped you see how they think about security, what their concerns are, and how willing and prepared they are to contribute to the security of your application. You can consider the misusers of the application in the same way. Misusers are those people who would — intentionally or otherwise — compromise the security of your application and your users; they are *attacking* the application. When you discover and list the attackers, it's best to include everyone you can think of. Leave discounting certain attackers until you've gotten enough candidates to usefully rank them in order of importance. Considering an unimportant attacker will waste some time, but failing to account for a likely case will undoubtedly cost time, money, and customer goodwill. Remember, too, that the attackers don't have to play by your rules, so don't discount a potential misuser because you find a certain type of exploitation distasteful. An important class of attack might fall through the cracks if you are unwilling to face the idea that the attacker exists. If your app will be used by a charity or religious group that could have enemies for ideological reasons, you need to consider the threat those enemies will pose.

You should collect two important categories of information in order to build up a profile of the attackers: who they are and what their motivation is in attacking your application and its users.

As with the users, create a persona for each class of attacker you have identified, with a mini-biography addressing each of the points described above. Two such personae are shown in the following "ThyTunes: Misusers" example.

Put the attacker's goal and motivations for achieving that goal in his or her own words — computer security can seem at times like a very abstract universe, so having a name and a face for your attacker will make the threats seem more real. Keep the attackers and the users together in the threat model — in this context, they are both classes of people who could misuse your app, for whatever reason.

Who are the attackers? Referring to the information you have already gathered about your users makes it easier to reason about who might be targeting them. If your application tracks online banking transactions and you expect a number of elderly customers, then there's a reasonable chance that an attack might come from a family member who wants to see how much money is in an account (or even change the amount). If your application deals with medical information there are a host of people who could potentially want unauthorized access.

THYTUNES: MISUSERS

The following discussion illustrates two distinct types of misusers: Tim and Bob.

THE HACKER: TIM

Tim is an unemployed computer science graduate and longtime ThyTunes user. As he currently doesn't have a job, he'd love to find a way to grab the music from the ThyTunes store without paying. He's got a good knowledge of programming and networking, but has use only of his own computer hooked up to DSL. He definitely wouldn't want to get caught in the act as that could destroy his chances of ever getting another job, but if he is successful at obtaining free music then he's likely to mention it on his social networking page. From there his story would undoubtedly be blogged and could even get into the press, which would not be good for the ThyTunes developers.

THE ACTIVIST: BOB

Bob is a member of Inph0free, an online activist group that believes the traditional record labels like Balony are treating their artists unfairly and stifling creativity. The group wants to show that applications like ThyTunes are fundamentally broken in order to pave the way for the next generation of digital music, which will be friendly toward independent artists. Bob doesn't really know what that generation will look like, but he won't stop until he's found a way to discredit ThyTunes for conspiring with Balony and other record labels.

As mentioned earlier, the users themselves could also be misusers, and could attack the application. Recall the example of Susan, the non-expert user of ThyTunes; do you think that if faced with a question about the app's configuration she would always choose the most secure option? If she does not, and compromises the application as a result, she has become an accidental misuser.

How technically competent are the attackers? Are they just going to try scripted attack "recipes" that they can find on the Internet, or will they have some advanced knowledge of the platform they can use to explore the target system? This is particularly relevant on the iPhone, where a less competent attacker may not know about or be able to use jail-breaking tools to drop their own programs onto the device. It's also related to the question of whether the attacker has the skills or inclination to learn specifically about the workings of your application in order to try to discover a flaw. Less able hackers will look for common problems like bad handling of malicious input but might not find issues that require detailed knowledge of your app.

Another factor that determines the type and severity of attack particular misusers are likely to mount is their adversity to risk. A politically motivated hacker could be willing to stop at nothing in an attack on your user; conversely a *script kiddy* may back down at the first sign of countermeasures. In fact, many remote login services display a banner message such as, "It is illegal to use this service without permission"; some systems administrators have found that even this simple deterrent reduces the rate of attack. (For more information on how login banners decrease the rate of attack, see *Practical Unix and Internet Security* 3rd Edition [Chapter 10], Garfinkel, Spafford, and Schwartz, O'Reilly Media, 2003.)

The reason I frequently call the attackers "misusers" is so I don't forget that not all security threats are intentional. The word "attackers" automatically conjures up images of criminals or invading armies; in other words, attackers are the "bad guys." Considering only the security risks born of malice will mean you miss whole classes of important vulnerabilities, specifically those that in being addressed lead directly to a better user experience.

Script kiddy *is a derogatory name for an inexperienced or would-be cyber-criminal who is trying to prove himself as a "hacker." The name comes from the stereotypical — but accurate — depiction of a teenager with few computer skills, whose ability is limited to downloading and running scripted attacks from sites such as SecurityFocus.*

For the type of attacker you have identified, how far do you think this person will go in order to complete an attack? Of course this depends in part on the value of the asset being attacked, which we will investigate in the next section.

The attacks that misusers may perform against your users depend on their goals. The possibility of politically motivated attackers seeking to discredit your users or your company has been described already. The profile of the victims and of the attackers, the publicity value of a successful attack, and whether the attackers intend to inconvenience or destroy their victims will all affect the types of attack that they will consider.

The type and scope of such an attack will differ from a personal "grudge" attack against an individual user. A misuser targeting one user will not be probing for vulnerable systems across the Internet, as he or she knows already who the victim is. On the other hand, such a misuser will be more likely to know personal information about the victim, which could be helpful to him or her, for example in guessing the user's password.

Don't forget to include indiscriminate attacks as well as those associated with your application specifically. The traditional view of the script kiddy falls into the first of these categories — script kiddies will be looking to "own" as many different computers as they can to prove to themselves and their online friends how "elite" they are, and will not have any reason for choosing your user's Mac over any other computer on the Internet. Attackers whose target is you as the application's developer, or even Apple as the provider of the platform, might use your application to achieve their goal.

What resources do the attackers have at their disposal? Will they try to brute-force a password using a beige G3 PowerMac, or a cluster of multi-core systems? Bear in mind that attackers will find it easy (and cheap) to access large amounts of computing power, whether in the form of a legitimate "cloud computing" service, a university computing laboratory, or an illegal "botnet" comprising previously compromised PCs. Even if these attackers are not very skillful, could they afford to contract an expert, and is attacking your app important enough that they might consider it? How much time can they dedicate to performing the attack? An employee using a 15-minute coffee break to try to access the payroll system will need to try different attacks from an outsider who can spend all night on the attempt — the initial position of the two is also different, which will affect their approaches and chances of success.

> **TITAN RAIN: A POLITICAL CYBERCRIME**
>
> A particularly famous example of a successful attack with apparent political motivation was code-named Titan Rain by the U.S. government. In 2003, attackers, located in China but of unknown affiliation, hid code on PCs located on U.S. and U.K. government networks, as well as those run by defense contractors, including Lockheed Martin. The attackers stole large numbers of files from the computers, which were transmitted to other systems located in a number of companies around Asia before finally being sent on to China. When knowledge of the attack became public, it became the subject of wide press coverage including articles in *Time* magazine: See `http://www.time.com/time/nation/article/0,8599,1098371,00.html` for an example.

The Assets That Can Be Taken

Notice that in the previous section, each of the example users and misusers had some object, real or abstract, that they were interested in. Susan, the application user, mentioned her identity, even if she didn't see the relevance of identity theft in the ThyTunes context. Roger, the music industry executive, was concerned about money from sales of the music. Tim, the unemployed hacker, had other reasons for being interested in the costs of songs. And Bob, the activist, wanted to damage the reputation of anyone associated with the traditional music industry. Each of these objects, or assets, is something that the application either controls or can provide access to, and that has some value to somebody. It could be that the asset has some value to the user, to you as the developer, or just to the attacker. It is this value that makes the asset important to protect and gives the attacker motivation to take or compromise the asset.

What Makes an Asset Important?

Leaving software aside for the moment, some things have value to you for different reasons. A heirloom may have monetary as well as sentimental value, while a bank statement contains useful information that makes it a valuable asset. An antique dealer would dismiss your bank statement as a worthless scrap of paper, while a loan arranger couldn't find out much about your finances from the antique. As objects in the real world can be valuable for different reasons, so the assets in an application have different properties that make them important.

Software security experts like to refer to the important properties of an asset with the acronym *CIA*, standing for *confidentiality, integrity, and availability.*

- **Confidentiality:** This means that the asset has some value in being kept a secret within the application. Attackers may wish to gain the secret for themselves, as is usually the case with a password — the benefit is that the attacker gets to use the password to access the same services as the victim (perhaps even while posing as the victim). On the other hand, there may be some confidential assets — company financial records perhaps — where a successful attack doesn't just disclose them to the user but makes them public. There are also cases in which both types of confidentiality loss can occur. This was the case in April 2009, when a Twitter administrator's password was discovered. The password was used to modify other Twitter accounts, and was also published to draw attention to the problems inherent in having a weak password. The password was "happiness" in this case.

The problems facing Twitter as a result of the disclosure of its administrator's password are described by the security firm Sophos at `http://www.sophos.com/blogs/gc/g/2009/05/01/twitter-security-breach-exposes-accounts-hackers/`.

- **Integrity:** This refers essentially to an asset's accuracy or correctness; what would be the damage were the asset to be modified in some way? Usually there are legitimate changes that can be made: for example, a log file can reasonably have events added to it. It is not desirable for an existing log message to be changed or removed, though. A blog-editing application should let users change their own previous blog posts, but not those of another blogger, unless he or she permits it.
- **Availability:** This property simply means that an asset can be used for its intended purpose. An attacker could stop the victim from using the application as intended; what would be the impact of that? Hijacking is, in a sense, related to availability; the assets are supposed to be available exclusively to the legitimate users. Threats that target the availability of an asset are frequently referred to as denial-of-service (DoS) attacks, as we shall see in the next section.

For each of the assets you identify in your application, think about whether any of these three properties is important. If so, how important are the properties with respect to other properties, and to the other assets on the system? If you could act to protect either the confidentiality of a password or the integrity of the billing process, which would you work on first? The importance of an asset may not entirely be your own decision; there could be laws, industry codes, or other regulations you must take into account. A billing process is a good example, since security standards such as PCI-DSS may be mandated, depending on your customers' requirements or those of your marketers, who may see compliance as a "feature" offering competitive advantage. (The PCI-DSS — Payment Card Industry Data Security Standard — is described at `https://www.pcisecuritystandards.org/security_standards/pci_dss.shtml`.)

Also think about which of the users you have identified should be able to use the asset during normal operation of the app — is it something users can access, or is there an administrator to take care of it? Does it ever get shared with a remote service, or a user on another computer? Without knowing what the legitimate uses of the asset are, it's impossible to know what uses are illegitimate.

The CIA properties should not be considered exhaustive. If there is an attribute of an asset in your application that doesn't seem to fit in any of these categories, it is important that you make note of that attribute rather than ignore it because it doesn't "work." Failing to keep track of an important asset in your threat model will result in unaccounted-for vulnerabilities in your app.

Exclusivity of an asset is another aspect that could be important in your threat model. A user's Internet connection is not confidential in itself (though the traffic certainly may be), but the user probably has an expectation that it's there to be used as desired, especially if the user is paying for it. An attack in which the connection is hijacked to send spam e-mails shows that this expectation has not been met.

Types of Assets

Many assets are tangible objects, often with meaning outside the application's context. Credit card records are good examples of this type of asset. They have some obvious presence in the application, often having been entered by the user through a form. They have an obvious relevance and value to the user, since the credit card information represents a way for the user to give other people access to the user's money. In fact, because the credit card information can be readily identified with a physical object — the real credit card — it's very easy for users to think about what value they place on the data, because they know what value they place on the real card. Payment records, similarly, are similar to sales receipts in the real world, so it's clear why the vendor and customer would want an accurate record of the transactions that have taken place. Customers want to track what they have spent and ensure that they have been charged the right amount for the right products; the vendor needs to have an accurate record of sales to see turnover and to pay the correct taxes.

A component of the application itself could be a valuable asset. If your application has a logging facility, which audits important actions (see Chapter 7 for more on auditing important operations), then the availability and integrity of that facility itself are important after an attack, for forensic purposes, in tracing the steps taken by an attacker. The attacker would therefore have a reason for targeting the logging component, even though it has no value outside the application.

Sometimes an asset is not valuable in itself, but can become targeted because it provides access to a different asset (or assets). Passwords are included in this category. The password itself is not useful information; it takes on meaning only when it is used to identify the user to some application or service. So an application that does not afford appropriate protection to the password is really giving up access to the user's identity. The value of the password is dependent on the value of the identity — a password for a one-click purchasing system has value equal to that of the money that could be lost through the purchasing process. It also follows that when users access multiple accounts with the same password, that password takes on a higher value — which is the reason for using a different password for each service. Of course it is the confidentiality of the password that is most important; the identity is protected by the password only when the password is secret.

Notice that assets like a password or private key can exist only when you have determined that something else needs protecting. There is no point in password protection that keeps people out of nothing. Similarly, requiring a password to access non-confidential information would be considered just annoying. So to determine that the application needs to have a password-protected component, you need to have already decided that something needs to be protected and that using a password is a good way to provide that protection. This demonstrates that a threat model must be considered iteratively — each countermeasure designed into the system certainly changes the security profile of the existing system. But it may not merely mitigate some existing risks; adding a countermeasure such as a password may introduce new threats that must be taken into account.

Still other assets do not have any tangible presence in the application, but can nevertheless be of value. Bob, the information freedom activist, wants to damage the reputation of the companies behind ThyTunes and its services. The reputation isn't a part of the application, and it isn't even stored on the computer. Nonetheless it has some worth and the application can be used to compromise it. But why would any attacker want to target your reputation? Possible reasons include:

- **Political motivation:** Perhaps your company is based in a country that has poor relations with the attacker's country.
- **Competitive discrediting of your company:** Your reputation can also be indirectly compromised by an attack targeting some other asset, simply because the attack was possible.

Any successful attack is also likely to damage that other important intangible asset, the confidence of the victim and your other users and customers.

Intangible assets can be the hardest to think of because they are often nebulous concepts, bearing only an indirect relation to the software and its purpose. Reputation and user confidence are great places to start thinking, though, because if these lose their value then it becomes hard to sell any software. At the time of writing, the online store for a popular browser maker has been unavailable for over a week since a security breach was discovered in the software running the store. In addition to the direct cost of lack of sales, how many people will question using the store once it does reopen? How many will question the security of the browser software?

There are also assets that are incidental to the application entirely. A commonly misused asset in many modern attacks is the network connection of the host computer. The network connection isn't "owned" by any application of course, but an attacker can use a vulnerable application to turn the computer into a "zombie" that connects to other systems, perhaps as part of a spam or distributed denial-of-service (DDoS) campaign. The attacker could also want to access the CPU time of the zombie computer, perhaps to try to crack an encrypted password. Remember that just because the asset isn't "yours," that doesn't mean the attackers won't use your app to get at it — they don't need to play by the rules.

THYTUNES: IMPORTANT ASSETS

The user's music in the ThyTunes application is the asset with the most direct relationship to the use cases. If the music were to be rendered unplayable, then the user would not have any reason to use the application If it were to be made publicly available, the record companies would lose sales. So the user is concerned about the availability of the music purchased, but the record label director is concerned about the confidentiality of that music.

Because users are able to purchase music through the ThyTunes store, there must be some way for them to present payment information, such as credit card authorization, to the application. Users will want to ensure that the confidentiality of their information is protected, so that their own credit cards cannot be used by other people. The developers of ThyTunes want to be certain of the integrity of the payment information, to avoid problematic disputes over questioned payments. The developers are also concerned over the availability of the payment-handling service, since any time this service is unavailable they are unable to sell any music.

Were there to be any public security problem with ThyTunes, the record labels would question their partnership with the developers. They see the application as being primarily about the relationship between the users and their music — and thus the labels as providers of that music are going to be affected by any damage to the user's trust. Any damage to the reputation of the ThyTunes developers as providers of a secure and trustworthy application could have a direct financial impact on the record labels' business.

Understanding the Data Flow

So far, to borrow the jargon of TV crime dramas, you have profiled your attacker by identifying and understanding who the misuser is. And by identifying the valuable assets in the application you've given the attacker a motive. You also know who your users are, i.e., who the victims would be in any attack. In order for a threat — or potential attack — to exist, there needs to be a modus operandi. There must be some way for the attacker to get to the asset to steal or compromise it.

Imagine that you are in charge of security at a museum, and have been tasked with securing a priceless diamond from theft. You would need to know where all the doors, windows, air-conditioning vents, and other ways to get into the building were. You would also want to understand how the would-be thief could get from any one of these entry points to the diamond, and then back out of the building. So it is with computer security: you have found your jewel thief and the next gem on her target list, now you need to know how she'll break in and get back out with the diamond.

Applications have entrances and exits just as buildings do. In the software case, these are any places data goes into or out of the application.

The User Interface

The user interface is a good place to start. Of course, the person using the interface is the user, isn't he? Well, not necessarily. All you really know is that the person using the interface is the person who currently has access to the keyboard and mouse. But if the user has left the computer and lets somebody else take control of the application, isn't that the user's problem? If you could simply deal that way with any of the security issues you encounter, now would be a good time to put the book down and release the app. Instead, you might consider the following possibilities:

- The user accidentally did something unexpected.
- The user was coerced into doing something unexpected.
- Someone deliberately misused the user interface.

Apple's Mac Human Interface Guidelines already give you a way to deal with the user who performs a potentially insecure operation, by creating a forgiving user interface. The guidelines (at `http://developer.apple.com/documentation/UserExperience/Conceptual/AppleHIGuidelines/XHIGHIDesign/XHIGHIDesign.html`) say:

> *Encourage people to explore your application by building in forgiveness — that is, making most actions easily reversible. People need to feel that they can try things without damaging the system or jeopardizing their data. Create safety nets, such as the Undo and Revert to Saved commands, so that people will feel comfortable learning and using your product.*
>
> *Warn users when they initiate a task that will cause irreversible loss of data. If alerts appear frequently, however, it may mean that the product has some design flaws. When options are presented clearly and feedback is timely, using an application should be relatively error-free.*
>
> *Anticipate common problems and alert users to potential side effects. Provide extensive feedback and communication at every stage so users feel that they have enough information to make the right choices.*

These are good ways to deal with either of the first two UI issues in the earlier bullet list, because when presented with the question of whether they want to go ahead with a damaging task, the users should (you hope!) ask that very question of themselves. However, as noted by Apple, if you ask repeatedly for confirmation it will be frustrating for the users. If you look at the interface for your application and decide that there are a number of different actions that should all be confirmed before they are carried out because they increase the risk to one or more assets, then perhaps the application should not permit those actions at all — i.e., they should possibly be removed from the user interface. That would certainly make it easier to protect the assets. There are other ways to communicate concerns to the user, including a warning message alongside the

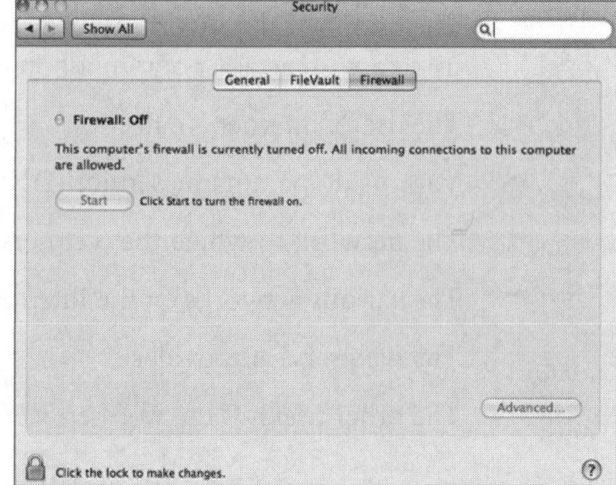

FIGURE 1-2: Configuration pane describes system's security status.

UI control that introduces the risk. The firewall configuration pane of System Preferences, shown in Figure 1-2, provides a good example: it allows the user to turn the firewall off without confirmation, but describes the security state of the system in a message on the pane.

Even the third possibility in the bullet list — that someone will abuse the application intentionally through the user interface — can be dealt with. On the Mac you can distinguish different users with varying levels of access to the application, and provide for a user who wants to perform some privileged operation using Authorization Services (see Chapter 2 for more on managing multiple users, and Chapter 6 on performing privileged tasks).

The iPhone does not have such a concept of multiple users, so the user is capable of performing any action that is available in the UI. This leaves three options:

- **Do not put that action into the UI:** This may be appropriate if users can get along without needing to perform the action, or if there is some alternative way to get at it. For example, you may not want to allow users to delete an account on a web service through the iPhone application, if they can log in at the browser to do that.
- **Provide your own "escalation" mechanism:** A good example is the iTunes application on the phone, which always prompts for the user's password before a purchase, even though it could store the password in the keychain. By forcing the user to re-enter the password, iTunes ensures that the escalation from "handset holder" to "iTunes account owner" is performed by only the correct person.
- **Documentation:** Explain to the user the importance of having the whole phone locked and PIN-protected through the Settings application when your app is installed, even when the user isn't using that app. This option is the least convenient for the user and is unlikely to work (will the user actually read your recommendation?), so its use should be considered carefully.

Data from External Sources

Not all the data in an app is necessarily going to come from the user working with the interface. Data could be coming from an external source such as a web service. Consider the large number of agencies involved in getting data from the web service to your application:

- The user's local network (which may not be the home network, of course; the user could be using a wi-fi access point in a hotel or coffee shop)
- The user's Internet connection
- Various domain name service (DNS) providers
- The network to which the web service's server is connected
- The various networks on the Internet between the user's network and the web service's network
- The web service provider
- The other users of the web service

It would be a very trusting soul who believed that none of these agents could be hostile. It pays to be very careful when dealing with remote data, as the outside world is the natural home of the attacker.

While there is, as we have already discussed, a chance that one of your users is misusing the application, there are plenty more potential misusers among the billions of other people on the Internet. How does the information that comes from remote sources get handled in the application? What components does it get passed between? Which assets do those components give access to?

If data of a certain type coming in through a particular entry point eventually causes problems in a certain method from a class in an entirely different module, then attackers could use that problem to their advantage. But such issues can be hard to track down, as it may not be clear that the other module is ever used during the handling of that data. The interfaces between components should thus be listed, as well as interfaces that are purely on the application's "surface," such as its connections to network resources. If a Mac application launches a background task or communicates with a daemon, then what can happen if the task is launched outside the app or the daemon is sent arbitrary requests? Is a string that it is safe to use in the network-communications component still acceptable when it is passed to the database module? Because the protocols used are different, the techniques that should be used to guard against misuse of each component differ. This reinforces the idea that every component should either mistrust what it is told, or should "trust, but verify."

The phrase "Trust, but verify" has been attributed to various people. I was first told the phrase by a manager who attributed it to Soviet leader Nikita Khrushchev. Since then I've seen it attributed to at least two U.S. presidents, as well as the writer Damon Runyon. And it's also been reported as a translation of a Russian proverb. Whoever said it first, it's good advice — as well as an illustration of how hard it is at times to verify something.

Such boundaries can include interface calls between different classes, particularly to or from loadable frameworks or bundles. The questions to ask here are which of the assets in the application can be accessed directly by the bundles, and which can be accessed through the application programming interface (API) exposed to the bundle — that is, whether through the published interface or as a result of the bundle's calling undocumented methods. The goal is to know everything that happens once some data enters the application — or at least to understand enough about where everything happens with that data to make reasonable guesses about which assets are at risk from abuse of that entry point.

Also think about how the application behaves if the interface is misused — for example, if the bundle calls methods out of sequence, or uses unexpected values for some parameters. How could your application deal with these cases? If it is possible to clean up the malformed parameters and carry on normally with the sanitized versions, this could allow the application to recover from some genuine mistakes including accidental bad input from the user or a bug in the bundle code. On the other hand, if the bundle really is going out of its way to misuse the API by calling methods out of sequence or with clearly malicious data in the parameters, then it could be best to avoid trying to honor its requests. Techniques for doing this range from ignoring the request (perhaps noting in the log that this was done) to aborting the whole application. That last suggestion seems quite extreme, but if it is detected that misuse of the application has already caused it to get into an inconsistent state with no hope of recovery, it could be the only safe measure to take. Attempting a more sophisticated form of recovery when dealing with inconsistent or malicious data could end up getting the application into a worse state than simply giving up and stopping, distasteful though it may seem. Some very nasty vulnerabilities have resulted from developers — particularly of web browsers — trying to be too clever in accepting malformed data.

There are cases in which the operating system will make the decision on your behalf that the security of your app has been irrevocably compromised. It will then kill the app without any alternative action offered. One example is the case of the stack canary, *a guard against attackers modifying the way an application exits from functions. Stack canaries in OS X are described by Amit Singh at* `http://www.kernelthread.com/publications/security/smemory.html`, *and in Apple's Leopard Security briefing:* `http://images.apple.com/au/macosx/leopard/pdf/MacOSX_Leopard_Security_TB.pdf`.

Coding for Security

It sounds as if the treatment of data entering, moving through, and leaving the application depends very specifically on the app's implementation, so shouldn't it be dealt with at the code level while you write the app? Yes, but there are good reasons to understand the data flow while designing the app, too. You're more likely to be thinking about the "big picture" and how the whole app fits together when designing it than when coding it, when you will be dealing with the specifics of individual classes or methods. This all means that it's much easier to see where the data is going while working on the design, and to identify relationships between distant parts of the app that might go unnoticed while you're knee-deep in the code. For example, your big picture view might identify sensitive data such as a password or some confidential data. Identifying the flow up front may enable you to define a strategy for consistent protection of this data — it's common for applications to encrypt data but forget the other points of access including the network service for which the password is used. Even a seemingly small application with only a few use cases can comprise several components.

SOME OF THE THYTUNES ENTRY POINTS

The external interfaces for ThyTunes include the Mac and iPhone user interfaces, which allow users to buy music through the store and organize their music libraries. Organizing these libraries includes the ability to delete music. The store is accessed over the Internet via a web service. Additionally, the Mac and iPhone applications communicate over a local network connection to synchronize music and playlists.

I have not listed any internal interfaces in the applications, because they really depend on the way the components in the application are hooked together. This is where knowledge of the specific design of the application will be necessary to work out where these interfaces are and how important each is.

It can be very useful to annotate any sketches or other design documentation you create with comments about the source and safety of data or callers, to act as an aide-mémoire when you (or another developer) write the code. If your design includes a skeleton of the source code, then writing these notes in code comments alongside the class or method descriptions is best; it will be much harder to ignore or forget about the security notes if they are staring back at you when you open Xcode. Such notes could explain who might have prepared the data that's being handled by this code, whether any change of privilege is involved, and any particular sanitization that you should deal with before using the data. For instance, a method for writing a Twitter message into an SQLite database would have an associated comment explaining that the message could have come from anyone on the Internet but will be in the privileged position of modifying the database asset, and should be cleaned of SQL injection attempts before being used.

DEFINING THREATS

Returning to the crime show analogy, you now know the victims, perpetrators, motives, and modus operandi. If any one of the perpetrators could use one of the MOs to achieve a goal, then there is the potential for a crime to be committed. The threat of crime hangs over your application.

What Is a Threat?

A threat is the risk that one of your attackers could use an entry point of the app in order to damage or take the asset the attacker willfully or accidentally targets. As with any risk, there are two important dimensions: the likelihood that this threat will actually occur and the impact, or amount of damage, that would happen if it did occur. There's no reason to go into very fine-grained analysis of either impact or likelihood; ratings of low, medium, and high will be sufficient to compare the threats with each other and identify those that should be dealt with first.

Visualizing the Threats

A useful way to visualize this information is on a graph of impact versus likelihood, with each threat plotted as a point on the graph. The risk you are willing to accept, or that you believe your users would be willing to accept, is drawn as a line separating the top-right and bottom-left corners of the graph. The more threats toward the top-right corner, the higher the risk the application is exposed to. When you have that graph, which will look like Figure 1-3, congratulations! You've now modeled the environment of your application in terms of the risks it will face. This is the first important milestone in the complete threat model — or, more correctly, in the initial version of the threat model. As the application changes, and features are added, bugs

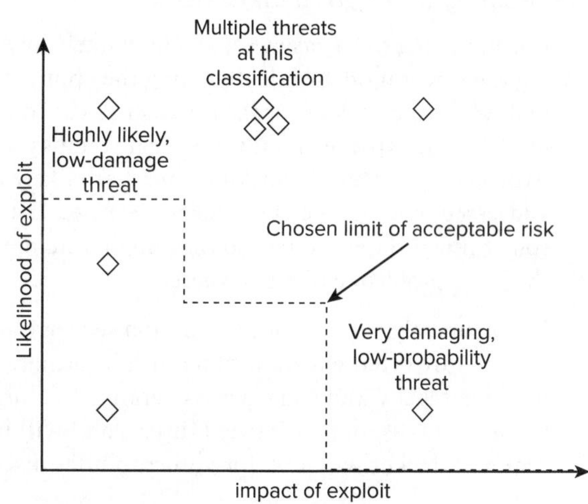

FIGURE 1-3: An example of a threat graph

are found, and countermeasures are designed in, the threat model should be updated to reflect the current state of the app. A static threat model representing the 1.0 release (or worse, the pre-alpha version) of the software you released two years ago will not help you understand the security of your application as it evolves.

It isn't strictly accurate to depict likelihood and impact as independent properties; if attackers can cause a lot of damage to a system in one way, they may be more inclined to attack in that way. That really depends on the profile of the attacker: if a vulnerability is going to be targeted only by script kiddies, then the attackers probably lack the skills or aversion to risk required to mount a continuous campaign to realize one particular attack. Similarly, if a threat is very likely to be realized, then the level of damage may come not just from the direct attacks on the target asset, but from the negative reviews of an app that is continually suffering from security problems.

For the first evaluation of an application's threat model, it should not be assumed that any countermeasures have been designed or implemented in the app. If the countermeasures already exist, then the tail is wagging the dog; the threat model is supposed to show you where to expend effort in protecting the app. If you assume that some countermeasures are in place before constructing the threat model, then you aren't considering the importance of the threats if those countermeasures are not in place. Thus you can't be sure that the countermeasures are truly the most effective, nor that it is a good use of your time to implement them. List and rank the threats first, then identify the vulnerabilities (see the next section) that should be protected against. Design countermeasures into the application to deal with those vulnerabilities. Now look at the threat model again, see how the countermeasures have mitigated some threats and created others, and draw the graph for the new state.

Similarly, do not worry yet about the specifics of how the attacker will perform the attack, as this could depend on details of the application that either do not yet exist or are inappropriately specific for a design-level analysis. The reason you are identifying threats is to consider what attackers might be trying to do to the application, how bad it would be if they managed to do this, and what the likelihood is of their pulling it off. The exact set of circumstances through which the attack might be successful constitutes a vulnerability, discussed later in this chapter.

Assessing a Threat's Likelihood

It is not going to be easy to assess how likely any of the threats you identify may be. If you are building the threat model while designing the application, then the app has not yet been exposed to the real world and so none of the threats has yet come to pass. Of course, if you are working on a threat model of an existing application, then you may already have had to deal with some security issues. Attackers (particularly unskilled ones) are likely to try variations on a theme, thinking that you have addressed only the specific problem revealed last time. Or maybe they just lack the skill to think of something different to try. So they might attempt the same attack on a different entry point, to see if the same problem exists elsewhere.

Unfortunately, victims of information security attacks — and the software vendors who supply them — are often reluctant to publish information about the attacks they have faced, though you might get lucky and come across details of vulnerabilities found in competing or related apps (a vulnerability is an unmitigated threat, and will be covered in the next section). The probability is that an attacker will look for vulnerabilities discovered in other, similar applications to use as a template when targeting yours — therefore the likelihood that the threat will affect your users in addition to your competitors' is increased.

A final way to determine the likelihood of any threat's coming to pass is to look in general at vulnerabilities reported in any other applications and try to discover trends. The U.S. government's National Vulnerabilities Database at `http://nvd.nist.gov/` *is a good place to look for current and historical security problems in well-known software, as is the SecurityFocus web site,* `http://www.securityfocus.com/`*. SecurityFocus also hosts the Focus-Apple mailing list (*`http://www.securityfocus.com/archive/142/description`*), a low-traffic list discussing "security involving hardware and software produced by Apple or that runs on Apple platforms." Apple announces security advisories for its own products on the security-announce mailing list at* `http://lists.apple.com/mailman/listinfo/security-announce`*.*

Once all the available facts have been exhausted, you must compare the relative likelihood of distinct threats using judgment or even intuition. Some are simple to dismiss; if a particular attacker has no physical access to the computer, then any threat performed by that attacker that requires physical access is unlikely. Consider the values of the assets that are threatened and how likely they are to be associated with each route into the system. If it would be obvious to people that a particular asset is accessed through a given entry point, then threats targeting that combination of asset and entry point seem likely. Also think about how many of the relevant class of misuser you might expect; a particular type of threat might be more common simply because there are many people who might try to perform the attack.

The impact of each threat is easier to evaluate than its likelihood. We have already considered the relative importance of each asset and which of the CIA properties is important. We can similarly classify each of the threats to understand how it affects the system (see the next section, "STRIDE classification"). If a threat is going to cause an important compromise of a valuable asset, then it is more important than a threat affecting only inconsequential assets.

STRIDE Classification

Simply knowing that a threat exists is not sufficient information with which to plan countermeasures to reduce or mitigate the threat. You also need to understand what it is the attacker gains (or you or your users lose) by any particular threat's being realized. The different possible effects that the threat can produce in the system are known by the acronym STRIDE. The categories in the STRIDE classification are not graded in the same way as the likelihood of a threat or the availability of an asset; they are yes/no properties of the threat. A threat either represents the possibility of realizing one (or more) of these effects or it does not. The effects are:

- **Spoofing:** The possibility that an attacker will be able to pass him- or herself off as a different person. An external agent might be able to perform a task as if the application's user had performed it, or one user could appear to be acting as a different user.

- **Tampering:** The realization of the threat would result in the modification of an asset that the attacker does not normally have the right to modify, or just not in the way made possible by this threat.
- **Repudiation:** It is not possible to demonstrate that the attacker accused of realizing a threat was really responsible for the attack. This can be an important property of a threat if an application must meet some legal or regulatory security requirement, like applications that process online payments. Such requirements are also common for corporate software systems. Without the ability to prove beyond reasonable doubt who the attacker is, it is impossible to place sanctions on the attacker, through either legal prosecution or corporate disciplinary measures.
- **Information disclosure:** The attacker has gained access to some confidential asset that this person should not normally be permitted to view.
- **Denial of service:** The availability of an asset has been compromised. There are many ways in which this could occur. The asset could be removed (which is often also a tampering event). It could become impossible to reach the asset; perhaps it is located on a remote system and the network connection has been rendered unavailable. The asset could also be slowed down or made so busy as to refuse or infrequently allow legitimate access; this is how the classic DDoS on the Internet works.
- **Elevation of privilege:** The attacker is able to perform some action that is not normally permitted for someone with the attacker's privilege level. This can often be the result of a spoofing attack, though that is not necessarily the case. Once an attacker has elevated his privilege level, he usually gains the ability to carry out attacks from any of the other threat classes listed here. Security analysts therefore treat privilege escalation as a very serious class of threat.

THYTUNES THREAT DISCOVERY AND CLASSIFICATION

Some of the threats that can be identified from the environment of ThyTunes are described here. The list is not complete but shows how knowledge of the app's environment can be used to consider the sort of attacks that might be likely. Figure 1-4 shows the three threats in a graph as described earlier. It should not be much of a surprise that the threats identified here all lie toward the top-right corner of the graph, as either high-impact or high-likelihood threats. By identifying the most important assets, attackers, and entry points you make it easy to selectively aim at the more threatening attacks the application will face.

The ThyTunes developers have decided that any low-impact or low-likelihood risk can be accepted, and the risk from any other threat must be mitigated. The amount of risk they are willing to accept is shown in Figure 1-4 by the dashed line, which shows that they will need to address each of the three threats discussed after the graph. Try to think of more threats that would be present during the use of ThyTunes, and place them on the threat graph relative to the threats shown. Will the developers need to mitigate all the threats you have identified? Do you agree with their choice of acceptable risk level?

DELETING ITEMS: DENIAL-OF-SERVICE THREAT

A regular user of the application, either at the Mac or iPhone interface, accidentally deletes purchased music while organizing the library. This is a denial-of-service threat in the STRIDE classification, as the availability of the purchased music has been compromised. Based on the profile of the users defined above, this threat would seem very likely. It would cause a single user severe problems, basically stopping this user from using the app for its intended purpose. But since it doesn't affect multiple users, the developers choose to rank its impact as medium.

STEALING SERVICES: CONFIDENTIALITY THREAT

The out-of-work attacker or the online activist targets the web interface to the online store in order to retrieve music without paying. This would probably be categorized as affecting the "confidentiality" of the music, since the record company sees the music as being licensed to legitimate customers when they purchase it and does not want it to be available to anybody else. This attack would also indirectly damage the relationship between the ThyTunes developers and the record company, which doesn't want record piracy to be possible in the online music world. This vulnerability could be exploited, allowing attackers access to information they should not have, and could potentially be a spoofing attack if the attacker poses as a paying customer. It's also a privilege escalation threat as the music is supposed to be available only to people who can pay for it. If one user found a way to purchase songs on behalf of all other users, the whole system could be thrown into chaos. The customers would expect refunds of all the spoofed purchases. The developers of ThyTunes could expend lots of effort in identifying all the attacker's orders and reversing those. They could refund every purchase made during the attack or insist that the payments stand. In any case, the story is likely to get into the press and damage the company's reputation with both ThyTunes users and with the record companies.

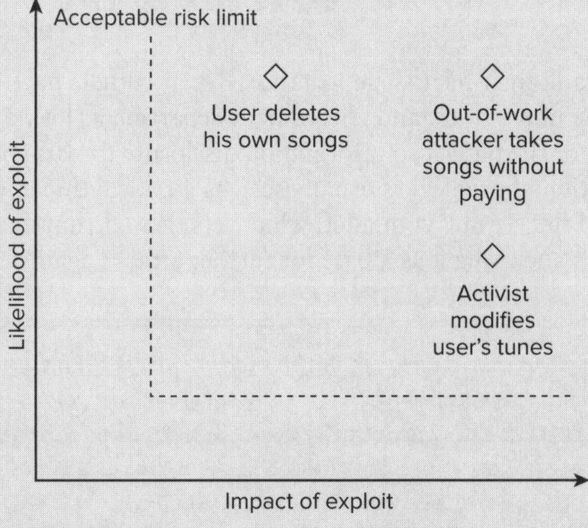

FIGURE 1-4: Threat graph for the ThyTunes application

continues

(continued)

The likelihood of this threat's being realized is probably high, as there are many attackers who might try it, and the end result — free music — is appealing. The potential consequence, that the record company withdraws its music from the ThyTunes store, strikes at the core of the ThyTunes business, so the expected impact is also high.

CHANGING THE INTERFACE: TAMPERING THREAT

The online music activist uses the library syncing network interface to replace tunes in a user's library with messages about the activist group's mission. This would attack the integrity and the availability of a user's library, and as with the previous threat could tarnish the developers' relationship with the record company (which is, after all, the real goal of the activist). This threat is classified under STRIDE as a tampering threat. It is also a privilege escalation threat, as the syncing interface is supposed to allow users to sync only their own computers and phones. As with the previous threat, the expected impact is high, since there is a threat to the business. It is not thought that there are many of these activist attackers with knowledge of the syncing mechanism, but the profile of such attackers suggests that they would expend some effort to attack the system. The likelihood of attack is therefore medium.

So now that you know all the constituent parts of a threat, and how to classify threats and rate their importance relative to each other, you can now start to consider countermeasures to mitigate those threats — reducing their likelihood, impact, or both to an acceptable level. The remaining chapters in this book all discuss aspects of Mac OS X or iPhone OS technology with a view to creating technical countermeasures, and as such will make use of the terminology and ideas described in this chapter. However, before we leave the world of the on-paper application design behind, there is one remaining aspect of an attack to consider. You have the victim, the perpetrator, the motive, and the MO — for the complete criteria for a crime the attacker needs an opportunity. This brings us to the unmitigated threat — the vulnerability.

Classifying the threats can also help to rank their relative importance. Recently there have been a number of news stories about companies, universities, and government departments losing personal information about customers, members, or the public, so information disclosure threats could resonate particularly with individual users. Elevation of privilege is usually seen as a critical threat, especially if it gives the attackers "root" privileges on the victim's computer, which lets them do anything with that system, including sending spam messages and using it as a base for further attacks against other victims.

Examples of the impact information disclosure has in the media can be found at `http://www.darkreading.com/insiderthreat/security/app-security/showArticle.jhtml?articleID=219400878`, `http://www.theregister.co.uk/2009/08/21/trade_body_data_policy/`, `http://www.dailycal.org/article/106339/campus_takes_steps_to_boost_server_security_after_`, *and* `http://www.guardian.co.uk/uk/2007/dec/11/northernireland.jamessturcke`.

DEFINING AND MITIGATING VULNERABILITIES

The previous section was about defining threats faced by your application: potential misusers and the ways in which they could target the app. This modeling of the hypothetical hostilities in the app's environment enabled you to balance risks against each other to find the most important ones, but of course it's only the ones that really happen that will cause problems when the app is deployed. If there exists a threat against which the app is unprotected, then the app is said to be vulnerable to that threat. The circumstances that result in the threat's being exploitable comprise a vulnerability.

Vulnerabilities as Unprotected Threats

For each of the threats you have identified as significant, try to think about how the attacker might go about targeting the application — how the threat could be realized. Some vulnerabilities are so common that tools have been written to automate their exploitation (which has the side effect of automating the detection of those vulnerabilities, too).

A discussion of a popular set of penetration-testing (or pen-testing*) tools can be found in Chapter 5 of* OS X Exploits and Defense *by Kevin Finisterre et al., Syngress Publishing Inc., 2008.*

The definition of the vulnerability is essentially a "use case" for the attacker's interacting with your application; perhaps a better term would be a "misuse case." A convenient way to describe use cases is with the user story, and that's also a handy way to describe misuse cases. We need to go into more detail than is usually present in user stories. (User stories are explored in detail in *User Stories Applied: for Agile Software Development* by Mike Cohn, Addison-Wesley, 2004.)

Common practice when writing user stories is to ignore, or rather actively avoid discussion of, the application's implementation. When writing a description of a vulnerability, you need to describe how the attacker is going to exploit the application in order to carry out the attack — that means that you must include details of what makes the application vulnerable. A complete misuser story must therefore describe which threat is being realized by which misuser, and what this misuser does to the app to make the threat happen. The amount of detail you go into is entirely up to you. The description should be sufficient to help you remember what the vulnerability is about — either when working on its mitigation or when discussing it with others — but not so long that either the security model becomes unmanageable or you spend inordinate amounts of time on creating and maintaining it. The sentence "Attacker uses SQL injection in the recipes field" could be a useful aide-mémoire, or you might want to go into more depth. Sometimes it might be quicker just to fix an obvious bug than to think about all the conditions and write out a description, even as a simple misuser story. You should use your own judgment, and take your company's processes and development lifecycle into account. I have worked on teams with very specific change control mechanisms, designed to ensure that all modifications made to the teams' products are understood and tested. In such situations an ad hoc change would not be welcome even though the alternative is more expensive.

For an app that still exists entirely on the whiteboard, this definition of vulnerabilities will take two forms: discovering and addressing vulnerabilities in the design of the application, and making notes of problems that could come up when you implement the application. Both types should be documented in the threat model. If you make a design choice based on security but fail to explain in the design why you made that choice, you might change the design later without remembering that the original choice was justified as a vulnerability mitigation. If you do not leave reminders to yourself or fellow developers on your team to defend against vulnerabilities when writing the code, then you or they will probably forget to do so. Remember the adage that every application has a team of at least three developers: you from six months ago, you, and you six months into the future. Your design and threat model should accommodate each of these developers.

A user story is complete when the user can complete the task identified in that story (or, more correctly, when the users accept that they can complete that task). The criteria for completing work on a misuser story are more nebulous: the story is completed when you or your customers can live with the remaining risk associated with the vulnerability. The most visible form of that completion is when the risk is reduced to zero; either the vulnerability is impossible to exploit or there is no impact caused by successful exploitation. If it is not possible to get to exactly zero risk, then you will need to decide what constitutes "acceptable" residual risk. The DREAD classification outlined below can help you to understand what makes a vulnerability likely or damaging, and then to decide which aspects of the vulnerability to address in mitigation of the risk.

The number of threats faced by any application may be fairly small; on one project I worked on, three developers brainstorming for a total of two hours ultimately came up with a list of around a dozen threats. Depending on the relative risk associated with each threat and the level of risk you choose to accept, you could easily decide not to deal with half the threats you list. However, when constructing the threat model for an app that is either still in the design phase or has never been the subject of security analysis, it could be easy to come up with a very long list of vulnerabilities. For example, a tampering threat in which the attacker is a local user of the computer implies that each file in the app could be vulnerable to a file-system-permissions or access-control attack, as could named sockets or pipes, temporary files created while the application is running, or listeners on loopback network connections.

The number of vulnerabilities that could appear as a result of the analysis might seem overwhelming. Vulnerabilities can be grouped if they are similar — a vulnerability in which the attacker sends too much data to an entry point and one in which the attacker sends too little data to the same entry point could both be classed as a data sanitization vulnerability of that entry point. The group of vulnerabilities can then be treated as a single issue to be addressed in the application. Be careful not to lose too much information in this process: the combined vulnerability descriptions should still be sufficient to remind you of the problems that must be dealt with. Forgetting to deal with one aspect of a vulnerability still leaves the application vulnerable.

Estimating Risk

As you have already defined a risk level for each of the threats identified, the risk associated with each vulnerability is roughly known. The information you have on the vulnerabilities can be used to refine your understanding of the risk associated with each threat, and the relative risk of each vulnerability needs to be known so that you can prioritize dealing with it. It is, after all, the vulnerabilities themselves that you will be addressing, not the abstract threats underlying them. Remember to take into account the information you have already gathered about the security profile of the application; will the attacker actually have the competence or tenacity to discover a complex vulnerability? Is a vulnerability that targets the confidentiality of public information worth spending any effort on?

If you were unable to find any vulnerabilities that realize a particular threat, then it's likely that this threat is not exploitable, or at least that the probability of its being exploited is lower than you might have initially thought. Conversely, if there is a huge pile of misuser stories all corresponding to one threat, then the threat is probably an important one to deal with.

Another thing to look out for is outlying vulnerabilities. The DREAD classification described in the next section will help you to identify the likelihood and damage associated with each vulnerability. If there's one that seems obviously exploitable or particularly dangerous, then it could indicate that you've underestimated that threat, and that it's worth trying to uncover other related vulnerabilities (or at least satisfying yourself that there are none). Outliers in the opposite direction, for example a very unlikely vulnerability in a sea of easy targets, can probably be dealt with last if at all.

DREAD classification

The properties by which security analysts classify vulnerabilities are a refinement and augmentation of the two dimensions of impact and likelihood that have so far been used. As with the STRIDE classification for threats, your consideration of these properties can both drive and be driven by the understanding of the importance of the risk associated with the vulnerability. Each of these properties should be given a rank on some simple scale, such as low-medium-high or 1–5. The DREAD classification system was first suggested by Microsoft: see *Writing Secure Code, Second Edition* by Michael Howard and David LeBlanc, Microsoft Press, 2003.

- **Damage:** The severity of the effect were this vulnerability to be exploited in the field. This property is related to the impact of the risk to which this vulnerability relates, as well as to user perception of the exploit. As has already been described, information disclosure attacks are currently garnering a lot of press coverage, so an information disclosure threat should be rated higher than any other threat that would otherwise be considered equally damaging.
- **Reproducibility:** The likelihood that the same series of actions on the part of the misuser will always lead to the vulnerability's being exploited. Evaluation of this criterion includes questions such as whether the vulnerability is time-related: a vulnerability in the default state of the app is inherently more reproducible than one that can be exploited only while certain operations are in progress, or when non-default features are enabled.
- **Ease of attack:** A measure of the simplicity of exploiting the vulnerability. This can incorporate issues like the required technical competence and time or resource investment of the misuser and any environmental prerequisites, such as whether the attacker must have physical access to the computer or phone and the level of privilege the attacker needs to perform the attack.
- **Affected users:** The fraction of the user base that could be affected by exploitation of this vulnerability. Does the vulnerability work only on particular models of the iPhone, or affect only users with specific releases of Mac OS X? Perhaps the application is vulnerable on 32-bit machines but safe in 64-bit mode; how many users have the vulnerable version? If the exploit relies on a custom app configuration, such as a certain feature's being enabled, how many of the users are likely to have that configuration?

Note that ease of attack and reproducibility are not necessarily linked. A vulnerability that requires 72 hours of manual preparation and a cluster of 10 Xserves to exploit but against which an attack always succeeds means an attack that is difficult but 100 percent reproducible. An exploit that can be run from an automatic script but that succeeds only once in every million attempts is easy to perform, but not very reproducible. A vulnerability that can be exploited both repeatably and rapidly can be catastrophic.

- **Discoverability:** How likely do you think it is that the vulnerability will actually be found in the field? This is quite a contentious issue — the authors of *Writing Secure Code* choose to assume that all vulnerabilities will eventually be discovered and assign this property the highest value every time. A cynical person might think that the discoverability is only recorded to add credence to the (probably back-formed) DREAD acronym. I think it is possible to use information about your misusers and the specifics of the vulnerability to answer the question, "Will the attackers find this vulnerability?" and that it's important to do so to get a better view of the likelihood that a given vulnerability will be exploited. If discovering an exploit would require in-depth knowledge of the design of your application that you don't expect the attacker to have, then it's probably going to be harder to find than a "well-known" vulnerability like a buffer overflow. In the case of a misuser exploiting the vulnerability by accident, are the odds good that this attacker will stumble on the circumstances required to damage the application?

By taking the average of each of the DREAD scores for a vulnerability, you will arrive at a final number representing the "importance" of that vulnerability. It's taken a long time to get here, from profiling the attackers through identifying how they might misuse the app and to what end, to discovering how the application lets them in to perform their attacks. But it's been worth it: by choosing to address the most important vulnerabilities first you can be confident that time spent in securing your app is time well spent.

SUMMARY

Users of your application will have concerns about being able to complete their tasks with the application without being exposed to unacceptable levels of risk. In constructing a threat model of the application, you discover what the risks are, which risks your users will be most concerned about, and whether it is appropriate to accept or mitigate those risks.

These risks exist because your app can potentially be misused by an attacker — the potential misuse being termed a threat. The application contains, or gives access to, assets that are valuable to the attacker, user, or both. Attackers threaten the application to damage, destroy, or gain access to one or more assets. To do so, attackers must use one or more entry points — interfaces between the application and the outside world. Understanding how each entry point can gain an attacker access to the application's assets is the key to assessing — and ultimately controlling — the security risk.

A vulnerability exists in your application if a threat can be realized by an attacker. You can class vulnerabilities using the DREAD system, rating the importance of the vulnerabilities by measuring various properties related to the likelihood and to the damage possible were any vulnerability to be exploited by an attacker.

While the users' worries and the threats they face in using the application do not relate to any specific technology, the details of a vulnerability and the most appropriate way to mitigate it in a Cocoa or Cocoa Touch application are strongly dependent on the Objective-C language and the features and APIs available in Apple's frameworks. The remaining chapters of this book describe how the various features of the Mac and iPhone platforms are relevant to the security of an application running on those platforms, the problems those features can introduce, and how you can use them to mitigate the risks faced by your users.

2

Managing Multiple Users

WHAT'S IN THIS CHAPTER?

- Why have multiple-user accounts?
- How user accounts and groups are handled
- Directory services
- Handling user preferences

Mac OS X and the iPhone OS both have their roots in UNIX, and very deep roots they are indeed. UNIX first escaped from the Bell Labs in AT&T back in the 1970s, and was frequently to be found on minicomputers such as the Digital Equipment Corporation's PDP-11. Minicomputers are "mini" in that they are the size of filing cabinets, rather than taking up entire rooms as the contemporary mainframes did.

As both the equipment expenses and the electricity bills associated with giving every employee his or her own minicomputer would have been enormous, it was usually the case that tens or even hundreds of people would be using each computer, originally by booking time slots with the operator. UNIX and other systems were given the ability to run multiple processes at the same time, so computers with many terminals connected could be used simultaneously by different users. The UNIX users system allowed these people to all share a system without getting in each others' way. Each user could have a personal *account* that allowed the system to identify him or her and assign "sandboxed" access to the computer's resources. Without these account sandboxes, a multi-user system would have been unusable — any one user could just stop everybody else's work when she wanted priority use of the computer.

Even as minicomputers were replaced by network-connected workstations such as those made by Sun Microsystems and NeXT Computer (whose own operating system, NeXTSTEP, was the direct forerunner of Mac OS X), with one for each worker, the multi-user paradigm grew in new ways to support the new environments. Information about the various user accounts was now stored in a central directory on the network, such as NetInfo. This allowed the accounts to have a consistent meaning on every workstation and server on the network, extending the user's sandbox to cover file servers, mail services and so on provided by remote systems.

The user account paradigm on modern UNIX systems including Mac OS X is largely unchanged from that of the workstations of the 1980s. We shall see below how the concept of multiple users provides security protection to the system our applications are running on, how to fit in and potential risks introduced by multi-user systems.

CAVEAT FOR IPHONE DEVELOPERS

The UNIX multiple-user paradigm is present in the implementation of the iPhone OS, but is not exposed via the iPhone SDK. Applications have their user accounts set up for them by the operating system, which then uses alternative access control methods to prevent disruption of each app by the other. The iPhone sandbox is described in "Playing in the Sandbox" in Chapter 4. The rest of this chapter may provide an interesting diversion to iPhone developers interested to see how a more general-purpose UNIX system works, but none of the rest of this chapter is directly applicable to iPhone apps.

WHY WE HAVE MULTIPLE USERS

Plenty of Macs are configured with multiple (human) user accounts. Home desktop systems may be used by different members of the family, each of whom has his or her own preferences about such things as which applications are visible in the dock or which is the home page in Safari. The users also have their own documents, which they may or may not wish to share with the other users. Some users might not be able to access some features. Children who have their own accounts may be unable to use the iTunes store, for example, or run particular applications.

Macs found in offices are more likely to have traditional workstation-style configurations, with user accounts provided by a directory service on the network such as Open Directory or Microsoft's Active Directory. In these cases the user's account on the Mac is likely to correspond to accounts on intranet applications, file servers and other network services. The user account will be able to access those services as well as providing the local sandbox functions. This remote access could be integrated with a single sign-on service like Kerberos, so that the user need log in only once to use the disparate systems.

It may seem like overkill to have a multi-user operating system on a laptop that is only ever used by a single person. Even with this setup, though, having several distinct accounts is a useful property of Mac OS X — although the other accounts are not actually used (usually) by human actors. The various other accounts make it possible to isolate different components of the system from each other. Before discussing how this works let's look at how the system distinguishes the different users. What follows is an example of a user account record from the local directory of a Snow Leopard system.

```
heimdall:~ leeg$ dscl localhost -read /Local/Default/Users/leeg
dsAttrTypeNative:_writers_hint: leeg
dsAttrTypeNative:_writers_jpegphoto: leeg
dsAttrTypeNative:_writers_LinkedIdentity: leeg
dsAttrTypeNative:_writers_passwd: leeg
dsAttrTypeNative:_writers_picture: leeg
```

```
dsAttrTypeNative:_writers_realname: leeg
dsAttrTypeNative:_writers_UserCertificate: leeg
AppleMetaNodeLocation: /Local/Default
AuthenticationAuthority: ;ShadowHash;
;Kerberosv5;;leeg@LKDC:SHA1.8EB3550A549C4CE53B593706D2C0C9C7A506F25E;LKDC:SHA1.8
EB3550A549C4CE53B593706D2C0C9C7A506F25E;
GeneratedUID: 33BF38CD-36EF-4E0F-8054-547A790C481B
JPEGPhoto: [Lots of data ...]
NFSHomeDirectory: /Users/leeg
Password: ********
Picture:
 /Library/User Pictures/Animals/Cat.tif
PrimaryGroupID: 20
RealName:
 Graham J Lee
RecordName: leeg
RecordType: dsRecTypeStandard:Users
UniqueID: 501
UserShell: /bin/bash
```

The important property to the operating system is the UniqueID (also known in much of the API as a UID); it is this property that is used to track which user is associated with resources such as files and processes. If there is another user account with a UID of 501 on the computer, the operating system treats the two accounts as indistinguishable. As an aside, 501 is an important UID to the login window application: it shows only those users in its list that have a UID of 501 or higher. The UIDs of 500 and below are reserved for accounts internal to the system, so they are not displayed in the user interface.

Many of the examples in this chapter use the directory services command-line tool, dscl, to display information about users, groups and the directory services configuration. The dscl tool is also capable of searching the directory services, and of updating records, including by changing the passwords of users in the directory. For more information about how the dscl tool works see its UNIX manual page. To view the manual page type the following command into the Terminal: **man dscl**

Notice that the account has two distinct name properties; the RealName is the one shown in the login window if it is set to display a list of users. It is the user's "Full Name" in the Accounts pane of System Preferences (see Figure 2-1) and can be used in some network services on a Mac, such as the file-sharing services. UNIX traditionally could handle only one-word user names with a limited number of characters, so accounts in Mac OS X also have a "short name" that is compatible with this limitation — it is the RecordName property in the preceding record. Many of the Darwin components in Mac OS X will use the short name when identifying users, particularly in Terminal output or log files. If I want to log in to my computer using the secure shell (ssh), I have to give my user name as "leeg" and not as Graham J Lee. The short name is also given to the user's home directory.

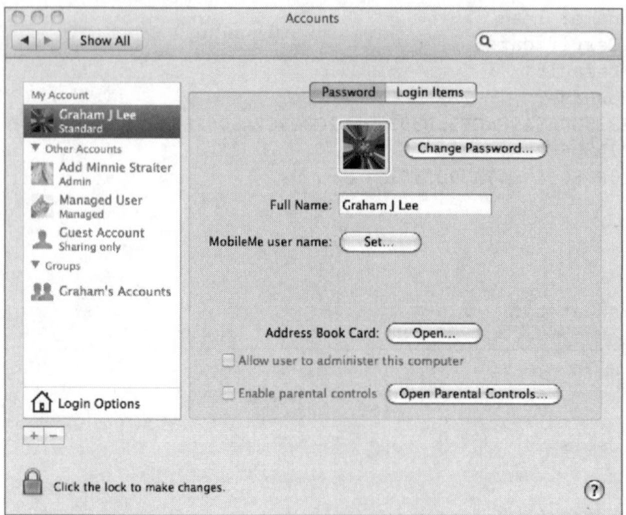

FIGURE 2-1: Configuring user accounts in System Preferences

Let's take a look at the complete list of users on the system:

```
heimdall:~ leeg$ dscl localhost -list /Local/Default/Users
_amavisd
_appowner
_appserver
_ard
_atsserver
_calendar
_carddav
_clamav
_coreaudiod
_cvmsroot
_cvs
_cyrus
_devdocs
_dovecot
_eppc
_installer
_jabber
_lda
_locationd
_lp
_mailman
_mcxalr
_mdnsresponder
_mysql
_pcastagent
_pcastserver
_postfix
_qtss
_sandbox
_screensaver
```

```
_securityagent
_serialnumberd
_softwareupdate
_spotlight
_sshd
_svn
_teamsserver
_timezone
_tokend
_trustevaluationagent
_unknown
_update_sharing
_usbmuxd
_uucp
_windowserver
_www
_xgridagent
_xgridcontroller
admin
daemon
leeg
manageduser
nobody
root
```

That's a long list of users! Of these, only three (leeg, manageduser, and admin) are accounts with which I can log in to the computer; they're also the only accounts listed in Figure 2-1 (the Guest Account entry allows the setting of some special configuration options, but is not a real account). The other accounts are all created by the operating system, and used to provide the resource sandboxing mentioned earlier.

To see what multiple user accounts provide to the system, imagine an operating system that cannot distinguish between different users. Anyone capable of interacting with the computer would be able to do anything, because the operating system would be unable to tell whether or not that person should be permitted to do so (even if it knew what the permissions should be, it would be unable to *identify* different users). There would be swaths of tampering, information disclosure and denial-of-service attacks possible against the operating system, as anybody with access could reconfigure or disable services and read data stored on the file system. There would be no elevation-of-privilege issues, but that's not much consolation when nobody needs any special privileges.

User accounts limit the ability of processes to interact with each other. The ability to signal a process, such as by requesting that it terminate, is limited to processes running under the same user ID. The following example shows what happens when I send the terminate signal (SIGTERM) to TextEdit, which is running as my leeg user, and launchd, which is running as root:

```
heimdall:~ leeg$ ps augxww
USER       PID  %CPU %MEM      VSZ    RSS   TT  STAT STARTED      TIME COMMAND
root         1   0.0  0.1  2456684   1224   ??  Ss    9:27AM   0:13.68
/sbin/launchd
leeg      2317   0.0  0.4  2763664   8968   ??  S     2:25PM   0:00.18
/Applications/TextEdit.app/Contents/MacOS/TextEdit -psn_0_364633
[lots of other output cut]
heimdall:~ leeg$ kill 2317
```

```
[TextEdit.app exits]
heimdall:~ leeg$ heimdall:~ leeg$ kill 1
-bash: kill: (1) - Operation not permitted
```

Because I am not running as the root user, I do not have permission to terminate root's processes. The launchd process does not receive the signal. The operating system also uses the user ID of processes to decide what level of access they have to the file system. File system permissions are explored in depth in Chapter 3.

The administrator on UNIX systems, including Mac OS X, can also impose his or her own restrictions, called *quotas*, on each of the users of that system. The admin could restrict the amount of disk space those users have access to, the number of processes they are allowed to run, the fraction of time a user's processes can spend on the CPU, and other resource usages. On Mac OS X the administrator can wield much greater control over the user than other UNIX operating systems permit, which is explored in "Accessing User Preferences and Managed Preferences" later in this chapter.

SPECIAL USERS: ROOT AND NOBODY

The root user is a special case on all UNIX systems. Also known as the *super-user*, root has an UID of 0. Processes running with UID 0 are not subjected to most of the same tests that other processes are, and so can perform tasks that would not be permitted to processes running as other users. The root user has traditionally been used to carry out administrative work on UNIX computers, because of the wide access the account grants to the system.

It is often said on the Web that the root account is "disabled" on Mac OS X. This does not mean that the account does not work, but it is not possible to log in as root on a default Mac OS X installation. This is not usually a problem, as administration can be carried out through other means, such as with Authorization Services (discussed in Chapter 6) or the sudo command in Terminal. Occasionally users will set a password for root and will log in and use applications as the super-user, so it's definitely worth testing your app as root. Additionally, the root user is enabled by default on Mac OS X Server, where its password is initially set as the same password the administrator entered for the initial user account.

Disabling login for the root user by default is a good security practice as it means that anybody trying to perform an administrative task is required to authenticate as a different, lower-privileged user first and then elevate his or her privileges to achieve the task. This offers both the opportunity to restrict each user's elevation to only the privileges required to get his or her task completed, and the opportunity to audit the attempts each user makes to gain additional privileges. The root account, with its ability to do nearly anything, is a very blunt instrument on any UNIX platform and should be treated with the cautious respect given to dangerously powerful tools in the real world. The root password can easily be enabled or disabled from the command line by means of the dsenableroot tool; in 10.5 it is also possible to configure the root user from the Directory Utility application in /Applications/Utilities; this app is no longer present in 10.6.

Root is also special to the networking features of UNIX and Mac OS X because only the root user can listen for TCP connections on the so-called "privileged ports" below port number 1024. The effect of this is that if your application is connecting to a privileged port on a UNIX system, such as a web server on port 80, you can trust that the server was configured by the administrator of the system. Whether you trust the administrator, and whether such configuration was intentional, are not addressed by this restriction.

Root has many other abilities, including the ability to change its own processes' user IDs to any other user IDs (see Chapter 4), give processes a higher priority than the default, or even write to a disk after the file system has started reporting that it is "full."

There is another special account called "nobody." The nobody account attempts to provide UNIX systems with the ability to run "unprivileged" processes. A process running as nobody has no access to user-based privileges for any user, and can access the file system only in ways that are available to everybody. In addition, it's used in Sun's NFS file system; most UNIX computers are configured to treat file access from root as if the request had been made by nobody. This stops people who have administrative access on one computer from automatically becoming superusers on any system that computer connects to.

So all those user accounts created by OS X are there to stop the various components of the operating system from interfering with one another. If an attacker manages to compromise a particular network service, such as the Apache web server running as user _www, he or she cannot then manipulate other components like the mail delivery server running as _postfix, because the _www user does not have permission to do so. Furthermore, a real user such as the leeg user does not have special access to either of these components, and must interact with them solely through the public interface: for example, by pointing a browser to port 80 in the case of the Apache web server. In this way the entry points to the components are restricted to only those that must be exposed for the component to work.

Processes, including Cocoa applications, can discover which user they are running as by using the POSIX getuid() API. The Collaboration Framework provides a simple way to get more information about user accounts. Listing 2-1 demonstrates using getuid() along with the Collaboration Framework to find the full name of the user who launched the program.

LISTING 2-1: Getting information about the current user [getuid.m]

Available for download on Wrox.com

```
#import <Foundation/Foundation.h>
#import <Collaboration/Collaboration.h>
#import <unistd.h>

int main (int argc, const char * argv[]) {
    NSAutoreleasePool * pool = [[NSAutoreleasePool alloc] init];

    //who am I?
```

continues

LISTING 2-1 *(continued)*

```
    uid_t myUID = getuid();

    /* find out some more about me
     * To find an identity in Collaboration Services, the API needs to be told
     * an identity authority to ask. The default authority means that it will
     * search the local and network identity databases.
     */
    CBUserIdentity *myIdentity = [CBUserIdentity userIdentityWithPosixUID:
myUID
                                                                   authority:
[CBIdentityAuthority defaultIdentityAuthority]];
    NSString *fullName = [myIdentity fullName];

    NSLog(@"My user is %@", fullName);
    [pool drain];
    return 0;
}
```

The program in Listing 2-1 produces the following output when I run it:

```
2009-08-28 16:29:14.456 GetUID[3485:a0f] My user is Graham J Lee
```

The full user name would actually have been much easier to retrieve using the Foundation convenience function NSFullUserName(). Where the Collaboration Framework really comes in useful is when you want your user to pick other users, often to grant access to some asset. The CBIdentityPicker class gives you a simple way to show a list of other accounts, available locally or on network services, from which the user can choose. It can even allow the user to choose identities based on entries in the address book that don't have accounts on the user's computer — passwords will be created for such identities. Listing 2-2 shows how the identity picker can be used; a screenshot is shown in Figure 2-2.

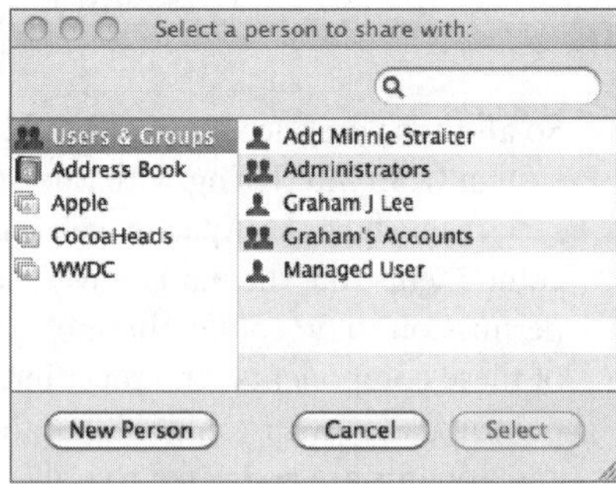

FIGURE 2-2: Choosing users with the identity picker

Available for download on Wrox.com

LISTING 2-2: Using the Collaboration framework identity picker

```
- (IBAction)pickUsers: (id)sender {
    CBIdentityPicker *picker = [[CBIdentityPicker alloc] init];
    [picker setAllowsMultipleSelection: YES];
    if ([picker runModal] == NSOKButton) {
        [[picker identities] enumerateObjectsUsingBlock: ^(id identity, NSUInteger
idx, BOOL *stop) {
            [self grantAccessForIdentity: identity];
        }];
    }
}
```

USER GROUPS

Users on UNIX systems can be organized into groups; any one user can be a member of multiple groups, but every user is a member of at least one group. The user record for the leeg user shown above has a PrimaryGroupID field; groups are identified by integers called GIDs just as users are identified by their UIDs. So the user leeg is a member of the group with GID 20, which is the system-provided staff group on OS X. But the groups command in Terminal shows that this is not the complete story:

```
heimdall:~ leeg$ groups leeg
staff localaccounts everyone com.apple.sharepoint.group.1
com.apple.sharepoint.group.2
```

The user is actually a member of five different groups. That information comes from the same source — either the local storage or a networked directory service — as the user records, as there are also records for each group. Let us take a look at the records for one of the groups that leeg is a member of:

```
heimdall:~ leeg$ dscl localhost -read
/Local/Default/Groups/com.apple.sharepoint.group.1
AppleMetaNodeLocation: /Local/Default
GeneratedUID: A372262C-6663-41AA-A50E-55068B529B69
GroupMembers: 33BF38CD-36EF-4E0F-8054-547A790C481B
GroupMembership: leeg
NestedGroups: ABCDEFAB-CDEF-ABCD-EFAB-CDEF0000000C
PrimaryGroupID: 101
RealName: Public
RecordName: com.apple.sharepoint.group.1
RecordType: dsRecTypeStandard:Groups
```

We see that in the GroupMembership field leeg is listed as the single user in the group (and the unique identifier — confusingly also referred to as a UID in this context — shown in the GroupMembers field is the same as leeg's GeneratedUID property). So it is from this record that the system discovers that leeg is in this group, and not from the user record for leeg.

Group membership is used in a number of contexts throughout the operating system: let us explore those by looking at some of the useful groups on a Mac OS X computer.

Administrative Users

All Mac users will be familiar with the idea that some operations — copying downloaded applications to the /Applications folder, installing software with the Installer app, adding new users in System Preferences and so on — require that they authenticate as administrators. How this process works will be detailed in Chapter 6. For the moment we want to see how the user is *identified* as being an administrator. The answer is that he or she is a member of a special group, the *admin* group.

```
heimdall:~ leeg$ dscl localhost -read /Local/Default/Groups/admin
AppleMetaNodeLocation: /Local/Default
GeneratedUID: ABCDEFAB-CDEF-ABCD-EFAB-CDEF00000050
GroupMembers: FFFFEEEE-DDDD-CCCC-BBBB-AAAA00000000 E0F3D7C1-D656-4BE7-9484-
83AFF750A03C
GroupMembership: root admin
```

```
Password: *
PrimaryGroupID: 80
RealName: Administrators
RecordName: admin
RecordType: dsRecTypeStandard:Groups
SMBSID: S-1-5-32-544
```

If a user is in the admin group — like users with the "Allow this user to administer this computer" checkbox ticked in the Accounts pane of System Preferences — then that user is identified as an administrator for the purpose of performing the tasks listed above.

The command-line interface also uses the admin group; the sudo command permits users to run commands as root (or any other user), and by default on a Mac; Sudo is configured to allow any user in the admin group to run any command via sudo after they entering his or her password. This configuration can be changed in the /etc/sudoers file. Note that this setup is different from those of some more traditional UNIX or UNIX-like distributions, which often use the wheel group (GID 0) for this purpose, particularly those that offer the su command instead of sudo.

Earlier I wrote that only the root user can change the user ID of its processes. But if sudo allows a non-root user to run commands as root, then it must also be able to change the user ID of that user's process to UID 0. How can that be?

The sudo executable is stored on the file system with the setuid permission bit set. This bit is also owned by root. Here is the directory listing for the executable:

```
heimdall:~ leeg$ ls -l /usr/bin/sudo
-r-s--x--x  1 root  wheel  272384 Jun 23 07:29 /usr/bin/sudo
```

This means that when a regular user runs the sudo command, it is actually running as the root user (its UID is set to 0, hence the name of the setuid bit). Code that is going to elevate the user to root like this should always be viewed with suspicion, as it is a natural hiding place for elevation-of-privilege vulnerabilities. Factor your application so that as little as possible runs with privileges, as described in Chapter 4.

Other Built-In Groups

Mac OS X does ship with a wheel group, which as described above is the traditional means by which UNIX systems determine which accounts are allowed to switch the user to root. In Mac OS X the wheel group is largely unused, and where it is consulted its effect is mostly identical to that of the admin group. Many of the system files are installed with the root owner and wheel group, but as root is the only member of the wheel group by default this is equivalent to ensuring that only root ever gets special access to the system files.

One of the system groups provided by Mac OS X is the procmod group. In Mac OS X 10.4 for Intel, Apple restricted the use of a particular API call, task_for_pid(), to code running with that effective group ID. The task_for_pid() call is frequently used as part of a technique to inject executable code into a different process. Because this could be part of an attack (malware could inject the malicious code into a different process to bypass access checks, evade appearing in auditing systems or give the user a false impression of why particular privileges are being requested), and because users are not by default members of the procmod group, the effect of this change was to ensure that administrators had to configure their systems to allow any attempt at task_for_pid() usage to succeed. Later in OS X 10.5 Apple introduced the taskgated process for deciding whether to allow requests to task_for_pid(); as well as procmod membership the taskgated process looks for a code signature and will allow any request from code signed with a safe identity. Code signing is discussed further in Chapter 10.

We saw earlier that leeg, a standard user without administrative privileges, has the staff group as its primary group ID. This is true for all regular users on a Mac, and users managed with parental controls. The fact that all of these users are in the same group makes it easy to share files between users on the same Mac. Conversely it makes it easy to disclose information to other users on the same Mac, so refer to Chapter 3 to ensure that the file system permissions on your assets are appropriate. As this group is the primary group for users of the system, any file they create will automatically have staff as its group. The permissions given to that group for accessing the file (as well as the folders in the path to that file, as explained in Chapter 3) will determine whether other users on the Mac can read or modify the file.

This is different from the way in which other UNIX systems, including many Linux distributions, operate. It's common to see each user's default group ID referring to a different group, with the group having the same name as the user account. No other accounts are in any of these groups. To share a file with other users of the same computer in this setup, the owner must deliberately change the file's group or allow access for everyone.

Custom Groups

To allow for sharing of file access between arbitrary subsets of users, UNIX permits the creation of custom groups. In Mac OS X the simplest way to create a new group is to use the Accounts pane in System Preferences. Clicking the plus button below the list of accounts invokes the new account sheet, and one of the types of account that can be created is a group. Users are offered only the ability to enter the full name of the group, though as with user accounts the group has a "short name" consisting only of characters acceptable to the POSIX API for dealing with groups.

Users may have good reason for sharing their documents with other users on the system: if two of the users are using your application to collaborate on a document then they might create a group containing just their two user accounts, and give that group read and write access to the document. You would not help those users by "correcting" the permissions on your app's document files if you think that group write access is too permissive.

Custom groups are also useful in *restricting* access to particular resources. Consider a network of Macs in a school, used by teachers, ancillary staff and students. The teachers use a grade-tracking application to record the progress of the students; this progress is confidential so they do not want the students to be able to view it. By making the grade data accessible only to users in the teachers group, the administrator denies access to the students; they also cannot be helped by ancillary staff (intentionally or otherwise), who also do not have access to the data. The administrator could go further and configure the *application* so that it can be used only by accounts in the teachers group; this denies access to the application as an entry point to the other users.

UNDERSTANDING DIRECTORY SERVICES

We have seen what information Mac OS X is using to identify users and groups, but where is it getting that information? How do the local and network-based sources, sharing their information over different protocols, combine to provide a consistent set of users and groups for the kernel to use in its access control tests? The answer lies in Open Directory.

Open Directory Architecture

Open Directory is an umbrella term that Apple uses for both the server and client aspects of its directory services infrastructure. The framework of APIs used to access information in Open Directory and provide custom information sources is known as Directory Services.

On the client side, requests for information about groups, users and other entries in the directory services are handled by a daemon process called DirectoryService. In earlier versions of Mac OS X, a process called lookupd performs the same function. This process provides a consistent interface to a number of separate plug-ins, each of which acts as a front-end to a particular store of directory information like NetInfo, local files, Active Directory and so on. This is shown graphically in Figure 2-3. The concepts behind Directory Services plug-ins, and their implementation, will be fully explored later in this chapter; for the moment let us investigate the API for finding and changing information in Open Directory.

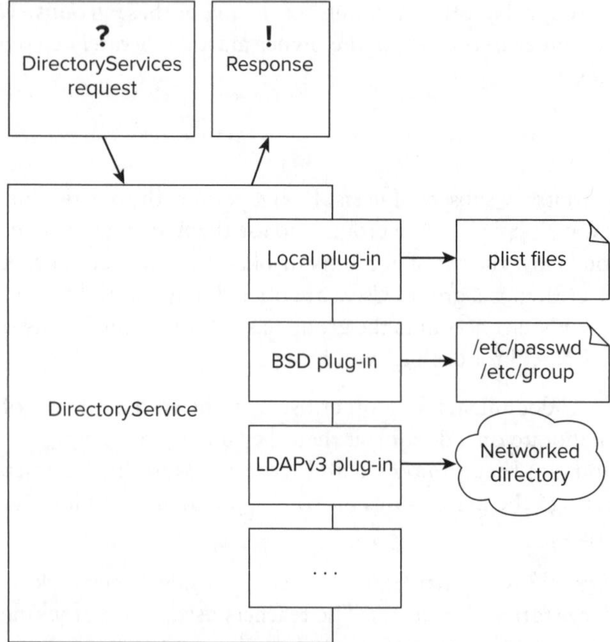

FIGURE 2-3: Open Directory client-side architecture

As the name Directory Services may suggest, Open Directory presents information in a structured fashion, wherein the structure is similar to the directory hierarchy of a file system. The hierarchy is represented as a tree of *nodes*: each node can contain other nodes (these are analogous to the folders in a file system) and records (analogous to files). Each record belongs to exactly one node, and each node is a child of one other node except the *root node*, which has no parent, like the / folder at the root of a file system. Records themselves are simple dictionaries; the values are considered to be opaque by Directory Services.

Just as two files with the same name cannot appear in the same folder but can be in different folders, so records within any node must all have different names *if they are of the same type*. Some of the more common types of records are listed in Table 2-1. It would be acceptable, for example, for the node containing the user record for leeg to also contain an AFP server record called leeg: however there could not be a second user called leeg in that node. A different node could contain another user record with the name leeg.

TABLE 2-1: Some Common Record Types in Directory Services

Record type	Description
`kDSStdRecordTypeUsers`	User account records.
`kDSStdRecordTypePeople`	Records describing people. These are used for contact information; the people do not necessarily have user accounts.
`kDSStdRecordTypeGroups`	Records for groups of users.
`kDSStdRecordTypeConfig`	Configuration information.
`kDSStdRecordTypeAFPServer`	AFP (Apple Filing Server) network file system records.
`kDSStdRecordTypeHosts`	Host records mapping computer names to network addresses.
`kDSStdRecordTypeComputers`	Computer records.
`kDSStdRecordTypeSMBServer`	SMB (Server Message Block. the standard Windows file-sharing protocol) network file system records.

You can see that a vast range of information beyond user account records is commonly accessed via Open Directory; one of the most common ways to use Directory Services, including Open Directory, is to access user and group records, so I will concentrate on that use during this discussion. Contact information (in a form frequently referred to as the Global Address Book) is also provided by Open Directory.

As the various records are all potentially provided by different services accessed through various plug-ins, it would be convenient to locate a record without knowing which node it is in, or knowing the path to that node from the root. We want to be able to search for a node that could be anywhere. For this purpose Open Directory provides a small number of search nodes at known locations in the hierarchy. These can be used to search for records appropriate to contexts such as authentication or finding contact information. Which plug-ins are consulted and in what order during the search is up to the administrator, who defines the search order using the Directory Utility application, found in /Applications/Utilities on 10.5 and before, and in /System/Library/CoreServices on 10.6. Listing 2-3 shows how to find the correct record for authenticating a user given the username, as might be performed by the login window or any other application that needs to verify the identity of a user. The listing uses the OpenDirectory.framework Objective-C interface, which was introduced in OS X 10.6; code that must support earlier versions of Mac OS X should use the C APIs in DirectoryServices.framework.

LISTING 2-3: Finding a user record in Directory Services [opendirauthentication.m]

Available for download on Wrox.com

```
- (ODRecord *)findUser: (NSString *)user error: (NSError **)error
{
    ODNode *searchNode = [ODNode nodeWithSession: [ODSession defaultSession]
                                            type: kODNodeTypeAuthentication
                                           error: error];
    if (searchNode == nil) {
        return nil;
    }
    /* query this node for the user record we're interested in.
     * We only need one result, which is why maximumResults is set to 1.
     */
    ODQuery *userSearch = [ODQuery queryWithNode: searchNode
                                  forRecordTypes: kODRecordTypeUsers
                                       attribute: kODAttributeTypeRecordName
                                       matchType: kODMatchEqualTo
                                     queryValues: user
                                returnAttributes: kODAttributeTypeStandardOnly
                                  maximumResults: 1
                                           error: error];
    if (userSearch == nil) {
        return nil;
    }
    /* For this example we'll use a synchronous search. This could take a while
     * so asynchronous searching is preferable.
     */
    NSArray *foundRecords = [userSearch resultsAllowingPartial: NO
                                                         error: error];
    if (foundRecords == nil || [foundRecords count] == 0) {
        return nil;
    }

    ODRecord *userRecord = [foundRecords objectAtIndex: 0];
    return [[userRecord retain] autorelease];
}
```

To avoid anyone with access to the directory tampering with the records, it is usually the case that an application needs to authenticate with Open Directory before it can make a change to a record, add a new record to a node or alter the directory in other ways. Listing 2-4 shows how to alter the full name of a user record, first authenticating with Open Directory. Note that Directory Services handles the business of authentication itself; there is no need for the calling code to concern itself with the mechanism involved in authentication. Accounts on standalone Macs (and local accounts on networked Macs) are usually authenticated via a *shadow hash*: a cryptographic hash of the user's password is stored in a file in /var/db/shadow/hash, which can be read only by the super-user. When the user tries to authenticate, the same function is used to generate a hash of the password he or she supplied, which is compared with the version on disk. In this way the confidentiality of the password is doubly protected: the password itself is not stored anywhere on the system, and the hash can be read only by a privileged user.

The code in Listings 2-4 and 2-5 requires that the user authenticate with the Directory Services framework, so that the DirectoryService daemon can determine whether the user has permission to make the attempted changes. If you are testing the examples or your own code on your own Mac, make sure that you do not make unintentional changes to production data. Consider making test user accounts in System Preferences to try the code against, so that any problems are contained. If things get really out of hand you can just delete the account without losing critical information.

In order to perform the authentication, the examples assume that a password has been passed in from somewhere. They do not demonstrate how such a confidential asset is handled by an application; this will be the topic of Chapter 5.

Available for download on Wrox.com

LISTING 2-4: Authenticating with Directory Services [changerecordsnippit.m]

```
- (BOOL)setName: (NSString *)newFullName forUser: (NSString *)userName error:
(NSError **)error
{
    NSError *dirSearchError = nil;
    ODRecord *foundUser = findUser(userName, &dirSearchError);
    if (foundUser != nil) {
        NSString *fullName = [[foundUser valuesForAttribute:
kODAttributeTypeFullName error: nil] objectAtIndex: 0];
        NSLog(@"username %@ currently has full name %@", userName, fullName);
        NSError *authError = nil;
        if ([foundUser verifyPassword: password error: &authError]) {
            NSError *nameChangeError = nil;
            if ([foundUser setValue: newFullName forAttribute:
kODAttributeTypeFullName error: &nameChangeError]) {
                NSLog(@"full name of user %@ successfully changed to %@",
userName, newFullName);
                return YES;
            }
            else {
                NSLog(@"could not change name of user %@: got error %@",
userName, nameChangeError);
                *error = nameChangeError;
                return NO;
            }
        }
```

continues

LISTING 2-4 *(continued)*

```
        else {
            NSLog(@"couldn't authenticate as user %@: got error %@", userName,
authError);
            *error = authError;
            return NO;
        }
    }
    else {
        NSLog(@"couldn't find user %@: got error %@", userName, dirSearchError);
        *error = dirSearchError;
        return NO;
    }
}
```

Listing 2-4 also demonstrates how attributes are retrieved and set for records using the ODRecord class. Any attribute can take multiple values, so the API for working with attributes always returns or accepts NSArray objects for the attribute's value. Each of the objects in this array can be either an NSString or NSData. In the interest of brevity, some additional checking code has been elided from the listing; it is assumed that the user record has a full name attribute with at least one value. To avoid denial-of-service problems caused by uncaught exceptions, real use of this API should test each of these cases. Before using any of the values of an attribute, the caller should check whether it is an NSString or NSData instance (or that it responds to the selectors that the calling code wishes to use). Future examples of the OpenDirectory.framework API will not even show as much validation code as Listing 2-4, in order to focus the examples on the API being discussed.

The method -[ODRecord verifyPassword:error:] used to authenticate against the directory in Listing 2-4 is a convenience to allow a user to modify his or her own user record; the general case is that some user (perhaps a directory administrator) wants to modify an arbitrary node in the directory by creating, removing or editing records at that node. The user must authenticate with the node that he or she intends to modify. Listing 2-5 shows how a user with sufficient permission could change a different user's full name attribute.

Available for download on Wrox.com

LISTING 2-5: Authenticating as one user to modify another's record

```
- (void)setFullName: (NSString *)newFullName forUser: (NSString *)userName asUser:
(NSString *)editingUser password: (NSString *)password error: (NSError **)error
{
    NSError *dirSearchError = nil;
    ODRecord *foundUser = findUser(userName, &dirSearchError);
    if (foundUser != nil) {
        NSError *authError = nil;
        if ([foundUser setNodeCredentials: editingUser password: password
error: &authError]) {
            NSError *nameChangeError = nil;
            if ([foundUser setValue: newFullName forAttribute:
kODAttributeTypeFullName error: &nameChangeError]) {
                NSLog(@"full name of user %@ successfully changed to %@",
```

```
userName, newFullName);
                }
            }
        }
    }
```

The reason the user authenticates with the node is that the user could have different access rights at different nodes, depending on which plug-in is providing those rights and the access control settings. That completes our look at the architecture of the client side of Open Directory. Now let us look at the architecture of the server side.

Mac OS X Server uses the same DirectoryService infrastructure (described earlier) to authenticate its users as the client version of the operating system. It also includes the software necessary to act as an Open Directory master or replica server, a source of directory information for multiple clients on a network. A master is the canonical source of directory information; replicas provide redundancy and high availability to avoid denial of service. The components that make up this server side of the system are shown in Figure 2-4.

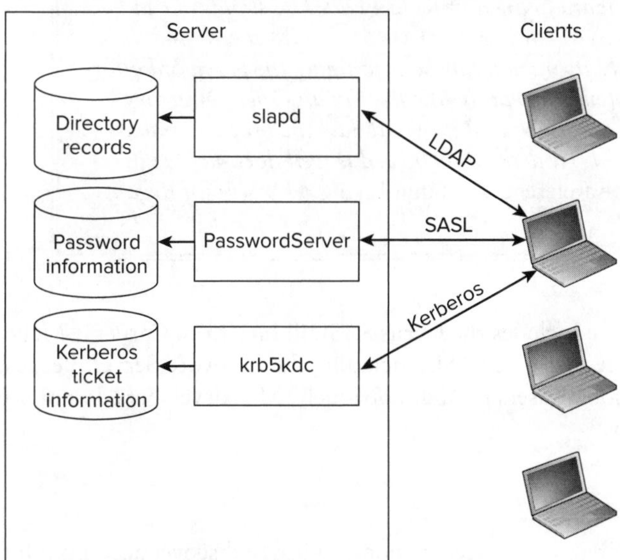

FIGURE 2-4: Open Directory server-side architecture

Clients that reference an Open Directory server primarily do so using LDAP (the Lightweight Directory Access Protocol) to search the directory on the server. The LDAP plug-in to DirectoryService supports this communication on the client side; the server end of the communication is provided by Apple's implementation of slapd, the server daemon from the OpenLDAP project at `http://www.openldap.org`. The database of records is stored in a Berkeley DB file on the server.

Further components on the server are involved when a client needs to authenticate a user whose account is provided by the Open Directory server. The ShadowHash method for local account authentication described earlier would not work for remote accounts, as the local system would not have access to the files containing the hashed passwords. There must be some way to authenticate the user without either locally knowing the account password or sending the password over the network in such a way that it could be intercepted.

In fact, two such methods are possible with an Open Directory server. Services that support Kerberos can authenticate the user with a ticket exchange using a Kerberos Key Distribution Center on the server. Kerberos is a large topic in itself and will be explored later in this chapter.

Another means available for authenticating Open Directory accounts, for cases in which Kerberos is not supported or the user does not have a ticket, is the Password Server. This daemon uses the SASL protocol (Simple Authentication and Security Layer) to verify the user's identity. In SASL exchanges, the password is typically not sent in the clear over the network; instead the Password Server issues a challenge to the client, which incorporates information about the challenge and the password into a response that it gives to the server. In this way not only is the password never sent over the network, but an attacker who manages to intercept the network traffic for one authentication attempt cannot replay the same data to spoof an authentication later, as the challenge will have changed.

SASL is a proposed Internet standard defined in RFC 4422. The standard can be found at `http://www.rfc-editor.org/rfc/rfc4422.txt`*.Kerberos and the SASL Password Server each keeps its own database containing the password information that it uses to validate attempts to authenticate. On an Open Directory Server each component is configured such that it will update the other's database when a user's password is changed. How this is achieved is well documented in* Mac OS X System Administration Reference, Volume 1, *edited by Schoun Regan (Peachpit Press, 2003).*

Mac OS X (both client and server versions) includes the Cyrus SASL library from Carnegie Mellon University for integrating with any service that uses SASL, including the Password Server. Because Open Directory handles the authentication of users to nodes opaquely, Mac developers do not need to directly interact with the SASL library.

Directory Services Plug-Ins

You can augment the services that the DirectoryService daemon can use to discover account information by creating plug-ins for the daemon. These plug-ins use the CFPlugin interface, which is very similar to Microsoft's COM technology. The plug-ins register a collection of callbacks, which the daemon uses to query the plug-ins about the state of the directory and to make changes. Plug-ins not provided by Apple should be installed in /Library/DirectoryServices/Plugins.

When a plug-in is loaded by DirectoryService, the daemon first calls the Initialize callback to set up the plug-in. If the plug-in is successfully initialized it becomes active and can participate in the Open Directory service. If it cannot initialize it is still loaded but is marked by the daemon as having failed to initialize. This stops the daemon from trying to load it again in the future.

There are two types of event that will cause the daemon to call an active plug-in. The daemon triggers a "caretaker" callback called PeriodicTask every 30 seconds, which the plug-in can use to perform housekeeping tasks such as updating caches or testing for the availability of network services. The other trigger is external events, which include searches for information by the Directory Services framework and other events like the daemon's getting ready for system sleep or waking from sleep. These events are handled by the ProcessRequest callback.

While custom DirectoryService plug-ins are obviously designed to provide access to information, you should still be aware of the possibility of information disclosure attacks involving your custom directory service. For each attribute exposed by the plug-in, consider whether it is really needed and, if so, who should be able to access it. The context passed to ProcessRequest includes information about the user making the request, so you can decide whether to complete the request or deny access.

Tampering attacks, particularly those that could lead to an elevation of privilege, are also important to defend against. If your plug-in allows a user to change details of his or her own account, then that user could change his or her UID to 0 in order to get super-user access. The ability to modify information about other users could be an annoying disruption or could lead to their being denied access to their Macs.

In the record for the user leeg, shown earlier in the chapter, you can see how local directory nodes include access control information alongside the other attributes in the account record. The attributes with names like _writers_realname describe which users are allowed to modify other attributes (in this case the full name attribute). The super-user (root) is always permitted to change local records, and no one else is unless his or her name is in the _writers_* access control attributes. In this way root gets to decide if anyone else may change the directory, and in what ways.

The following are some of the common plug-ins you'll find in use on multi-user Mac networks. Where the source code for these plug-ins is available a reference is given: the source for a real-world plug-in is a great reference to use when writing your own and for identifying how particular issues are solved.

Local

The Local plug-in provides access to the locally-defined collection of user accounts on the Mac. It is always enabled in the DirectoryService daemon. The plug-in stores the records in XML property lists, which can be found in /var/db/dslocal/. The record files on the file system are readable and writable only by root so that the Local plug-in can arbitrate over whether particular information should be available to users.

The source code for the Local plug-in is available as part of the Darwin DirectoryService project, which also includes the source for the DirectoryService daemon, some of the other system-supplied plug-ins and the API framework for interacting with Directory Services. The source code for the DirectoryService project as shipped with OS X 10.6 is located at `http://www.opensource.apple.com/source/DirectoryService/DirectoryService-621/`.

This being a very simple plug-in, it is very educational to see how the local records are handled. Listing 2-6 shows how the plug-in looks up the value for a particular attribute.

LISTING 2-6: Getting an attribute from the local directory

Available for download on Wrox.com

```
try
{
//records have unique IDs, fInRecRef is the ID we're interested in
    recRefNumber = CFNumberCreate( NULL, kCFNumberIntType, &inData-
>fInRecRef );
```

continues

LISTING 2-6 *(continued)*

```
        //retrieve the property list for this record
        CFMutableDictionaryRef openRecordDict = RecordDictForRecordRef( inData-
>fInRecRef );
        if ( openRecordDict == NULL ) throw
BaseDirectoryPlugin::GetRecAttrValueByID( inData );

        CDSLocalPluginNode *node = NULL;
        nodeDict = this->CopyNodeDictandNodeObject( openRecordDict, &node );
        if ( nodeDict == NULL ) throw( ePlugInDataError );

        CFMutableDictionaryRef mutableRecordAttrsValues =
(CFMutableDictionaryRef)CFDictionaryGetValue( openRecordDict,
            CFSTR( kOpenRecordDictAttrsValues ) );
        if ( mutableRecordAttrsValues == NULL )
            throw( ePlugInDataError );
        //discover which attribute the caller is interested in
        stdAttrType = CFStringCreateWithCString( NULL, inData->fInAttrType-
>fBufferData, kCFStringEncodingUTF8 );
        if ( stdAttrType == NULL )
            throw( eMemoryAllocError );

        CFStringRef recordType = (CFStringRef)CFDictionaryGetValue(
openRecordDict, CFSTR( kOpenRecordDictRecordType ) );
        if ( recordType == NULL ) throw( ePlugInDataError );

        // get the attribute value
        CFStringRef nativeAttrType = this->AttrNativeTypeForStandardType(
stdAttrType );
        //here is where the acces control is handled
        if ( node->AccessAllowed(nodeDict, recordType, nativeAttrType,
eDSAccessModeReadAttr) == false )
            throw( eDSPermissionError );

        CFTypeRef attrValue = NULL;
        siResult = node->GetAttributeValueByCRCFromRecord( nativeAttrType,
mutableRecordAttrsValues, inData->fInValueID, &attrValue );
        if ( siResult != eDSNoErr ) throw( siResult );

        size_t attrValueLen = 0;

        CFTypeID attrValueTypeID = CFGetTypeID(attrValue);
        if ( attrValueTypeID == CFStringGetTypeID() )
        {
            dataValue = CStrFromCFString( (CFStringRef)attrValue, &cStr,
&cStrSize, NULL );
            if ( dataValue == NULL ) throw( eMemoryAllocError );
            attrValueLen = strlen( (char *)dataValue );
        }
        else // must be CFDataRef; Directory Services only deals with strings
             // and data
        {
            dataValue = CFDataGetBytePtr( (CFDataRef)attrValue );
```

```
            attrValueLen = (size_t) CFDataGetLength( (CFDataRef)attrValue );
        }

        size_t attrValueEntrySize = sizeof( tAttributeValueEntry ) +
attrValueLen  + 1 + eBuffPad;
        attrValueEntry = (tAttributeValueEntry*)::calloc( 1, attrValueEntrySize
);
        if ( attrValueEntry == NULL ) throw( eMemoryAllocError );

        attrValueEntry->fAttributeValueID = inData->fInValueID;
        attrValueEntry->fAttributeValueData.fBufferSize = attrValueLen;
        attrValueEntry->fAttributeValueData.fBufferLength = attrValueLen;

        ::memcpy( attrValueEntry->fAttributeValueData.fBufferData, dataValue,
attrValueLen );
        // return the attribute value by reference
        inData->fOutEntryPtr = attrValueEntry;

        attrValueEntry = NULL;
    }
    catch( tDirStatus err )
    {
        DbgLog( kLogPlugin, "CDSLocalPlugin::GetRecAttrValueByID(): Got error
%d", err );
        siResult = err;
    }
```

NetInfo

Although it is no longer shipped with Mac OS X, NetInfo is still common in environments with older Macs because it was the default directory service for local accounts on Mac OS X up to version 10.4; in 10.5 it was replaced by the Local plug-in already described. Until OpenLDAP was introduced in OS X Server version 10.3, NetInfo was the main means of setting up networked directory services in Mac networks.

NetInfo services are arranged into domains. Each system that uses NetInfo locally therefore has a local domain, providing information unique to that system. The domains can be organized in a hierarchy with any number of subdomains, and at most a single parent domain. When responding to an information request, NetInfo first searches the local domain, and if it cannot find the information there will continue up the hierarchy toward the root domain.

It is difficult, or impossible, to deploy a NetInfo-based directory in a secure manner. NetInfo offers no way to encrypt the data transferred across the network, meaning that any computer that can intercept traffic on the network is able to read the NetInfo exchanges taking place, and read sensitive information about the users and groups in the directory. Netinfo does not verify the identity of any of the computers taking part in a NetInfo hierarchy — if a computer at the expected network address accepts NetInfo connections, then the service will believe that that computer is part of the domain, and will give it access to all the data in the directory. An early reported vulnerability in Mac OS X used the fact that early versions would, by default, look for a NetInfo domain in configuration information provided by a DHCP server, and would bind to the domain provided as the parent to the local domain. Because a DHCP client accepts configuration data from whichever server first responds to its request, attackers could easily pose as a "parent" domain to any computer and act as a provider for its NetInfo directory. An attacker could effectively set any password for root or other users on the system by providing custom user account records in the parent domain.

The source code for NetInfo is available from Apple at `http://www.opensource.apple.com/source/netinfo/netinfo-369.6/`.

BSD Flat File and NIS

Traditionally UNIX systems would retrieve their user and group information from a number of plain-text files stored in the /etc/ folder. The user records came from a file called /etc/passwd, or later /etc/master.passwd on BSD platforms. The format of this file is a colon-separated table of user records, one per line.

```
nobody:*:-2:-2::0:0:Unprivileged User:/var/empty:/usr/bin/false
root:*:0:0::0:0:System Administrator:/var/root:/bin/sh

daemon:*:1:1::0:0:System Services:/var/root:/usr/bin/false
```

Initially the encrypted password for the user was stored in the second field of the passwd file, but because this file had to be readable by everybody it was easy for attackers to retrieve the password hashes and attempt to recover the password by brute force. This was also true of Mac OS X, including computers using NetInfo, until version 10.3. The solution to this problem was to move the passwords into a file (called /etc/shadow in the BSD plug-in) that can be read only by root. This meant that login programs (which must run as root so that they can switch to the user who authenticates) could still function, but unprivileged users no longer get to read the encrypted passwords. Similarly, group information is stored in a file called /etc/group.

Mac OS X still has master.passwd and group files, but they are used only when the computer is booted into *single-user mode* (a recovery mode that disables many of the operating system functions, including DirectoryService). The files can be used in normal operation through the BSD plug-in. On a 10.6 Mac, the plug-in is always enabled but is not configured to add any account nodes to Open Directory. By configuring the plug-in through Directory Utility, you can enable look-up of users and groups in the /etc/ files.

The same plug-in is also used to look up records in the Network Information Service, or NIS. NIS is an early directory service created at Sun Microsystems, and is popular on a wide variety of UNIX platforms. It is a very simple service that distributes tables of information in the same format as passwd and group files. NIS (or more usually a later version called NIS+) is frequently found on heterogeneous UNIX networks which have not yet moved to a later directory such as OpenLDAP.

LDAPv3

The server parts of Open Directory publish directory information through the LDAP protocol, as already described. The LDAPv3 plug-in on the client side is where the two sides of the Open Directory architecture meet, although the plug-in can be used to access any LDAP service which conforms to the protocol. LDAP servers can be manually added to the plug-ins list using the Directory Access utility, or it can automatically find servers which are advertised via DHCP.

BRUTE FORCE

Brute force is a trial-and-error approach to solving a problem, in which every possible solution is tried until the correct one is found. In finding a user's password, the brute force approach is to try every permutation of characters until the true password is discovered. Brute force approaches commonly start by attempting more likely potential passwords, including dictionary words and pet names, to reduce the amount of time required to guess the correct password.

Try entering an incorrect password at the Mac OS X login window. The login window freezes for a couple of seconds, before shaking to indicate that the login attempt failed. To guess a password by entering all the possibilities into the login window would take a very long time, but if an attacker can recover the encrypted password he or she can write brute force software that doesn't wait between failed attempts. The password cannot be recovered from the encrypted text (the algorithm is not reversible), but the rate at which the permutations can be tried is now limited only by the time taken for the computer to encrypt each guess.

Passwords in the early versions of Mac OS X — before shadow passwords were implemented — were stored via a very old encryption algorithm called DES. It did not take a contemporary computer very long to encrypt a password guess using DES, so a non-dictionary password could be found in a few months on a single machine. A modern implementation of a brute force cracker using GPU programming techniques like OpenCL, and other optimizations including "rainbow tables" — sequences of pre-calculated hashes — might take a few days: which is why more time-consuming algorithms are used now.

Other Plug-Ins

Open Directory plug-ins also exist for various proprietary directory services. Mac OS X includes a plug-in for Microsoft's Active Directory. Third-party plug-ins provide a rich set of Active Directory features, and support other directory services such as eDirectory. Because of the extensible architecture described here, the likelihood is that if any other directory service not listed here becomes popular, someone will write a plug-in to support it in Open Directory.

Kerberos

Accounts on Open Directory servers are usually able to authenticate using Kerberos, and an increasing number of services can use Kerberos to identify and authenticate users. But what is it?

Kerberos, named after the three-headed dog that guards Hades in Greek mythology, is a system for providing identification and authentication services across a network that contains multiple user systems as well as multiple servers. It supports *Single Sign-On* (SSO), so the user authenticates only once to access of the different services he or she might use in a single session. Kerberos also allows for *mutual authentication*, so the user can verify that he or she is interacting with the legitimate servers. All of this is mediated via a Key Distribution Center, or KDC.

Documentation on deploying Kerberos authentication frequently recommends locating the KDC on a separate physical server from all users and the service activity. This is because the KDC is the gateway to doing anything as any user in any service on the network: the ability to tamper with the KDC is therefore so powerful that all steps should be taken to isolate it from attack. Particularly because, as you will see, the authentication component of the KDC has access to every user's password hash, which is the same as the hash generated at the user's machine when he or she attempts to log in. Recovering the user's hash from the KDC's database would give an attacker the ability to spoof interaction as that user. Isolation reduces the attacker's ability to exploit a different service on the same machine to gain access to the KDC.

Open Directory as configured through Apple's Workgroup Manager tool does not use this configuration; instead the KDC and the slapd directory server reside on the same server (usually also the server where the services that are Kerberos clients are located).

The KDC has two capabilities: it can authenticate users and it can grant tickets. The authentication is performed without the password's ever having to pass from the user's workstation to the KDC. When the user has entered his or her password, the workstation creates a request for a *ticket-granting ticket* (TGT), which identifies the user and the network address of the workstation. This request is sent to the KDC, along with the current time, which is encrypted with the user's password. The KDC looks at the request to find the user, and looks up that user's password hash in its database. If it can use that hash to decrypt the time — and the time is indeed current to within a few minutes — then the user is authenticated to the KDC. It prepares a TGT that is sent back to the user's computer, but that can only be decrypted by the KDC. The TGT contains a *session key*, which the workstation can decrypt with the user's password. The session key is used to encrypt further communications with the KDC.

Merely being able to authenticate is not much use in itself; users authenticate with computers only because they want to perform tasks for which their identities must be verified. The user who has begun a Kerberos session now wishes to use an AFP file server on a remote Mac OS X Server machine. The workstation does not ask the AFP server for permission; instead it contacts the KDC, sending a request to access the AFP service. This request is encrypted with the session key that was sent in the TGT. The KDC checks whether the user can access the service, and if so responds with a *service ticket* for the AFP service. Part of this service ticket is encrypted with a password known only to the KDC and the AFP server: the workstation passes this component on to the AFP server. When decrypted, this component tells the server which user at which network address can use the service, and the time at which the session expires. Additionally, the user's workstation verifies that the AFP server is the legitimate server, using an additional authentication step. Both the client and server components of the service ticket include a further session key: the server encrypts a timestamp with this key and sends it to the workstation. This interaction among the three systems (the KDC, the user's workstation and the file server) is depicted in Figure 2-5.

REPLAY ATTACKS

If a user's password is sent over the network, even if it is hashed or otherwise obfuscated so that the real password cannot be recovered, an attacker who can intercept the network traffic during authentication will be able to pose as that user. In other words, a spoofing vulnerability still exists.

The attack works by listening on the network for the password hash that is sent to the server, then connecting to the server. When the server asks the attacker to authenticate, the attacker just sends the same hash (i.e., *replays* the data) that was intercepted earlier. The server accepts that hash and the attacker has spoofed the user. An example of a service with this vulnerability is HTTP Digest mode authentication. Digest mode is superior to basic mode in that the plain password does not get sent over the network, but even so the digest (hash) sent in its place can be replayed by an attacker.

The timestamp sent in Kerberos authentication represents an attempt to mitigate this attack. Because the password encrypts a timestamp, the time during which the authentication data can be replayed is restricted. This imposes the requirement on a network using Kerberos authentication that the systems must all synchronize their clocks using a protocol such as NTP, otherwise no authentication will succeed as every request would be interpreted as a replay attack.

The KDC acts as a *trusted third party* in the interaction between the AFP server and the user's workstation. The only way the user can have gotten a service ticket to send to the AFP server is by having gotten it from the KDC using a ticket-granting ticket; this means that the KDC believes the user's identity claim, which is sufficient for the AFP server to do so. The only way the AFP server can have gotten the session key to encrypt a timestamp is by having decrypted the service ticket; it can do that only if it has the same password that the KDC has for that service, meaning that the KDC believes the server's identity, which is sufficient for the workstation. Neither the workstation nor the server need trust each other until the other has proven that the KDC vouches for it — this makes Kerberos a good choice for authentication over a network, on which the authentication traffic could potentially be redirected to a

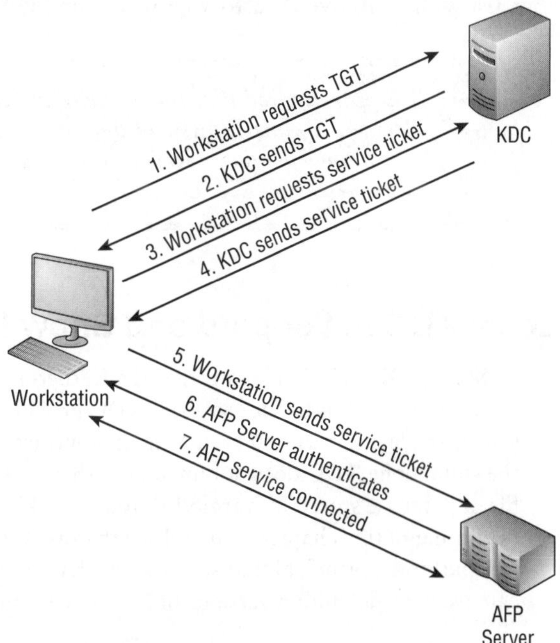

FIGURE 2-5: Client, server, and KDC interaction in Kerberos

computer under hostile control. Note that the server never communicates directly with the KDC, they just share the service password.

Both the user and the service are authenticated when a service is "kerberized," so each of these entities is identifiable to the KDC by a unique name, which can be authenticated via the password. Users and services alike must have accounts in the KDC. An account in Kerberos is known as a *principal*, and indeed there are user principals and service principals. Each is of the form *realm:accountname@hostname*, where the account name will be either the user's short name or a service name, like vnc for a VNC screen-sharing service or cifs for a Windows file server. The hostname is the network name of the computer at which the user or service is located. Because the hostname is important for identifying both a user who wishes to use a service and the service itself, it is important that a network using Kerberos have a robust DNS (domain name service) provision.

Hosts that take part in a Kerberos authentication system using the same KDC are said to be part of the same *realm*. A realm is usually coincident with a DNS domain, so all the hosts in the domain example.com would be in the EXAMPLE.COM realm (Kerberos realms are traditionally named all in uppercase). It is possible to set up trust relationships between KDCs of different realms, so that principals identified in one realm can take part in authentication in a different realm. Such cross-realm trust could be used in large federated networks such as universities: users in the PHYSICS.EXAMPLE.EDU realm could acquire TGTs from their KDC and access services in the CHEMISTRY.EXAMPLE.EDU realm without being added to the Chemistry realm and without the Chemistry servers' being in the Physics realm. Cross-realm trust can also be used to integrate networks based on different technologies: an Open Directory network run by Mac IT staff can share trust with an Active Directory network run by Windows IT staff.

It is not required that the name of a Kerberos realm and DNS domain be coincident. Administrators can define custom maps of Kerberos realms to KDC host names using the Kerberos configuration file, which on a Mac is located at `/Library/Preferences/edu.mit.Kerberos`.

Local KDC in Leopard and Snow Leopard

In Mac OS X 10.5, Apple introduced a Kerberos KDC running on every Mac, both client and server variants. The "standalone" or local KDC provides single sign-on access to the local file-sharing and screen-sharing services on each Mac. In contrast with the KDC in an Open Directory configuration, the standalone KDC does not interact with a password server. It keeps passwords stored in a *keytab* file, a database stored in /var/db/krb5kdc. Looking back at the user account record for leeg at the beginning of this chapter, you will see that its AuthenticationAuthority field mentions the Kerberosv5 scheme, and a principal that starts with LKDC:leeg@LKDC. The local KDC can be used to authenticate users by default on versions of Mac OS X that ship with the feature.

The main benefit to users of the local KDC is realized when you use peer-to-peer networks — not the infamous file-sharing networks like KaZaA or eDonkey, but local networks without a central server. Since version 10.2 of Mac OS X, Macs have been able to discover services running on different systems on the local network using Bonjour, originally called Rendezvous (Bonjour is explored in depth in Chapter 8). If a single computer offered multiple services to the local network, then a user taking advantage of each of them would need to authenticate numerous times, once for each service. The local KDC reduces the plethora of authentication steps to one per machine, by allowing a user to acquire a TGT that is good for all the kerberized services on the same system. Figure 2-6 shows the TGT owned by user leeg on one system (heimdall) who has connected to a different system (mabinogi) on the local network, which offers authentication using the local KDC.

The Kerberos tickets available to any user are shown in the Ticket Viewer.app utility, which is found in /System/Library/CoreServices. In versions of Mac OS X prior to Snow Leopard, the utility is called Kerberos.app.

Kerberos for Developers

The APIs required to integrate an application with Kerberos on Mac OS X are all available in Kerberos.framework. The framework provides access to the Global Single Sign-on interface (GSS-API), a cross-platform library that abstracts Kerberos details behind a generic interface for single sign-on authentication. GSS-API is fully documented as a proposed Internet standard in RFC 2744 (`http://www.rfc-editor.org/rfc/rfc2744.txt`), and the example code supplied by Apple with the Xcode tools includes a project Kerberos GSS, which demonstrates how a network client and server can negotiate sign-on using GSS-API as supplied in the Kerberos.framework. In Listing 2-7 the client-side code from Apple's example for connecting to the server is reproduced, with comments explaining how the authentication is achieved.

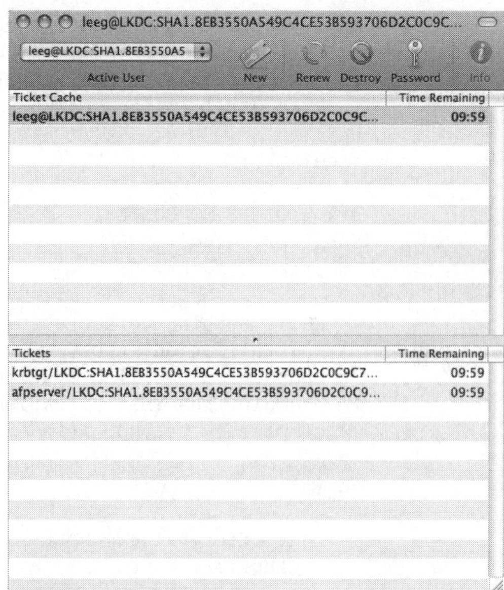

FIGURE 2-6: Kerberos tickets acquired from a local KDC during connection to another Mac

LISTING 2-7: Annotated use of GSS-API to connect to a Kerberized server [gssclient.c]

Available for download on Wrox.com

```
/*
 * This function creates a socket connection to the server and returns the
 * socket descriptor. It is assumed that the server supports GSS-API
 * negotiation of login - in this case it does, through Kerberos.
 */
fd = connectHost(server, port);

printf("connected to %s\n", server);
```

continues

LISTING 2-7 *(continued)*

```
    /*
     * Build a GSS-API host service name (service@hostname) and pass
     * it into gss_import_name(). Notice that the service name is very similar
     * to a Kerberos principal - GSSAPI will map the service to a
     * principal
name
     * when it determines that it must use Kerberos to negotiate the

     * connection.
     */

    asprintf(&str, "%s@%s", service, server);
    namebuffer.value = str;
    namebuffer.length = strlen(str);

    major_status = gss_import_name(&minor_status, &namebuffer,
                                   GSS_C_NT_HOSTBASED_SERVICE, &aname);
    if (major_status != GSS_S_COMPLETE)
        gss_err(1, major_status, minor_status, "gss_import_name");

    free(str);

    ctx = GSS_C_NO_CONTEXT;
    inbuffer.value = NULL;
    inbuffer.length = 0;
    /*
     * Fully setting up the authentication context can require multiple
     * initialization steps, with certain capabilities of the client-server
     * connection becoming available as the context is filled out. In this
     * example, the initialization code is looped until the context is
     * completely set up.
     */
    do {

        outbuffer.value = NULL;
        outbuffer.length = 0;

        major_status = gss_init_sec_context(&minor_status,
                                            GSS_C_NO_CREDENTIAL, // use default
credential
                                            &ctx,
                                            aname, // name of the service
                                            GSS_C_NO_OID, // allow any
mechanism
                                            GSS_C_MUTUAL_FLAG|GSS_C_REPLAY_FLAG|
                                            GSS_C_CONF_FLAG|GSS_C_INTEG_FLAG,
                                            GSS_C_INDEFINITE, //time of
validity
                                            GSS_C_NO_CHANNEL_BINDINGS,
                                            &inbuffer,
                                            NULL, // Don't really care about
actual mechanism used
```

```
                                      &outbuffer,
                                      &ret_flags,
                                      NULL);
        /*
         * Even in case of an error, if there is an output token, send
         * it off to the server. The mechanism might want to tell the
         * acceptor why it failed.
         */
        if (outbuffer.value) {
            send_token(fd, &outbuffer);
            gss_release_buffer(&junk, &outbuffer);
        }

        if (inbuffer.value) {
            free(inbuffer.value);
            inbuffer.value = NULL;
            inbuffer.length = 0;
        }

        /* Print a report on any error found. The program will quit in
         * gss_err() if there is an error. */
        if (GSS_ERROR(major_status)) {
            gss_delete_sec_context(&junk, &ctx, NULL);
            gss_err(1, major_status, minor_status, "gss_init_sec_context");
        }

        /* If we are not done yet, wait for another token from the server */
        if (major_status & GSS_S_CONTINUE_NEEDED)
            recv_token(fd, &inbuffer);

    } while (major_status != GSS_S_COMPLETE);

    /* If there was a failure building the context, fail */
    if (major_status != GSS_S_COMPLETE)
        err (1, "gss_accept_sec_context");

    /*
     * Check that context flags are what we expect them to be, with
     * confidentiality and integrity protected. This step is important; if you
     * decide that the network traffic needs some form of protection, you
     * should not use a channel which does not provide it.     */
    if ((ret_flags & GSS_C_CONF_FLAG) == 0)
        errx(1, "confidentiality missing from context");
    if ((ret_flags & GSS_C_INTEG_FLAG) == 0)
        errx(1, "integrity missing from context");
```

ACCESSING USER PREFERENCES AND MANAGED PREFERENCES

Both iPhone and Mac apps can use the User Defaults mechanism to store user settings and preferences. The settings are managed and accessed in code by an instance of the NSUserDefaults class called the *shared defaults* object, in which preference values are indexed by keys, just as in a dictionary.

NSUserDefaults hides a lot of complexity behind this very simple interface. Values returned by the shared defaults can come from any of the following locations, or domains:

- Command-line options of the form -PreferencesKey Value
- User defaults, in ~/Library/Preferences
- Local (i.e., per-machine) defaults, in /Library/Preferences
- Network defaults, in /Network/Library/Preferences
- "Factory" settings, which you can configure within the app by calling -[NSUserDefaults registerDefaults:]

Additionally, preferences stored in any of the three Preferences folders can come from a property list file specific to each app, or from NSGlobalDomain, a list of preferences shared among all apps, with the app-specific preferences being preferred. Listing 2-8 demonstrates registering and then querying a value in the defaults database for an app. Notice that there is just a single call to look up the value; the complexity of looking up all the different domains listed above is hidden in the NSUserDefaults class.

Available for download on Wrox.com

LISTING 2-8: Accessing preferences through user defaults [userdefaults.m]

```
#import <Foundation/Foundation.h>

void registerDefaults() {
    NSDictionary *defaults = [NSDictionary dictionaryWithObject: @"John Doe"
                                                         forKey: @"Name"];
    [[NSUserDefaults standardUserDefaults] registerDefaults: defaults];
}

int main (int argc, const char * argv[]) {
    NSAutoreleasePool *pool = [[NSAutoreleasePool alloc] init];

    registerDefaults();
    NSString *preferredName = [[NSUserDefaults standardUserDefaults]
                               stringForKey: @"Name"];
    NSLog(@"My preferred name is %@", preferredName);
    [pool drain];
    return 0;
}
```

As iPhones do not have a multi-user networked file system, and iPhone apps cannot be run from the command line, only one preferences file is accessible in addition to the application's registered defaults. The interface to the preferences is the same, though, with the change in implementation being transparent to the application.

You can see that as the per-user and command-line defaults are the first to be consulted, even if a systems or network administrator sets a preference in the appropriate domain, a regular user can override any of the administrator's settings. The user does not have permission to tamper with the files in /Library/Preferences or /Network/Library/Preferences, but can provide a new file in his or her home folder, to which the user does have write permission. The contents of the user's file is used in preference to the administrator's file.

It is not always desirable to allow users to set their own preferences. On a corporate network the business's IT policy may require particular settings be fixed to certain values. A family system could have accounts for children, who should not be able to configure their environments arbitrarily. For these situations the user defaults includes *managed* preferences, which cannot be overridden by the user. Managed settings are stored in users' account records in Directory Services, or in the Managed Preferences folder in the various Library locations. Preferences defined as managed settings always get applied, and users cannot change them. Applications use the `-[NSUserDefaults objectIsForcedForKey:]` method to find out whether the value for any defaults key is fixed as a managed preference. If the value is forced, the application should disable the user interface to configure that value. The "Forced Preferences" project in this book's sample code shows how this can be done: the application delegate method that determines whether the preferences value is managed is excerpted in Listing 2-9.

Available for download on Wrox.com

LISTING 2-9: Testing whether a user default's value is managed [Forced_PreferencesAppDelegate.m]

```
- (void)applicationDidFinishLaunching:(NSNotification *)aNotification {
    BOOL forced = [[NSUserDefaults standardUserDefaults]
                   objectIsForcedForKey: @"Name"];
    [nameField setEnabled: !forced];
}
```

On a network setup with Open Directory, the administrator configures such managed settings using the WorkGroup Manager application, where the feature is referred to as MCX (Managed Client for OS X). A limited set of managed preferences can be configured through the Parental Controls preference pane on a standalone Mac.

SUMMARY

The design of user accounts and user groups on Mac OS X has its roots in standalone time-sharing computers of yesteryear, but is still useful today in allowing multiple people to use the same computer without getting in each others' way. The operating system provides each user account with its own restricted access to the computer's resources; users usually cannot interact with resources owned by other users.

User account information is stored in databases known as directories. There are multiple different sources of directory data, some designed for single computers and others for managing accounts across large networks. Mac OS X's DirectoryServices.framework provides a common interface to all these directory services, so that application developers do not need to deal with the details of each specific directory type.

Kerberos can be used to provide a "single sign-on" experience, in which a user authenticates once to obtain a ticket that is subsequently used to gain access to multiple services. There is a local Kerberos

Distribution Center on every Mac, so single sign-on can even be provided on ad hoc networks such as those created with Bonjour. Kerberos is based on a published standard, so Macs using Kerberos can interoperate with other operating systems on the network for account identification.

One of the uses of multiple user accounts on a Mac is to allow users to choose individual preferences and settings for the applications they use, which are exposed to applications through the NSUserDefaults class. There are contexts in which it is important to be able to control the settings for a user, so preferences can be managed. Applications can detect when preferences are being managed so that they do not allow the user to change those preferences in the UI.

3

Using the Filesystem Securely

WHAT'S IN THIS CHAPTER?

- Filesystem permissions and access controls
- Encrypted filesystems
- Networked filesystems
- Layout of a Mac OS X filesystem
- Quarantining downloaded files
- How to ensure a "deleted" file really is deleted

The default filesystem used by Mac OS X and the iPhone OS, HFS+, has a venerable history. HFS+ is derived from the classic Mac OS's HFS filesystem, which was introduced in 1989 and itself borrowed concepts from Apple's earlier Lisa computer. It also includes a multiple-user permissions system based on the UNIX filesystem, access control lists based on the Windows model, and extended attributes borrowed from BeOS. In addition, Mac OS X supports numerous other filesystem types, including networked filesystems. In this chapter you'll find out about the security concerns relevant to working with files and filesystems.

UNIX PERMISSIONS

The simplest form of access control provided by the Mac OS X and iPhone filesystems is the UNIX permissions model. This model builds on the concepts of users and groups introduced in Chapter 2. Every file and folder has a single owner, which corresponds to one of the user accounts on the computer. Each file also belongs to a single user group. The permissions stored for each file record the access available to three classes of user — the file's owner, members of the owning user group, and everybody else (the catch-all).

There are three permission bits that can be set for each of the three user classes: read, write, and execute. When the permissions are applied to a file, each bit does what you might expect: it indicates whether a user in that class can read the file's contents, write to the file, and/or run it as a program or script. The permissions are often written as three groups of the letters r (read), w (write), and x (execute), with the permissions for the owner, group and others being written from left to right. A permission that is *not* set for a class is replaced by a hyphen, so the permissions for a file that everyone can read, but only the owner can write to or execute, are written as rwxr--r--. This is how the permissions are presented by the ls command in Terminal. The collection of permissions settings for all three capabilities (read, write, and execute) for all three classes of user (the owner, group, and others) is known as the *access mode* for a file.

The access mode has a different meaning when applied to a folder. The read bit indicates whether a user can list the contents of the folder using ls or any other method. The write bit indicates whether the user can modify the folder contents — adding or removing files. The execute bit indicates whether the user can access files and folders contained within this folder. The presence of the execute bit does not mean that users get the ability to read a directory listing — that is provided by the read bit. If users know that a file or folder with a particular name is inside another folder for which they have execute permission, they can work with that file or folder. Users could still guess the names of other files inside the folder and access them; if they had been told about two files called January.doc and March.doc then they might guess that other files named after months appear in the same folder, and would be able to open those.

The ability to delete a file is not granted by having write access to the file, but rather by having access to the directory where that file is located. A user who cannot write to a file, but who can write to its directory, can delete the file and create a new one with the same name. That ability is usually equivalent to being able to alter the file's contents, as applications and people alike often use the file names to identify files.

Never assume that a file is inaccessible to an attacker just because it is stored in a folder with restrictive permissions. Because of the way in which Mac OS X's filesystem works, it's still possible for the attacker to get to a file, even if its folder has appropriate permissions. A file is stored on the disk as a sequence of bytes, written across one or more *blocks* (numbered areas on the disk, usually 4KB in size). The file has a record, called the *inode* (index node) in UNIX-speak (or *cnode* — catalogue node — in the Mac world), that describes which blocks contain the file's contents, the times at which the file was created, last modified and last accessed, its permissions, and its ownership. A directory is just a file listing the names of the files in the directory, and which inode is referred to by each file name. The file is said to be linked in the directory in which it is named. Usually each file is linked once — so a file appears with a single name in a single folder. There is nothing stopping a file from being linked with different names, or even in different folders on the same filesystem (this capability is emulated on HFS+, but users and administrators see an abstracted layer called the *virtual filesystem* that has this multiple link capability). A file could be linked in two different folders, each of which has different permissions, but the file's permissions will be the same in both cases because its permissions are associated with the same inode in each case. It is only the permissions on the file that restrict its use.

The file links described earlier, also known as *hard links*, should not be confused with *symbolic links*, another feature of UNIX filesystems. A symbolic link is a file stored in a folder that names a different file, potentially in another folder, as its target. (In HFS+, it has a type code of SLNK and a creator code of RHAP, short for Rhapsody, which was an early code-name for Mac OS X.) When an application tries to open a symbolic link, the process is redirected to the target file. The user must have appropriate permissions on the target file *and* on the folder structure in which it is stored to be able to open the file, which is not true for hard links.

The API for creating files and changing permissions takes a numeric representation of the permissions flags. The easiest (and as a result the conventional) way to translate a set of permissions such as rwxr-x--x to its numerical form is to use octal (base 8) notation. Each of the three class groups in the permission is then a separate octal digit: rwx, r-x, --x. Each letter represents a binary 1 and each hyphen a binary 0, with x in the units position, w in the 2s position and r in the 4s position. Adding these together, the three digits become 7, 5, 1, so the octal representation is 0751 (because in C and Objective-C, octal numbers must be prefixed with a 0).

It is possible to test a file's access mode to determine whether the current user is capable of reading, writing or executing a file or folder, using the access() function, or the NSFileManager methods of the form -isReadableFileAtPath:. This capability is never useful and is occasionally dangerous. The file could have its permissions changed or even be deleted between the call to access() and the attempt to use the file, so the result of the permissions test is meaningless. The access mode may not even apply if the file also has flags or an access control list set. It is always better to attempt whatever operation your application needs to perform, dealing with any error appropriately.

In processes running with a different user or group from the user or group that launched it (see the discussion on setuid and setgid permissions below), access() reports on the capabilities of the real user. So if user joeuser runs a program that is set to run as root, access() determines the rights that joeuser has on the filesystem. Relying on the results of this test is dangerous: the tested file could be replaced by an attacker between testing and use of the file. Because the program is running as root, there would be nothing to stop it working with the replaced file, potentially changing the content of any other file on the machine.

Privileged programs doing work on behalf of a regular user should always relinquish those privileges whenever they are not required, as discussed in Chapter 4. If the setuid program were to drop privileges to work with the filesystem as joeuser, it would not be able to edit files that joeuser is not permitted to edit.

Permissions on a file can be changed by the file's owner, or the super-user. Cocoa and Cocoa Touch applications can use the NSFileManager class to do this, as demonstrated in Listing 3-1; another option is the portable chmod() function which works in a very similar way.

Available for download on Wrox.com

LISTING 3-1: Changing a file's permissions [changeposixperms.m]

```
#import <Foundation/Foundation.h>

int main (int argc, const char * argv[]) {
    NSAutoreleasePool * pool = [[NSAutoreleasePool alloc] init];

    //create a file for the purposes of changing its permissions
    system("/usr/bin/touch /tmp/testfile");
    //change the permissions to r--------, i.e. only the user can read the file
    NSNumber *desiredPermission = [NSNumber numberWithUnsignedLong: 0400];
    NSDictionary *fileAttributes = [NSDictionary
                                    dictionaryWithObject: desiredPermission
                                    forKey: NSFilePosixPermissions];
    NSError *permissionsError = nil;
    BOOL didChange = [[NSFileManager defaultManager]
                      setAttributes: fileAttributes
                      ofItemAtPath: @"/tmp/testfile"
                      error: &permissionsError];
    if (!didChange) {
        //handle the error
    }

    [pool drain];
    return 0;
}
```

The permissions of a file can also be chosen when the file is created. The NSFileManager method -createFileAtPath:contents:attributes: takes a numeric permissions representation as a member of the attributes dictionary, in the same way that -setAttributes:ofItemAtPath:error: did in Listing 3-1. If access permissions are not explicitly set when the file is created, the operating system will choose a standard set. The user can configure the standard permissions using a setting called the *file creation mask* or umask, a number that will be subtracted from the default access mode. The default permissions on a newly created file are 0666 (which is rw-rw-rw-), so if the user has a umask of 0022, new files will have permissions set to 0644 (or rw-r--r--). The permissions on a new folder will be 0777 (rwxrwxrwx) minus the umask. You can find the umask appropriate for a Cocoa application using the umask() function; umask() sets a new value for the umask and returns the previous value, so it must be called twice — the first time to find out the current value and the second time to set the umask back to that value. This process is shown in Listing 3-2. The umask change applies only to the current process and any child processes, so your application must avoid working with files or launching any other programs in between calls to umask; there are no security issues associated with changing the umask, but particular care must be taken in multi-threaded code to ensure that no such events happen between the two calls.

Available for download on Wrox.com

LISTING 3-2: Using umask() to find the file creation mask [findumask.m]

```
#import <Foundation/Foundation.h>
#import <sys/stat.h>

int main (int argc, const char * argv[]) {
```

```
    NSAutoreleasePool * pool = [[NSAutoreleasePool alloc] init];

    unsigned long currentUmask = umask(0); // set the umask to anything, to see
                                           // the previous value
    umask(currentUmask); // and now set it back
    NSLog(@"This process's umask: %#lo", currentUmask);
    [pool drain];
    return 0;
}
```

The umask can be configured for a login session with launchd. A line of the form "umask 022" can appear in the file /etc/launchd.conf, which will set the umask for every process on the Mac. If the same line appears in /etc/launchd-user.conf, it will affect all user logins but not system processes. Finally, each user can set her own umask value in ~/.launchd.conf.

Document files created by your application should certainly have permissions that reflect the user's file creation mask, as it represents a level of confidentiality and integrity protection that the user expects of every application and process on the Mac. Consider very carefully any instance in which you want to give a file a more permissive set of rights than suggested by the umask — it is likely that users know more about the trust they have in their environment than you do.

'Sticky' Folders

How is it that world-writable folders, such as the /private/tmp folder used for caches and temporary files, don't result in anarchy? If a folder can be written by every user on the computer, then any one of them can delete or replace the files created by any other.

There is an additional permission bit that can be applied to a folder to restrict users from meddling in each other's affairs if multiple users can write to the folder. This permission is known as the "sticky" bit. A user with write permission to a sticky folder can create files and folders in that folder, and can move or rename any files or folders that he created. He *cannot* move, rename, or delete any object in this folder that was created by a different user. The sticky bit then reduces, but does not eliminate, the chance of one user's spoiling another's use of a commonly writable folder. If one user needs to write a file of a given name, another user can create that file first and block the original user from doing so.

The sticky bit is the first bit higher than the user-read permission in a permissions mode, so a folder that everyone can read, write to, and execute, and that is sticky, has mode 01777.

Sticky *is an odd name for a permission that restricts modification of a folder. The sticky bit was originally used for executable files and libraries, to indicate that they should be kept in memory even after they are no longer in use — in other words they should "stick" to the RAM. The decision about which executables to cache is now dealt with by the kernel, so "stickiness" of executables is no longer used. However, the same bit was borrowed for this folder restriction, as folders can't be loaded like executable files.*

Setuid and Setgid Permissions

There are two remaining permissions bits in the UNIX permissions model, which can be applied to both folders and files. These are the setuid and setgid permissions, which behave in the same way but relate to user and group settings, respectively. The following discussion explains the setuid bit; the discussion is valid for the setgid bit if you remember that it operates on group IDs instead of user IDs.

When setuid is applied to a folder, any file or folder created within that folder will belong to the owner of the folder instead of the user who created it; in other words it sets the user ID of the folder's contents to that of the folder's owner. The setuid capability on folders allows users to subvert filesystem quotas, so it is disabled by default on Mac OS X; for a bit to be enabled on a filesystem, that filesystem must be remounted with the suiddir option.

When setuid is applied to an executable file, that program is launched with the user ID of the owner rather than that of the user who launched the program. Setuid binaries allow users to gain privileges their accounts do not normally permit them: as an example the top command, which prints out resource usage on the computer, is owned by root and has setuid because users cannot normally get statistics on all the processes on a Mac. Some games implement a global high-score table as a file in a group to which no user belongs (the "highscore" group, perhaps) and set the group ownership of the game to "highscore," enabling the setgid permission. Any user who plays the game can add a score to the high-score table, but none of them can edit the table in a text editor.

The setuid bit must be carefully handled to avoid elevation-of-privilege vulnerabilities. Processes that can themselves launch other processes based on user input, such as login shells, should either not be setuid or should have limited capabilities when running as setuid. How to handle setuid in your own applications is discussed in the next chapter.

The operating system automatically applies certain restrictions to the setuid bit to avoid common privilege escalation problems. It will ignore the setuid bit on removable media, so that an attacker cannot prepare a shell with the setuid flag and root ownership on the attacker's own machine to use on a different computer. If a file with setuid is written to, or has its owner changed, the OS will automatically remove the setuid permission. If it did not, then it would be possible to replace setuid programs with arbitrary other programs once they had been installed.

UNIX Permissions and Removable Media

When a removable device such as an external hard drive is plugged in to a computer, a decision of trust must be made. If the filesystem supports multiple users, as HFS+ does, it could be convenient and useful to honor the user and group IDs assigned to each file and folder. Alternatively, that could allow access to some files to users who should not have it, and deny access to some users who should, if the user IDs on the removable volume do not correspond to those of the users on the computer. So should the ownership on the media be honored?

Mac OS X allows either approach to be taken. When filesystems are mounted, the option MNT_IGNORE_OWNERSHIP can be set so filesystem user and group IDs will be ignored. The permissions are still intact, but all the files are owned by a special user and group called _unknown. Whenever a user tries to work with a file owned by _unknown, the kernel tests the permissions as if that user were the real owner of the file. For example, a file with permissions rw-r----- owned by _unknown can be written to by any user. In directory listings, files on filesystems in which ownership is ignored will appear to be owned by the user who requested the listing, and to be in that user's default group. The MNT_IGNORE_OWNERSHIP option is exposed in Finder as the "Ignore ownership on this volume" checkbox in a volume's Info window, as shown in Figure 3-1.

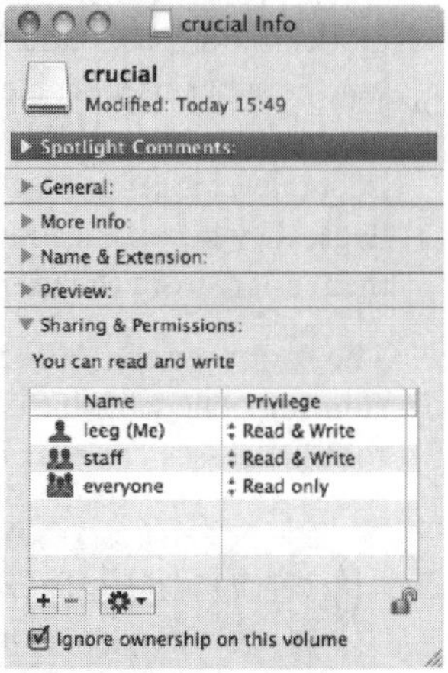

When the option to ignore ownership is not set, the user and group IDs for files recorded in the filesystem will be used. The filesystem stores numerical IDs rather than user names, so if the user has UID 501 on one computer and UID 502 on another, then files he creates on one machine will not belong to his user on the second when he moves the removable device to the second computer.

FIGURE 3-1: File ownership on removable media

FILESYSTEM FLAGS

HFS+ supports some extensions to the basic UNIX permissions described earlier, inherited from the BSD family of UNIX platforms. These extensions also take the form of binary flags (i.e., a task is either permitted or denied on a file or folder) but are separate from a file's access mode. The name and meaning of each flag is given in the following table.

TABLE 3-1: Flags Defined by the BSD File Flags Mechanism

FLAG NAME	PURPOSE OF FLAG
UF_NODUMP	Do not dump the file. Dump is an archaic UNIX filesystem backup utility: it ignores files and folders with this flag set.
UF_IMMUTABLE	The file cannot be modified or deleted (user version).
UF_APPEND	The file cannot be arbitrarily written to but can have data appended. This flag is useful for log files, in which content must be added but the log must not be tampered with (user version).
UF_OPAQUE	A folder with this flag is "opaque" when its filesystem is mounted as a union with another filesystem. If the underlying filesystem also contains a folder with the same name at the same location, the contents of that folder won't be available.
UF_HIDDEN	The file or folder should be hidden from the user interface. The Finder honors this flag; the command-line ls tool does not.
SF_ARCHIVED	The file has been archived.
SF_IMMUTABLE	The file cannot be modified (system version).

Flags with the UF prefix are *user flags,* which can be set on a file by its owner or the super-user. These flags can also be removed by those users. Setting the immutable flag on a user's file does not stop that user from modifying the file, though it may stop accidental changes because the user will need to jump through hoops before being able to edit it.

Flags with names prefixed by SF are *system flags,* and they may only be set on a file by root, or someone acting as root with sudo. The behavior of Mac OS X with regard to these flags depends on a kernel sysctl variable called kern.securelevel. The default value of kern.securelevel is 0, also known as insecure mode, in both 10.5 and 10.6. In this mode no user may override the effects of any of the system flags, but the super-user is able to turn any of the flags off. A process running as root is therefore at liberty to modify files with the SF_IMMUTABLE or SF_APPEND flag set, simply by removing the flag. If kern .securelevel is set to 1 or 2 (the only higher levels), even the root user cannot remove any of the system flags; they become a simple form of mandatory access control. It is their mandatory nature that sets them apart from the user equivalents, UF_IMMUTABLE and UF_APPEND.

The root user can raise the kern.securelevel variable with the sysctl command while Mac OS X is running. The variable cannot subsequently be lowered without the computer's being rebooted, so root processes cannot circumvent system flags by reducing kern.securelevel to 0.

The kern.securelevel variable affects more of the system than the system flags. A good discussion of how it is used and its results is on the NetBSD wiki: `http://wiki.netbsd.se/Kernel_secure_levels`.

There is no high-level Objective-C API for filesystem flags, so Cocoa applications must use the UNIX interface to get or change the flags. A file's status, reported by the stat() function, includes the flags currently set on the file. You can use the chflags() function to set flags on a file. Listing 3-3 sets the user-immutable flag on a file passed to the program in the command-line arguments.

LISTING 3-3: Setting the user-immutable flag on a file [setimmutable.c]

Available for download on Wrox.com

```
#include <stdio.h>
#include <sysexits.h>
#include <sys/stat.h>
#include <unistd.h>

int main (int argc, const char * argv[]) {
    if (argc != 2) {
        fprintf(stderr, "usage: setimmutable <filename>\n");
        return EX_USAGE;
    }
    const char *fileName = argv[1];
    struct stat fileStatus;
    if (0 != stat(fileName, &fileStatus)) {
        // report the error
        return EX_NOINPUT;
    }
    int flags = fileStatus.st_flags;
    flags |= UF_IMMUTABLE; // set the immutable flag with bitwise OR
    if (0 != chflags(fileName, flags)) {
        // report the error
        return EX_IOERR;
    }
    return EX_OK;
}
```

Notice that the program must find the set of flags already enabled, and modify that set to incorporate its changes, rather than just setting the flag it is interested in. Calling chflags(UF_IMMUTABLE), i.e., specifying only the user-immutable flag, would also cause an attempt to clear all the other flags, resulting in either an error or an unintended permissions change.

ACCESS CONTROL LISTS

The UNIX approach to permissions considered so far is limited in its applicability. Imagine an application designed to support managers writing performance reviews of the employees under their charge. Each report is written by a manager who must also be able to read it and create new reports. An employee must be able to read and write to his or her own report, but not those of other employees. Staff in the human resources department must be able to read any of the reports, but not write to any of them; the head of the employee's department must have the same rights. No one may delete a report that has already been written. These permissions could not be expressed in the UNIX model, but represent the requirements of a real application.

HFS+ in Mac OS X has supported access control lists (ACLs) since version 10.4, based on the definition of ACLs in the POSIX standard. The HFS+ ACLs are also very similar to the access control capabilities of the Windows NTFS filesystem. An ACL is an ordered list of Access Control Elements (ACEs), each of which expresses a single rule about the permissions granted to the file or folder to which the ACL is attached. An ACL can contain an arbitrary number of ACEs.

Each element is a single rule that says that a user or group of users is either allowed or denied the right to perform a particular operation on the file. The ls command provides a flag, -e, to display ACLs where files have them: they are written in a readable English-like form, e.g., "user:admin allow delete." When a process attempts to use a file with an ACL, the ACEs will be examined in the order in which they appear in the list. The first ACE that matches the process's user and the operation it is trying to perform will define whether the operation is permitted. If a user named joeuser is in the staff group, and a file has the following ACL:

```
0: group:staff deny read
1: user:joeuser allow read
```

— then joeuser will *not* be allowed to read the file, because the ACE saying members of the staff group cannot read it comes before the ACE saying that joeuser can. If no ACE matches, then the UNIX access mode is used.

The capabilities to which ACLs gate access are more fine-grained than those protected by the UNIX access mode. The capabilities applicable to files are as follows:

- **read:** The permission to read a file's contents
- **write:** The permission to modify a file
- **append:** The permission to append to but not arbitrarily modify a file
- **execute:** The permission to run a file as an application or script

ORDERING ENTRIES IN AN ACL

Because the effects of an ACL depend on the order of the ACEs in the list, it is easy to tie yourself in knots trying to work out what the impact of any change is, especially on an ACL of nontrivial length. The best way to order an ACL is to put all the deny elements first, then all the allow elements. In this way you can be sure that if there are conflicting rules the deny rule will be followed.

This is an example of *fail-safe* thinking. If it is possible for something to go wrong, an application should go wrong in the most secure way possible. With an ACL, if the deny rules come first, "going wrong" means that someone who should have access to an asset does not: an annoyance, surely, but one with limited impact. Were the rule to be written with the allow rules first, then to go wrong would be to allow access to those who should not have it, a breach of confidentiality with potentially disastrous consequences.

There is no provision in OS X's ACLs for an ACE to affect everyone — instead the UNIX permissions are used if an ACL doesn't specify the rule for a particular user. Wherever possible, make the UNIX access mode completely empty (i.e., 000) for files with ACLs. Again, this makes the application fail-safe; if you forget a particular user or group in constructing your ACL, access to the asset will be denied to that user or group.

The read, write, and execute permissions of file ACLs do not apply to folders in the same way that the rwx bits in an access mode do. There are separate access control permissions for folders, which are as follows:

- **list:** List the contents of the folder, like the read bit on a folder's access mode.
- **search:** Go to a file or folder in this folder if its name is known, like the execute bit on a folder's access mode.
- **add_file:** Create a new file inside this folder.
- **add_subdirectory:** Create a new folder inside this folder.
- **delete_child:** Remove an object stored in this folder.

Additionally, the following permissions may be controlled for any filesystem object:

- **chown:** Change the object's owner. Notice that allowing users to change ownership of their files may allow them to circumvent storage quota limits. Operating Systems usually implement system quotas by calculating the total size of all files owned by each account; a user with chown permission could relinquish ownership of large files to avoid reaching the quota.
- **readsecurity:** View the ACL.

- **writesecurity:** Change the ACL or the object's access mode. The existence of this permission avoids an obvious chicken-and-egg problem with ACLs — if an attacker doesn't have permission to read a file but can change the ACL, then he or she can add an ACE to gain read permission; the attacker should not be able to do this. But doesn't that mean having access controls on the access control list? It is important to ensure that the writesecurity permission is given only to those users who need it, since it opens up access to all the other permissions.
- **readattr:** View the object's basic attributes (its stat() information).
- **writeattr:** Change the basic attributes.
- **readextattr:** Read the extended attributes of the object. Extended attributes are small pieces of metadata that can be attached to a file or folder. In Snow Leopard their uses include the implementation of compressed files and the Launch Services quarantine feature discussed later in this chapter.
- **writeextattr:** Write the extended attributes.
- **delete:** Remove the object.

There is a clear conflict between the delete permission on an object and the delete_child permission on its enclosing folder. Figure 3-2 shows the resulting behavior when both of these permissions are explicitly allowed or denied.

As with the file access mode, the super-user is not subject to restrictions imposed by ACLs. If a file has an access control element saying user:root deny read, a process running as root can still read the file.

FIGURE 3-2: The effects of combining delete and delete_child access

ACL Inheritance

A folder protected with an access control list can extend the same protection to objects created inside that folder through ACL inheritance. Each ACE in a folder ACL includes a flag to indicate whether it is inherited; when a new file or folder is created inside that folder, the inherited ACEs are automatically added to the new object's ACL. Notice that if an inherited ACE is added to a folder that already contains some files, those files do not automatically gain the same ACE. Only new files and folders will inherit the ACEs. Similarly, if an existing file is linked in a folder with inheritable ACEs, the file will not inherit those access controls. The flags that define inheritance rules for an ACE are as follows:

- **file_inherit:** Files created inside this folder will inherit this ACE.
- **directory_inherit:** Folders created inside this folder will inherit this ACE.
- **only_inherit:** While files or folders inside this folder will inherit this ACE, the ACE should not be processed when determining access rights to this folder.

- **limit_inherit**: While a folder created inside this folder will inherit this ACE, files and folders created inside that new folder will not inherit it. Without the limit_inherit flag, folders inherit the inheritance rules of their parent folders when they are created, and the ACL inheritance is arbitrarily deep. With limit_inherit, inheritance is "shallow" and restricted to the top level of a folder.

Using inherited access control can be a simple way for you to ensure that all data files created by an application have appropriate access restrictions, by creating them in a folder where the correct rules are inherited. Of course the writesecurity permission on the parent folder must be correctly restricted, to stop attackers from tampering with the inherited access controls.

Using the ACL API

Inspecting and manipulating access control lists in code is more complicated than working with access modes, because of the greater complexity of the underlying access model. Listing 3-4 demonstrates adding a single ACE to a file's ACL, and therefore shows the important features of the API. The function deny_myself_read() adds an element denying the current user read access to a file, so if it is in a program run by the user joeuser, the ACE "user:joeuser deny read" will be added to the file's ACL.

LISTING 3-4: Adding an access control element to a file [addaccesscontrol.c]

Available for download on Wrox.com

```
//add an access control element restricting this user's read permission
bool deny_myself_read(const char *filename) {
    //get the file's existing access control list
    bool result = false;
    acl_t accessControlList = acl_get_file(filename, ACL_TYPE_EXTENDED);
    if (NULL == accessControlList) {
        //there is no existing ACL, create a new one
        accessControlList = acl_init(1);
        if (NULL == accessControlList) {
            fprintf(stderr, "could not create an ACL for %s: %s\n", filename,
strerror(errno));
            return false;
        }
    }
    /* A new entry must be added to the ACL. As it's a deny entry, it will be
     * best to insert it at the top of the list, so use the OS X-specific
     * interface which allows control over the insertion order.
     */
    acl_entry_t newEntry = NULL;
    if (-1 == acl_create_entry_np(&accessControlList, &newEntry,
ACL_FIRST_ENTRY)) {
        fprintf(stderr, "could not create a new ACE: %s\n", strerror(errno));
        goto drop;
    }
    if (-1 == acl_set_tag_type(newEntry, ACL_EXTENDED_DENY)) {
        fprintf(stderr, "could not set the deny tag on the ACE: %s\n",
strerror(errno));
```

```
        goto drop;
    }

    /* The user or group to which an ACE applies is identified by its UUID.
     * The following API is a convenience wrapper to DirectoryService to look up
     * the UUID for a user - DirectoryService featured in Chapter 2.
     */
    uuid_t myUUID = {0};
    uid_t myuid = getuid();
    int uuidLookup = mbr_uid_to_uuid(myuid, myUUID);
    if (0 != uuidLookup) {
        fprintf(stderr, "could not look up this user's UUID: %s\n",
strerror(uuidLookup));
        goto drop;
    }
    if (-1 == acl_set_qualifier(newEntry, &myUUID)) {
        fprintf(stderr, "could not set the ACE qualifier: %s\n", strerror(errno));
        goto drop;
    }
    // Now set the read permission in the entry's permission set
    acl_permset_t permissions = NULL;
    if (-1 == acl_get_permset(newEntry, &permissions)) {
        fprintf(stderr, "could not retrieve permissions set for ACE: %s\n",
strerror(errno));
        goto drop;
    }
    if (-1 == acl_add_perm(permissions, ACL_READ_DATA)) {
        fprintf(stderr, "could not set the read permission in the ACE: %s\n",
strerror(errno));
        goto drop;
    }

    /* The ACL is complete, but is only an in-memory representation. It must be
     * applied to the file to actually take effect.
     */
    if (-1 == acl_set_file(filename, ACL_TYPE_EXTENDED, accessControlList)) {
        fprintf(stderr, "could not set the ACL for file %s: %s\n", filename,
strerror(errno));
        goto drop;
    }
    result = true;
drop:
    acl_free(accessControlList);
    return result;
}
```

The function initially attempts to retrieve the current ACL for the file using acl_get_file(), but if this fails it creates a new ACL with acl_init(). The object returned by acl_get_file() represents the state of the ACL *at the time the function was called*. Changes to this object do not automatically update the file's ACL, and changes to the ACL by other processes do not get reflected in the object. In the interests of keeping the code example short, some error-checking has been elided here; you should check whether the process has permission to retrieve the ACL (i.e., that it is allowed the readsecurity access right), and that the filesystem supports ACLs, both of which are reflected in the errno variable if the acl_get_file() call fails.

The next step performed by deny_myself_read() is to create a new entry — a new ACE — in the ACL with the acl_create_entry_np() function call on line 19. As described in the "Ordering Entries in an ACL" sidebar earlier, it is preferable to put deny ACEs before allow ACEs, so that if the same user or group is accidentally given both rights, the effect will be to deny that user or group access. Therefore, deny_self_read() inserts its ACE at the head of the list. An ACE is formed from a *tag* defining whether it is an allow or deny element, a *qualifier* identifying the user or group it applies to, *permissions* indicating which rights it grants or restricts, and *flags* affecting the inheritance. The function deny_myself_read() creates a file ACE and does not set any inheritance flags, but the other parts of the ACE must all be set.

At line 23 the tag is set to ACL_EXTENDED_DENY. Its meaning, and that of its alternative ACL_EXTENDED_ALLOW, should be clear: this ACE will be a deny element. The two are mutually exclusive: a single element cannot both deny and allow access to the same user (though two conflicting elements can appear in the same list).

Lines 28 through 42 set the qualifier to represent the current user. The qualifier is a UUID found in the directory entry for a user or group, so deny_myself_read() uses a call to DirectoryService to retrieve the correct UUID.

The ACE now defines a deny rule for the current user, but does not specify what that user is denied permission to do. The permissions set associated with the ACE is retrieved at line 45, and the read permission added to it at line 49.

Finally, in line 57 the new ACL is applied to the file via acl_set_file(). This will work as long as the filesystem supports ACLs, the file exists (it could have been deleted while the function was working), and the process's user has the writesecurity permission for the file.

In adding a permission to an ACL, you may find it appropriate to find an element with a matching tag and qualifier, and to add the permission to that elements permission set — the ACE "user:joeuser deny write" could be changed to "user:joeuser deny read,write." If you choose to do this, you should make sure that the position of the ACE in its list is appropriate for your new permission setting. Additionally, you must decide what to do in the case of *antonymic* elements: if a file already has "group:staff deny write" and your user wants to allow write access to staff, should the deny element be removed as the allow element is added? The chmod command will not remove the conflicting element, but will order the two elements so that access is still denied; is that what the user meant?

FILEVAULT AND OTHER ENCRYPTION OPTIONS

For high-confidentiality assets, restricted access through UNIX permissions and access control lists may still be insufficient. An attacker who acquires access to the owner's account or the root account can read the asset. An attacker with physical access to the computer can plug the hard drive into a different computer, or use target disk mode to mount the disk on his own system — either of these attacks will thwart any access restrictions imposed on the files. To remain secret when access controls fail, a file must be encrypted.

FileVault

Apple introduced FileVault as a configuration option in version 10.3 of Mac OS X. A user can enable FileVault for his home folder — when he does, the contents of the home folder are moved into an encrypted disk image, which is protected by the user's password (and a *master password* for every account on the system, which can be used if the user ever forgets his own). The user's documents and settings are now available only when the user is logged in, or to people who know the password and can mount the disk image directly. In either case, the files cannot be retrieved offline by someone unfamiliar with the password. Online is a different matter — if the user logs in, mounting his home folder, and then leaves the computer unattended, an attacker could retrieve any files by using removable media and the Finder. Additionally, if an application writes files to a location outside the user's home directory, like /tmp or /Users/Shared, those files will not be protected by FileVault.

Applications cannot enable FileVault on behalf of their users, and even if they could, to do so would probably be considered a rude intervention in most circumstances. The effects of having FileVault configured on a user account extend beyond any one application. It is possible, on the other hand, to test whether a user has FileVault enabled. Where your application stores its cache or other temporary files could depend on the confidentiality associated with those files, and whether users have FileVault encryption on their accounts. To determine if the current user has FileVault enabled, inspect the output of the /usr/bin/hdiutil info command. A FileVault-protected home folder will appear as a disk image mounted at the user's home folder path, as shown here.

```
mabinogi:~ leeg$ /usr/bin/hdiutil info
framework        : 199
driver           : 10.5v199
================================================
image-path       : /Users/.leeg/leeg.sparsebundle
image-alias      : /Users/.leeg/leeg.sparsebundle
shadow-path      : <none>
icon-path        :
/System/Library/PrivateFrameworks/DiskImages.framework/Resources/CDiskImage.icns
image-type       : sparse bundle disk image
system-image     : TRUE
blockcount       : 155755872
blocksize        : 512
writeable        : TRUE
autodiskmount    : TRUE
removable        : TRUE
image-encrypted  : TRUE
mounting user    : root
mounting mode    : -rwx------
process ID       : 89
/dev/disk1    Apple_partition_scheme
/dev/disk1s1 Apple_partition_map
/dev/disk1s2 Apple_HFS     /Users/leeg
```

Encrypted Disk Images

FileVault is built on top of encrypted disk images, but use of these images is not limited to FileVault. An application could create such a disk image as a simple way to store confidential information without having to deal with the encryption of contents at a low level.

Creating and using disk images is done through the hdiutil command-line tool, which can be driven through shell scripts or the NSTask class. In this section all the examples will be presented as shell commands. If you are driving hdiutil with NSTask, remember that the -plist option causes hdiutil to output property lists that are easy to read in Cocoa code.

The disk image capabilities are also exposed through a framework called DiskImages.framework. This framework is private and undocumented by Apple. Security-conscious developers should stay away from undocumented interfaces, as not all the effects of using them will be clear. Changes in behavior in later versions of the framework could introduce vulnerabilities, including denial-of-service problems in applications relying on the private framework.

A writable, encrypted disk image can be made with the create option to hdiutil. The following command creates an encrypted, password-protected "sparse bundle" — the same format as is used by FileVault — with a maximum size of one gigabyte:

```
heimdall:~ leeg$ hdiutil create -size 1g -encryption AES-128 \
-type SPARSEBUNDLE -stdinpass secrets.sparsebundle -fs HFS+
Enter disk image passphrase: <enter the password>
created: /Users/leeg/secrets.sparsebundle
```

While the maximum size of the disk image is one gigabyte, the fact that it is stored in "sparse" format means that it takes up only as much space as is required to store the contents and metadata. The disk image will automatically expand up to the maximum size as more files are added. The tool hdiutil can be used to verify that this disk image is encrypted:

```
heimdall:~ leeg$ hdiutil isencrypted secrets.sparsebundle/
encrypted: YES
blocksize: 4096
uuid: D5CB77DA-4E4B-4837-85E6-8BC244F363EA
private-key-count: 0
passphrase-count: 1
max-key-count: 1
version: 2
```

The passphrase that was used to create the disk image must be provided when the disk image is mounted, for the operating system to be able to decrypt it:

```
heimdall:~ leeg$ hdiutil attach secrets.sparsebundle/
Enter password to access "secrets.sparsebundle": <wrong password>
hdiutil: attach failed - Authentication error
heimdall:~ leeg$ hdiutil attach secrets.sparsebundle/
Enter password to access "secrets.sparsebundle": <correct password>
/dev/disk2              GUID_partition_scheme
/dev/disk2s1            Apple_HFS                       /Volumes/untitled
```

Once the disk image is mounted, the filesystem acts like any other: files may be created, deleted, read, or written to by any process with appropriate privileges. For the files to be rendered inaccessible again, the disk image must be unmounted.

```
heimdall:~ leeg$ hdiutil detach /Volumes/untitled/
"disk2" unmounted.
"disk2" ejected.
```

With the disk image unmounted, the only way to access the files is to attach it again (or otherwise decrypt the disk image), which requires knowledge of the password.

The master password feature of FileVault, allowing access to all FileVault home folders on a system, even if the users forget their passwords or can no longer be contacted, works by protecting the disk image with a secondary certificate. Assuming a certificate created and stored in the keychain/Library/Keychains/master.keychain, and exported as a CER file on the Desktop as Certificate.cer, the disk image would be created in this way:

```
heimdall:~ leeg$ hdiutil create -size 1g -encryption AES-128 -type \
SPARSEBUNDLE
-stdinpass -certificate ~/Desktop/Certificate.cer \
secrets.sparsebundle -fs HFS+
Enter disk image passphrase: <enter the password>
created: /Users/leeg/secrets.sparsebundle
```

Now even if the password is lost, if the person who knew it is no longer available, or if it was never recorded in the first place, the disk image can still be attached by means of the -recover option. You pass it the path to the keychain file where the private key associated with the certificate is stored.

```
heimdall:~ leeg$ hdiutil attach -recover /Library/Keychains/master.keychain
secrets.sparsebundle/
<Mac OS X prompts for the master password>
/dev/disk2                    GUID_partition_scheme
/dev/disk2s1                  Apple_HFS                        /Volumes/untitled
```

Block Encryption

Applications on the iPhone cannot create and work with encrypted disk images, as the hdiutil program is unavailable on the iPhone and there is no API equivalent. On the Mac it may not always be appropriate to work with encrypted disk images, particularly if you're dealing with very small files for which the time spent in dealing with the disk image environment could dwarf the time taken to actually work with the file.

In both environments the CommonCrypto library is available to perform symmetric encryption operations. CommonCrypto is part of libSystem, the library used in every nontrivial Mac OS X process, which contains the C standard library, mathematical functions, and other basic capabilities.

SYMMETRIC AND ASYMMETRIC ENCRYPTION

The encryption algorithms provided by CommonCrypto are *symmetric* algorithms, which means that the same key is used for encryption and decryption — or at least that the two are trivially related. This is also referred to as a *shared secret* encryption scheme.

Think of the *substitution ciphers* used by Julius Caesar to send secret messages across Gaul back to Rome, in which he would replace each letter in the alphabet with a different letter: perhaps a becomes c, b becomes d, and so on. If you know that this is Julius's rule, you can both construct ciphered messages and recover the original messages from cipher texts. The same information is used both to encrypt and decrypt — hence the "shared" in "shared secret." The rule must be kept secret to prevent attackers from reading your secret messages, or being able to write their own messages that seem to come from Caesar.

Symmetric encryption with a strong algorithm and a shared secret gives you the confidence that a message cannot be read by people who do not have the secret. But now there's a chicken-and-egg problem; how do you get the secret to the right people without its being intercepted by the wrong people? And how do you ensure that if you receive a key, it came from the person you actually want to talk to, rather than from an attacker?

Asymmetric encryption is frequently used for distributing the keys used in symmetric encryption. In asymmetric encryption algorithms, the key used for encryption (the *public key*) and the key used for decryption (the *private key*), while related to each other, cannot be derived from each other. As the names suggest, the public key can be distributed freely, while the private key must be kept secret by the key holder. Messages encrypted with the public key can therefore be read only by the holder of the private key, ensuring that the correct person receives the message.

Asymmetric encryption can also be used to verify the identity of a message's sender. The sender of a message can use her private key to generate a message *signature*, which can be verified with her public key. The verification will succeed only if the correct public key is used (i.e., if the sender is correctly identified) and the message has not been tampered with since being signed.

If asymmetric encryption has these advantages, why is it often used just to encrypt a symmetric key? Modern asymmetric algorithms are much more computationally intensive than symmetric algorithms that offer a similar level of confidentiality. This is why it is common to generate a random *session key* for two computers to use to communicate over a symmetrically encrypted channel, a key that is passed between the two systems via an asymmetrically encrypted channel. The session key is therefore known to both ends to be the correct one and not to have leaked, and the cheaper symmetric encryption can be used.

> The one remaining challenge is to ensure that the public key you have for an agent is the correct one; in other words, to *authenticate* its identity. Two techniques for doing this are to ask the agent for the *fingerprint* of the agent's public key, which you can generate for yourself and verify, and to use a *trusted third party* to confirm the identity of the agent.

CommonCrypto provides efficient implementations of standard symmetric encryption algorithms used in internal operating system functions, in addition to being available as public API. Some algorithms can be used in *block cipher* operations, which act on a 64-bit or 128-bit block of data at a time, others in *stream cipher* operations, which work a bit or byte at a time. Block mode is appropriate for encrypting files, which are of known length and usually much bigger than the block size. Processors can churn through block encryption much faster than through stream encryption. The final few bytes of the file to be encrypted will need to be padded so that the total length is a multiple of the block size, but that won't usually waste much space. Listing 3-5 encrypts the contents of an NSData object, returning the encrypted content as another NSData object along with the *encryption artifacts*, which will be explained in the discussion following Listing 3-5.

LISTING 3-5: Symmetric encryption of a file using CommonCrypto [GLFileEncryptor.m]

Available for download on Wrox.com

```
- (NSDictionary *)encryptFile: (NSData *)plainText error: (NSError **)error {
    //generate a key
    char *keyBytes = malloc(kCCKeySizeAES128);
    if (NULL == keyBytes) {
        *error = [NSError errorWithDomain: GLFileEncryptorErrorDomain
                                     code: GLFileEncryptorOutOfMemory
                                 userInfo: nil];
        return nil;
    }
    int randomFD = open("/dev/random", O_RDONLY);
    int bytesRead = read(randomFD, keyBytes, kCCKeySizeAES128);
    if (bytesRead < kCCKeySizeAES128) {
        *error = [NSError errorWithDomain: GLFileEncryptorErrorDomain
                                     code: GLFileEncryptorKeyGenError
                                 userInfo: nil];
        free(keyBytes);
        close(randomFD);
        return nil;
    }
    NSData *key = [NSData dataWithBytes: keyBytes length: kCCKeySizeAES128];
    free(keyBytes);

    //generate an IV
    char *ivBytes = malloc(kCCBlockSizeAES128);
    if (NULL == ivBytes) {
        *error = [NSError errorWithDomain: GLFileEncryptorErrorDomain
                                     code: GLFileEncryptorOutOfMemory
                                 userInfo: nil];
        close(randomFD);
```

continues

LISTING 3-5 *(continued)*

```
        return nil;
    }
    bytesRead = read(randomFD, ivBytes, kCCBlockSizeAES128);
    close(randomFD);
    if (bytesRead < kCCBlockSizeAES128) {
        *error = [NSError errorWithDomain: GLFileEncryptorErrorDomain
                                     code: GLFileEncryptorIVGenError
                                 userInfo: nil];
        free(ivBytes);
        return nil;
    }
    NSData *iv = [NSData dataWithBytes: ivBytes length: kCCBlockSizeAES128];
    free(ivBytes);
    // the key and the iv are the "encryption artefacts"

    /* call the encryption routine once, to find out how much space is needed
     * as the data will be padded to a multiple of the block length
     */
    size_t bytesNeeded = 0;
    CCCryptorStatus cryptResult = kCCSuccess;
    cryptResult = CCCrypt(kCCEncrypt,
                          kCCAlgorithmAES128,
                          kCCOptionPKCS7Padding,
                          [key bytes],
                          [key length],
                          [iv bytes],
                          [plainText bytes],
                          [plainText length],
                          NULL,
                          0,
                          &bytesNeeded);
    if (cryptResult != kCCBufferTooSmall) {
        *error = [NSError errorWithDomain: GLFileEncryptorErrorDomain
                                     code: GLFileEncryptorCryptFailed
                                 userInfo: nil];
        return nil;
    }
    char *cipherBytes = malloc(bytesNeeded);
    size_t bufferLength = bytesNeeded;
    if (NULL == cipherBytes) {
        *error = [NSError errorWithDomain: GLFileEncryptorErrorDomain
                                     code: GLFileEncryptorOutOfMemory
                                 userInfo: nil];
        return nil;
    }
    // now actually encrypt the file
    cryptResult = CCCrypt(kCCEncrypt,
                          kCCAlgorithmAES128,
                          kCCOptionPKCS7Padding,
                          [key bytes],
                          [key length],
```

```
                                  [iv bytes],
                                  [plainText bytes],
                                  [plainText length],
                                  cipherBytes,
                                  bufferLength,
                                  &bytesNeeded);
        if (kCCSuccess != cryptResult) {
            *error = [NSError errorWithDomain: GLFileEncryptorErrorDomain
                                         code: GLFileEncryptorCryptFailed
                                     userInfo: nil];
            free(cipherBytes);
            return nil;
        }
        NSData *cipherText = [NSData dataWithBytes: cipherBytes
                                            length: bytesNeeded];
        free(cipherBytes);
        return [NSDictionary dictionaryWithObjectsAndKeys:
                cipherText, GLEncryptedFile,
                key, GLEncryptionKey,
                iv, GLInitializationVector,
                nil];
    }
```

The code first generates the "encryption artefacts." These are the encryption key itself, which is the secret required to decrypt the data once it has been ciphered, and an *initialization vector* (IV). The IV is required because the encryption is operating in a mode called Cipher-Block Chaining (CBC) mode. If all the blocks to be encrypted were worked on entirely independently, then any two blocks encrypted with the same key would result in the same encrypted data. This is not desirable because if an attacker can have his own files encrypted by your application, he can inspect the encrypted files to build up a map between plain and cipher data. Even if the attacker cannot prepare his own encrypted files, he can spot identical blocks in encrypted files and potentially learn something about the contents of the files based on the patterns and frequencies of identical blocks. Such statistical patterns make the attacker's job of discovering the plain data much easier. The Caesar ciphers discussed earlier could be broken by knowing the frequency with which each letter appears in a message, and guessing from the frequency of symbols in the encrypted message which symbol maps to which letter. For example, in English prose the letter "e" occurs more frequently than any other. A very similar technique was used in deciphering German messages encrypted with Enigma during the second world war: analysts assumed that names of command posts and German army ranks appeared in the messages, and searched for decryption keys that led to those words appearing in the deciphered text.

CBC mode avoids the predictability problem by combining the plain data of block n with the encrypted result of block n–1 before encrypting it. The encrypted data thus depends on the contents of the file preceding the block in addition to the contents of the block itself. The IV is combined with the first block to ensure that the result of encrypting block 0 is not predictable. Both the key and the IV must be known to a user in order for him to decrypt the cipher text correctly. The key must be kept secret and the IV must not be tampered with: otherwise an attacker can change it and the first block of the file, but in such a way that the rest of the file is unaffected. CommonCrypto also offers Electronic Code Book (ECB) mode, which does not protect against predictable output.

Both the key and the IV are created by reading random data from the /dev/random file. In fact /dev/random is not a regular file but a special device node. The device provides a stream of data, created by a pseudo-random number generating algorithm (PRNG). A PRNG generates a stream of numbers that are (or should be, at least) statistically similar to a stream of numbers created entirely at random. The actual sequence created by the PRNG depends on its state, so the generator behind /dev/random is periodically updated by the operating system with empirically gathered random data. This input data is derived from measurements of the timing of some events in the kernel, which depend on how the computer is being used, on delays introduced by mechanical components, and on inconsistencies of the oscillation frequencies of some of the timing circuits in the computer. Such input to a PRNG is known as *entropy*, though it has nothing to do with the concept in thermodynamics of the same name.

An application that requires "more random" random numbers than the operating system provides natively can collect its own entropy and feed it to the PRNG by writing to the /dev/random file. Good sources for entropy are the timing of events on input devices like keyboards and mice. How random the entropy gathered truly is depends on context: the hard drive's Sudden Motion Sensor may be a good choice for a laptop being used on a bus trip, but is less likely to provide entropy in a rack-mounted server.

At line 49 the encryption routine is called, to determine how much memory will be needed to store the encrypted data. The size of the encrypted output is not known in advance because the amount of padding needed has not been determined. CommonCrypto adds padding in the format described by PKCS #7 (`http://www.rfc-editor.org/rfc/rfc2315.txt`).

At line 75 the required memory has been allocated and the encryption routine is called again, this time to actually store the encrypted data in the buffer. CCCrypt() is a one-shot function that blocks until all the encryption has been done. By changing the flag passed to CCCrypt() from kCCEncrypt to kCCDecrypt, the same function will recover the original file from the encrypted data. Listing 3-6 demonstrates this.

LISTING 3-6: Decrypting an encrypted file with CommonCrypto [GLFileEncryptor.m]

Available for download on Wrox.com

```
- (NSData *)decryptFile: (NSDictionary *)cipherText error: (NSError **)error {
    NSData *encryptedData = [cipherText objectForKey: GLEncryptedFile];
    NSData *key = [cipherText objectForKey: GLEncryptionKey];
    NSData *iv = [cipherText objectForKey: GLInitializationVector];
    size_t bytesNeeded = 0;
    CCCryptorStatus cryptResult = kCCSuccess;
    cryptResult = CCCrypt(kCCDecrypt,
                          kCCAlgorithmAES128,
                          kCCOptionPKCS7Padding,
                          [key bytes],
                          [key length],
                          [iv bytes],
                          [encryptedData bytes],
```

```
                                 [encryptedData length],
                                 NULL,
                                 0,
                                 &bytesNeeded);
    if (kCCBufferTooSmall != cryptResult) {
        *error = [NSError errorWithDomain: GLFileEncryptorErrorDomain
                                     code: GLFileEncryptorCryptFailed
                                 userInfo: nil];
        return nil;
    }
    char *plainText = malloc(bytesNeeded);
    if (NULL == plainText) {
        *error = [NSError errorWithDomain: GLFileEncryptorErrorDomain
                                     code: GLFileEncryptorOutOfMemory
                                 userInfo: nil];
        return nil;
    }
    size_t bufferLength = bytesNeeded;
    cryptResult = CCCrypt(kCCDecrypt,
                                 kCCAlgorithmAES128,
                                 kCCOptionPKCS7Padding,
                                 [key bytes],
                                 [key length],
                                 [iv bytes],
                                 [encryptedData bytes],
                                 [encryptedData length],
                                 plainText,
                                 bufferLength,
                                 &bytesNeeded);
    if (kCCSuccess != cryptResult) {
        *error = [NSError errorWithDomain: GLFileEncryptorErrorDomain
                                     code: GLFileEncryptorCryptFailed
                                 userInfo: nil];
        return nil;
    }
    NSData *decryptedFile = [[NSData alloc] initWithBytes: plainText
                                                   length: bytesNeeded];
    return [decryptedFile autorelease];
}
```

The one-shot approach demonstrated in the previous two code listings is useful for encrypting and decrypting small amounts of data. To encrypt a large file requires twice its length in memory allocated (for both the plain and cipher text), and the CCCrypt() function blocks until the operation is completed. To reduce the memory requirement and allow applications to report on the status of encryption operations, CommonCrypto provides a staged API. An object called CCCryptorRef is initialized to represent a cryptographic operation, to which data can be added in sequential calls. The CCCryptorRef must be finalized to indicate that all the data has been submitted, and can now be released. In Listing 3-7 this behavior is encapsulated in a single function to show how the sequence is carried out. Note that for the sake of brevity, error-handling code not directly related to the cryptography function has been elided.

LISTING 3-7: Using the staged approach to building an encrypted file [SimpleCCCrypt.c]

Available for download on Wrox.com

```
int SimpleCCCrypt(char *fileName, void *key, size_t keyLength, void *iv,
                  char *cipherFileName) {
    CCCryptorRef cryptObject = NULL;
    CCCryptorStatus ccResult = kCCSuccess;
    ccResult = CCCryptorCreate(kCCEncrypt,
                               kCCAlgorithmAES128,
                               kCCOptionPKCS7Padding,
                               key,
                               keyLength,
                               iv,
                               &cryptObject);
    switch (ccResult) {
        case kCCSuccess:
            //nothing to do here in that case
            break;
        case kCCMemoryFailure:
        case kCCBufferTooSmall:
            errno = ENOMEM;
            return -1;
            break;
        case kCCParamError:
        default:
            errno = EINVAL;
            return -1;
            break;
    }
    int plainFile = open(fileName, O_RDONLY);
    if (-1 == plainFile) {
        //open() will have set errno appropriately
        return -1;
    }
    int cipherFile = open(cipherFileName, O_WRONLY | O_CREAT, 0400);
    if (-1 == cipherFile) {
        int error = errno;
        close(plainFile);
        errno = error;
        return -1;
    }

    size_t bytesRead;
    do {
        bytesRead = 0;
        char input[BUFSIZ], *output = NULL;
        bytesRead = read(plainFile, input, BUFSIZ);
        if (-1 == bytesRead) {
            //handle the error and clean up
            return -1;
        }
        size_t bytesOut = CCCryptorGetOutputLength(cryptObject,
                                                   bytesRead,
                                                   false);
        output = malloc(bytesRead);
```

```
        if (NULL == output) {
            // malloc will have set errno; cleanup code skipped for brevity
            CCCryptorRelease(cryptObject);
            return -1;
        }
        CCCryptorStatus status = kCCSuccess;
        size_t actualBytesOut = 0;
        status = CCCryptorUpdate(cryptObject,
                                 input,
                                 bytesRead,
                                 output,
                                 bytesOut,
                                 &actualBytesOut);
        if (kCCSuccess != status) {
            CCCryptorRelease(cryptObject);
            return -1;
        }
        int bytesWritten = 0;
        bytesWritten = write(cipherFile, output, actualBytesOut);
        free(output);
        if (-1 == bytesWritten) {
            CCCryptorRelease(cryptObject);
            return -1;
        }
    } while (0 != bytesRead);

    close(plainFile);
    //not quite finished, the padding must be written to the output file.
    size_t finalBufferSize = CCCryptorGetOutputLength(cryptObject,
                                                      0,
                                                      true);
    char *finalBuffer = malloc(finalBufferSize);
    if (NULL == finalBuffer) {
        CCCryptorRelease(cryptObject);
        return -1;
    }

    size_t actualFinalSize = 0;
    ccResult = CCCryptorFinal(cryptObject,
                              finalBuffer,
                              finalBufferSize,
                              &actualFinalSize);
    if (ccResult != kCCSuccess) {
        CCCryptorRelease(cryptObject);
        return -1;
    }
    int finallyWritten = write(cipherFile, finalBuffer, actualFinalSize);
    close(cipherFile);
    free(finalBuffer);
    CCCryptorRelease(cryptObject);

    return (-1 == finallyWritten) ? -1 : 0;
}
```

The CCCryptorRelease() function, called to clean up the cryptor object once it has been finished with, does more than just free the memory used by the library. It also overwrites the memory that was used by the cryptor object. Doing so is good practice, as it reduces the chance that an attacker with access to either the process's memory or the kernel's view of all memory on the computer — both available with debuggers — can extract confidential information from the process, such as the key. If a file's content is considered so confidential that it is worth encrypting, then it must be worth protecting from even administrators or the super-user, in addition to Trojan horse applications that the current user may inadvertently be running in other processes.

NETWORK FILESYSTEMS

Remote filesystems accessed over network connections present security issues similar to those of removable media — the pool of potential misusers must be expanded to cover anyone with access to the server, and everyone with access to a computer that can connect to the same shared filesystem. Different network protocols provide their own challenges.

The two protocols most commonly used on Mac systems are AFP (the Apple Filing Protocol) and SMB (Server Message Block). AFP is an Apple proprietary system, while SMB is provided by the open-source Samba component to allow interoperability with Windows and other operating systems. Both permit users to authenticate with the server and assume the access rights granted to the accounts they authenticate with, but they both also permit "guest" access. The permissions granted to a user connected as a guest depend on the rights given to other users on files and folders; in other words, the guest user is never treated as either the owner of a file, or a member of the group owning that file.

Neither SMB nor AFP provides an encrypted channel for transferring files by default. SMB will send passwords in an encrypted form, but all subsequent data is transferred in the clear. AFP uses a Diffie-Helman key exchange process to avoid sending passwords over the network, but still sends data in the clear once an authenticated connection has been created. Each can also use Kerberos to perform authentication, which also avoids transmitting passwords across the network, as discussed in Chapter 2 Mac OS X Server offers the ability to create a *secure tunnel* over which an AFP session can occur: the client and server will automatically negotiate an encrypted SSH connection and send the AFP traffic through that connection. If the two computers fail to negotiate the SSH connection, they will fall back to an unencrypted channel.

Mac OS X also supports hosting and connecting to NFS servers. NFS is an old UNIX file-sharing protocol developed by Sun Microsystems. The versions supported by Mac OS X have a very permissive approach to security: clients do not have to authenticate to connect to servers, but servers can restrict which IP addresses are allowed to mount which shared folders. There is no authentication; instead, user and group account IDs on the clients and servers are assumed to match, so if a file on the server is owned by a user with account 501, then a user with account 501 on the client is taken to be the owner of the file. The only limitation is support for *root squashing*, in which user 0 (the super-user, root) on the client is always given "nobody" privileges when using the shared folder. Additionally, a user with read *or* execute permission on a file can read that file over an NFS connection. That is because either reading a file or executing a program implies the ability to retrieve the file's content from the server.

While many administrators assume that IP-based restrictions are robust, as they correctly identify specific devices, the IPv4 protocol allows for easy spoofing. An attacker can easily assume any IP address and use it to connect to a server, needing to guess only an appropriate account ID. This style of security is extremely weak.

The latest version of NFS, version 4, supports authentication over Kerberos as well as integrity and confidentiality protection for transmitted data. However, the documentation for NFS in Snow Leopard cautions that the NFSv4 support is "alpha quality" and not yet ready for production use.

LAYOUT AND SECURITY OF A TYPICAL MAC OS X FILESYSTEM

The locations of files on a Mac are very different from the locations of equivalent files on other operating systems. Applications, frameworks and files are organized into *domains*, each of which permits modification by different users. The contents of each of these domains is roughly the same, so the users with access at each level can customize each aspect of the environment for a different subset of the users. The concept of the same content's being found in different domains has already been seen in Chapter 2 with regard to user preferences. The domains are as follows:

- **System domain:** Files are stored in the /System folder, which can be modified only by root. This domain is supposed to be reserved for Apple's use, containing key parts of the operating system: the Cocoa frameworks, the Finder and Dock applications, kernel extensions, and launchd jobs controlling the basic services of the computer.
- **Local domain:** Files are stored at the root level of the filesystem, i.e., in the / folder. This folder is writable by any administrator account (with the sticky bit, discussed previously) and as such is where systems administrators can install applications and plug-ins and make configuration changes that affect all the users on the computer. Important folders in the domain, including /Applications and /Library, are protected from deletion by ACLs.
- **Network domain:** The Network domain does not exist by default, but a network administrator can create it by defining networked filesystems that are mounted in folders in /Network. The access control is chosen by the administrators, but would typically permit modification only by network administrators. The Network domain is suitable for software and configuration that must apply to all computers on a network, so an administrator could choose to install site-wide software in /Network/Applications.
- **User domain:** The folders in a user's home folder mirror the layout of other filesystem domains: the home folder contains a Library folder and can additionally contain an Applications folder. The folder is usually writable only by the user who owns it, and is where that user can apply his or her own specific configuration changes or deploy applications that are not shared with other users.
- **Developer domain:** The Xcode Tools folder — usually /Developer but the location is configurable — also represents a separate domain, suitable for the deployment of developer tools. Folders in this domain are writable by any administrator, and lack the sticky bit, so any administrator can delete files created by any other.

Some of the folders in these domains are the mandatory locations for files in the operating system. The launchd service will search only the Library/LaunchDaemons and Library/LaunchAgents folders for jobs to load. Fonts are installed only if they are located in the Library/Fonts folder of a domain — though by choosing which domain, the administrator can install the fonts for different sets of users.

Other files have only an advisory location in the domain structure. While applications are conventionally installed in the /Applications folder (and in other domains in /Network/Applications, ~/Applications, or /Developer/Applications), the Launch Services system that detects and runs applications in response to user events will use applications located anywhere except in a Trash folder.

The different levels of access available to different users in each domain should be a factor you consider when choosing where to store application files. If an asset is confidential to the current user of the application, it should probably be stored in the User domain so that each account has an individual and private version of that asset. If the integrity is important, the Local and Network domains can be modified by a restricted group of users. However, be careful not to artificially restrict deployment options for your application by requiring filesystem access rights that some users cannot acquire. The issue of deployment location and permissions will be discussed further in Chapter 10.

ALIASES AND BOOKMARKS

Some files do not contain any content themselves, but act as pointers to other files. You have already encountered symbolic links in the discussion of UNIX permissions; a symbolic link is a file that contains a path to a different file. When an application tries to open a file that is really a symbolic link, it is redirected to the file located at the referenced path. If there is no file at the referenced path, then the attempt to open the symbolic link fails.

Mac OS X also supports file system aliases, a type of reference file inherited from the classic Mac OS and specific to HFS and HFS+ filesystems. An alias stores both the path to the aliased file, and the cnode ID (CNID) at which the file is located. If the target file is moved, the alias will still be able to resolve it. However, the operating system resolves the alias's path first, so if a file is moved and a new file created at its original location, the alias points to the replacement file, not to the original. If the target file has not moved but cannot be accessed through its path, because either the permissions on the file or an enclosing folder do not allow it, the user will not be able to open the file. This behavior is identical to resolving a symbolic link.

Aliases may refer to files on a different volume from the one on which the alias is stored, but if an aliased file is moved from one volume to another, aliases to that file can no longer follow it; that's because the file is really copied from one volume to the other, then deleted from its original location.

In Mac OS X 10.6 the format of alias files was changed to a new structure called a *bookmark*; the behavior of aliases is the same as in earlier versions of Mac OS X, except that third-party applications can now create and store bookmarks using Cocoa's NSURL API or the CoreFoundation CFURLRef interface; previously only the Finder could create alias files.

QUARANTINING DOWNLOADED FILES

Starting in version 10.5, OS X's Launch Services component provides a quarantine feature. A file downloaded by applications such as Safari and iChat is marked with an extended attribute named com.apple.quarantine, indicating that it possibly comes from an untrusted source. The first time a user tries to open that file through Launch Services (typically by double-clicking the file in the Finder), Launch Services determines whether it is a potentially dangerous file (an application, shell script, or installer package would be considered potentially dangerous) and, if it is displays a dialog providing some information about the file and where it came from. The dialog asks whether the user really wants to open the file. If so, the file is opened, and if the user can write to the file's extended attributes the quarantine attribute is cleared so the question will not be asked again.

Approaching a security-related problem by asking the user what to do in this way is not always a very productive solution. The user already indicated that he wanted to open the file by double-clicking it in the Finder; will he really have changed his mind by the time your application asks him whether he wants to open the file? Probably not.

Unfortunately, in cases like these there is not enough information to decide on the user's behalf what to do. Snow Leopard will, in certain circumstances, detect Mac malware (malicious software) but will still allow the user to open the file if he chooses to do so. There's always the slight but real possibility that the user is either a malware researcher or a masochist and does want to open a file even once he knows it is dangerous.

By asking the user to confirm an action that he has already tried to take, you hope that the chance the user will slow down, think the action through rationally, and choose the correct response outweighs the frustration he might derive from being interrupted. Is it? Equally, without extremely cautious interface design, such repetitive questions can simply train the user to give a certain response, making the situation worse when the user really does need to think about a given action.

The quarantine feature of Launch Services can be used by third-party applications. The simplest way to adopt the feature is to put the following property into your application's Info.plist file:

```
<key>LSFileQuarantineEnabled</key>
<true/>
```

Any file created by applications with this property set to true will automatically have a quarantine attribute set. The dialog presented to a user attempting to work with such a file is shown in Figure 3-3; it lacks information such as the URL from which the file was downloaded because the operating system cannot determine that information on the application's behalf.

FIGURE 3-3: The generic file quarantine dialog

The LSFileQuarantineEnabled key is useful for applications that cannot control the files they create: interpreting script files and loading code bundles are situations in which an application could write arbitrary data to a file over which the application's author has no control. In each of these cases the application could create a dangerous file at any time, so imposing the quarantine behavior on all files created could help a user to understand that any such file needs to be verified before being used.

For other applications it is easier to understand when they might create a potentially dangerous file. A file transfer application, for example an FTP client, creates files at predictable times, the contents of which are unknown. These applications can use the Launch Services API to add quarantine attributes to those files they download, to indicate that just these files are suspicious. By limiting their use of the quarantine attribute in this way, these applications expose users to fewer confirmation dialogs, which some security experts hope will lead to the users' paying more attention to those that do appear. Listing 3-8 shows an application using LaunchServices.framework to attach a quarantine attribute to a file.

LISTING 3-8: Attaching a quarantine attribute to a newly created file [create_quarantined_file.m]

Available for download on Wrox.com

```
BOOL create_quarantined_file(NSString *fileName) {
    NSString *content = @"#!/bin/sh\n\necho \"arbitrary code...\"\n";
    NSURL *saveToURL = [NSURL fileURLWithPath: fileName];
    [content writeToURL: saveToURL
             atomically: YES
               encoding: NSUTF8StringEncoding
                  error: nil];
    //for demo purposes, invent a source for this file
    NSURL *originURL = [NSURL URLWithString: @"http://www.example.com/"];
    NSURL *dataURL = [NSURL URLWithString: [@"http://www.example.com/somefile.txt"
                                        stringByAppendingString: fileName]];
    NSDictionary *attributes = [NSDictionary dictionaryWithObjectsAndKeys:
                                kLSQuarantineTypeOtherDownload,
kLSQuarantineTypeKey,
                                originURL, kLSQuarantineOriginURLKey,
                                dataURL, kLSQuarantineDataURLKey,
                                nil];
    //LaunchServices works with the Carbon file system reference type
    FSRef carbonFileReference;
    BOOL converted = CFURLGetFSRef(saveToURL, &carbonFileReference);
    if (!converted) {
        // there isn't much to be done, the quarantine attribute can't be set
        return NO;
    }
    OSStatus quarantineResult = LSSetItemAttribute(&carbonFileReference,
                                                   kLSRolesAll,
                                                   kLSItemQuarantineProperties,
                                                   attributes);
    return (noErr == quarantineResult);
}
```

The dialog presented to users trying to open files that have been quarantined in that way contains more information than the generic version, as demonstrated by Figure 3-4. The two URLs provided to LSSetItemAttribute serve different purposes: the *data URL* is the location from which the file was actually downloaded, while the *origin URL* is the location the user would recognize as

FIGURE 3-4: Quarantine dialog displayed when custom quarantine attributes are set

the download site. When the user clicks the Show Source button in the quarantine dialog, the origin URL is opened in a web browser.

SECURELY DELETING FILES

You have seen in the discussion on file permissions that files are stored on the disk as blocks of data, which are associated with each other through a record called an inode. An inode is given a name and a location in the folder hierarchy by being linked to a file name in a particular folder. To remove a file, then, all you need to do is *unlink* it, to destroy its association with a name in the filesystem.

That is indeed how removing a file works on Mac OS X. Each inode has a *link count,* which is like a retain count for the file. Every time an inode is linked to a file name, its link count is incremented. The unlink() system call (which is used by the NSFileManager methods -removeItemAtPath:error: and -removeItemAtURL:error:) removes the link entry for the file name that is unlinked, and decrements the inode's link count. Once the link count has reached 0, the inode is no longer in use and the space consumed by its data can be reused.

Note that I say "*can*" be reused, not *will* be reused. This is an important distinction. The area on the disk where the file was stored is no longer reserved for the file, but the data in that area is not immediately replaced. The contents of the file still exist and you can recover them by creating a new file record to refer to that data, which is how commercial file-recovery software works. Of course, once the file has been unlinked its permissions and ownership are no longer recorded, so the file can be recovered by any user who can read the disk — if the file's contents were previously being kept secret from other users, they are paradoxically no longer secret after the file is deleted.

To be removed from the hard disk completely, the data must be overwritten. Simply overwriting the whole file with zeroes is not considered good enough for many applications, as the underlying data can still theoretically be recovered, so a seven-pass system is usually used. The file's contents are overwritten with ones (i.e., the byte 0xFF, in which every bit is "on"), then zeroes (0x00), ones again, then random data, zeroes, ones, and finally more random data. Those seven passes are thought to make recovery of underlying data *from a hard disk* impossible. The appropriate method on other media could be different. Developers should always be aware of the profile of the device and the operating system behaviors.

Because the seven-pass system involves writing to the file, an application that does this must have permission to write to the file as well as to delete objects from the folder that contains the file.

There is no library function for performing safe file deletion. The tool /usr/bin/srm can securely delete files and can be called from system() or via NSTask. Notice that if a file is linked multiple times (with hard links, not symbolic links), the srm command does not actually overwrite the contents.

Additionally, the Finder can securely delete files with the Secure Empty Trash menu item, which is also available through Finder's AppleScript API:

```
tell application "Finder"
    empty trash with security
end tell
```

It isn't a very good idea for an application to empty a user's Trash without warning, as the user may have other files in there that they want to review before deleting. Secure Empty Trash and srm both take a long time to complete.

DISK ARBITRATION

Once a file has been copied to a removable device, applications on the original computer no longer have any control over what happens to the file's data. Any access control in place may be ignored when the device is attached to a different computer, and the meanings of the user accounts will have changed anyway. Even encrypting the content may not be sufficient protection: the original user might decrypt the file on an untrustworthy computer, or even copy and paste the content onto an unencrypted file on the removable media.

Some assets may be considered sufficiently confidential that users should not be able to create copies of them on external drives or USB devices, or should be able to create copies only on approved devices, such as those with built-in encryption. As the ownership and permissions settings on such volumes cannot be trusted to provide good access control (and, as you have already seen, may not be honored by the operating system anyway), the only way to mitigate the risk of files being copied onto removable devices is to block those devices from being mounted at all.

Blocking removable devices from being mounted affects all applications and all users on the computer. Ensure that users and administrators understand the impact your application will have on their work and accept that impact before taking such drastic action.

Removable devices are automatically mounted by Mac OS X when they appear, but applications have the capability to intercept these events and decline them, based on information provided by the operating system about the devices. This capability is provided by the DiskArbitration framework, and also allows applications to detect and react to volumes appearing and disappearing, including networked filesystems. Listing 3-9 demonstrates how an application can deny any attempt to automatically connect a removable volume.

Available for download on Wrox.com

LISTING 3-9: Blocking access to removable media with DiskArbitration [disk_arbitration.m]

```
#import <Foundation/Foundation.h>
#import <DiskArbitration/DiskArbitration.h>

DADissenterRef approvalCallback(DADiskRef disk, void *context) {
    // none of the mounts shall be approved
    DADissenterRef response = DADissenterCreate(NULL,
                                                kDAReturnNotPermitted,
                                                @"This volume is blocked.");
    NSDictionary *diskProperties = DADiskCopyDescription(disk);
    NSLog(@"refused to mount volume: %@", diskProperties);
    return response;
}

int main (int argc, const char * argv[]) {
    NSAutoreleasePool * pool = [[NSAutoreleasePool alloc] init];
```

```
    DAApprovalSessionRef session = DAApprovalSessionCreate(NULL);
    if (NULL == session) {
        NSLog(@"couldn't create a DiskArb session");
        return -1;
    }
    DARegisterDiskMountApprovalCallback(session,
                                        NULL,
                                        approvalCallback,
                                        NULL);
    CFRunLoopRef runLoop = [[NSRunLoop currentRunLoop] getCFRunLoop];
    DAApprovalSessionScheduleWithRunLoop(session,
                                         runLoop,
                                         kCFRunLoopDefaultMode);
    //run the run loop forever - the process must be killed to stop its effect
    [[NSRunLoop currentRunLoop] run];
    // this is how the clean-up code should go, but this tool won't get here
    DAApprovalSessionUnscheduleFromRunLoop(session,
                                           runLoop,
                                           kCFRunLoopDefaultMode);
    DAUnregisterApprovalCallback(session,
                                 approvalCallback,
                                 NULL);
    CFRelease(session);

    [pool drain];
    return 0;
}
```

When run, the program will refuse to allow any removable media to mount, though it does not affect networked filesystems. The information available to the application looks like this:

```
2009-11-05 14:56:04.572 disk arbitration[1898:903] refused to mount volume: {
    DAAppearanceTime = "279125764.051253";
    DABusName = EHC2;
    DABusPath = "IODeviceTree:/PCI0/EHC2@1A,7";
    DADeviceInternal = 0;
    DADeviceModel = "USB DRIVE";
    DADevicePath = "IOService:/AppleACPIPlatformExpert/PCI0/AppleACPIPCI/EHC2@1A,7/
AppleUSBEHCI/USB DRIVE@fa410000/IOUSBInterface@0/IOUSBMassStorageClass/
IOSCSIPeripheralDeviceNub/IOSCSIPeripheralDeviceType00/IOBlockStorageServices";
    DADeviceProtocol = USB;
    DADeviceRevision = "1.11";
    DADeviceUnit = 6;
    DADeviceVendor = CRUCIAL;
    DAMediaBSDMajor = 14;
    DAMediaBSDMinor = 7;
    DAMediaBSDName = disk2s1;
    DAMediaBSDUnit = 2;
    DAMediaBlockSize = 512;
    DAMediaContent = "Apple_HFS";
    DAMediaEjectable = 1;
    DAMediaIcon =     {
        CFBundleIdentifier = "com.apple.iokit.IOStorageFamily";
        IOBundleResourceFile = "Removable.icns";
```

```
        };
        DAMediaKind = IOMedia;
        DAMediaLeaf = 1;
        DAMediaName = "Untitled 1";
        DAMediaPath = "IODeviceTree:/PCI0/EHC2@1A,7/@6:1";
        DAMediaRemovable = 1;
        DAMediaSize = 128927232;
        DAMediaWhole = 0;
        DAMediaWritable = 1;
        DAVolumeKind = hfs;
        DAVolumeMountable = 1;
        DAVolumeName = crucial;
        DAVolumeNetwork = 0;
        DAVolumeUUID = "<CFUUID 0x100300d20> A17423CC-15A4-39BE-9311-CF0459A3091F";
    }
```

You can use any of these properties to restrict the devices for which the callback will be invoked, by passing a dictionary of properties with values to be filtered on to the DARegisterDiskMountApprovalCallback() function.

Note that a technically adept user can still mount a removable volume after a DiskArbitration callback has rejected it. The DiskArbitration behavior only limits the function of the automatic mounter in OS X; the device is still registered in I/O Kit and because of this a device node in /dev is created for it. A non-technical attacker would probably be deterred by the failure of the automatic mounter, making this technique sufficient to stop casual or accidental data leakage. A more competent attacker will not be stopped so easily. By using the mount command from the Terminal, a user can still attach the device to the filesystem.

SUMMARY

The access users are granted to files and folders on the filesystem shapes the confidentiality, integrity and availability of assets stored on the hard disk. Mac OS X provides different ways to restrict access to the filesystem: UNIX access modes, filesystem attributes, and access control lists.

In some circumstances — those involving removable disks and networked filesystems that can both be used on multiple computers — relying on the filesystem access controls to protect assets is insufficient. The application can either forbid such devices from being connected or encrypt confidential assets so that only the original user can recover them. Encryption also protects assets from being viewed by the super-user, who has the privilege of being able to use any file.

Applications that download content from the network cannot necessarily trust that content. The suspicious nature of such files can be indicated to the user through Launch Services quarantine attributes, so the user is given information about when and from where files were retrieved before agreeing to open them.

Deleting a file from the hard disk does not actually remove the file's contents, which can still be recovered by commercial undeleting applications. To ensure that sensitive data is really removed you must overwrite it a number of times, such as by using the srm tool.

Handling Multiple Processes

WHAT'S IN THIS CHAPTER?

- When to use multiple processes and how to design a multiple-process application
- How to handle switching between different users
- Communicating between different processes
- Limiting processes' access to resources
- Verifying a program's identity

Splitting an application into multiple processes can impart significant design benefits. A system comprising a user-interfacing foreground application communicating with a background daemon can carry on its work while the user is not working in the app, or not even logged in. A helper tool can perform some tasks in parallel with the user interface without adding the complication of multi-threaded programming. Applications can take advantage of services provided by other applications and by the operating system through inter-process communication (IPC). The interfaces between these processes must be considered as entry points to the whole system, so both the design and implementation of multi-process systems must be carefully thought out to avoid the introduction of vulnerabilities.

PRIVILEGE SEPARATION

A process that can be controlled by an attacker could potentially be used to perform any task for which the process has the required privileges. If the process is used only for making network connections but also has the ability to replace files in the /Applications folder, then an attacker can subvert it for this second purpose, which isn't even a feature of the application. It is desirable to minimize the rights given to any process in an application, so that the risk associated with threats unrelated to its intended function is reduced.

The *principle of least privilege* (PoLP) is a design rule that takes such mitigation into account. A system designed according to the PoLP has no more privileges than are required to do its work. There are actually two principles at work here: first, that an application should never have a privilege it is not designed ever to use, and second, that if it needs to gain additional privileges to perform a task it should relinquish them as soon as it has completed that task. The first of these principles reduces the risk that an application can be hijacked to do something unrelated to its function, and the second reduces the window of opportunity for exploiting privileges that the application uses only infrequently.

An application will often need different rights on the system to perform unrelated tasks. As an example, consider an application for creating and modifying user accounts on a Mac. This app needs to connect to the WindowServer so that it can draw its user interfaces and accept input events. It must read account information from Directory Services, and write changes to Directory Services when it needs to make them. If the application has any preferences or auto-saving information, it must be permitted to write to the user's Preferences folder. All these abilities are shown diagrammatically in Figure 4-1.

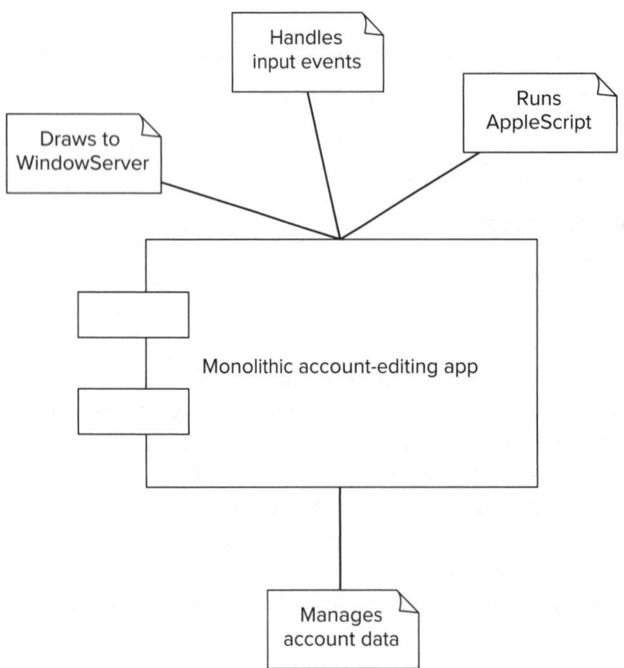

FIGURE 4-1: A single application with multiple responsibilities

The ability to work with the WindowServer — a standard requirement of Cocoa apps — seems entirely disconnected from the ability to work with Directory Services. Because these different portions of the app are separated into different processes, as shown in Figure 4-2, each can have a separate restricted set of privileges with which to access the operating system. The graphical application runs whenever a user launches it, but uses a helper process to work with Directory Services. The helper process does not need the complexity of AppKit with its multiple entry points, but does need to be able to change records in Directory Services. The privileges required to complete the application's use cases have been separated into different processes.

Dividing an application in this way is known as *factoring* it. A factored app calls on helpers with different privileges when it needs to use those privileges, and doesn't keep the helpers around when the privileges are unnecessary. The privileges have been factored out of the main application process into the helper tools. In this way, factored apps are better able to adhere to the principle of least privilege than monolithic apps.

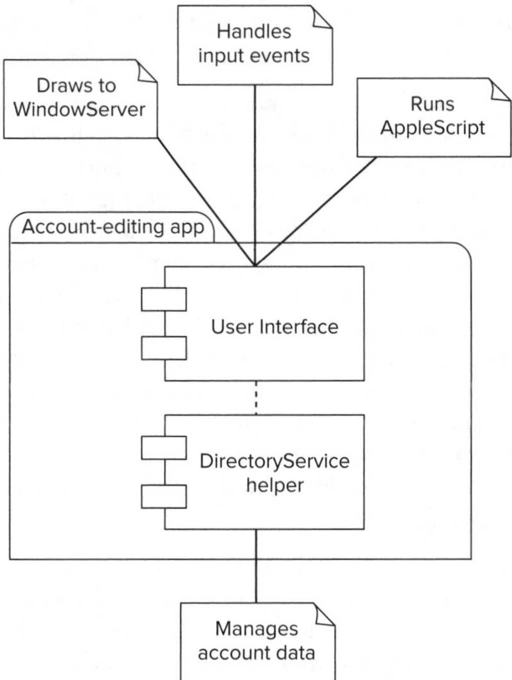

FIGURE 4-2: Factoring a complicated app into multiple processes

DESIGNING MULTIPLE-PROCESS SYSTEMS

You have seen that splitting an application into multiple processes limits the access to operating system resources and privileges required by any one of the processes. Such limitation in turn reduces the scope for damage should any one of the processes be compromised by an attacker. Referring back to Figure 4-2, if the graphical application were compromised, it would have no way of directly changing the Directory Services information. An attacker could use it to communicate with the helper process, but this is true of any compromised application or Trojan horse on the target computer. The Directory Services helper process can potentially be misused to alter directory information, but if it's only launched when needed, the window of opportunity to exploit the helper is reduced. The helper process does not need to make network connections or write files on the disk, so it should not be given those privileges. Without those abilities, the helper process is less useful in arbitrary attacks on the computer.

The interface between the different processes in a complex system represent *privilege boundaries*, where processes without the capability to perform particular tasks can request that other processes carry them out. This is the trade-off inherent in multiple-process systems: the reliance on privileged access to resources is minimized, but the system must defend a higher number of entry points. For the system to work together, a process with one set of privileges must be able to communicate with processes that have different sets of privileges. One process can request of another that it perform some task that the first process does not have the right to do. These privilege boundaries can be sources of privilege-escalation threats, if attackers can use the privileged processes for their own needs.

The process boundary is also a natural place to perform security checks on the request being made, and on the entity making the request. The real-world analogy is a port on a country's border (which allows people from other countries to enter): this is the best place to locate passport control (which identifies people and decides whether they have permission to enter). By choosing which requests to honor at the process boundary, a process can turn away malicious requests without having to handle them at all. To further the analogy, a country's perimeter is not one long port extending all the way around the nation. By concentrating entry and exit in a small number of ports located around the border, the country can focus its passport control and other security efforts at these ports, relying on passive defenses like fences or geographic features around the rest of its borders to stop people entering anywhere that isn't a port. Similarly, each component of a multi-process system should have the minimum required number of entry points, so that access-control efforts can be focused on a few locations. If each process has only one interface to the outside world, the work of defending each process from inappropriate access is as easy as possible.

In some types of software, access to the graphical interface itself can be the privilege that is infrequently required. Consider the File Sharing facility in Mac OS X, which provides an AFP server for other Macs to connect to. The AFP server must be available whenever the computer is switched on and needs to make network connections and access the file system. It does not, however, usually need to present a user interface — and must be available at times when no user is logged in to interact with a UI. Users must be able to configure the sharing facility, though. The system is factored into multiple processes, with the configuration UI being presented as a plug-in to the System Preferences application. Users configure the AFP server through System Preferences, although the server itself is always available when it is enabled.

Applications sometimes use multiple processes so that they can drop privileges that are required only during initialization. The Remote Login facility in Mac OS X, also known as Secure Shell or SSH, is an example of a system that behaves in this way. The facility must listen on TCP port 22 for incoming connections, and listening on any port with a number less than 1024 requires super-user access. Once a client has connected, and identified and authenticated its user, SSH must start a login session for that user, who also needs super-user privileges. From that point on the session is acting on behalf of the authenticated user, and does not need to do anything this user could not do. The SSH service is actually handled by three processes. The launchd event manager (described in detail in the next section) is running as root, and listens on port 22. When a connection is made, launchd starts an instance of the SSH daemon, sshd, also running as root. Launchd hands the socket to this sshd, which handles the authentication stage. Once the root sshd has determined which user is connecting, it starts another sshd process, which switches to the user ID of the connecting user and handles the rest of the login session.

MANAGING PROCESS LIFECYCLES WITH LAUNCHD

The launchd daemon provides a unified interface for responding to numerous different events. In addition to handling the system startup (the event of turning on the computer) launchd can start processes at scheduled times, when network connections are made (as with SSH, discussed earlier), when files or folders change, when users log in, when file system sockets are connected to, or when volumes are mounted. The processes can be monitored by launchd as a watchdog, so that they are restarted if they exit. In this way launchd is responsible for the availability of processes and services in Mac OS X. It also pays attention to the code signature of the executables under its control, and in this way maintains the integrity of loaded jobs in a way that would be cumbersome for applications to take care of themselves.

A specification of a task to be run by launchd and the preconditions for launching that task are known as a *job*. All the jobs started in the same context are in the same *session*. The system daemons and system-wide services run in the system session, which is created as part of the operating system's boot process. Each time a user logs in, a new launchd session is created to handle that user's login session. Users can add jobs to and remove jobs from their own login sessions, but only privileged users can modify the jobs in the system session (specifically, processes must have acquired the com.apple.ServiceManagement.daemons.modify right in Authorization Services). Users cannot change the jobs loaded in other users' login sessions.

Each job is defined by a dictionary of properties, which tells launchd under what conditions the job should be launched, and what to do when those conditions are met. These dictionaries can be stored on the hard disk as XML property lists: launchd will automatically load property lists found in the Library/LaunchDaemons and Library/LaunchAgents folders of the file system domains when new sessions are started. The ServiceManagement framework lets an application retrieve information about the jobs loaded in the system launchd session, and in the same login session as the application. Listing 4-1 shows how to find the system session's jobs.

LISTING 4-1: Finding the launchd jobs in the system launchd session. [findlaunchdjobs.m]

Available for download on Wrox.com

```
#import <Foundation/Foundation.h>
#import <ServiceManagement/ServiceManagement.h>

int main (int argc, const char * argv[]) {
    NSAutoreleasePool * pool = [[NSAutoreleasePool alloc] init];

    NSArray *allJobs = SMCopyAllJobDictionaries(kSMDomainSystemLaunchd);
    for (NSDictionary *job in allJobs) {
        NSString *label = [job objectForKey: @"Label"];
        NSString *program = [job objectForKey: @"Program"];
        if (nil == program) {
            program = [[job objectForKey: @"ProgramArguments"]
                        objectAtIndex: 0];
        }
        NSLog(@"job: %@ program: %@", label, program);
    }
    [allJobs release];
```

continues

LISTING 4-1 *(continued)*

```
    [pool drain];
    return 0;
}
```

Each job is identified with a label, which is usually named in a reverse DNS format (e.g., com .example.yourapplication.job) in order to ensure that the labels are unique. A job is associated with a program that will be run when the job is triggered, so the path of that program is part of the job dictionary. There are two places where the program name might appear: the Program key or the first element of the ProgramArguments array (just as the program name is also the first element of the argv[] array inside the main() function). There were about 150 jobs on one Mac when I ran the preceding tool, the (abbreviated!) output of which looks like this:

```
2009-11-13 10:34:42.565 findlaunchdjobs[504:a0f] job: com.apple.racoon program:
/usr/sbin/racoon
2009-11-13 10:34:42.566 findlaunchdjobs[504:a0f] job: com.apple.loginwindow program:
/System/Library/CoreServices/loginwindow.app/Contents/MacOS/loginwindow
2009-11-13 10:34:42.567 findlaunchdjobs[504:a0f] job:
com.apple.TrustEvaluationAgent.system program:
/System/Library/PrivateFrameworks/TrustEvaluationAgent.framework/Resources/
trustevaluationagent
2009-11-13 10:34:42.567 findlaunchdjobs[504:a0f] job: com.apple.portmap program:
/usr/bin/sandbox-exec
2009-11-13 10:34:42.568 findlaunchdjobs[504:a0f] job: com.apple.hdiejectd program:
/System/Library/PrivateFrameworks/DiskImages.framework/Resources/hdiejectd
2009-11-13 10:34:42.569 findlaunchdjobs[504:a0f] job: com.apple.periodic-weekly program:
/usr/sbin/periodic
2009-11-13 10:34:42.570 findlaunchdjobs[504:a0f] job: 0x100114e30.anonymous.launchd
program: launchd
```

The last job in the list has a label that doesn't match the usual reverse-DNS naming scheme. This is not a real launchd job, but a placeholder for an unmanaged program that has made a launchd request. Let's take a look at one of the jobs in more detail to discover what some of the other job properties are. The loginwindow process is responsible for authenticating users who attempt to use the computer locally (i.e., who sit in front of the screen with the keyboard and mouse, although screen sharing admittedly clouds the image slightly) and who initiate their login sessions when they successfully authenticate. The loginwindow application, as with other system services, is started by launchd in the system session. Listing 4-2 shows how ServiceManagement.framework can be used to get the details of the loginwindow job.

LISTING 4-2: Discovering information about a launchd job [getjobinfo.m]

Available for download on Wrox.com

```
#import <Foundation/Foundation.h>
#import <ServiceManagement/ServiceManagement.h>

int main (int argc, const char * argv[]) {
    NSAutoreleasePool * pool = [[NSAutoreleasePool alloc] init];
```

```
    NSDictionary *loginWindow = SMJobCopyDictionary(kSMDomainSystemLaunchd,
                                                   @"com.apple.loginwindow");
    NSLog(@"loginwindow: %@", loginWindow);
    [loginWindow release];

    [pool drain];
    return 0;
}
```

The dictionary returned by launchd looks like this:

```
{
    Label = "com.apple.loginwindow";
    LastExitStatus = 0;
    LimitLoadToSessionType = System;
    MachServices =     {
        "com.apple.O3Master" = 1801678675;
    };
    OnDemand = 0;
    PID = 39;
    ProgramArguments =     (
        "/System/Library/CoreServices/loginwindow.app/Contents/MacOS/loginwindow",
        console
    );
    TimeOut = 30;
}
```

Most of these properties reflect permanent attributes of the job, and can be configured through the job's property list file (in this case /System/Library/LaunchDaemons/com.apple.loginwindow.plist). A couple of the properties depend on the instantaneous state of the job. The LastExitStatus key records whether or not the job's process terminated with an error the last time it ran. It is possible to choose whether or not the job restarts based on whether it exits cleanly. The PID is the process ID of the program associated with the job that launchd has started — in this case the process ID of the loginwindow process. Launchd determines when a job has finished by watching for the process it launched to terminate. It is therefore necessary for a system using launchd to avoid exiting this process before it has completed its work. This is different from many other UNIX platforms, where the process launched by init or inetd is expected to spawn a child process and quit, usually through the daemon() function.

As we explore the various ways to configure a launchd job, you will discover that there is no way to record a job's dependencies. That is, you cannot indicate that com.example.job1 must wait for com.apple.job2 to start before it can be launched. This is not a design oversight; jobs should expect their dependencies to be present and allow launchd to resolve absences on demand. If job1 requires a socket connection provided by job2, it should just launch and attempt to connect to the socket when it needs to. Assuming job2 advertises the socket in its launchd job, then when job1 connects to that socket, launchd will automatically start job2. In this way, the load on the system and the start time are kept to a minimum, as services are not launched until they are actually used.

Jobs do not need to be loaded at the beginning of a launchd session. Applications can submit and remove jobs in a session at any time, as long as they have the right to modify the target session. An application can submit a helper after the app has been launched, and remove the helper from the launchd session before it terminates. The following program, in Listing 4-3, submits a launchd helper job (the example is just the sleep program, demonstrating the position a helper takes without adding the complexity of communicating with a full helper process) to run every few seconds while the program is alive, and removes it before the program exits.

Available for download on Wrox.com

LISTING 4-3: Submitting and removing a launchd job in the user launchd session [submitlaunchdjob.m]

```
#import <Foundation/Foundation.h>
#import <ServiceManagement/ServiceManagement.h>

static NSString *kLaunchdJobLabel =
@"info.thaesofereode.cocoasecurity.examplejob";

void submitLaunchdJob(void) {
    NSString *path = @"/bin/sleep";
    NSArray *args = [NSArray arrayWithObjects: path, @"15", nil];
    NSDictionary *keepAlive = [NSDictionary dictionaryWithObject:
                               [NSNumber numberWithBool: NO]
                                                           forKey:
                              @"SuccessfulExit"];
    NSDictionary *jobSpec = [NSDictionary dictionaryWithObjectsAndKeys:
                            args, @"ProgramArguments",
                            kLaunchdJobLabel, @"Label",
                            [NSNumber numberWithBool: YES], @"RunAtLoad",
                            [NSNumber numberWithInt: 20], @"StartInterval",
                            keepAlive, @"KeepAlive",
                            nil];
    NSError *submitError = nil;
    BOOL submitResult = SMJobSubmit(kSMDomainUserLaunchd,
                                    jobSpec,
                                    NULL,
                                    &submitError);
    if (NO == submitResult) {
        NSLog(@"error submitting job: %@", submitError);
    }
}

void removeLaunchdJob(void) {
    NSError *removeError = nil;
    BOOL removeResult = SMJobRemove(kSMDomainUserLaunchd,
                                    kLaunchdJobLabel,
                                    NULL,
                                    NO,
                                    &removeError);
    if (NO == removeResult) {
        NSLog(@"error removing job: %@", removeError);
    }
}

int main (int argc, const char * argv[]) {
    NSAutoreleasePool * pool = [[NSAutoreleasePool alloc] init];
```

```
        submitLaunchdJob();
        //run for a short time before removing the job
        NSDate *stopDate = [[NSDate date] dateByAddingTimeInterval: 60.0];
        [[NSRunLoop currentRunLoop] runUntilDate: stopDate];
        removeLaunchdJob();

        [pool drain];
        return 0;
    }
```

If you keep the Activity Monitor program open while running Listing 4-3, you will observe the sleep process appearing and disappearing as it gets run by launchd. The program configures the job through the KeepAlive key to automatically restart the process if it ever exits with an error; in the case of the sleep tool, this will happen only if it's terminated with a signal. In this way launchd supports the availability of the helper by restarting it if it ever exits prematurely. For an asset with a strong availability requirement this can be a useful supporting feature, but should not be relied on as the sole availability defense. If an attacker can cause the helper to continually exit with an error, service may be denied or severely affected for other users, and launchd will eventually throttle back its attempts to restart the process.

DEBUGGING LAUNCHD JOBS

Handing control of a helper job over to launchd can introduce some uncertainty in the development of your application. Until you are confident that you have the launchd job parameters correct, it can be hard to determine whether a problem is caused by the code being run by the job, or by launchd's not loading the job on the occasions you expect.

There are a couple of devices available to assist with such debugging. The launchd job dictionary can contain a key, Debug, that if set to Boolean YES will cause launchd to emit extra debug messages when handling the job. These messages do not appear in the Console by default — you will need to direct them to a log file by configuring the Apple System Logger. Using sudo and a text editor such as vi or nano, add a line like this to /etc/syslog.conf:

```
*.debug                                         /Library/Logs/Debug.log
```

Then send syslogd the hang-up signal so that it rereads its configuration:

```
jormungand:~ leeg$ sudo killall -HUP syslogd
```

Now the debug messages will appear in /Library/Logs/Debug.log, which can be viewed in the Console application.

Launchd can also be configured to start a job when it is triggered, but to delay execution until a debugger such as gdb is attached. You can then watch the behavior of the job's process in the debugger, change its state, and perform all the other debugging tasks as if you had started the process from the Xcode debugger — although it is still triggered on demand by launchd and inherits its usual context.

The third argument to both SMJobSubmit() and SMJobRemove() is an authorization reference, which can be NULL when you are working with the user launchd domain. To change jobs in the system domain (for example, to install a daemon), the authorization reference must contain the com.apple.ServiceManagement.daemons.modify privilege so that unprivileged users cannot tamper with the system services. You will see how to acquire this privilege in Chapter 6.

Most launchd helper and daemon jobs will be triggered on a socket connection, either a network connection from another computer or an IPC connection from a user application. In either case, the daemon needs to check in with launchd before it hands over the socket to the tool. Checking in is accomplished with launchd's IPC interface, defined in <launch.h>. A process sends the LAUNCH_KEY_CHECKIN message to launchd. The reply to this is a dictionary of its job properties, although the socket descriptions specified when the job was submitted are replaced by file descriptor numbers corresponding to the streams associated with each socket in the process. The process can then use this dictionary to identify each of its IPC or RPC connections.

Launchd still has the look of an all-or-nothing service. Launchd jobs are either user agents running in each user's session on behalf of that user, or system daemons running in the system session as the super-user. The principle of least privilege suggests that you not use higher privilege than is really required, so what should you do if you need to provide a system daemon but it does not need super-user privileges?

If the daemon will never need to operate as root, its launchd job can specify that launchd should switch to a different user and group before executing the daemon process. This is signified by the UserName and GroupName properties in the job plist, which indicate the short names of the user and group as the ones the daemon should run. These properties are observed only in the system launchd domain (or the root user's domain), because in other domains the launchd process doesn't have the right to change users. If the situation is more complicated (for example, if the daemon must perform some initial work as the super-user before dropping the privileges), then the daemon must rely on setting its own user ID.

HOW TO USE SETUID AND SETGID

You have already come across the concept of a process running under a different user or group ID from that of the user who invoked the process, when we examined the setuid and setgid bits of the UNIX access mode. Those bits made a process launch with the user or group ID specified in the executable file's ownership, although the process can still find out which user launched it. This is because there are actually multiple user and group IDs associated with any process, but usually they all happen to be the same. The *real* UID and GID represent the user and group accounts that launched the process, and so are suitable for accounting purposes. The permissions accorded to the process are determined by its *effective* UID and GID. Consider a tool that reports on the tool's real and effective UID and GID, like this:

```
#include <stdio.h>
#include <unistd.h>

int main(int argc, const char *argv[]) {
    uid_t realUid, effectiveUid;
    gid_t realGid, effectiveGid;
```

```
    realUid = getuid();
    effectiveUid = geteuid();
    realGid = getgid();
    effectiveGid = getegid();

    printf("real UID: %ld effective UID: %ld\n", realUid, effectiveUid);
    printf("real GID: %ld effective GID: %ld\n", realGid, effectiveGid);
    return 0;
}
```

If that tool is compiled and run as usual, with no special file system permissions, the result is that the real and effective UIDs are equal, both set to the user ID and primary group ID of the user who launches the tool:

```
heimdall:~ leeg$ ls -l showuids
-rwxr-xr-x  1 leeg  staff  8896 Nov 17 14:21 showuids
heimdall:~ leeg$ ./showuids
real UID: 501 effective UID: 501
real GID: 20 effective GID: 20
```

Now change the ownership on the tool, and set both the setuid and setgid permission bits. If the same user again launches the tool, the real UID and GID will remain the same, but the effective IDs will become those of the executable file's owning user and group:

```
heimdall:~ leeg$ sudo chown root showuids
heimdall:~ leeg$ sudo chmod u+s showuids
heimdall:~ leeg$ sudo chgrp daemon showuids
heimdall:~ leeg$ sudo chmod g+s showuids
heimdall:~ leeg$ ./showuids
real UID: 501 effective UID: 0
real GID: 20 effective GID: 1
```

If a process makes any attempt to use resources protected by some form of access control, like file system objects, it is the effective user and group IDs that are used to calculate the process's rights. A process can change its effective user and group IDs. It can set them to either the process's real IDs or the initial values of the effective IDs; in other words it can switch between these two identities. The initial effective identities are often called the *saved* UID and GID, because the kernel stores these values to keep track of which IDs the process can switch between. If the saved IDs of a process are the same as its real IDs (i.e., the process was launched without any setuid or setgid provision), then it cannot change either ID. This is useful when a setuid process must perform an operation on behalf of the invoking user, usually writing a data file or performing an audit operation.

Be careful when using setuid executables to ensure that the correct user and group IDs are used under all circumstances. When a process's ID has been set with setuid, all users will have identical access to resources used by the process. It is easy in this situation to introduce vulnerabilities that damage the confidentiality or integrity of assets, since each user has the same right to read and write the process's files.

The seteuid() function is used to change the effective UID; similarly, setegid() is used to change the effective GID. Listing 4-4 demonstrates the use of seteuid(); note that after compiling this tool you must add the setuid permission and run it by a user other than its owner to see the seteuid() behavior.

LISTING 4-4: Changing a process's effective uid [seteuidexample.c]

Available for download on Wrox.com

```
#include <errno.h>
#include <stdio.h>
#include <string.h>
#include <unistd.h>

int main (int argc, const char * argv[]) {
    uid_t realUid, effectiveUid;
    realUid = getuid();
    effectiveUid = geteuid();
    if (realUid == effectiveUid) {
        printf("Nothing to do, I am not setuid\n");
        return 0;
    }
    printf("current euid: %d\n", effectiveUid);
    if (0 == seteuid(realUid)) {
        printf("new euid: %d\n", geteuid());
    }
    else {
        fprintf(stderr, "couldn't change euid: %s\n", strerror(errno));
        return -1;
    }

    return 0;
}
```

A process can also change its real and saved IDs to be the same as its current effective ID, using the setuid() and setgid() functions. In this way it can either completely assume its set identity, or completely assume the identity of the user who launched it. Such a change is permanent: as the real, saved, and effective identities all become identical, the process no longer has the right to change its effective identity.

The preceding restrictions, on which identities a process can modify with seteuid(), setuid() and the equivalent group ID functions, do not apply if the process is running as root — in other words if its effective UID is 0. A process with euid 0 can switch its effective UID and GID to any value, and can also use the setuid() and setgid() functions to switch real, effective, and saved IDs to any value. A root process that changes identity with setuid() or setgid() is said to *drop privileges,* because from that moment it can no longer acquire root status. It is this technique that is used by programs that manage login sessions, like loginwindow and sshd. Having authenticated their user as root, they launch a new process that drops privileges to the identity of the authenticated user before starting the login session.

COMMUNICATION BETWEEN PROCESSES

If a system comprises numerous processes, these processes should be able to share information in order to act as a concerted whole and perform the system's use cases. At a simple level, processes can share information by use of common files — a configuration utility could write preferences files, which are read by the process doing the real work. The file system permissions models discussed in Chapter 3 can then be used to control access to the shared files, enforcing limits on which users can modify or view the preferences. When communication needs become more complex — i.e., when tools need to share information in both directions, need a faster interface, or require good synchronization — inter-process communication (IPC) APIs must be used. Note that while the communication methods discussed here are called "inter-process," they can also be used for sharing data between different threads in the same process.

Mach Ports

Communication over Mach ports is the primitive form of IPC on both Mac OS X and iPhone OS, all other IPC mechanisms being implemented on top of Mach ports. Mach IPC has an access-control mechanism based on providing processes with the right to send or receive messages on a particular port. Developers sometimes use this rights-based access control as a generic access-control implementation, by encapsulating the interface to an asset behind a Mach port so that permission to use the asset is provided by permission to use the port interface.

Messages received from a Mach port include a trailer that can, if requested, include a security token. You request the security token by setting the option MACH_RCV_TRAILER_TYPE(MACH_RCV_TRAILER_SENDER) or MACH_RCV_TRAILER_TYPE(MACH_RCV_TRAILER_AUDIT) when receiving a message in the Mach API. The security token is in the following format, defined in /usr/include/mach/message.h:

```
typedef struct
{
  unsigned int                val[2];
} security_token_t;
```

The first element of the security token (i.e., val[0]) is the effective UID of the process that sent the message. The second element is the process's effective GID. These values are not controlled by the sending process, but are instead written by the kernel. It is therefore not possible for the sending process to submit false information about the account for which it is acting. The security token can be requested for messages on any port to which a process has receive rights, including those to which it has given another process the send-once right.

Distributed Objects

Cocoa provides a very high-level IPC interface called Distributed Objects (DO). A Distributed Objects connection looks just like a regular Objective-C object in code, albeit with a slightly more involved initialization process. The object is actually a proxy, and messages sent to it are actually forwarded over an IPC connection (or even an RPC connection, in which case the recipient is on a different machine on the network) to be run by a different process that actually hosts the object.

The details of the connection are mainly kept hidden from the application making use of DO, and are handled automatically by Cocoa.

Each application that publishes a DO connection attaches a single object called the *root object* to the connection, and publishes the name of the connection in a name server. Any process that can find the name of the connection in the name server can connect to the application, retrieve a proxy to the connection's root object, and use it to send arbitrary messages to that object in the publishing process. It is desirable to mitigate the possibility of misuse of the connection where it provides access to any asset with confidentiality requirements (arbitrary processes should not be able to view the asset), or integrity requirements (arbitrary changes to the asset should not be permitted).

Distributed Objects provide the ability for processes taking part in DO communication to authenticate each other through methods on the NSConnection's delegate object. The process making a DO request calculates an authentication token for the request with its delegate's -authenticationDataForComponents: method. The receiving process recalculates the token in -authenticateComponents:withData: and compares the calculated token with the received token. If the two match, the request is authenticated and acted upon; otherwise it is rejected and an exception raised in the requesting process.

A client and server taking part in an authenticated DO connection are shown in the following code listings. The processes calculate a *Hashed Message Authentication Code* (HMAC) using the CommonCrypto functionality in libSystem. (CommonCrypto was initially introduced in Chapter 3, to encrypt files.) Using an HMAC allows the verifying process to discover not only that the incoming request is authentic (i.e., that it was sent by the legitimate client process) but that it has not been tampered with since being constructed. The two processes must share a secret key to generate the same authentication codes from identical data; in this example the key is simply a character array compiled into each executable. The processes must also, of course, use the same algorithm to generate authentication codes. The class used as a connection delegate in both server and client processes is implemented in Listing 4-5.

Available for download on Wrox.com

LISTING 4-5: Authentication in a Distributed Objects connection delegate [GLConnectionDelegate.m]

```
#import "GLConnectionDelegate.h"
#import <CommonCrypto/CommonHMAC.h>

const NSString *secretKey = @"This is the secret key";

@implementation GLConnectionDelegate

- (NSData *)authenticationDataForComponents:(NSArray *)components {
    CCHmacContext ctx;
    CCHmacInit(&ctx,
               kCCHmacAlgMD5,
               [secretKey cStringUsingEncoding: NSUTF8StringEncoding],
               [secretKey lengthOfBytesUsingEncoding: NSUTF8StringEncoding]);
    for (id component in components) {
        // only NSData components should be used in calculating the HMAC
        if ([component isKindOfClass: [NSData class]]) {
```

```
            CCHmacUpdate(&ctx, [component bytes], [component length]);
        }
    }
    char *hmac = malloc(CC_MD5_DIGEST_LENGTH);
    if (NULL == hmac) {
        //error in allocating the memory
        return nil;
    }
    CCHmacFinal(&ctx, hmac);
    NSData *authData = [NSData dataWithBytes: hmac length: CC_MD5_DIGEST_LENGTH];
    return authData;
}

- (BOOL)authenticateComponents:(NSArray *)components withData:(NSData *)data {
    NSData *localHmac = [self authenticationDataForComponents: components];
    return [localHmac isEqualToData: data];
}

@end
```

The server process, including the object published as the connection's root object, is implemented in Listing 4-6.

Available for download on Wrox.com

LISTING 4-6: Distributed Objects server process [do_servermain.m]

```
#import <Foundation/Foundation.h>
#import "GLConnectionDelegate.h"

@interface GLVendedObject : NSObject {}
-(NSString *)serverMessage;
@end

@implementation GLVendedObject
-(NSString *)serverMessage {
    return @"A message from the DO server";
}
@end

int main (int argc, const char * argv[]) {
    NSAutoreleasePool * pool = [[NSAutoreleasePool alloc] init];
    GLVendedObject *vo = [[GLVendedObject alloc] init];
    GLConnectionDelegate *delegate = [[GLConnectionDelegate alloc] init];
    //get the default DO connection
    NSConnection *conn = [[NSConnection new] autorelease];
    [conn setDelegate: delegate];
    BOOL status;

    //set which object we vend, and register with the name server
    [conn setRootObject:vo];
    status = [conn registerName: @"DOExample"];
    if(NO == status) {
        NSLog(@"Couldn't register with the name server");
        exit(-1);
```

continues

LISTING 4-6 *(continued)*

```
    }

    //now wait for connections
    [[NSRunLoop currentRunLoop] run];

    [pool release];
    return 0;
}
```

A client process is shown in Listing 4-7.

Available for download on Wrox.com

LISTING 4-7: Distributed Objects client process [do_clientmain.m]

```
#import <Foundation/Foundation.h>
#import "GLConnectionDelegate.h"

int main (int argc, const char * argv[]) {
    NSAutoreleasePool * pool = [[NSAutoreleasePool alloc] init];

    NSConnection *connection = [NSConnection connectionWithRegisteredName:
                                                                @"DOExample"
                                                                host: nil];
    GLConnectionDelegate *delegate = [[GLConnectionDelegate alloc] init];
    [connection setDelegate: delegate];

    id clientObject = [connection rootProxy];
    if (nil == clientObject) {
        NSLog(@"Error: did not get a proxy object");
        exit(-1);
    }

    NSString *message = [clientObject serverMessage];
    NSLog(@"received message from server: %@", message);
    [delegate release];
    [pool release];
    return 0;
}
```

The client and server demonstrated in the preceding listings use the same algorithm and key for generating message authentication codes, so they have no problem communicating.

```
heimdall:~ leeg$ ./do_client
2009-11-23 14:28:54.006 do_client[858:903] received message from server: A message from
the DO server
```

If they could not agree on the HMAC, the server would not reply to the client.

```
heimdall:~ leeg$ ./do_client
2009-11-23 14:54:06.051 do_client[923:903] *** Terminating app due to uncaught exception
'NSFailedAuthenticationException', reason: '[NOTE: this exception originated in the
server.]
*** Received message without authentication'
```

The server process has thrown an exception which was caught in the client (terminating the client, as it did not have an exception handler). The functionality of the server is not affected, but it will not respond to requests from this client, as it cannot verify the client's identity.

Notifications

Notifications provide a very simple form of communication between different processes. They work like the bell in a hotel lobby: when an interesting event occurs (in this case, a guest's approaching the check-in desk) the bell is rung and everybody in the lobby can hear it. What each person chooses to do on hearing the bell depends on that person's function — a porter might start loading the guest's suitcases, a receptionist might go to greet the guest, and another guest will probably ignore the bell. Such a system can save employees from having to monitor the desk constantly, so they are available to perform their other functions. However, nothing stops people from ringing the bell when there isn't a guest waiting to check in, so the receptionist and porter may end up wasting a lot of time going to the check-in desk only to find there is no one to greet, and no suitcases to carry.

The same risk is present in the notification IPCs available on Mac OS X — both Cocoa-distributed notifications and the lower-level "notify" library. Notifications can be posted by any process, and so could easily be introduced to a system by a process under an attacker's control. A system cannot expect the state of its components to be well known at the time a given notification is received, as the notification could actually be posted at any time by an external agent. Similarly, processes that need a lot of resources to handle a notification — CPU time, network bandwidth, or file system space — could easily be coerced into a denial-of-service situation by a process repeatedly posting the notification. Not only could notifications occur when the event they signal has not happened, but if that event happens multiple times in quick succession it is not guaranteed that a process will receive a notification for each occurrence. Notifications are posted via a finite-length queue, and if too many of the same notifications are added to the queue, subsequent notifications will be dropped.

Processes that accept incoming notifications should be able to deal with them quickly, at least determining whether the situation is appropriate before launching into a costly handling mechanism. They should be ready to handle floods of identical notifications, including those in which interesting events are dropped in a flurry of other notifications — whether legitimately or falsely sourced. In the components of your application that legitimately post notifications, consider the volume of notifications that will be generated. Notification systems let you reduce coupling in your application design and react to events efficiently, but do not scale up well. The operating system won't assist you with getting the scale correct, so you need to manage it yourself.

PLAYING IN THE SANDBOX

There are occasions when the access-control configuration for a particular class of resource is very simple — when an application process should have no need for accessing that resource. A music encoder has no need to make network connections or use the file system; it can simply take data in from an application process and return encoded data to the same process. Even if running as the unprivileged nobody user, the encoder process still could have the capability to perform some of those actions, which could in turn result in its being a valuable entry point a hacker could use to get into the encoding application and onto the user's computer. It would be advantageous to remove completely the encoder's ability to interact with the file system and network, so that even if it gets compromised the possibilities for exploitation are minimal.

Both Mac OS X and iPhone OS provide a *Mandatory Access Control* policy engine known as a *sandbox*. The sandbox gives processes restricted access to the operating system resources, which processes cannot break out of (i.e., they cannot play outside the sandbox). The controls and limitations imposed by the sandbox are mandatory in that the processes are always forced to work within the sandbox restrictions, unlike such *discretionary* access controls as file permissions that can be changed by the owner of a file.

Mac Sandbox

The sandbox provision on Mac OS X is voluntary: applications must opt in to have their capabilities restricted, or a user must deliberately launch an application in a sandbox context. To launch an application in a restricted sandbox context, the user invokes the application via the sandbox-exec command, specifying a profile as an argument to sandbox-exec. The operating system ships with some profiles, stored in /usr/share/sandbox, which are written in the Scheme programming language, although in all versions of Mac OS X that implement the sandbox functionality this configuration format is undocumented and stated to be subject to potential change. Each profile comprises a list of rules, which specify whether the process is allowed to perform a particular operation on a particular object (files, folders, network connections, and devices are all objects in the rule definitions).

Profiles imposed on a process by sandbox-exec apply from the moment the process is launched. If the profile forbids the process from performing some action, the process will never be able to perform that action while it runs. Sandbox profiles are inherited by child processes, so if a sandboxed application launches a helper process through NSTask or fork(), that process will be subject to the same restrictions as the application.

The public API to the sandbox functionality permits a process to dynamically inherit one of a few restrictive profiles. The sandbox policy is evaluated (by a kernel extension called seatbelt) when a process tries to *acquire* access to a resource, not when it tries to *use* that access. This has an important effect on the ordering of tasks affected by the sandbox policy. Consider a tool that opens a file for writing, then adopts a policy denying it any write access to the file system. The tool can still write to the file handle it has already opened, but cannot subsequently open any other file for writing. This is demonstrated in Listing 4-8.

LISTING 4-8: Restricting a process's activity with the sandbox API [sandbox_demo.c]

```
#include <errno.h>
#include <fcntl.h>
#include <sandbox.h>
#include <stdio.h>
#include <string.h>

#define FILENAME_ONE "/tmp/fileone"
#define FILENAME_TWO "/tmp/filetwo"

int main (int argc, const char * argv[]) {
```

```
    int fd1 = open(FILENAME_ONE, O_WRONLY | O_CREAT, 0600);
    if (-1 == fd1) {
        fprintf(stderr, "couldn't open %s: %s\n",
                FILENAME_ONE,
                strerror(errno));
    }
    char *sbError = NULL;
    // adopt a sandbox profile which prohibits writing to the filesystem.
    int sbResult = sandbox_init(kSBXProfileNoWrite, SANDBOX_NAMED, &sbError);
    if (0 != sbResult) {
        //show the error for debugging; it isn't supposed to be presented to
        //the user as it contains developer information.
        fprintf(stderr, "couldn't initialize sandbox: %s\n", sbError);
        //clean up the memory allocated for the error
        sandbox_free_error(sbError);
    }
    int fd2 = open(FILENAME_TWO, O_WRONLY | O_CREAT, 0600);
    if (-1 == fd2) {
        fprintf(stderr, "couldn't open %s: %s\n",
                FILENAME_TWO,
                strerror(errno));
    }

    //it should still be possible to write to fd1 as it was opened before the
    //restrictive profile was adopted.
    int bytesWritten = write(fd1, "Hello file one", 15);
    if (bytesWritten == -1) {
        fprintf(stderr, "couldn't write to %s: %s\n",
                FILENAME_ONE,
                strerror(errno));
    }
    close(fd1);
    return 0;
}
```

The sandbox_demo program in Listing 4-8 is not permitted to open the second file, but still can write to the first file.

```
heimdall:~ leeg$ ./sandbox_demo
couldn't open /tmp/filetwo: Operation not permitted
heimdall:~ leeg$ cat /tmp/fileone
Hello file one
```

Unlike with the many discretionary access-control measures available in Mac OS X, even the super-user is not permitted to perform denied actions.

```
heimdall:~ leeg$ sudo ./sandbox_demo
Password:
couldn't open /tmp/filetwo: Operation not permitted
```

The full list of profiles available to you when you use sandbox_init() is shown in Table 4-1.

TABLE 4-1: Named Sandbox Profiles

PROFILE NAME	EFFECT OF ADOPTION
kSBXProfileNoInternet	Process cannot connect to or listen on TCP sockets.
kSBXProfileNoNetwork	Process cannot use any networking sockets.
kSBXProfileNoWrite	Process cannot write to any file on the file system.
kSBXProfileNoWriteExceptTemporary	Writing to the file system is forbidden, except in the /var/tmp folder and the *user temporary folder*, the path of which is in the _CS_DARWIN_USER_TEMP_DIR confstr() variable.
kSBXProfilePureComputation	No operating system resources are available to the process.

iPhone Sandbox

The sandboxing behavior of the iPhone OS is built into the operating system in such a way that all applications are subject to mandatory access controls, unlike on the Mac, where the controls are optional. There is no API for changing the policy that applies to an application. The effects of the iPhone's sandbox policy are as follows:

- Each application has its own area on the file system, cannot write outside its own area, and cannot read the documents and temporary files created by other applications.
- Applications can access some data — address book contents, music files, and photos — only through Cocoa Touch APIs, not by accessing the files directly.
- Applications cannot directly interact with the network devices on the phone or iPod.

GUARANTEEING CODE'S ORIGIN

If confidential information is going to pass between two processes, it can be important to verify the identity of the other process. Similarly, a process that accepts commands from another process may need to ensure that the commanding process has a legitimate provenance, to protect the integrity of the assets being commanded. A user who has made a decision regarding the security policy or configuration of an application does not expect this decision to be ignored after he or she updates the application to a new version, so it should be possible to confirm that two different applications are actually versions of the same product from the same developer.

The iPhone OS does not permit any application to run unless it has been *signed* by Apple. Signing is a way to verify the integrity of a message (on the iPhone, the "message" is an application) and the identity of its originator using asymmetric cryptography techniques. The originator — in this case Apple — combines its private key with the message to generate a signature. Anyone in possession of the originator's public key can use it to verify both that the message has not been tampered with and that the originator signed it. The public key is embedded in a *digital certificate*, a sequence of countersigned identities indicating a chain of trust between the message originator and a root *certificate authority*, and also indicating the uses for which the key pair is appropriate. If an agent verifying a signature with the originator's public key trusts any of the identities defined in the certificate, this agent has some reassurance that the originator's identity is genuine.

iPhone apps from the App Store are signed by a certificate issued by Apple as root certificate authority, so there is no chain of trust to any third-party entity or organization. The extent to which identity claims made by real-world commercial certificate authorities can be trusted has been questioned: see `http://searchsecurity.techtarget.com/expert/KnowledgebaseAnswer/0,289625,sid14_gci1253295,00.html` *for a general discussion of the problem, and* `http://my.opera.com/securitygroup/blog/2009/01/30/md5-in-certificates-what-is-happening` *for details of a particular attack against the public key infrastructure (PKI) system.*

Apple also has the ability to ensure that applications submitted for inclusion in the App Store are submitted by the developers who claim it is their app, and that the app has not been tampered with since it was built and submitted to iTunes Connect. Developers must sign applications with a certificate issued by Apple through the developer program portal before uploading the applications with iTunes Connect. This ensures that malicious developers cannot pass their own apps off as those written by other developers, provided the legitimate developers keep their private keys secret.

Xcode will automatically sign both Mac and iPhone applications with an appropriate certificate if it is specified in the build settings. The Code Signing Identity build setting should be set to the name of a certificate that can be used for code signing, for which the private key is available, and that is stored in the default keychain search list for the user who will build the app. Keychain is described in much more detail in the next chapter; the default keychain (login) is suitable for storing code signing identities. Configuring the code signing identity is shown in Figure 4-3.

An identity for signing iPhone applications must be created through the iPhone developer program portal, as the iPhone has restrictions on the identities it will accept. For experimenting with code signing on the Mac, a self-signed certificate is sufficient. Self-signed certificates do not carry any validation of the owner's identity, because they have not been countersigned by any third parties. To test the code-signing capabilities of the operating system using your own code on your own computer, it's not really required that you have independent verification of your identity. To generate a self-signed certificate, open the Keychain Access application in /Applications/Utilities and navigate to the application's menu, then the Certificate Assistant submenu, and choose Create a Certificate. Enter a name for the code-signing identity and configure the certificate as shown in Figure 4-4.

Applications can be signed and their signatures verified by the "codesign" tool on the command line. To sign an application with the certificate generated in Figure 4-4:

```
heimdall:~ leeg$ codesign -s "Example Codesign Certificate" Example.app/
```

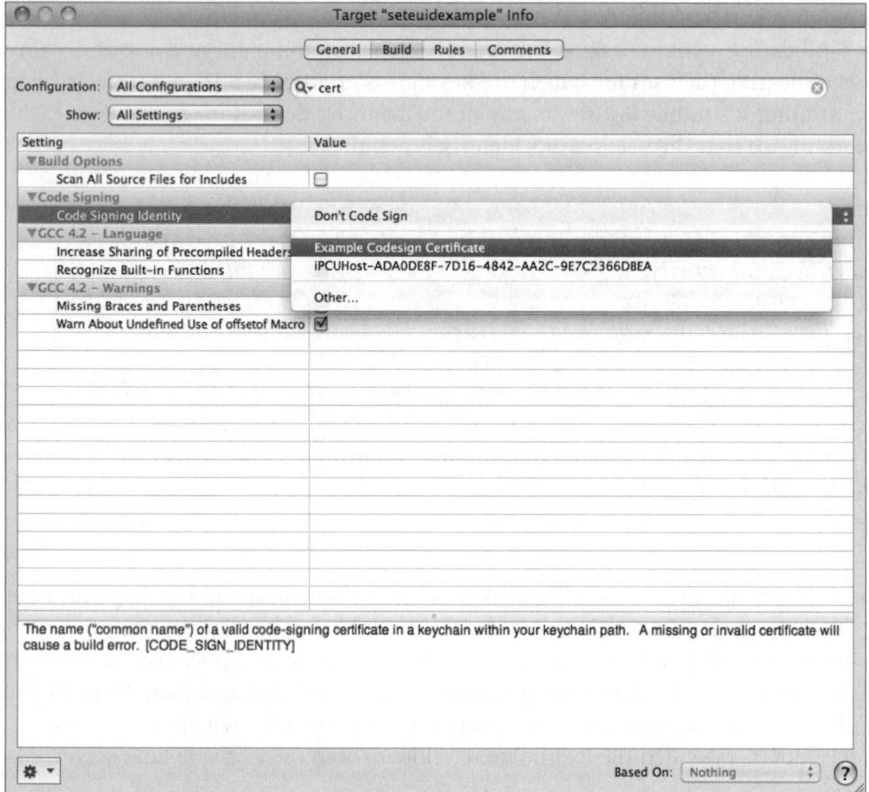

FIGURE 4-3: Choosing an identity with which to sign an application

FIGURE 4-4: Creating a self-signed certificate for code signing

The operating system will ask whether the codesign tool can have access to the signing identity; choose Allow or Always Allow to complete the signing process. The process embeds a signature into the application binary and separately stores a hash of each of the resource files (NIBs, managed object models, and image and sound files). The presence of the signature and the identity of the signer can be verified as follows:

```
heimdall:~ leeg$ codesign -dvv Example.app/
Executable=/Users/leeg/Example.app/Contents/MacOS/Example
Identifier=info.thaesofereode.Example
Format=bundle with Mach-O thin (x86_64)
CodeDirectory v=20100 size=355 flags=0x0(none) hashes=11+3 location=embedded
Signature size=1439
Authority=Example Codesign Certificate
Signed Time=2009 11 26 11:36:13
Info.plist entries=12
Sealed Resources rules=4 files=3
Internal requirements count=1 size=104
```

You can also determine if a modification to a file has been detected.

```
heimdall:~ leeg$ vi Example.app/Contents/Info.plist # make a change to the file
heimdall:~ leeg$ codesign -dvv Example.app/
Example.app/: code or signature modified
```

But what difference does it make whether an application is signed? The operating system will make use of the signature in evaluating some access-control rules. Two applications with the same identifier, signed with the same identity, are treated as different versions of the same application. Any firewall, parental control, or keychain access rules configured for one version of the application will automatically apply to the other. If the applications are unsigned, the operating system must ask the user whether that user wishes to continue trusting the modified application.

There are APIs that can be successfully called only by signed applications, or any app running as the super-user. At the moment the only APIs with this limitation are the Developer Tools Access interfaces, including task_for_pid(), which allows a process to get send rights to the Mach port for another process on the system.

Applications can also make use of the signing facility. Signatures can include options that change the operating system's treatment of the signed application. The kill option instructs the OS to terminate the application if its identity is ever invalidated (e.g., if it dynamically loads unsigned code). The hard option tells the OS that if the result of accessing some resource would be for the app to invalidate its identity, it should be denied access to that resource. The requirements governing whether an identity is considered valid can also be overridden at the time an application is signed. Examples of custom requirements:

- **info NSPrincipalClass = NSApplication:** The NSPrincipalClass key in the application's Info.plist has the value NSApplication.
- **anchor trusted:** The root certificate must be trusted by the user.
- **anchor apple:** The root certificate must belong to Apple, Inc.

An application can also perform its own checking of code identity using the Code Signing Services API. The API is designed to allow processes to dynamically inspect the identity of their own code and that of bundles loaded into their process, and to allow bundles to inspect the identity of their host processes.

Checking the identity of a bundle before launching it (using the codesign tool) is not a safe operation. If the executable is replaced between the time when its identity is validated and the time when it is launched, your application will still start an untrusted process. Always aim to validate an external object after *loading it but* before *interacting with it. However, if the bundle includes code that will be run when it is linked, such as an Objective-C +load method, that code will get a chance to run before the host process is able to inspect the code's identity. In such circumstances, if maintaining the identity of all running code is required, the hard or kill signing flag must be used.*

Code Signing Services can be used to determine whether a process's executable satisfies its internal requirements or to verify custom requirements designed by the application developer. In Listing 4-9 an application determines whether it has a valid signature and displays some information about itself retrieved from Code Signing Services.

LISTING 4-9: Retrieving signature information and verifying identity with Code Signing Services

Available for download on Wrox.com

```
#import <Foundation/Foundation.h>
#import <Security/SecCode.h>

int main (int argc, const char * argv[]) {
    NSAutoreleasePool * pool = [[NSAutoreleasePool alloc] init];

    OSStatus secError = noErr;
    // retrieve this process's code object
    SecCodeRef myCode;
    secError = SecCodeCopySelf(kSecCSDefaultFlags, &myCode);
    if (noErr != secError) {
        NSLog(@"unable to retrieve code object, security error %d", secError);
        return -1;
    }

    // validate the process's identity, using the internal requirements
    secError = SecCodeCheckValidity(myCode, kSecCSDefaultFlags, NULL);
    switch (secError) {
        case noErr:
            NSLog(@"this process has a valid signature");
            break;
        case errSecCSUnsigned:
            NSLog(@"this process's executable is unsigned");
            break;
        case errSecCSSignatureFailed:
```

```
            NSLog(@"this process has an invalid signature");
            break;
        default:
            NSLog(@"error %d validating signature", secError);
            break;
    }

    // get the static code object, representing the executable on disk
    SecStaticCodeRef fileCode;
    secError = SecCodeCopyStaticCode(myCode, kSecCSDefaultFlags, &fileCode);
    if (noErr != secError) {
        NSLog(@"unable to get static code object, security error %d", secError);
        CFRelease(myCode);
        return -1;
    }

    //some basic information about the code signature
    NSDictionary *signingInfo = nil;
    secError = SecCodeCopySigningInformation(fileCode,
                                             kSecCSDefaultFlags,
                                             &signingInfo);
    if (noErr != secError) {
        NSLog(@"cannot get signing information, security error %d", secError);
    }
    else {
        NSLog(@"signing info: %@", signingInfo);
        [signingInfo release];
    }


    CFRelease(myCode);
    CFRelease(fileCode);
    [pool drain];
    return 0;
}
```

When run without a signature, Code Signing Services reports very little information about the executable.

```
2009-11-27 12:18:41.573 own_identity[720:a0f] this process's executable is unsigned
2009-11-27 12:18:41.594 own_identity[720:a0f] signing info: {
    "main-executable" =
"file://localhost/Users/leeg/Documents/Security%20Book/chapter%204/own_identity/build/
     Debug/own_identity";
}
```

The signing information includes details about the signature itself when the executable has been signed.

```
2009-11-27 12:25:13.065 own_identity[750:a0f] this process has a valid signature
2009-11-27 12:25:13.079 own_identity[750:a0f] signing info: {
    format = "Mach-O thin (x86_64)";
    identifier = "own_identity";
    "main-executable" =
"file://localhost/Users/leeg/Documents/Security%20Book/chapter%204/own_identity/build/
```

```
        Debug/own_identity";
        source = embedded;
        unique = <46a34d17 9fac8f48 c0b22cad 81215968 cdee54e8>;
    }
```

SUMMARY

An application needing multiple disparate privileges will be best positioned to provide a secure user experience if it follows the principle of least privilege (PoLP). This principle directs an application to use the fewest privileges required to get its work done, and to acquire each for the shortest time possible. A good way to adhere to the principle of least privilege is to break the application into multiple processes, each of which holds a subset of the privileges and is launched only when those privileges are needed.

Constructing a multiple-process system increases the number of entry points in the application, each of which must be protected against misuse. This means that the inter-process communication must be carefully designed to keep attackers from entering the system by posing as any of the component processes. When modeling potential attack vectors, always think of connections as a chain of events across interacting components. A seemingly insignificant modification can alter system behavior significantly at a later stage in processing

The integrity and authenticity of application code on both Macs and iPhones are protected by code signatures. By validating the signature of an executable or loadable bundle, an application can ensure both that the program comes from a trusted source and that it has not been modified since the trusted source signed the executable.

5

Storing Confidential Data in the Keychain

WHAT'S IN THIS CHAPTER?

- What the keychain is
- Why use the keychain
- How to use the keychain on the Mac and iPhone

Both Mac OS X and the iPhone OS provide a *keychain*, a service for storing, retrieving, and manipulating secret information — in fact, the Classic Mac OS also provided a keychain. In addition to providing developers with a common way to securely deal with confidential assets, the Keychain Access utility gives users a single entry point for configuring and managing their secrets. Applications that take advantage of the keychain make it easy for users to understand how their passwords and other confidential information are used.

WHAT IS THE KEYCHAIN?

Passwords are dangerous pieces of information. Access to a user's password for a service allows an attacker to pose as that user to the service protected by the password. Remember the categorization in Chapter 1 of spoofing, tampering, repudiation, information leak, denial of service and elevation of privilege (STRIDE). A leaked password allows a spoofing attack, under which the attacker can view protected data (information disclosure) and modify it (tampering), potentially with elevated privileges. If you consider that the attacker can probably now choose to terminate the account he's logged in with, and that he appears to be acting as the user, a password loss comes under the repudiation and denial of service categories, too. One attack that checks all the threat boxes!

Unfortunately, as we have become accustomed to using more online services, the number of passwords we need to keep track of has increased. There are three natural reactions to this high number of passwords: use the same password for multiple scenarios (although security policies in some corporate environments forbid this, it is a hard condition to detect); use simple passwords that are easy to remember; or write down each of the passwords. Each of these reactions leads to an easier time for attackers trying to compromise any of the password-protected services.

Using the same password for multiple different services means that a password compromised for one service could be used elsewhere. If an attacker can discover a victim's password for some inconsequential service, then use the same password to access that victim's bank account online, the problem is significantly worse than if only the first account had been compromised.

Simple passwords offer the possibility of compromise through the simple expedient of guesswork — an attack commonly called *brute force,* as the attacker has to go through the unsubtle process of trying every possible password. Writing all the passwords down allows users to choose distinct, complicated passwords in each case, but presents a new problem: that notebook or text file is a valuable resource for attackers. If passwords are dangerous like military weapons, then the user just created a stockpile.

Military bases often have large collections of weapons. Were the weapons left strewn around the base, they would always be available — to both attackers and defenders. The weapons are usually stored in a single armory or gun cabinet, with defenses concentrated around the arsenal. Instead of having to protect the entire base against potential weapon theft or accepting the risk of weapons' being stolen, the base commanders can now deploy heightened security focused on the location where the weapons are stored. A keychain is like an armory for secret data. While it is now possible for an attacker who compromises the keychain to access all the secrets, the concentrated defenses of the keychain should make it hard to do.

So a keychain is an armory for passwords. The passwords (and other confidential information) are stored in an encrypted way, only accessible by someone with the correct key, and access to each password can (on Mac OS X) be restricted to particular applications. The key required to unlock the keychain is a password on Mac OS X, but on the iPhone it's a device-specific string stored in the phone's firmware. Note the requirement on a Mac to have a password in order to get at the passwords: this might seem like a chicken-and-egg problem but really it means that the user has only one password to remember herself; therefore that password can be strong and doesn't need to be shared with any other services.

Keychains are files containing encrypted passwords, along with metadata describing the account each password is used for. Users can have multiple keychains and store different passwords in each, though in practice most users each have a single keychain that is created by the operating system when their user accounts are constructed. The user's login keychain is therefore often referred to as "the keychain."

The question of what constitutes a "strong" password has been discussed on many occasions; see for example pages 76–79 of Practical Unix & Internet Security, *3rd Edition, Simson Garfinkel, Gene Spafford and Alan Schwartz, O'Reilly Media, 2003.*

So far I've mainly been describing the keychain's contents as a collection of passwords. That is how applications frequently use the keychain, but in fact it can be used to store a number of different types of data. Passwords are stored as either *generic passwords* or *Internet passwords*, depending on the meta-data associated with the password. An Internet password is associated with a URI, defining the service on the Internet for which the password is to be used. Certificates can also be stored in the keychain, as can encryption keys (public, private, or symmetric keys). Another type of keychain item not available through Keychain Services is the *secure note*, simply a piece of encrypted text with a title and access control settings.

On both Macs and iPhones, applications can manage their own confidential information in the user's keychains using the Keychain Services APIs. Additionally, on a Mac the application can use Keychain Services to define its own custom keychain; or the user can administer her own keychains using the Keychain Access application, with which she can also edit secure notes. Users typically have one private keychain at ~/Library/Keychains/login.keychain, but can use Keychain Access to create others. Each user has full read and write access to keychains in her user domain. Other file-system domains can contain keychains in the appropriate Library/Keychains folder: one example is the local domain's /Library/Keychains/System.keychain, which stores the system's trusted root certificates.

Each keychain is stored as a single file in one of the locations mentioned earlier. This makes it easy to use filesystem permissions or access control to manage which users have access to the keychains, in addition to the Keychain Services access controls.

The keychain files are managed by Keychain Services, which provides and augments certificate management and data storage components of the Common Data Security Architecture. Keychain Services on the Mac is part of Security.framework, which must be linked to any application that works with keychain content. Because of this the keychain content can be managed through either the Keychain Services API or the Common Services Security Manager interface; this chapter will focus on Keychain Services, which is available on both Mac OS X and iPhone OS in similar forms and is much more straightforward to work with.

COMMON DATA SECURITY ARCHITECTURE

The CDSA is defined by the Open Group, which also defines the Single UNIX Specification to which Mac OS X conforms. CDSA is designed to be a platform for security-aware applications, and version 2 (implemented by Mac OS X) is defined at `http://www.opengroup.org/security/l2-cdsa.htm`.

The core services provided by CDSA are accessed by the Common Services Security Manager APIs, or CSSM. CSSM defines five categories of security service: data storage, cryptography, trust policy, certificate management, and authorization computation. The architecture allows for "layered services" on top of these five categories, and the Keychain Services API is one such layered service.

The contents of each keychain are encrypted, and the encryption key is usually protected by a password. The default password for a login keychain is the same as the user's account password.

Keychain Services will "unlock" access to a keychain upon being presented with the correct password, and will subsequently lock the keychain again if the user requests it. The user can also configure automatic locking of the keychain in Keychain Access, either after a time delay or when the screen is locked or the computer put to sleep. The password does not have to be the same as the login password; if it is not, the keychain is not automatically unlocked when the user logs in.

Notice that all the keychain's content is protected by the same key and thus the same password — unlocking a keychain makes all the content available. Each item has additional access control settings that determine how it can be used. The access control defines which applications may use the item's secret data, and whether the user should be asked for the keychain's password before the content is revealed to the application.

WHY SHOULD I USE THE KEYCHAIN?

In its default configuration, the keychain makes it simple for users to employ multiple distinct passwords for the many services they use. The burden of remembering many passwords, and remembering which service requires which password, is lifted from the user, who now must remember only his account password. Even in this liberal configuration the keychain is able to offer some protection to the user's passwords, by using encrypted storage to hide the passwords from those who can't log in to the user's account. To re-implement the same protection as custom code would require not only reinventing the encryption wheel, but separately prompting the user for a password to unlock the password store — using one password to protect one other password is not a great convenience.

Users can, as described in the previous section, configure custom access control settings for items in the keychain, so that they are notified if applications they don't expect try to gain access to the passwords. That ability offers some protection against Trojan horse attacks, as the malware will need to rely on the user's permitting it access to the confidential data. By changing the keychain's password and lock settings, users can also protect their passwords from snooping while they are logged in. Even if an attacker manages to take control of a user's machine while she is using it, the attacker cannot retrieve the keychain's secrets without knowing the password to unlock that keychain. The point of using the keychain to store your own app's confidential information is that it reduces the burden on the user, by ensuring that the passwords or other secrets used by your own application are managed in the same way as all the others. If users decide to adopt a more restrictive treatment of their passwords, your application automatically fits in with their choices. They do not have to separately work out how to configure the password security for your app — assuming that you provided an implementation at all.

Losing control of the protection of a confidential asset may seem at odds with the idea, presented in Chapter 1, of mitigating risks to that asset's confidentiality. Don't forget that you can still assume that some of the risk — the threat of an offline attack — has been mitigated, however the user's keychain has been configured. Ultimately you are writing the application for the user's benefit, so if he has chosen to assume a certain amount of risk in his password management in return for a certain amount of convenience, that level of risk should be accepted in your threat model (with appropriate, helpful warnings to the user).

HOW TO TAKE ADVANTAGE OF THE KEYCHAIN

The Keychain Services API is conceptually the same on both Mac and iPhone; however, the functions available on each platform are different. In this section the Mac interface is explored. The iPhone version is discussed in the section "Keychain on the iPhone."

The different classes of data that can be stored on the keychain are used in different circumstances. This exploration of Keychain Services will look at each class separately, focusing on the tasks appropriate to each type of confidential item.

General Passwords

A general password is also known as an *application password*, the secret data being simply a string representing the password. Associated with a general password are the following meta-data items:

- **Name:** An identifier for the password
- **Account:** The username for the account to which the password provides access
- **Location:** Used to distinguish accounts on different servers, or for use on different network locations
- **Comments:** User-editable notes about the keychain item
- **Access control list:** Specifies which applications may automatically have access to the keychain item

The application shown in Figure 5-1 presents a very simple username and password dialog; it will use the username and password to attempt to authenticate against Directory Services. If the credentials are valid, the user is asked whether he wants to store the details in the keychain. Note that the user probably wouldn't want to store an invalid password, so the application does not offer to save the credentials if it cannot use them successfully. Additionally, if there already is an appropriate keychain item when the application launches, it will automatically fill in the username and password fields.

FIGURE 5-1: Password acquisition user interface

The part of the application delegate that manages the keychain is shown in Listing 5-1. The -applicationDidFinishLaunching: method is used to discover whether the keychain item already exists, and if so to populate the user name and password fields with the account information.

Available for download on Wrox.com

LISTING 5-1: Creating and using a general password item in the keychain [general_passwordAppDelegate.m]

```
- (void)applicationDidFinishLaunching: (NSNotification *)aNotification {
    //find out whether the Keychain item already exists
    OSStatus keychainResult = noErr;
    SecKeychainItemRef keychainItem;
    char *keychainData;
```

continues

LISTING 5-1 *(continued)*

```
    UInt32 passwordLength;
    keychainResult = SecKeychainFindGenericPassword(NULL,
                                                    strlen(serviceName),
                                                    serviceName,
                                                    0,
                                                    NULL,
                                                    &passwordLength,
                                                    &keychainData,
                                                    &keychainItem);
    if (noErr != keychainResult) {
        NSString *errorString = SecCopyErrorMessageString(keychainResult,
                                                          NULL);
        NSLog(@"no keychain item: error %@", errorString);
        [errorString release];
    }
    else {
        [self setValue: [[[NSString alloc] initWithBytes: keychainData
                                                  length: passwordLength
                                                encoding: NSUTF8StringEncoding]
                        autorelease]
               forKey: @"passWord"];
        SecKeychainItemFreeContent(NULL, keychainData);
        //the username is an attribute of the generic password item
        SecItemAttr itemAttributes[] = { kSecAccountItemAttr };
        SecExternalFormat externalFormats[] = { kSecFormatUnknown };
        SecKeychainAttributeInfo info = { 1, itemAttributes, externalFormats };
        SecKeychainAttributeList *attributes = NULL;
        keychainResult = SecKeychainItemCopyAttributesAndData(keychainItem,
                                                              &info,
                                                              NULL,
                                                              &attributes,
                                                              NULL,
                                                              NULL);
        CFRelease(keychainItem);
        if (noErr != keychainResult) {
            NSString *errorString = SecCopyErrorMessageString(keychainResult,
                                                              NULL);
            NSLog(@"could not get attributes: error %@", errorString);
            [errorString release];
        }
        else {
            SecKeychainAttribute accountAttribute = attributes->attr[0];
            [self setValue:[[[NSString alloc] initWithBytes:accountAttribute.data
                                                      length:accountAttribute.length
                                                    encoding:NSUTF8StringEncoding]
                            autorelease]
                   forKey: @"userName"];
            SecKeychainItemFreeAttributesAndData(attributes, NULL);
        }
    }
}

- (void)addKeychainItem {
```

```
    char *accountChars = [self.userName UTF8String];
    char *passwordChars = [self.passWord UTF8String];
    OSStatus keychainResult = SecKeychainAddGenericPassword(NULL,
                                                        strlen(serviceName),
                                                        serviceName,
                                                        [self.userName length],
                                                        accountChars,
                                                        [self.passWord length],
                                                        passwordChars,
                                                        NULL);
    if (noErr != keychainResult) {
        NSString *errorString = SecCopyErrorMessageString(keychainResult,
                                                          NULL);
        NSLog(@"error writing to keychain: %@", errorString);
        [errorString release];
    }
}

- (IBAction)doLogin: (id)sender {
    //attempt to authenticate as this user
    NSError *dirSearchError = nil;
    ODRecord *foundUser = findUser(self.userName, &dirSearchError); //chapter 2
    if (nil != foundUser) {
        NSError *authError = nil;
        if ([foundUser verifyPassword: self.passWord error: &authError]) {
            //successful authentication, find out whether to store the password
            if (self.storePassword) {
                [self addKeychainItem];
            }
            [label setStringValue: @"authenticated"];
        }
        else {
            [label setStringValue: @"incorrect username or password"];
            NSLog(@"didn't authenticate: error %@", authError);
        }
        [label setHidden: NO];
    }
    else {
        NSLog(@"couldn't find user, error: %@", dirSearchError);
    }
}
```

This application still has some fundamental problems — once the user has saved login details in the keychain, the application will never modify them, and there is no way inside the app to remove the stored credentials. In Listing 5-2, the -addKeychainItem method is extended to modify an existing keychain item if the appropriate one is found.

LISTING 5-2: Modifying a keychain item [improved_general_passwordAppDelegate.m]

Available for download on Wrox.com

```
- (void)addKeychainItem {
    char const *accountChars = [self.userName UTF8String];
    char const *passwordChars = [self.passWord UTF8String];
    //see if the item already exists
```

continues

LISTING 5-2 *(continued)*

```
    SecKeychainItemRef keychainItem;
    OSStatus keychainResult = SecKeychainFindGenericPassword(NULL,
                                                             strlen(serviceName),
                                                             serviceName,
                                                             0,
                                                             NULL,
                                                             NULL,
                                                             NULL,
                                                             &keychainItem);
    if (noErr == keychainResult) {
        //just update the existing keychain item
        SecKeychainAttribute accountAttribute;
        accountAttribute.tag = kSecAccountItemAttr;
        accountAttribute.length = [self.userName length];
        accountAttribute.data = accountChars;
        SecKeychainAttributeList attributes;
        attributes.count = 1;
        attributes.attr = &accountAttribute;
        keychainResult = SecKeychainItemModifyAttributesAndData(keychainItem,
                                                  &attributes,
                                                  [self.passWord length],
                                                  passwordChars);
        if (noErr != keychainResult) {
            NSString *errorString = SecCopyErrorMessageString(keychainResult,
                                                              NULL);
            NSLog(@"error updating keychain item: %@", errorString);
            [errorString release];
        }
        CFRelease(keychainItem);
    }
    else {
        //add a new item to the keychain
        keychainResult = SecKeychainAddGenericPassword(NULL,
                                                       strlen(serviceName),
                                                       serviceName,
                                                       [self.userName length],
                                                       accountChars,
                                                       [self.passWord length],
                                                       passwordChars,
                                                       NULL);
        if (noErr != keychainResult) {
            NSString *errorString = SecCopyErrorMessageString(keychainResult,
                                                              NULL);
            NSLog(@"error writing to keychain: %@", errorString);
            [errorString release];
        }
    }
}
```

Listing 5-3 demonstrates a way to remove the item from the keychain if the user no longer wants it to be stored. The SecKeychainItemRef object, which represents the keychain item to the application, is not destroyed by deletion of the underlying item, and must be released (or made collectable, if your application has garbage collected memory management) after the item is deleted.

LISTING 5-3: Deleting a keychain item [improved_general_passwordAppDelegate.m]

Available for download on Wrox.com

```
- (void)removeKeychainItem {
    //find the appropriate item
    SecKeychainItemRef keychainItem;
    OSStatus keychainResult = SecKeychainFindGenericPassword(NULL,
                                                             strlen(serviceName),
                                                             serviceName,
                                                             0,
                                                             NULL,
                                                             NULL,
                                                             NULL,
                                                             &keychainItem);
    if (noErr == keychainResult) {
        //remove it
        SecKeychainItemDelete(keychainItem);
        CFRelease(keychainItem);
    }
    else {
        NSString *errorString = SecCopyErrorMessageString(keychainResult,
                                                          NULL);
        NSLog(@"error removing keychain item: %@", errorString);
        [errorString release];
    }
}
```

Internet Passwords

Internet password items are very similar to general passwords, though with additional meta-data describing each item. Associated with an Internet password are the following:

- **Server name:** The remote server for which the password should be used
- **Security domain:** An account domain (Kerberos realm or Active Directory domain) for the account
- **Path:** The path of the protected resource on the server (e.g., if the password is for `http://www.example.com/secrets/`, the path is `/secrets`)
- **Protocol:** The network service over which the account is used, such as http or ftp
- **Port:** The port number on which the service is listening
- **Authentication type:** How the server expects the application to present its credentials

Not all of these properties are required in every case; a server may use the same credentials to authenticate users on both http and afp connections. They do not all need to be specified whenever an Internet password is created. The APIs for creating and looking up Internet passwords,

SecKeychainAddInternetPassword() and SecKeychainFindInternetPassword(), are very similar to the functions for general passwords, with the addition of the preceding properties.

An Internet password is likely to be easily exploitable by an attacker, who can use the meta-data to work out how to connect to the service for which the password is valid. But this feature is also useful to legitimate apps, which can find out whether the user has already added a password for a service to the keychain and thus use it on the user's behalf, without asking for the password again. For example, both a web browser and an FTP application could use the same credentials for an FTP service. It would be appropriate to initially confine an Internet password's access to the application that created it, to let the user decide which other applications may access the data. In that way, Trojan horse applications will not automatically be able to retrieve the password from the keychain, even if the keychain is unlocked. The programmatic interface to the access control lists is demonstrated in Listing 5-4.

LISTING 5-4: Adding an access control list to a keychain item [acl_internet_password.m]

Available for download on Wrox.com

```
OSStatus restrictKeychainItemToSelf(SecKeychainItemRef item, char *myPath) {
    //only this process should be a trusted application.
    SecTrustedApplicationRef me = NULL;
    OSStatus result = SecTrustedApplicationCreateFromPath(myPath,
                                                          &me);
    if (noErr != result) {
        return result;
    }
    CFArrayRef trustedApplications = CFArrayCreate(NULL,
                                                   &me,
                                                   1,
                                                   &kCFTypeArrayCallBacks);
    SecAccessRef accessObject = NULL;
    result = SecAccessCreate(@"Example internet password", // shown in the UI
                             trustedApplications,
                             &accessObject);
    CFRelease(trustedApplications);
    if (noErr != result) {
        return result;
    }
    //now add that ACL to the item
    result = SecKeychainItemSetAccess(item,
                                      accessObject);
    CFRelease(accessObject);
    return result;
}
```

The user will need to agree to the application's setting an access control list on a keychain item. With the ACL defined by Listing 5-4 set, the user will be prompted if any application other than the creating application attempts to use the password created. The access control list can be modified in the Keychain Access application; Figure 5-2 shows what this ACL looks like after it has been created by an application.

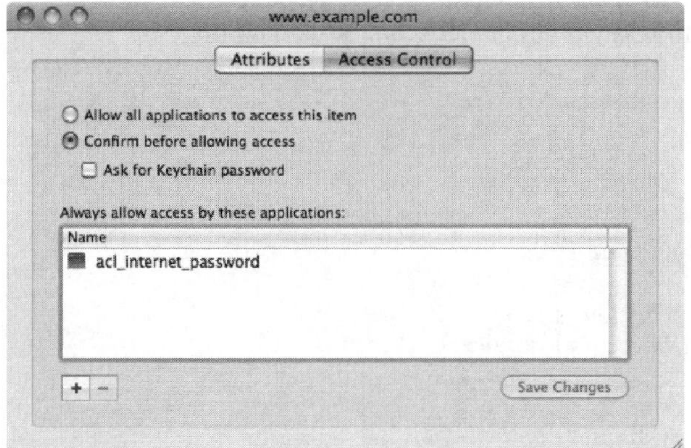

FIGURE 5-2: An access control list on an Internet password

Secondary Keychains

All the examples in the preceding sections have used whichever keychain the user has selected as the default for creating items (usually the user's login keychain), and the default keychain search path for retrieving items. An application can also create its own keychain, to provide dedicated storage (whether permanent or temporary) with no chance for "collision" with other applications, or to try to hide its secrets even from the user. Secondary keychains can also be used to provide a "master password" effect, whereby the user must know a single password in order to unlock other confidential information — but the default setup of the keychain already provides very similar functionality.

If a keychain is locked with a password and that password can be retrieved by a user, then that user can view and change the secrets in the keychain. For instance, passwords stored in a custom keychain are no different from passwords stored in the login keychain, if the password for the custom keychain is itself stored in the login keychain. Consider the technical capability of your users and attackers, along with the expected lifetime of items in the keychain, to determine how strongly the password for a custom keychain needs to be protected, or whether it even needs to be locked at all.

An application can create a custom keychain with SecKeychainCreate(), which returns a reference to the new keychain object; by passing that object to the item APIs already discussed the application manipulates confidential data in that new keychain. In Listing 5-5 a custom keychain is created and a password added to it. The code generates a random password to lock the new keychain, rather than prompting the user for a password. If the application is using the keychain for temporary storage, it should remove it with SecKeychainDelete() after the keychain is finished with. Like deleting items from a keychain, deleting the keychain itself does not release the object in memory, which must still be explicitly freed.

LISTING 5-5: Creating and using a custom keychain file [custom_keychain.m]

```
#import <Foundation/Foundation.h>
#import <Security/Security.h>

char *userName = "username";
char *passWord = "secret1234";
char *serviceName = "custom keychain entry";

int main (int argc, const char * argv[]) {
    NSAutoreleasePool * pool = [[NSAutoreleasePool alloc] init];

    //create a random password
    int fd = open("/dev/random", O_RDONLY);
    if (-1 == fd) {
        NSLog(@"couldn't open /dev/random: %s", strerror(errno));
        exit(-1);
    }
    char password[32] = {0};
    int bytesRead = read(fd, password, 32);
    if (bytesRead < 0) {
        NSLog(@"couldn't read from /dev/random: %s", strerror(errno));
        exit(-1);
    }
    close(fd);

    //now make the keychain
    NSString *keychainPath = [NSTemporaryDirectory()
                              stringByAppendingString: @"temp.keychain"];
    SecKeychainRef newKeychain = NULL;
    OSStatus result = noErr;
    result = SecKeychainCreate([keychainPath fileSystemRepresentation],
                               32,
                               password,
                               NO,
                               NULL, //specify custom access controls here
                               &newKeychain);
    if (noErr != result) {
        NSString *error = SecCopyErrorMessageString(result, NULL);
        NSLog(@"couldn't create keychain: %@", error);
        [error release];
        exit(-1);
    }

    // add an item to this keychain
    result = SecKeychainAddGenericPassword(newKeychain, //the custom keychain
                                           strlen(serviceName),
                                           serviceName,
                                           strlen(userName),
                                           userName,
                                           strlen(passWord),
                                           passWord,
```

```
                                              NULL);
        if (noErr != result) {
            NSString *error = SecCopyErrorMessageString(result, NULL);
            NSLog(@"couldn't add item to keychain: %@", error);
            [error release];
            exit(-1);
        }
        CFRelease(newKeychain);

        [pool drain];
        return 0;
    }
```

You can inspect the new keychain file using the Keychain Access utility, by opening the file from the Terminal:

```
heimdall:~ leeg$ open $TMPDIR/temp.keychain
```

It will not be possible for the user to see the password stored therein, as the password required to unlock the keychain is unknown.

Certificate Management and the Keychain

Keychain Services can be used to store and retrieve digital certificates, which were introduced in the discussion in Chapter 4 on code signing. The Security framework also provides facilities for determining whether certificates are trusted according to certain policies and criteria, known as Certificate, Key and Trust Services. Because the acts of storing and working with certificates are so closely related, the tasks associated with handling certificates in the keychain will be introduced here alongside the appropriate Certificate, Key and Trust Services material.

Certificates are usually distributed in one of a few standard formats:

- **Privacy Enhanced Mail (PEM):** Format encoded in Base 64 so that files contain only a restricted range of characters, suitable for sending over e-mail (also known as PKCS #7 which is a standard based on PEM)
- **Distinguished Encoding Rules (DER):** The same information as in a PEM file, but in binary format
- **PKCS #12:** A standard encrypted format for personal information

The Security framework can take files in any of these formats and create objects that refer to the certificates or identities therein, suitable for adding to the keychain. The user can extract the contents from a PKCS #12 file only if he knows the password necessary to decrypt the file's contents, meaning that such files are suitable for distributing private keys in addition to certificates.

Given a path to a DER-formatted certificate, the function in Listing 5-6 adds the certificate to the default keychain.

LISTING 5-6: Extracting a certificate from a file and adding it to the default keychain [import_der.m]

Available for download on Wrox.com

```
OSStatus importCertificateFromFile(NSString *path) {
    NSData *certData = [NSData dataWithContentsOfFile: path];
    if (nil == certData) {
        NSLog(@"cannot read file at %@", path);
        return errSecParam;
    }

    SecCertificateRef newCert = SecCertificateCreateWithData(NULL,
                                                             certData);
    if (NULL == newCert) {
        NSLog(@"cannot get certificate from %@", path);
        return errSecParam;
    }

    OSStatus addResult = SecCertificateAddToKeychain(newCert, NULL);
    CFRelease(newCert);
    if (noErr != addResult) {
        NSString *error = SecCopyErrorMessageString(addResult, NULL);
        NSLog(@"cannot add certificate to keychain: %@", error);
        [error release];
    }
    return addResult;
}
```

Relying on a certificate to identify the originator of a message means trusting the entities that have issued or signed the certificate to have correctly validated the identity, and trusting the identified entity to appropriately protect the associated private key against misuse. Depending on the source of the certificate and the technical capabilities of your users, it may be inappropriate for your application to automatically import a certificate without asking the user what she thinks of the certificate and trust path. The SecurityInterface framework contains a view class, SFCertificateView, which can display information about a certificate given the SecCertificateRef object. The view is shown in Figure 5-3.

The SFCertificateView can optionally be used to allow the user to modify *trust settings* for the certificate. Certificates can be used as validation of identity in numerous scenarios, including in e-mail, instant messaging, and code signing. Users can choose whether to trust (or distrust) a certificate presented in each of these scenarios on a case-by-case basis, or to delegate trust decisions to the operating system. The trust settings available in the SFCertificateView are shown in Figure 5-4.

The trust settings for a certificate can also be modified programmatically, which is appropriate when the application has a good reason to assert the trustworthiness (or otherwise) of a certificate — for example, a certificate received over a secure channel from the vendor. The trust settings are represented as an array of dictionaries, each of which specifies a set of operations for which a certificate could be used in a given context, and whether the certificate is to be trusted for those operations. There are two special values that the trust array can take — an empty array means that the certificate is always trusted for any action, and the NULL pointer means that the default operating system policy should be applied.

FIGURE 5-3: A certificate viewed in SFCertificateView

FIGURE 5-4: Editing trust settings for a certificate

In Listing 5-7, a certificate is always trusted for SSL operations if it is presented by the host `www.example.com`. The trust settings are modified for the current user, who is presented with a dialog she must accept before the settings will be changed — modifying certificate trust settings is thus not possible in a context in which no GUI is available. It is also possible to change the system-wide trust settings, which requires administrative privileges.

Available for download on Wrox.com

LISTING 5-7: Modifying the trust settings for a certificate [import_der.m]

```
OSStatus trustForSSLOperations(SecCertificateRef cert) {
    CFMutableDictionaryRef trustSSL = CFDictionaryCreateMutable(NULL,
                                                                100,
```

continues

LISTING 5-7 *(continued)*

```
&kCFTypeDictionaryKeyCallBacks,

&kCFTypeDictionaryValueCallBacks);
    //for www.example.com...
    CFDictionarySetValue(trustSSL,
                         kSecTrustSettingsPolicyString,
                         CFSTR("www.example.com"));
    //...for any use of the certificate...
    CFDictionarySetValue(trustSSL,
                         kSecTrustSettingsKeyUsage,
                         [NSNumber numberWithInt: kSecTrustSettingsKeyUseAny]);
    //...this certificate should be trusted...
    CFDictionarySetValue(trustSSL,
                         kSecTrustSettingsResult,
                         [NSNumber numberWithInt:
                             kSecTrustSettingsResultTrustAsRoot]);
    //...when evaluating the SSL trust policy.
    SecPolicyRef SSLPolicy = SecPolicyCreateSSL(true,
                                                CFSTR("www.example.com"));
    CFDictionarySetValue(trustSSL,
                         kSecTrustSettingsPolicy,
                         SSLPolicy);
    CFRelease(SSLPolicy);

    //now apply these trust settings to the specified certificate.
    OSStatus trustResult = SecTrustSettingsSetTrustSettings(cert,
                                                    kSecTrustSettingsDomainUser,
                                                    trustSSL);
    if (noErr != trustResult) {
        NSString *error = SecCopyErrorMessageString(trustResult, NULL);
        NSLog(@"cannot apply custom trust settings: %@", error);
        [error release];
    }
    CFRelease(trustSSL);
    return trustResult;
}
```

The effect of this custom trust policy can be seen in Figure 5-5. The certificate, which is actually issued to an academic department in the UK, would be trusted by this user if it were presented by the `www.example.com` server in the act of establishing a Secure Sockets Layer connection.

Of course the ability to decide whether to trust the identity behind a certificate is only useful if applications are going to use those policies when performing operations that rely on the certificates. One important aspect of Certificate, Key and Trust Services is the ability to *evaluate* trust — to decide whether an identity is reliable. A trust management object defines the certificate under consideration, along with the policy or policies to be used in evaluating the trusted status of the certificate. This is how a trust object is set up:

```
SecTrustRef trustObject = NULL;
CFArrayRef certificates = CFArrayCreate(NULL,
```

```
                                                   &cert,
                                                   1,
                                                   kCFTypeArrayCallBacks);
SecPolicyRef defaultPolicy = SecPolicyCreateBasicX509();
OSStatus trustResult = SecTrustCreateWithCertificates(certificates,
                                                      defaultPolicy,
                                                      &trustObject);
if (noErr != trustResult) {
    // handle error
}
```

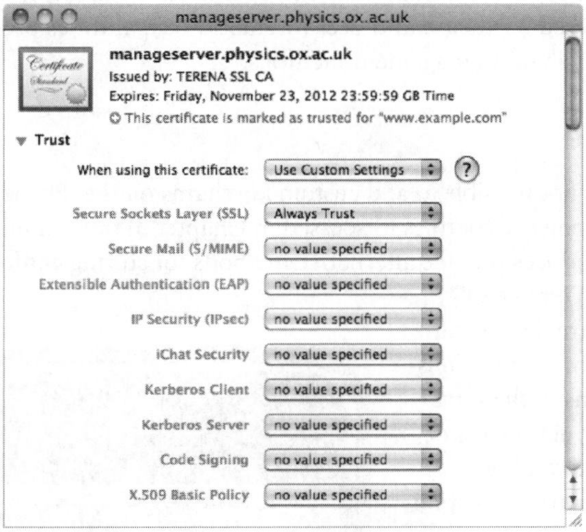

FIGURE 5-5: Custom trust settings set for a certificate

The act of evaluating a trust object returns a number reflecting the result:

```
SecTrustResultType resultType;
trustResult = SecTrustEvaluate(trustObject, &resultType);
if (noErr != trustResult) {
    // handle error
}
else {
    // work with the result
}
CFRelease(trustObject);
```

The result is not as simple as "yes" or "no". The policy could require that the user supply confirmation before continuing. The result of trust evaluation could be a "recoverable" failure, in which case there are conditions under which the trust evaluation would succeed. Typically a recoverable failure occurs when the certificate is either expired or not valid yet, in which case the user could be asked whether to proceed anyway, or the date for which the evaluation is being requested could be changed. For example, consider a mail application verifying the trust on a certificate used to sign the content of an e-mail. Even if today the certificate has expired, it could be appropriate to determine whether the certificate would have been trusted *at the time the document was signed*, as that will tell the user something about the identity of the signer at the time of signing. Once a trust object has been evaluated, it holds a reference to the result of the evaluation that can be acquired via SecTrustGetResult().

KEYCHAIN ON THE IPHONE

The iPhone OS version of Security.framework is simpler than its desktop counterpart. The iPhone does not provide access to an underlying CDSA environment, so only the operations available in the Security API are possible. Because of the restricted hardware and user interaction capabilities presented by the phone, there are fewer custom keychain management facilities.

Keychain Administration and Use

Each iPhone has a single keychain database. It is not possible to add custom keychains on the iPhone, though files encrypted with CommonCrypto symmetric routines (discussed in Chapter 3) or asymmetric algorithms from Certificate, Key and Trust Services provide alternative methods for storing confidential assets. The Keychain Services interface in iPhone OS implements a form of sandbox. Keychain items are, by default, available only to the application that created them; applications can optionally open items up to other applications in the same group, but this requires cooperation between the developers of each app involved in the sharing. The risk of a Trojan horse application's stealing the passwords from a different application should therefore be mitigated.

The iPhone keychain is not protected by a password as the keychains on Macs are, but rather by a key stored in the device firmware. If an attacker manages to get a copy of the device's filesystem, for example from the iTunes backup, the attacker is not able to unlock the keychain. However, if an attacker is able to get access to a user's phone, all the keychain items are available in each application.

The Keychain Services API for storing and recovering passwords is very similar to the Mac version, though with fewer conveniences. Keychain items are defined and identified as dictionaries, so to add either a generic or Internet password to the keychain involves constructing a dictionary with all the relevant keys defined. Figure 5-6 shows the user interface for an iPhone application that takes a username and password, storing it in the keychain. If the application finds the password in the keychain at launch, it automatically populates the fields with the stored values.

FIGURE 5-6: User interface for inputting account details

Listing 5-8 shows the code for storing the password , including code for updating an existing keychain item if the password has previously been stored.

LISTING 5-8: Storing a password in the iPhone keychain [iphone_passwordViewController.m]

Available for download on Wrox.com

```
- (IBAction)storePassword: (id)sender {
    NSDictionary *searchAttributes = [NSDictionary dictionaryWithObjectsAndKeys:
                                      [@"info.thaesofereode.samplepassword"
                                       dataUsingEncoding: NSUTF8StringEncoding],
                                      kSecAttrApplicationTag,
                                      kCFBooleanTrue, kSecReturnAttributes,
                                      nil];
    NSDictionary *foundAttributes = nil;
    NSMutableDictionary *attributesToStore = nil;
    OSStatus searchResult = SecItemCopyMatching(searchAttributes,
                                                &foundAttributes);
    NSData *passwordData = [self.passwordField.text
                            dataUsingEncoding: NSUTF8StringEncoding];
    if (noErr == searchResult) {
        // the password already exists, update it
        attributesToStore = [foundAttributes mutableCopy];
        [attributesToStore
         setObject: self.userNameField.text forKey: kSecAttrAccount];
        [attributesToStore
         setObject: passwordData forKey: kSecValueData];
        OSStatus result = SecItemUpdate(foundAttributes, attributesToStore);
    }
    else {
        // the password needs to be added
        attributesToStore = [searchAttributes mutableCopy];
        [attributesToStore setObject: self.userNameField.text
                              forKey: kSecAttrAccount];
        [attributesToStore setObject: passwordData
                              forKey: kSecValueData];
        [attributesToStore setObject: kSecClassInternetPassword
                              forKey: kSecClass];
        [attributesToStore setObject: @"www.example.com"
                              forKey: kSecAttrServer];
        [attributesToStore setObject: kCFBooleanTrue
                              forKey: kSecReturnPersistentRef];
        [attributesToStore setObject: @"Sample password"
                              forKey: kSecAttrDescription];
        [attributesToStore setObject: @"password label"
                              forKey: kSecAttrLabel];
        [attributesToStore removeObjectForKey: kSecReturnAttributes];
        NSData *persistentRef = nil;
        OSStatus result = SecItemAdd(attributesToStore, &persistentRef);
        NSLog(@"item was%@ added, return code %d", result?@"n't":@"", result);
        [persistentRef release];
    }
    [attributesToStore release];
    [foundAttributes release];
}
```

Listing 5-9 shows how the password is recovered from the keychain. In this example application the password is used only by the login view, so the password is retrieved during the view controller's initialization.

Available for download on Wrox.com

LISTING 5-9: Populating an iPhone app user interface from the keychain [iphone_passwordViewController.m]

```
- (void)viewDidLoad {
    [super viewDidLoad];
    // try to find the password
    NSDictionary *foundAttributes = nil;
    NSDictionary *searchAttributes = [NSDictionary dictionaryWithObjectsAndKeys:
                                      [@"info.thaesofereode.samplepassword"
                                       dataUsingEncoding: NSUTF8StringEncoding],
                                      kSecAttrApplicationTag,
                                      kCFBooleanTrue, kSecReturnAttributes,
                                      nil];
    OSStatus searchResult = SecItemCopyMatching(searchAttributes,
                                                &foundAttributes);
    if (noErr == searchResult) {
        // populate the UI with the keychain details
        NSString *password = [[NSString alloc]
                              initWithData: [foundAttributes objectForKey:
kSecValueData]
                              encoding: NSUTF8StringEncoding];
        self.passwordField.text = [password autorelease];
        self.userNameField.text = [foundAttributes objectForKey: kSecAttrAccount];
        [foundAttributes release];
    }
}
```

Persistent Keychain References

The keychain implementation in iPhone OS introduced *persistent references*, which are handles to keychain items that work as long as the keychain item exists. An application can retrieve a persistent reference to an item it needs to use multiple times and store that reference as a file on the iPhone's filesystem. The next time the app needs to use the password — even after the app has been quit and relaunched — it passes the persistent reference to Keychain Services instead of building a dictionary of search parameters. Referring back to Listing 5-8, when the password was added to the keychain, SecItemAdd returned a CFDataRef in the persistentRef object. That data can be used to recover the keychain item:

```
NSData *persistentRef = nil;
NSArray *matchItems = [NSArray arrayWithObject: persistentRef];
NSDictionary *searchDict = [NSDictionary dictionaryWithObjectsAndKeys:
                            matchItems, kSecMatchItemList,
                            kCFBooleanTrue, kSecReturnRef,
                            nil];
CFTypeRef realItem = NULL; /*really a SecKeychainItemRef, which isn't
                            *defined in the Security framework header files.
                            */
```

```
SecItemCopyMatching(searchDict, &realItem);
//use the keychain item
CFRelease(realItem);
```

SUMMARY

The storage of confidential assets associated with an application requires special consideration, to reduce the risk that the assets can be discovered by attackers. The protection offered by filesystem permissions can be insufficient, especially if the asset should not be visible to the root user or might be stored on a portable device.

Both Mac OS X and the iPhone OS provide Keychain Services, an API that provides access to an encrypted storage facility. Functions for storing and retrieving passwords, along with associated meta-data, make it easy to implement secure account management, and access controls stop the secrets from being discovered by Trojan horse applications. It is always worth assuming that users will have heightened privileges when interacting with your application (most users are regrettably administrators!), and some of the measures described in this chapter can provide better protection in such a scenario.

Performing Privileged Tasks

WHAT'S IN THIS CHAPTER?

- Separated privileges
- Creating factored applications
- Administering custom privileges
- User interaction for privilege escalation

In Chapter 4, the principle of least privilege was introduced. Applications conforming to this principle use as little privilege as they need to get their work done, for as little time as they need it. Granting a privilege to an app means escalating the capabilities of that app — but how does the operating system decide when that may be permitted? The operating system must be able to *identify* the user of an application, as described in Chapter 2, and then to decide whether that user is *authorized* to obtain the privilege requested by an application. If it is authorized, the application gains the *right* to perform the privileged task.

HOW TO ACQUIRE RIGHTS

Since the ability to perform any privileged task is based on the application's obtaining a right to that task, there needs to be a way for the operating system to calculate which users have which rights. In fact, users do not automatically have any rights, but can *acquire* rights when an application needs to use them. Acquisition of a right depends on being able to satisfy the *rules* defined for that right in the authorization database.

The design of Authorization Services is such that an application does not need to know the details of the rules, or how the user can adhere to them, in order to obtain a right. The application simply requests a right, and finds out whether the right was obtained. Should the user need to authenticate to acquire the right, or even authenticate as a different user, whether by entering a password or by providing a smart card, this will all be handled by the operating system.

The authorization database is a property list at /etc/authorization, which is consulted by the *security daemon*, securityd. When an application needs a right it sends a request to securityd, which looks up the rules associated with that right in the database. Securityd evaluates the rules, which may involve loading plug-ins implementing custom evaluation mechanisms or communicating with a GUI agent to present an authentication dialog. If the rules are successfully met, securityd assigns the right to the requesting application. Otherwise, securityd refuses to grant the right, and the application must handle the error.

What Is a Right?

The definition of any right in Authorization Services is simply a string, conventionally in reverse-DNS format, uniquely identifying that right. The name of the right usually identifies the facility and application for which the right is used, so the com.apple.Xcode.distcc.admin right allows the user of Apple's Xcode software to administer the distcc facility. The reason rights are this way has to do with how the rules are evaluated by the security daemon, a topic discussed later in this chapter.

There is no need to register a new right when a third-party application needs to use a hitherto unseen right; applications can request rights of any name. If the right has not been recorded in the authorization database, securityd will evaluate a default rule to decide whether to grant the right. The default rule is that the user must be able to authenticate as a member of the admin group, with a five-minute "grace period" during which a successfully authenticated administrator does not need to re-enter his credentials. Applications are thus automatically protected against privilege escalation attacks by permitting only administrators to acquire Authorization Services rights. Registering a right is possible, which gives you control over the initial rules associated with the right. Because adding a right implies editing the (root-owned) authorization database, the ability to do so is itself protected by an authorization right (the rights with names starting with "config" followed by a period govern modification of the database).

While it is not necessary to register a right with the security daemon, doing so makes things more convenient for systems administrators. If an administrator wants to change the rules associated with your application's right, he or she can find and modify the entry for that right created in the database when your application registered it. If the right was not registered, a new entry must be created from scratch: this task is more likely to introduce errors.

The rights system implemented by Authorization Services is discretionary. The security daemon does not really give a process that acquires rights any additional privileges; it simply provides a secure means by which applications can relate user identities to a system-wide policy on rights-granting. In other words, an application that owns any particular right has no more capabilities than an application that does not own the right — if the authorized app can perform some task, then the unauthorized one can also do it. Authorization Services can be used inside an application to limit the ability of some users to perform particular tasks within the application, and to allow the systems administrator to control the policy. Apple's documentation on Authorization Services refers to applications that limit access to their features in this way as *self-restricted applications*. A child-friendly web browser could limit access to untrusted web sites to a particular group of users (presumably the adults): this browser would be a self-restricted application.

The "security" of Authorization Services is mainly that it is tamper-resistant, as the policy database is owned by the super-user and can be modified only by the super-user or through rights delegated by that user, ensuring that an attacker cannot give himself permission to modify the rules or circumvent the policy. Authorization Services is also resistant to repudiation, as any acquisition of a right is logged by the security daemon to /var/log/secure.log — users who perform privileged tasks by acquiring rights cannot later claim they did not do so, without also tampering with the log (again requiring super-user privileges).

Applications composed of multiple processes running as different users can use Authorization Services tests as checkpoints at the privilege boundaries between different processes. The user application acquires a right, which it passes to the helper process to demonstrate that the user is permitted to request the privileged task.

Getting a Right

The process for attempting to acquire a named right is shown in Listing 6-1. Authorization Services is part of the Security framework, which must be added to the project for this code to run successfully.

LISTING 6-1: Acquiring a right through Authorization Services [gain_right.m]

Available for download on Wrox.com

```
#import <Foundation/Foundation.h>
#import <Security/Security.h>

int main (int argc, const char * argv[]) {
    NSAutoreleasePool * pool = [[NSAutoreleasePool alloc] init];
    //create a connection to the security daemon
    AuthorizationRef auth = NULL;
    OSStatus authResult = errAuthorizationSuccess;
    authResult = AuthorizationCreate(NULL,
                                     kAuthorizationEmptyEnvironment,
                                     kAuthorizationFlagDefaults,
                                     &auth);
    if (errAuthorizationSuccess != authResult) {
        NSLog(@"couldn't create authorization object, error %d", authResult);
        exit(-1);
    }

    //define the right set that this application tries to acquire
    AuthorizationItem item = { 0 };
    item.name = "com.example.gain_right.sample_right";
    item.valueLength = 0;
    item.value = NULL;
    item.flags = 0;
    AuthorizationRights requestedRights;
    requestedRights.count = 1;
    requestedRights.items = &item;

    //request that this application's rights be extended to include that right
```

continues

LISTING 6-1 *(continued)*

```
    AuthorizationRights *grantedRights = NULL;
    authResult = AuthorizationCopyRights(auth,
                                         &requestedRights,
                                         kAuthorizationEmptyEnvironment,
                                         kAuthorizationFlagDefaults |
                                         kAuthorizationFlagExtendRights |
                                         kAuthorizationFlagInteractionAllowed,
                                         &grantedRights);

    //was the right authorized?
    switch (authResult) {
        case errAuthorizationSuccess:
            NSLog(@"successfully authorized com.example.gain_right.sample_right");
            // perform the privileged task
            break;
        case errAuthorizationDenied: //user cannot be authorized
        case errAuthorizationCanceled: // user declined to authorize
            NSLog(@"could not authorize com.example.gain_right.sample_right");
            // do not perform the task
            break;
        default:
            NSLog(@"failed authorizing right, error %d", authResult);
            // do not perform the task
            break;
    }
    AuthorizationFreeItemSet(grantedRights);
    AuthorizationFree(auth, kAuthorizationFlagDefaults);
    [pool drain];
    return authResult;
}
```

The AuthorizationCopyRights() function takes a list of rights to be acquired, though in this case only one right was requested. If the list contains more rights, then authorization succeeds only if all rights can be gained. This behavior is changed by the passing of the kAuthorizationFlagPartialRights flag, in which case Au thorization Services evaluates each right individually and returns any that were successfully acquired.

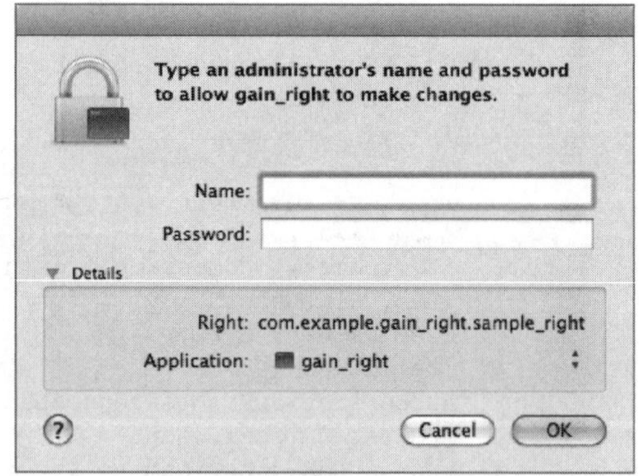

FIGURE 6-1: User authentication as part of Authorization Services

In Listing 6-1 the kAuthorizationFlagInteraction-Allowed flag was also specified, allowing the security agent to present the authentication dialog (shown in Figure 6-1) if required. Without this flag the security daemon will grant the right only if it can be acquired without user interaction. Denying user interaction is appropriate for a "faceless" process such as a daemon, which may not be running in a context where displaying windows is possible (e.g., if no users are logged in).

It is possible to define an *authorization environment* passed to AuthorizationCopyRights(), which can contain credentials supplied on a user's behalf. An application can securely store a password (in the keychain) to present to the security daemon even if user interaction is not available. Listing 6-2 demonstrates the modifications to Listing 6-1 that would be necessary to achieve that.

Available for download on Wrox.com

LISTING 6-2: Authorization with programmatically-supplied credentials [gain_right_credentials.m]

```
//the authorization environment will contain user credentials
AuthorizationItem credentials[2];
credentials[0].name = kAuthorizationEnvironmentUsername;
credentials[0].valueLength = strlen(username);
credentials[0].value = username;
credentials[0].flags = 0;
credentials[1].name = kAuthorizationEnvironmentPassword;
credentials[1].valueLength = strlen(password);
credentials[1].value = password;
credentials[1].flags = 0;
AuthorizationEnvironment environment;
environment.count = 2;
environment.items = credentials;
//request that this application's rights be extended to include that right
AuthorizationRights *grantedRights = NULL;
authResult = AuthorizationCopyRights(auth,
                                     &requestedRights,
                                     &environment,
                                     kAuthorizationFlagDefaults |
                                     kAuthorizationFlagExtendRights,
                                     &grantedRights);
```

Listing 6-2 sets up an authorization environment with two items: the username and password that the security daemon should use to identify the user on whose behalf the right is being requested. The environment could also provide a localized prompt to display in an authentication dialog and a custom icon. In this instance the tool cannot present a user interface even if the supplied credentials are insufficient, as the kAuthorizationFlagInteractionAllowed flag was not passed, so the prompt and icon will not be used.

In each of the two preceding listings the flag kAuthorizationFlagExtendRights was passed to AuthorizationCopyRights(). This important flag signifies to Authorization Services that if the application doesn't already have the right, it should attempt to acquire it. Without this flag, Authorization Services tests whether the application currently has the requested right, but if not it will not try to gain that right. This is useful in factored applications, in which rights are passed between different processes.

When registering a new right, the application can set default rules for evaluating the granting of that right, as shown in Listing 6-3.

Available for download on Wrox.com

LISTING 6-3: Registering a new right in the Authorization Services database [register_right.m]

```
#import <Foundation/Foundation.h>
#import <Security/Security.h>

#define kRightName "com.example.register_right.sample_right"

int main (int argc, const char * argv[]) {
    NSAutoreleasePool * pool = [[NSAutoreleasePool alloc] init];

    //check whether the right exists
    OSStatus authResult = AuthorizationRightGet(kRightName, NULL);
    if (errAuthorizationSuccess != authResult) {
        // no it doesn't, add the right to the database
        AuthorizationRef auth = NULL;
        authResult = AuthorizationCreate(NULL,
                                         kAuthorizationEmptyEnvironment,
                                         kAuthorizationFlagDefaults,
                                         &auth);
        if (errAuthorizationSuccess != authResult) {
            NSLog(@"couldn't create authorization object, error %d", authResult);
            exit(-1);
        }
        //ensure we have the right to add the right
        AuthorizationItem item = { 0 };
        item.name = "config.add." kRightName;
        item.valueLength = 0;
        item.value = NULL;
        item.flags = 0;
        AuthorizationRights requestedRights;
        requestedRights.count = 1;
        requestedRights.items = &item;
        authResult = AuthorizationCopyRights(auth,
                                             &requestedRights,
                                             NULL,
                                             kAuthorizationFlagDefaults |
                                             kAuthorizationFlagInteractionAllowed |
                                             kAuthorizationFlagExtendRights,
                                             NULL);
        if (errAuthorizationSuccess != authResult) {
            NSLog(@"don't have the right to modify the authorization database");
            exit(-1);
        }
        NSDictionary *rules = [NSDictionary dictionaryWithObject:
                               CFSTR(kAuthorizationRuleClassDeny)
                                                           forKey:
                               @"class"];
        authResult = AuthorizationRightSet(auth,
                                           kRightName,
                                           rules,
                                           NULL,
                                           NULL,
                                           NULL);
        if (errAuthorizationSuccess != authResult) {
```

```
            NSLog(@"couldn't add the right, error %d", authResult);
        }
        AuthorizationFree(auth, kAuthorizationFlagDefaults);
    }
    else {
        NSLog(@"the right already exists, no need to add it");
    }

    [pool drain];
    return authResult;
}
```

The right to be added is passed to the AuthorizationRightSet() function along with a dictionary specifying how the right should be granted — in this case a generic-rule class denying all access is used (so that the systems administrator must explicitly grant access to chosen users by modifying the database); other canned rules are defined in SecurityDB.h. The rule from another right could be copied, or a fresh dictionary constructed from scratch. The example tool in Listing 6-3 takes the precaution of ensuring that it has the right to add a new right — usually this step is redundant because the right is always allowed, but if the administrator had restricted access to that privilege, the step would be necessary.

FACTORED APPLICATIONS WITH AUTHORIZATION SERVICES

As described in Chapter 4, complicated applications may need a variety of distinct privileges. To reduce the damage that can be done if the application is compromised, the different privileges can be divided among separate processes, sharing data through an IPC mechanism. If any of the components of the application are compromised, it should be harder for the attacker to leverage the services provided by other components.

Identify the Privilege Boundaries

Choosing how to divide a complex system into multiple processes can be difficult, but one very obvious condition applies: if two sections of the system require unrelated privileges, then they should (and sometimes must) be separate processes. For example, a (very) simple application to manage network services could do two things: let the user see the state of each service and switch services on or off as the user requests. This application needs to show a user interface (which means interacting with the Window Server on behalf of the logged-in user), and it also needs to configure system daemons (which means working with the system launchd process). These two capabilities are not related, so they should be in separate processes — now an attack against the user interface process has a lower risk of being able to target the daemons. Designing the application in this way also introduces an obvious "funnel" where tests for valid data and behavior can be inserted, at the boundary between the two processes. Any assumptions about the preconditions for configuring daemons (including whether the user is authorized) and the changes that will be requested should be checked at this boundary.

The graphical application component of this system no longer needs any special privileges at all, as it just functions as a regular app. Because it can communicate with the daemon-configuration helper, it follows that any unprivileged user can request configuration changes of the helper. This represents a *privilege escalation* threat, as without this system in place there would be no way for regular users to configure system daemons like that. To mitigate this threat, the application and helper tool need to agree on a way to identify whether the user is authorized to perform the privileged function, and the helper must do its work only if it receives such authorization. And, unsurprisingly, Authorization Services can be used to implement both parts of this agreement.

Another place applications can be split into multiple processes is where they link against multiple, unrelated frameworks. If a single process uses both AppKit and OpenDirectory, for instance, that application can be exploited via vulnerabilities that exist in either of those frameworks. If the application is split into two processes, each of which handles tasks related to one of the two frameworks, the entry points presented by the application are shared between the two processes. The assets are similarly divided, so the overall risk is reduced.

Some frameworks are inappropriate for use in certain situations, which can lead to an enforced separation of concerns. The AppKit framework relies on a connection to the Window Server process, which is available to the current console user only. A process that must run as a background user (such as the super-user) therefore cannot rely on using AppKit classes and functions itself, but must communicate with another process that does run in the appropriate context.

Writing the Application

To perform the privileged operation, the application (i.e., the process with which the user is interacting) must verify that the user has the authority to get the task done, then launch the privileged helper tool and inform the helper of the user's authorization. This division of responsibility mirrors the division of labor between the two processes — the application works with the user, so it is the app's responsibility to identify and authorize the user; the helper does the work, so the helper uses the authorization to ensure that it really should start on the privileged task.

The specifics of getting the privileged helper launched in its appropriate context are not covered here. A general method of launching processes on demand in predefined environments is to use launch daemons, as described in Chapter 4.

The user application's role in this two-stage authorization process is known as *pre-authorization*, as the application verifies that the user is authorized for the requested right, but does not complete authorization by gaining the right. Instead, the application packages its authorization reference into an external form, which it then passes to the helper through an IPC channel. The application itself never acquires the right to the privileged task, which would not be useful anyway if the operating system's permissions model were to stop the application from completing the task.

Any process can use the external form of an authorization reference to acquire rights that have been pre-authorized by the process that created the external form. The external form should therefore be considered confidential and shared between the application and helper appropriately.

In Listing 6-4 the application component of a multiple-process system pre-authorizes a right and sends its authorization reference to the helper component. The system enables or disables the SSH daemon, and uses a right defined by the operating system for modifying the system launchd domain, com.apple.ServiceManagement.daemons.modify.

Available for download on Wrox.com

LISTING 6-4: An application pre-authorizing a right before launching a privileged tool [SSH_ControlAppDelegate.m]

```
- (IBAction)toggleSSHState: (id)sender {
    //pre-authorize the right to change the system launchd domain
    AuthorizationRef auth = NULL;
    OSStatus authResult = AuthorizationCreate(NULL,
                                              kAuthorizationEmptyEnvironment,
                                              kAuthorizationFlagDefaults,
                                              &auth);
    if (errAuthorizationSuccess != authResult) {
        NSLog(@"couldn't create an AuthorizationRef: %d", authResult);
        return;
    }

    AuthorizationItem right = { 0 };
    right.name = kSMRightModifySystemDaemons;
    right.valueLength = 0;
    right.value = NULL;
    right.flags = 0;
    AuthorizationRights requestedRights = { 0 };
    requestedRights.count = 1;
    requestedRights.items = &right;
    AuthorizationRights *grantedRights = NULL;
    authResult = AuthorizationCopyRights(auth,
                                         &requestedRights,
                                         kAuthorizationEmptyEnvironment,
                                         kAuthorizationFlagDefaults |
                                         kAuthorizationFlagExtendRights |
                                         kAuthorizationFlagInteractionAllowed |
                                         kAuthorizationFlagPreAuthorize,
                                         &grantedRights);
    //check that the right was pre-authorized
    if (NULL == grantedRights) {
        NSLog(@"didn't pre-authorize the right, status %d", authResult);
        return;
    }
```

continues

LISTING 6-4 *(continued)*

```
    int i;
    for (i = 0; i < grantedRights->count; i++) {
        if ((strncmp(grantedRights->items[i].name,
                     kSMRightModifySystemDaemons,
                     strlen(grantedRights->items[i].name)) == 0) &&
            (grantedRights->items[i].flags & kAuthorizationFlagCanNotPreAuthorize))
        {
            NSLog(@"couldn't pre-authorize the right, status %d", authResult);
            AuthorizationFreeItemSet(grantedRights);
            return;
        }
    }
    AuthorizationFreeItemSet(grantedRights);

    //package the rights into external form
    AuthorizationExternalForm externalForm;
    authResult = AuthorizationMakeExternalForm(auth,
                                               &externalForm);
    if (errAuthorizationSuccess != authResult) {
        NSLog(@"unable to create external form, status %d", authResult);
        return;
    }

    //launch the helper
```

Because the application, and not the helper, is responsible for pre-authorization, the application's name appears in the dialog presented by the security agent (Figure 6-2). The application then just starts the helper and sends it the authorization external form over NSPipe or another IPC mechanism.

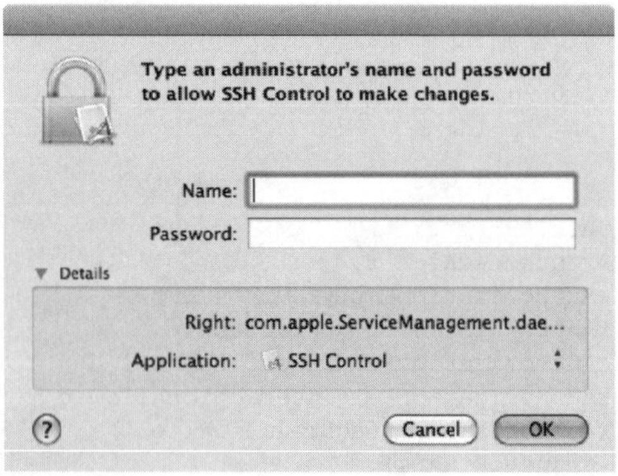

FIGURE 6-2: The pre-authorizing app, not the helper tool, is named in the authorization dialog.

The Helper Tool

The first task of the helper is to recover the authorization from the external form passed to it by the application. It then carries out the authorization proper, to confirm that the application did legitimately pre-authorize the user. Once the helper has confirmed that it has the right it needs, it can perform its work. This flow is shown in Listing 6-5 — note that the helper does not allow user interaction in its authorization call, as any required user interaction should have been carried out by the pre-authorizing app.

Available for download on Wrox.com

LISTING 6-5: Using a pre-authorized right in a privileged helper [launchdHelper.c]

```
//read the external form of the AuthorizationRef
AuthorizationExternalForm externalForm;
int bytesRead = read(STDIN_FILENO,
                     &externalForm,
                     kAuthorizationExternalFormLength);
if (bytesRead < kAuthorizationExternalFormLength) {
    fprintf(stderr, "couldn't read the authorization ref\n");
    return -1;
}

AuthorizationRef auth;
OSStatus authResult = AuthorizationCreateFromExternalForm(&externalForm,
                                                          &auth);
if (errAuthorizationSuccess != authResult) {
    fprintf(stderr, "not allowed to internalize this external form\n");
    return -1;
}

//check that we actually got the appropriate right
AuthorizationItem right = { 0 };
right.name = kSMRightModifySystemDaemons;
right.valueLength = 0;
right.value = NULL;
right.flags = 0;
AuthorizationRights requestedRights = { 0 };
requestedRights.count = 1;
requestedRights.items = &right;
authResult = AuthorizationCopyRights(auth,
                                     &requestedRights,
                                     kAuthorizationEmptyEnvironment,
                                     kAuthorizationFlagDefaults |
                                     kAuthorizationFlagExtendRights,
                                     NULL);
if (errAuthorizationSuccess == authResult) {
    //yes, do the privileged task
```

The right pre-authorized by the app and the right authorized by the helper must agree, as the helper will almost certainly not be able to acquire any other right without user interaction.

The helper tool should be capable of performing only the task for which it was designed. It can seem tempting to write the privileged tool as a form of UNIX shell or sudo-style command, so that the same helper can be used for any privileged task. The problem with that approach is that if the entry point to the helper through the application is compromised, an attacker can easily get the tool to perform arbitrary tasks — a privilege-escalation vulnerability. When an administrator or computer forensics expert looks at the system to diagnose what happened, even if the logs have not been tampered with she will find only that the right to launch your privileged tool was gained: this is sufficient to raise the question of whether the victim should carry on using your software, but of no help in showing what the attacker did. In other words, the generic nature of the tool can also provide a repudiation threat to the system.

THE AUTHORIZATION DATABASE

The whole system of rights is useful only if there are controls on who can acquire which rights; in other words there must be *rules* governing the allocation of rights to user accounts. The same /etc/authorization database in which the rights are specified also defines the rules to be used in deciding whether a user should be granted any right. The database is in an XML property list format that can be modified by administrators using standard text editors, and can also be edited via the Authorization Services APIs by applications that have themselves acquired the rights to modify the database.

What Are Rules?

A rule is simply a statement of a condition that securityd can test when deciding whether to grant a right to a user. So the statement "user can be authenticated as a member of the admin group" is an appropriate rule; if a user wants to gain a right that is determined by the rule, and cannot identify himself as a member of the admin group, he is denied that right. Conversely, if he can identify himself as a member of the group, the right is granted.

The preceding rule is defined in the authorization database and given the name authenticate-admin. Its definition looks like this in the XML database:

```
...
<key>authenticate-admin</key>
<dict>
      <key>class</key>
       <string>user</string>
       <key>comment</key>
       <string>Authenticate as an administrator.</string>
       <key>group</key>
       <string>admin</string>
       <key>shared</key>
       <true/>
       <key>timeout</key>
```

```
        <integer>0</integer>
</dict>
...
```

The rule has a comment, describing it to viewers and editors of the database. It is a user class of rule, indicating that it will test a property of the user account at the time of attempted acquisition — in this case whether the user belongs to a particular group. Specifically (and as expected), it requires that the user belong to the admin group. The other rule classes are as follows:

- **allow:** The rule is always satisfied.
- **deny:** The rule can never be satisfied.
- **evaluate-mechanisms:** The security daemon must defer to plug-ins that provide custom processing of the security environment.
- **rule:** The rule delegates to one or more named rules.

The rule has the shared property, which indicates that the Security Daemon can use a credentials cache on successful authentication. If multiple rights are requested within a short time and they all require that the same be evaluated, the requests can all share the result of the first test. The authenticate-admin rule has a timeout, but it is set to 0. If the same process tries to use rights protected by this rule more than once, that process must satisfy this rule every time it calls AuthorizationCopyRights(). If the timeout is set to some number of seconds, subsequent tests of this rule within that many seconds of the first successful test will automatically pass. Because this timeout could be set to any value, it is important that applications using Authorization Services do not assume that when they initially acquire a right they can use indefinitely the privileges conferred. Each attempt to perform a protected task should be preceded by acquisition of the appropriate right or rights, so that the timeouts set by the administrator are honored.

Now that the authenticate-admin rule is defined, you can use it as a prerequisite for any right by naming this rule in the definition of that right.

```
<key>config.modify.</key>
<dict>
        <key>class</key>
        <string>rule</string>
        <key>comment</key>
        <string>Wildcard right for modifying rights.  Admins are allowed to modify
 any(non-wildcard) rights.  Root does not require authentication.</string>
        <key>k-of-n</key>
        <integer>1</integer>
        <key>rule</key>
        <array>
                <string>is-root</string>
                <string>authenticate-admin</string>
        </array>
</dict>
```

The definition here is not for a single right called config.modify. — an entry in the rights database ending with a period represents a *wildcard* that Authorization Services can use if there is no specific right defined that matches the right being requested. An application that needs to change the rules for a right called com.example.right1 must first gain the right config.modify.com.example.right1, but as this is not specifically listed in /etc/authorization the security daemon will try to evaluate config.modify.com.example., and then config.modify.com., and finally config.modify. when it finds a match to the wildcard and evaluates the rules.

The definition of the right itself contains the rule that controls whether it is granted. In this case the rule is of the rule class, so it must delegate evaluation to another, named rule. There are in fact two rules named in the definition of the config.modify. wildcard: one is authenticate-admin, which you have already seen, and the other is is-root, which, perhaps unsurprisingly, is met if the user requesting the right is the super-user. But the user does not need to be an admin *and* root in order to gain this right. That's because the rules are combined in a k-of-n fashion on this wildcard. Ordinarily, if the k-of-n association is not specified, all the rules must be satisfied in order for a right to be granted. The k-of-n number means that if *any* k of the rules is satisfied, the right can be granted. In this case k equals one, so the right is gained if either of the two rules is satisfied.

Creating Custom Rules

When you're adding a right to the database with AuthorizationRightSet(), as seen earlier in Listing 6-3, the definition of the right must include the rule by which access to the right will be gated. That allows new rights to delegate to existing, named rules and plug-in mechanisms, to create a single custom user-class rule, or to use the trivial allow and deny classes. The access for any existing right can similarly be changed through AuthorizationRightSet(), as long as the application requesting the change has the appropriate config.modify. right. But how can an application add a new, named rule?

The short answer is that there is no way to do so. You can create custom, named rules by modifying the /etc/authorization file, either programmatically with NSDictionary or with a text editor, although Apple discourages that approach as it regards the format of the database to be subject to change without notice. Authorization Services provides API only for modifying rights in the database, not rules. To use the same rule for multiple rights is still straightforward, though. Retrieve the rule for the "master" right with AuthorizationRightGet(), then apply the same dictionary to each right you wish to "paste" the rule onto.

Modification of the rule associated with any right involves acquiring a right, which is usually permitted only to administrators, and therefore will often involve the presentation of an authentication dialog. Even so, it is a good idea to seek explicit confirmation from an administrator regarding the details of any change you want to make to the authorization rules. If a change would potentially override the administrator's custom policy, it could not be a good change to make; perhaps the administrator knows more about the customer's network and users than you do, and has deliberately hardened or relaxed the restriction on acquisition of your application's rights.

WHY NOT TO LAUNCH PRIVILEGED TASKS WITH AUTHORIZATION SERVICES

Authorization Services does provide a facility for launching helper tasks as root, but it is not a good idea to rely on it. Using AuthorizationExecuteWithPrivileges() is a lot like using the setuid bit on the filesystem or the sudo command, in that it will allow any code to be run as the super-user. The right it requires, system.privilege.admin, is similarly broad in its application, allowing a multitude of effects across the whole operating system. Using AuthorizationExecuteWithPrivileges() to launch the helper tool causes the same problems described in the warning about generic helper tools: this makes it too easy for an attacker with access to the unprivileged part of the application to change the behavior of the privileged portion.

The best approach to starting privileged helper tasks on modern versions of Mac OS X is to use an on-demand launchd job, so that the task is started in a controlled environment by the core operating system. To subvert such a setup once it is installed should, with appropriate filesystem protections (see Chapter 3), require at least the same access to the system as would be gained by a successful completion of the attack, making it an unattractive proposition to any would-be attacker.

The one remaining possibility is that the attacker could modify the privileged portion of the application during the install process. Secure software deployment is covered in Chapter 10.

THE PADLOCK

Most Mac OS X users are familiar with the padlock view — at the bottom-left of the screenshot in Figure 6-3 — and its interaction. Some of the controls on the page are currently disabled. By clicking the padlock a user can authenticate to gain the right to work with those controls.

The padlock view is part of the public interface of a framework, SecurityInterface.framework, supporting drop-in authorization UI for Cocoa applications. You have already encountered SecurityInterface.framework in Chapter 5, where views for working with certificates and trust were introduced. Through the rest of this section you will see how you can add this view (called SFAuthorizationView) to an application by extending the SSH control app presented earlier in the chapter.

After adding SecurityInterface.framework to the application's Xcode project, the next step is to put the SFAuthorizationView into the user interface in Interface Builder. You cannot directly add instances of SFAuthorizationView to windows or panels in Interface Builder as it does not natively support that class. Instead, drag a Custom View object into place on the UI and use the object inspector to change its class identity to SFAuthorizationView. The result is shown in Figure 6-4. Note that the text alongside the padlock image takes up a lot of space, particularly in some localized translations.

The authorization view cannot be used until it knows what rights it is supposed to acquire. For complicated rights sets, the view can be passed an AuthorizationRights structure detailing the rights, but for this simple case a string naming the single right can be given to it. In Listing 6-6 the view is configured in the application delegate object's -applicationDidFinishLaunching: method, with the SFAuthorizationView having previously been connected to an outlet in the app delegate class. Having told the SFAuthorizationView which right it is managing, the app delegate determines whether the process already owns that right and enables or disables the other controls appropriately. It also tells the SFAuthorizationView to automatically update itself, so that if the right times out the view will reflect this event.

FIGURE 6-3: The authentication padlock control in situ in System Preferences

FIGURE 6-4: Adding an authorization view to the user interface in Interface Builder

LISTING 6-6: Initializing an SFAuthorizationView [SSH_Control2AppDelegate.m]

Available for download on Wrox.com

```
- (void)applicationDidFinishLaunching:(NSNotification *)aNotification {
    /* configure the authorization view
     * note that the string should be a C string, not an NSString
     */
```

```
[authView setString: kSMRightModifySystemDaemons];
[authView setAutoupdate: YES];
[authView setDelegate: self];
// set initial state of the checkbox
[enableButton setEnabled:
 ([authView authorizationState] == SFAuthorizationViewUnlockedState)];
//...
```

The -authorizationState method on SFAuthorizationView will report to the application whether the view has acquired its rights, but this property cannot be observed via Cocoa Bindings or Key-Value Observation. The class instead provides delegate methods to notify the app when its authorization state changes — methods which in this example are also implemented on the app delegate class (Listing 6-7). They need do nothing other than update the state of the other user interface elements.

Available for download on Wrox.com

LISTING 6-7: SFAuthorizationView delegate method implementations [SSH_Control2AppDelegate.m]

```
- (void)authorizationViewDidAuthorize:(SFAuthorizationView *)view {
    [enableButton setEnabled: YES];
}
- (void)authorizationViewDidDeauthorize:(SFAuthorizationView *)view {
    [enableButton setEnabled: NO];
}
```

The sole remaining task to complete before the SFAuthorizationView is completely adopted is to use its AuthorizationRef object (with the SFAuthorizationView-supplied right already acquired) in the action method, rather than constructing a new authorization object. Listing 6-8 is a modified version of Listing 6-4, using the Authorization Services objects provided by the view object.

Available for download on Wrox.com

LISTING 6-8: Using an SFAuthorizationView's authorization object [SSH_Control2AppDelegate.m]

```
- (IBAction)toggleSSHState: (id)sender {
    //get the right from the authorization view
    AuthorizationRef auth = [[authView authorization] authorizationRef];
    //package the rights into external form
    AuthorizationExternalForm externalForm;
    authResult = AuthorizationMakeExternalForm(auth,
                                               &externalForm);
    if (errAuthorizationSuccess != authResult) {
        NSLog(@"unable to create external form, status %d", authResult);
        return;
    }

    //launch the helper...
```

Notice how much shorter this extract is than Listing 6-4. If you allow the SFAuthorizationView to manage all the complexity associated with Authorization Services, you have to write only the code for your application's functionality, and therefore reduce the chance of introducing bugs in uninteresting boilerplate code.

One final word on working with SFAuthorizationView — the AuthorizationRef object in Listing 6-8 had to be acquired in two stages, via an intermediate object called SFAuthorization. This class is an Objective-C wrapper to some of the functions in Authorization Services, but contains no novel functionality and so will not be considered further.

AUTHORIZATION PLUG-INS

The most customizable approach to authorization is to take over evaluation of the authorization itself, by instructing the security daemon to delegate evaluation to your own custom code deployed in a plug-in. An Authorization Services plug-in contains one or more *mechanisms*, and the evaluate-mechanisms class of rule tells the security daemon that it should execute the appropriate mechanism and use its result to decide whether to grant a right. The mechanism can take information from the authorization environment passed by the requesting application, can present a user interface, and can enforce any arbitrary requirements when evaluating the request.

Remember that information in the authorization environment has been prepared by the requesting application, which may not be trustworthy. Relying on that information as a critical part of the authorization decision is taking a big risk regarding the accuracy of that information. Consider using it as supplementary information, but not for anything critical. For example, if the application passes the name of its user, you could consider pre-populating an authentication dialog with that user's details, but should not assume before authentication that the application is working on behalf of the named user.

An authorization plug-in runs either as root or as an unprivileged user with no other responsibilities — the choice is made in the authorization database, but using the unprivileged environment allows plug-ins to interact with the user interface. The plug-ins are never loaded into the security daemon itself, so malicious or buggy plug-ins cannot compromise either the availability or the integrity of the daemon. Instead they are loaded into special helper processes that communicate with securityd over IPC, just as modern web browsers load content plug-ins into external processes. The interface is based on C callback functions called in a particular sequence, as shown in Figure 6-5.

The plug-in creation function is the entry point to all the plug-in functionality, and must be named AuthorizationPluginCreate(). It is responsible for filling in a table of the callback functions to be used for the rest of the plug-in's behavior. While each plug-in can host multiple mechanisms, there is only a single callback for each of the mechanism-related functions; in other words, the same function is called to invoke any of the mechanisms in a plug-in. The mechanism callbacks can distinguish which mechanism is expected, as its name is passed as a parameter, so the different mechanism names could be used to indicate variations on the same procedure, such as versions with debugging logs or varying parameters. It is not a good idea to have functionally distinct mechanisms in the same plug-in, as it makes the plug-in code unnecessarily complex.

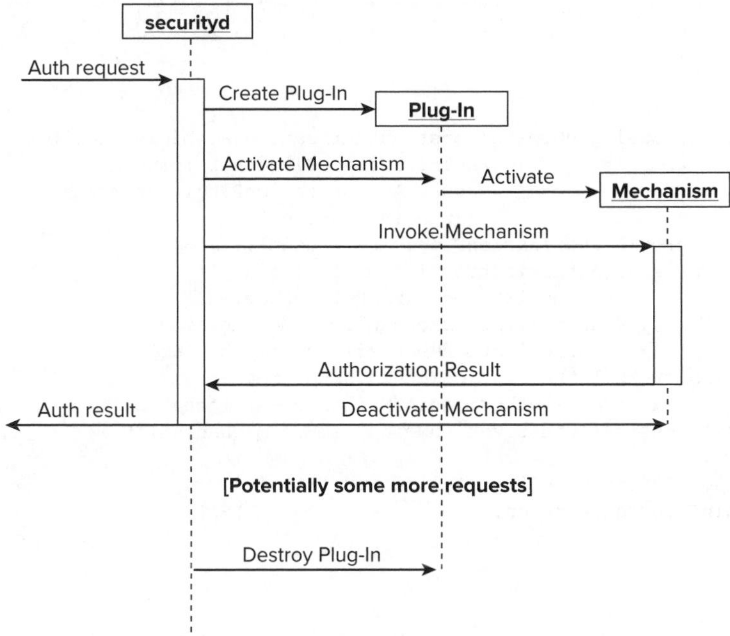

FIGURE 6-5: Lifecycle of an Authorization Services plug-in

Listing 6-9 implements an authorization plug-in that denies authorization at certain times of day. That behavior could easily be combined with other rules demanding authentication and membership of certain groups, but adds an extra dimension to the authorization process. It also serves to prove the point that the information used by authorization plug-ins to grant or deny rights can be entirely arbitrary.

The use of time as an authorization requirement, believe it or not, is a genuine requirement from an academic system I worked on. Professors and lab demonstrators were allowed to grade students if they had authenticated, but were additionally restricted to entering grades only when the labs were open. Threat analysis had concluded that computer-literate students who wanted to tamper with the grades would be most likely to do so in the evenings or at night, when they were less likely to be in class.

LISTING 6-9: A custom authorization plug-in [NineToFiveAuth.c]

Available for download on Wrox.com

```
#include <CoreServices/CoreServices.h>
#include <Security/AuthorizationPlugin.h>
#include <Security/AuthSession.h>
#include <Security/AuthorizationTags.h>
#include <stdlib.h>
```

continues

LISTING 6-9 *(continued)*

```
#include <time.h>

extern OSStatus AuthorizationPluginCreate(const AuthorizationCallbacks *callbacks,
                                          AuthorizationPluginRef *plugin,
                                          const AuthorizationPluginInterface
                                          **pluginInterface);
static OSStatus PluginDestroy(AuthorizationPluginRef plugin);
static OSStatus MechanismCreate(AuthorizationPluginRef plugin,
                                AuthorizationEngineRef engine,
                                AuthorizationMechanismId mechanismId,
                                AuthorizationMechanismRef *mechanism);
static OSStatus MechanismInvoke(AuthorizationMechanismRef mechanism);
static OSStatus MechanismDeactivate(AuthorizationMechanismRef mechanism);
static OSStatus MechanismDestroy(AuthorizationMechanismRef mechanism);

static AuthorizationPluginInterface gPluginCallbackTable = {
    kAuthorizationPluginInterfaceVersion,
    &PluginDestroy,
    &MechanismCreate,
    &MechanismInvoke,
    &MechanismDeactivate,
    &MechanismDestroy
};

struct nineToFivePlugin {
    AuthorizationCallbacks *callbacks;
};

extern OSStatus AuthorizationPluginCreate(const AuthorizationCallbacks *callbacks,
                                          AuthorizationPluginRef *plugin,
                                          const AuthorizationPluginInterface
                                          **pluginInterface) {
    /*
     * tell the plug-in host which callback functions to use.
     */
    *pluginInterface = &gPluginCallbackTable;
    // give the host a unique handle for this plug-in.
    *plugin = malloc(sizeof(struct nineToFivePlugin));
    if (NULL == *plugin) {
        return mFulErr;
    }
    struct nineToFivePlugin *pluginPtr = *plugin;
    pluginPtr->callbacks = callbacks;
    return noErr;
}

static OSStatus PluginDestroy(AuthorizationPluginRef plugin)
{
    free(plugin);
    return noErr;
}
```

LISTING 6-9 *(continued)*

```
struct nineToFiveMechanism {
    AuthorizationPluginRef plugin;
    AuthorizationEngineRef engine;
    char *mechanismId;
};

static OSStatus MechanismCreate(AuthorizationPluginRef plugin,
                                AuthorizationEngineRef engine,
                                AuthorizationMechanismId mechanismId,
                                AuthorizationMechanismRef *mechanism) {
    /*
     * this plug-in doesn't use the mechanism ID, but needs the plugin reference
     * and engine reference to record the result of authorization. However,
     * we'll keep and track it all for purposes of demonstration.
     */
    struct nineToFiveMechanism *myMechanism = malloc(sizeof(struct
                                                  nineToFiveMechanism));
    if (NULL == myMechanism) {
        return mFulErr;
    }
    myMechanism->plugin = plugin;
    myMechanism->engine = engine;
    myMechanism->mechanismId = (char *)mechanismId;
    *mechanism = myMechanism;
    return noErr;
}

static OSStatus MechanismInvoke(AuthorizationMechanismRef mechanism) {
    // this is where the work is done - check the time
    time_t theTime = time(NULL);
    struct tm *localTime = localtime(&theTime);
    int auth = (9 <= localTime->tm_hour && localTime->tm_hour < 17)
    ? kAuthorizationResultAllow
    : kAuthorizationResultDeny;
    struct nineToFiveMechanism *myMechanism = mechanism;
    struct nineToFivePlugin *myPlugin = myMechanism->plugin;
    OSStatus result = myPlugin->callbacks->SetResult(myMechanism->engine, auth);
    return result;
}

static OSStatus MechanismDeactivate(AuthorizationMechanismRef mechanism) {
    // there's nothing to do to deactivate, but signal that deactivation was done
    struct nineToFiveMechanism *myMechanism = mechanism;
    struct nineToFivePlugin *myPlugin = myMechanism->plugin;

    OSStatus result = myPlugin->callbacks->DidDeactivate(myMechanism->engine);
    return result;
}

static OSStatus MechanismDestroy(AuthorizationMechanismRef mechanism) {
    free(mechanism);
    return noErr;
}
```

Before this plug-in can be used, it must be correctly deployed. In addition to being located in the correct folder (/Library/Security/SecurityAgentPlugins) and owned by user root, group wheel, it must have the appropriate property list entries, as shown in Listing 6-10 — in particular, the bundle package type and bundle signature must be identical to those in the listing, and the bundle identifier must be unique.

LISTING 6-10: Info.plist for an Authorization Services plug-in [Info.plist]

Available for download on Wrox.com

```
<?xml version="1.0" encoding="UTF-8"?>
<!DOCTYPE plist PUBLIC "-//Apple//DTD PLIST 1.0//EN"
"http://www.apple.com/DTDs/PropertyList-1.0.dtd">
<plist version="1.0">
<dict>
       <key>CFBundleDevelopmentRegion</key>
       <string>English</string>
       <key>CFBundleExecutable</key>
       <string>NineToFiveAuth</string>
       <key>CFBundleIdentifier</key>
       <string>com.example.ninetofiveauth</string>
       <key>CFBundleInfoDictionaryVersion</key>
       <string>6.0</string>
       <key>CFBundlePackageType</key>
       <string>BNDL</string>
       <key>CFBundleShortVersionString</key>
       <string>1.0</string>
       <key>CFBundleSignature</key>
       <string>hmdr</string>
       <key>CFBundleVersion</key>
       <string>1.0</string>
</dict>
</plist>
```

When developing and debugging an Authorization Services plug-in, ensure that your debug builds are compiled for the same architecture that the security infrastructure is using. On Snow Leopard, this means that debug builds must be x86_64 (as must release builds).

With the plug-in bundle deployed, it is now possible to define rights that are gated by the code in this bundle. You do this as before, but with changes to the rights dictionary used to invoke the plug-in, as in Listing 6-11.

LISTING 6-11: Using the Authorization Services plug-in mechanism [auth_plugin_use.m]

Available for download on Wrox.com

```
#import <Foundation/Foundation.h>
#import <Security/Security.h>

#define kRightName "com.example.auth_plugin_use.timed_right"

int main (int argc, const char * argv[]) {
    NSAutoreleasePool * pool = [[NSAutoreleasePool alloc] init];
    AuthorizationRef auth = NULL;
    OSStatus authResult = AuthorizationCreate(NULL,
                                              kAuthorizationEmptyEnvironment,
```

```
                                    kAuthorizationFlagDefaults,
                                    &auth);
    if (errAuthorizationSuccess != authResult) {
        NSLog(@"couldn't create authorization object, error %d", authResult);
        exit(-1);
    }

    authResult = AuthorizationRightGet(kRightName, NULL);
    if (errAuthorizationSuccess != authResult) {
        /*
         * The format of a mechanism name is plugin:mechanism. The mechanism in
         * this case can be anything as the plug-in ignores it; note that by
         * appending ",privileged" to the mechanism name the plug-in is loaded
         * into a root-owned process.
         */
        NSArray *mechanisms = [NSArray arrayWithObject: @"NineToFiveAuth:blah"];
        NSDictionary *rules = [NSDictionary dictionaryWithObjectsAndKeys:
                               @"evaluate-mechanisms", @"class",
                               mechanisms, @"mechanisms",
                               @"Office Hours Only", @"comment",
                               nil];
        authResult = AuthorizationRightSet(auth,
                                           kRightName,
                                           rules,
                                           NULL,
                                           NULL,
                                           NULL);
        if (errAuthorizationSuccess != authResult) {
            NSLog(@"couldn't add the right, error %d", authResult);
        }

    }
    else {
        NSLog(@"the right already exists, no need to add it");
    }

    //now authorize me for that right
    AuthorizationItem nextitem = { 0 };
    nextitem.name = kRightName;
    nextitem.valueLength = 0;
    nextitem.value = NULL;
    nextitem.flags = 0;
    AuthorizationRights nextRequestedRights;
    nextRequestedRights.count = 1;
    nextRequestedRights.items = &nextitem;
    AuthorizationRights *grantedRights = NULL;
    authResult = AuthorizationCopyRights(auth,
                                         &nextRequestedRights,
                                         kAuthorizationEmptyEnvironment,
                                         kAuthorizationFlagDefaults |
                                         kAuthorizationFlagExtendRights |
                                         kAuthorizationFlagInteractionAllowed,
                                         &grantedRights);
    switch (authResult) {
        case errAuthorizationSuccess:
```

continues

LISTING 6-11 *(continued)*

```
            // it must be office hours...
            break;
        case errAuthorizationDenied: //user cannot be authorized
        case errAuthorizationCanceled: //user declined to authorize
        default:
            NSLog(@"failed authorizing right, error %d", authResult);
            // do not perform the task
            break;
    }
    AuthorizationFreeItemSet(grantedRights);
    AuthorizationFree(auth, kAuthorizationFlagDefaults);

    [pool drain];
    return authResult;
}
```

As expected, this right is permitted between 9 a.m. and 5 p.m.

```
Jan  7 16:12:33 heimdall com.apple.SecurityServer[22]: Succeeded authorizing right
'com.example.auth_plugin_use.timed_right' by client '/Users/leeg/Dropbox/Security
Book/chapter 6/gain_right/build/Debug/auth_plugin_use' for authorization created by
'/Users/leeg/Dropbox/Security Book/chapter 6/gain_right/build/Debug/auth_plugin_use'
```

But it is rejected at other times.

```
Jan  7 17:01:17 heimdall com.apple.SecurityServer[22]: Failed to authorize right
'com.example.auth_plugin_use.timed_right' by client '/Users/leeg/Dropbox/Security
Book/chapter 6/gain_right/build/Debug/auth_plugin_use' for authorization created by
'/Users/leeg/Dropbox/Security Book/chapter 6/gain_right/build/Debug/auth_plugin_use'
```

SUMMARY

Authorization is an important part of many security systems — it isn't sufficient to know who someone is (identification) or be confident of that fact (authentication). You must decide whether that agent is permitted to perform some task.

Authorization Services provides a way to define a securely managed policy that describes the conditions under which various actors have the right to do certain things with your application or with the operating system, and it also provides a way to test that policy and discover whether the conditions are met. It is a discretionary measure, in that if an application has the capability to perform the task it can go ahead and do so without asking the authorization system, should it so choose. By combining Authorization Services with privilege escalation via user accounts and permissions, you can ensure that only authorized users interact with the components of your application.

Developers can customize the authorization process in multiple ways: by defining new rights, by changing the rules evaluated for existing rights, and by creating custom plug-ins that apply arbitrary calculations in determining whether rights should be granted. Most uses of Authorization Services are very straightforward, though, and the SecurityInterface framework provides a view class that manages the usual use case with minimal developer effort.

7

Auditing Important Operations

WHAT'S IN THIS CHAPTER?

- Examples of auditing in action
- Using the operating system auditing facilities
- Auditing and the Common Criteria security standards

It can initially seem as if auditing allows administrators only to close the stable door after the horse has bolted. Wouldn't it be better to invest money and effort in preventative security measures than to watch what an attacker does after breaking in? Not necessarily — as discussed in Chapter 1, the aim of secure application development is to reduce the risk of attack, which means reducing either the likelihood of successful exploitation or the impact of an attack on the system. Auditing can serve to limit the impact of an exploit by making it easier to detect and react to. It can reduce the damage to your company's or customer's reputation by making it possible to understand the limits of any successful attack on the system — publicizing that 1 percent of personal records were compromised may be bad, but it's not as bad as publicizing that an unknown percentage of the records were compromised.

Auditing also gives you a chance to learn from and react to changes in the attackers' behavior and mistakes made in your original threat analysis. You are only likely to find out if attackers are misusing your application in novel or unexpected ways if you have records of what has happened to the app — and someone reviewing those records. The threat-modeling process defined in Chapter 1 should be iterative: make sure you give yourself enough information to get value out of the second and subsequent iterations.

Auditing serves to reduce the risk of repudiation as a component of any attack against the application. It is hard for an attacker to deny carrying out a particular attack if you have records of the operations performed on the system. Indeed, sufficient audit records can form the first step in identifying the attacker in order to initiate punitive processes. The cost of implementing reactive security measures could easily outweigh the benefits of adding successive layers of protective or deterrent mechanisms.

When you implement auditing you must take into account the confidentiality of the audit information, in addition to the integrity of that information. Audit records can reveal information about the structure and policies of the user's IT environment, which could be used by an attacker to target that user. On the other hand, an attacker who believes his or her actions are being recorded may be more reluctant to carry an attack through to its conclusion. Logs that have been modified by an attacker provide no useful information about the attack.

Some applications have an "in emergency, break glass" mode: in abnormal situations like emergencies, some of the preventative security measures get disabled as continuity of operation is preferred over correct but time-consuming security procedures. The 1983 movie *WarGames* featured such a mode: while the WOPR computer was trying to brute-force the missile launch codes, NORAD staff contemplated unplugging the computer. That would have been interpreted by the launch sites as the destruction of the military complex housing WOPR, so the missiles would have been automatically launched without the need for launch codes to be entered. The emergency situation (destruction of NORAD headquarters) led to alternative security processes (launch codes no longer required). In such "in emergency, break glass" situations a record of what has happened helps when normal service is restored, so that administrators can review the effects of the emergency on their applications' operations.

Finally, depending on the area of business your application addresses, there could be external forces driving the need to audit machinery — customer IT policy, or procedures for insurance or legal purposes. In these cases the question of cost versus benefit becomes much simpler: no audit, no customers.

EXAMPLES OF AUDITING

Mac OS X already provides logs and audits of a variety of operating system procedures, and exploring these defenses can help improve your picture of what auditing capabilities provide as part of an overall security approach.

Authorization Services

You already saw in Chapter 6 that Authorization Services maintains a log at /var/log/secure.log, detailing when processes attempt to gain authorization rights, and the results of such attempts. The log may be written to only by root (who also owns the securityd process), and is in a folder that likewise only root can modify. In order to repudiate any claim of having misused a privileged task, an attacker would need super-user access to the filesystem in order to remove the evidence from the log, which one may hope would be at least as hard as performing the initial misuse. Certainly, once an attacker has gotten root privilege on a system, the security game is usually up.

A typical sequence of entries in secure.log, in this case pertaining to installing a software update from Apple, is as follows:

```
Jan 11 15:47:26 heimdall com.apple.SecurityServer[21]: UID 501 authenticated as user
admin (UID 502) for right 'system.privilege.admin'
Jan 11 15:47:26 heimdall com.apple.SecurityServer[21]: Succeeded authorizing right
'system.privilege.admin' by client '/System/Library/CoreServices/Software Update.app'
```

```
for authorization created by '/System/Library/CoreServices/Software Update.app'
Jan 11 15:47:26 heimdall com.apple.SecurityServer[21]: Succeeded authorizing right
'system.install.admin.user' by client
'/System/Library/PrivateFrameworks/PackageKit.framework/Versions/A/Resources/installd'
for authorization created by '/System/Library/CoreServices/Software Update.app'
Jan 11 15:47:26 heimdall com.apple.SecurityServer[21]: Succeeded authorizing right
'system.privilege.admin' by client
'/System/Library/PrivateFrameworks/SoftwareUpdate.framework/Versions/A/Resources/suhelpe
rd' for authorization created by '/System/Library/CoreServices/Software Update.app'
Jan 11 15:47:40 heimdall com.apple.SecurityServer[21]: Succeeded authorizing right
'system.privilege.admin' by client '/System/Library/CoreServices/Software Update.app'
for authorization created by '/System/Library/CoreServices/Software Update.app'
```

You can see from this log that the user authenticated to acquire the system.privilege.admin right in the Software Update application, which then called on a couple of helper processes during installation of the update. Suspiciously, the user who was logged in (user ID 501, on this computer the leeg user) is not the user who authenticated to gain the right (user ID 502, shown in the log to be admin). One of the following possibilities must be considered:

- The admin credentials have been compromised and are available to leeg.
- The admin user and leeg worked together to complete the update.

In this case I know that the leeg and admin accounts are both controlled by the same person (me), so there is no need to be concerned by the audit records. Had the information in the log file not been available, it would not have been possible to perform that reconstruction of the event.

Sudo Logs

The sudo facility allows users to perform tasks on a Mac with the permissions of another account. Consider two users, imaginatively named Alice and Bob, working at an online bookstore. On one of the company's Mac servers, Bob is allowed to configure the web service but Alice is not. The administrator has configured sudo so that Alice can access the web service configuration tools as Bob's user. On one of the company's biggest sales days, the web site becomes unavailable. Investigation of the web server shows that the web service was misconfigured — but did Alice or Bob do it? Alice says that only Bob has permission to modify the web server, but Bob correctly points out to the disciplinary board that if Alice changed the configuration, it would look as if Bob had made the change.

Luckily the sudo system keeps a record of its use. Whenever a user attempts to use sudo to gain access to another user's account, the attempt is logged, along with which two user accounts are involved and the command that sudo was to run as the switched-to account. This auditing includes failed attempts, which are useful in identifying a user trying to guess the passwords of other users. The forensics team analyzing the compromised web service above could use the sudo log to determine whether Alice had gained access to Bob's account — information which is crucial to reconstructing the events leading up to the service failure, and finding out who was responsible.

The information collected by sudo is passed to a system-wide audit facility called Apple System Logger. It is therefore stored in the default system log, which can be read in Console.app, and administrators can configure custom destinations for sudo log events, including remote computers. Later in the chapter you will see how to use the Apple System Logger facility in your own applications.

User Account Logging

The very act of logging into a Mac — whether with the loginwindow application, over a remote login session like SSH, or through the automatic log-in facility — represents a change in privilege level: the user goes from an unknown entity to being identified with the holder of a system account, with all the potential for spoofing, privilege escalation, and repudiation problems entailed. It is definitely important for forensic purposes to be able to track when login sessions occur and for which users. Auditing user sessions also helps administrators in other ways: if a network administrator needs to distribute an operating system patch to the workstations on the administrator's network, he or she can see when people are using the workstations and install the update when it will cause the least disruption.

The effect of logging into a computer can be restated: a user demonstrates the authority to initiate a login session for a user account on the computer. It is, then, not surprising to find that the loginwindow application (which not only displays the log-in window it is named for, but manages the creation of users' log-in sessions at the console) uses Authorization Services to decide whether a user has permission to log in. The full interaction between loginwindow.app and securityd for initializing a session is therefore captured in secure.log:

```
Jan 12 09:32:36 heimdall com.apple.SecurityServer[25]: Session 0x33bc62 created
Jan 12 09:32:36 heimdall com.apple.SecurityServer[25]: Session 0x33bc62 attributes 0x30
Jan 12 09:32:37 heimdall loginwindow[42]: Login Window Started Security Agent
Jan 12 09:32:38 heimdall SecurityAgent[133]: Showing Login Window
Jan 12 09:35:20 heimdall SecurityAgent[133]: User info context values set for leeg
Jan 12 09:35:21 heimdall SecurityAgent[133]: Login Window Showing Progress
Jan 12 09:35:21 heimdall SecurityAgent[133]: Login Window done
Jan 12 09:35:21 heimdall com.apple.SecurityServer[25]: Succeeded authorizing right
'system.login.console' by client '/System/Library/CoreServices/loginwindow.app' for
authorization created by '/System/Library/CoreServices/loginwindow.app'
Jan 12 09:35:21 heimdall loginwindow[42]: Login Window - Returned from Security Agent
Jan 12 09:35:21 heimdall com.apple.SecurityServer[25]: Succeeded authorizing right
'system.login.done' by client '/System/Library/CoreServices/loginwindow.app' for
authorization created by '/System/Library/CoreServices/loginwindow.app'
```

When a user logs out, Authorization Services logs the termination of the security session created for that user's (log-in) session.

```
Jan 12 11:55:58 heimdall com.apple.SecurityServer[25]: Session 0x33bc62 dead
Jan 12 11:55:58 heimdall com.apple.SecurityServer[25]: Killing auth hosts
Jan 12 11:55:58 heimdall com.apple.SecurityServer[25]: Session 0x33bc62 destroyed
```

Working with secure.log to derive user session history is not very easy. Not only are the log entries hard to parse, but other services, such as SSH, record different information in the same log.

```
Jan 12 11:59:50 heimdall sshd[768]: in pam_sm_authenticate(): Failed to determine
Kerberos principal name.
Jan 12 11:59:57 heimdall sshd[765]: Accepted keyboard-interactive/pam for leeg from ::1
port 50655 ssh2
Jan 12 11:59:57 heimdall com.apple.SecurityServer[25]: Session 0x313a47 created
Jan 12 11:59:57 heimdall com.apple.SecurityServer[25]: Session 0x313a47 attributes 0x20
Jan 12 12:00:11 heimdall com.apple.SecurityServer[25]: Session 0x313a47 dead
```

```
Jan 12 12:00:11 heimdall com.apple.SecurityServer[25]: Killing auth hosts
Jan 12 12:00:11 heimdall com.apple.SecurityServer[25]: Session 0x313a47 destroyed
```

Going from Authorization Services events to log-in sessions would involve knowing every possible authorization event that leads to a login session's being created — a set of events that could change at any time if new facilities are added to the operating system by Apple or by third parties. Indeed, in the example above, sshd didn't actually authorize a right at all — it just happens that the authentication module it uses logs to the same file as the security daemon. Furthermore, identifying which security server session maps to which login session based just on the contents of the security log is not possible; nowhere is the user account "owning" each new security session identified.

Mac OS X provides another method to audit user login sessions, inherited from its UNIX background. The start and conclusion of user sessions, along with events such as shutdowns and system reboots, are logged to a database at /var/run/utmpx. This file's contents can be examined by users and administrators from the command line:

```
heimdall:~ leeg$ last
leeg      ttys002  localhost        Tue Jan 12 11:59 - 12:00  (00:00)
leeg      ttys001                   Tue Jan 12 11:59   still logged in
leeg      ttys000                   Tue Jan 12 11:56   still logged in
leeg      console                   Tue Jan 12 11:56   still logged in
leeg      ttys000                   Tue Jan 12 11:31 - 11:55  (00:24)
leeg      console                   Tue Jan 12 09:35 - 11:55  (02:20)
reboot    ~                         Tue Jan 12 09:31
shutdown  ~                         Mon Jan 11 18:01
admin     console                   Mon Jan 11 10:22 - 10:27  (00:05)
leeg      ttys000                   Mon Jan 11 09:35 - 18:01  (08:25)
leeg      console                   Mon Jan 11 09:22 - 18:01  (08:38)
reboot    ~                         Mon Jan 11 09:21
[...]
heimdall:~ leeg$ who
leeg     console  Jan 12 11:56
leeg     ttys000  Jan 12 11:56
leeg     ttys001  Jan 12 11:59
```

As far as log-in sessions are concerned the utmpx database is much more flexible, allowing applications to track both historical information and current active sessions. It also tracks events in which the system clock was changed, invaluable information in forensic analysis of audit records as it tells you how reliable time stamps on other data are. Log-in management and reporting applications can interact with the database through the API declared in <utmpx.h>, though only applications with super-user privileges can add entries to the database.

The tool in Listing 7-1 uses the utmpx database to work out how long the log-in session in which it is run has been in progress. Because the same user may have multiple log-in sessions at any time, it uses the tty name to identify its session. The word *tty* comes from archaic *teletypewriter* devices that used to be attached to UNIX systems, and identifies the device file in the /dev/ folder through which input and output on the current session is directed. Sessions initiated by loginwindow (i.e., graphical user sessions with a Dock, Finder and other applications available) are identified by the tty name "console"; other tty device files are dynamically created as required for sessions created by SSH, Terminal.app or the command-line "login" session manager.

LISTING 7-1: Use account audits to find out how long the current log-in session has been in progress [sessiontime.c]

```
#include <libgen.h>
#include <stdio.h>
#include <string.h>
#include <unistd.h>
#include <utmpx.h>

int main (int argc, const char * argv[]) {
    char *tty = basename(ttyname(0));
    char *username = getlogin();
    struct utmpx prototype = { 0 };
    strncpy(prototype.ut_line, tty, _UTX_LINESIZE);
    struct utmpx *entry = NULL;

    do {
        entry = getutxline(&prototype);
    } while (entry &&
             strncmp(entry->ut_user, username, _UTX_USERSIZE) != 0);

    if (entry) {
        struct timeval currentTime;
        gettimeofday(&currentTime, NULL);
        int secondsSinceStart = currentTime.tv_sec - entry->ut_tv.tv_sec;
        int minutesSinceStart = secondsSinceStart / 60;
        int secondsCounter = secondsSinceStart % 60;
        printf("session for user %s on tty %s\nstarted %d min, %d sec ago.\n",
               username,
               tty,
               minutesSinceStart,
               secondsCounter);
        return 0;
    }
    else {
        fprintf(stderr, "accounting information for this session could not be
found.\n");
        return -1;
    }
}
```

The sessiontime tool reads through utmpx records until it finds one matching the current user and tty name; then it reports on the time since that event was recorded:

```
heimdall:Debug leeg$ ./sessiontime
session for user leeg on tty ttys000
started 255 min, 18 sec ago.
```

The records are returned with the most recent first, so this record will pertain to the current session and not some earlier session with coincidentally identical user and tty names. The entries in utmpx are maintained by the Apple System Log facility, which is available to third-party applications and discussed later in this chapter.

Firewall Log

Mac OS X has two firewall components; the one that is configured through System Preferences (and therefore the one most users will work with) is an application firewall. It uses the code identities present in signed applications to distinguish various applications and operating system services, to which it permits or denies the ability to accept incoming network connections according to its configuration. A network administrator or security officer reviewing the firewall configuration could need information about both permitted and forbidden connection attempts. The two potential problems with firewall configurations (in fact, with any filtering process, from anti-spam software to cancer-screening procedures) are false acceptance, in which an application that should be denied network access is granted it, and false rejection, in which an application that should be granted access is denied. If the firewall were to log only failed network connection attempts, then any false acceptances could go unnoticed. This is a common security mistake in many implemented systems, not just firewalls. Administrators and developers will tend to focus on failed events, forgetting the importance of success events in auditing. Increasingly, with compliance standards growing more specific and threat vectors more prolific, it is key that appropriate complete auditing be the default.

The application firewall records events in the file /var/log/appfirewall.log, and as the following excerpt shows, it logs both rejections (the UDP "stealth mode" entries represent blocked connections) and acceptances (for which the Spotify application is allowed to listen on its port).

"Stealth mode" changes the way in which the firewall responds to traffic that falls outside the rules for permissible communication. A computer will normally reply to a connection attempt on a filtered port with a "reset" response, indicating that the computer does not accept packets sent to that port. With stealth mode enabled, the computer does not send any response, making it harder for attackers to discover the host's existence.

```
Jan 14 10:33:11 heimdall Firewall[65]: Stealth Mode connection attempt to UDP
192.168.1.4:59715 from 8.8.4.4:53
Jan 14 10:41:42 heimdall Firewall[65]: Spotify is listening from 0.0.0.0:42459 proto=6
Jan 14 10:42:53 heimdall Firewall[65]: Stealth Mode connection attempt to UDP
192.168.1.4:54464 from 8.8.8.8:53
```

Filesystem Change Tracking

When a computer has been targeted by an attacker, knowing which files were compromised and how this was done is useful to a forensic analyst as part of understanding the scope and impact of the incursion. The kernel records three distinct time stamps with regard to each file in the filesystem:

- **Access time:** The time at which the file was last read
- **Modification time:** The time at which the file was last written to
- **Change time:** The time of the most recent change to the inode

The extent to which these values can be relied upon is limited. It is possible to mount filesystems with the noatime flag, which disables tracking of access times. Access time auditing is often switched off on server filesystems, where fast performance is more important than keeping a record of which files have been read. In addition, both the access and modification times of a file can be set to arbitrary values by the super-user or the owner of the file by means of the utimes() interface. Only the inode change time is guaranteed to reflect real events — assuming that the system clock can be trusted. A common mistake in systems administration is to underestimate the value of time synchronization and the importance of this service in allowing forensics across multiple services or systems. While some network services — notably Kerberos — require consistent timekeeping across all computers, synchronized time reporting makes tracking an attacker across multiple hosts much easier.

The filesystem may track modification times, but you will not be able to discover what the modification was without more information. While some filesystems (notably those used on VMS, and Sun's Zettabyte File System) do maintain previous versions of files, that is not true of HFS+. To recover earlier versions of modified files, you must have access to reliable backups or detailed change records — which must not themselves have been tampered with. This implies that you should have multiple levels of change backup — otherwise you might have synchronized the tampered file by the time you realize you have a problem!

Process Accounting

Knowing what commands and applications have been run on a system can go a long way toward your understanding what has happened to the data on that computer. This is particularly true of servers, where the administrator can easily know the "expected" processes on the system and identify any inconsistencies — for example, an ftpd process (FTP daemon) running on a database server would probably be suspicious. Recording every process also means making the super-user's activity more visible than it is made by the sudo log, which records only the process launched by sudo. If a user invokes a shell with sudo, the root account actions will not be adequately captured.

By enabling the process-accounting feature of Mac OS X, administrators ensure that the kernel logs every use of the exec() family of functions. Therefore, any attempt to launch a new tool, application, or daemon is recorded. Auditing is enabled with the accton command, or the acct() API function, and the default location for the log is /var/account/acct. From that moment on, all new processes are recorded. The log of recent commands can be reviewed with the lastcomm command.

```
bash-3.2# lastcomm
SFLIconToo -S       leeg     __            0.00 secs (null) (0:00:00.11)
lastcomm   -        root     ttys001       0.00 secs Tue Jan 19 15:16 (0:00:00.02)
login      -S       leeg     __            0.03 secs (null) (0:00:07.48)
bash       -S       leeg     ??            0.00 secs (null) (0:00:07.33)
ls         -        leeg     ??            0.00 secs (null) (0:00:00.00)
bash       -F       leeg     ??            0.00 secs (null) (0:00:00.03)
path_helpe -        leeg     ??            0.00 secs (null) (0:00:00.03)
accton     -S       root     ttys001       0.00 secs Tue Jan 19 15:16 (0:00:00.02)
```

Notice that the log entries are in reverse order, so the most recently launched process is at the top of the list. The flags in the second column represent processes started by the super-user (S), and processes that forked but did not call the exec() function (F). Lastcomm also reports on processes that exit because they receive a signal (an X flag). More verbose reports on the accounting logs, and commands to summarize and condense the entries, are available through the sa command.

USING APPLE SYSTEM LOGGER

Mac OS X provides a system-wide logging facility called Apple System Logger, or ASL. The design of ASL makes it a good facility on which to base an auditing system.

If you are familiar with older versions of Mac OS X or other UNIX platforms, you will have come across the syslog facility, and ASL is an extension of syslog with more flexible behavior. Events are recorded by means of messages sent to the ASL facility (specifically, the syslogd daemon), which are then recorded in a database. The database keeps all messages received over the previous seven days, but ASL can also be configured to write messages to separate files that are kept indefinitely. Each message consists of a dictionary of keys and values, which are filled in by the process sending the message. The dictionary keys that are attached by default to a new message, and that are provided with values if these are not supplied by the client, are as follows:

- **Message:** The text description of the event to appear in log files
- **Facility:** Identity of the client that sent the message
- **Sender:** The name of the process that sent the message
- **PID:** Process number of the sending client
- **UID:** The user account under which the client process was running
- **GID:** Group identifier of the ASL client process
- **Level:** An indication of the message's severity (sometimes also called the message's *priority*), from "debug" through "informational," "notice," "warning," "error," "critical," "alert," and "emergency"
- **Time:** The time associated with the event (by default, the time at which syslogd received the message)
- **Host:** The host name of the computer on which the message originated

Because these values (except the time) can be set by the calling process, you should be aware that the contents are not necessarily reliable. Applications using the facility to view log events can assume that every message sent by a particular client has been logged, but not that every message in the log comes from whom it claims to come from.

Notice that the sender of any message is identified in multiple, distinct ways: by process name, process identifier, and facility name. This apparent redundancy allows coalescence of log entries from multiple components of a complex system into a single audit facility. Consider Example Corp's BigApp application, made up of the BigGUI user interface and the LittleHelper privileged process. If both these processes use ASL and log with the com.example.BigApp facility, users working with the ASL database can choose to view a holistic log or just those events from one of the two components. A user experiencing a particular problem can narrow the search further, to look for messages associated with his or her user ID or a specific instance of one of the application processes.

The default facility name, used if none is provided by the logging application, is user. This is a throwback to the earlier syslog logging component, which had only a limited number of pre-supplied facility names. The user facility will also be applied to a message if any process that is not owned by the super-user attempts to use the com.apple.system prefix.

Applications can search the ASL database for messages matching conditions predicated on any of the messages' keys. Apple provides one application as a front end to the ASL database — the Console application in /Applications/Utilities. It allows users to search for interesting messages that have been logged using ASL, in addition to allowing them to page through text-format log files.

Getting a Message into ASL

The simplest route to logging some text message in ASL is a one-liner:

```
asl_log(NULL, NULL, ASL_LEVEL_INFO, "The answer is %d", 42);
```

The only parameter that must be specified other than the message content itself is the log level, an indication of the severity of the message. The ASL library fills in all the other default fields automatically, using the facility name user, the process's name, ID, and account identifiers, the current time, and the computer name.

Administrators use the log level of messages to filter issues according to priority and deal with them with different levels of urgency. On one network I administered, I configured server messages of "error" or higher priority to go to a terminal window that was permanently open on my desktop, with "critical" and higher being broadcast to all available consoles. Other administrators I have worked with even used pagers to receive high-priority log messages.

Misusing higher levels of log criticality ensures that your application's log events get noticed, but for the wrong reason; your application annoys administrators who find that their alert systems are "spammed" by irrelevant notices, which may lead them to filter out all messages created by your app — a digital retelling of the story of the boy who cried wolf. Choose the severity at which you log each event wisely. Early versions of UNIX famously included the error message "printer on fire," which if true would be an appropriate event to log as an emergency. "Welcome to my great application" is significantly less important.

To fill the fields of the message with custom values, the application must create an ASL message and set the values for each key it needs to change. The process for creating and filling out a message structure is shown in Listing 7-2.

Available for download on Wrox.com

LISTING 7-2: Defining custom parameters for ASL messages [asl_message.c]

```
#include <asl.h>
#include <stdio.h>

int main (int argc, const char * argv[]) {
    //create a new message
    aslmsg message = asl_new(ASL_TYPE_MSG);
    //configure some properties
    asl_set(message, ASL_KEY_FACILITY, "com.example.logger");
    asl_set(message, "LoggerServerName", "www.example.com");
    //now log this message
    asl_log(NULL, message, ASL_LEVEL_INFO, "attempting connection");
    asl_log(NULL, message, ASL_LEVEL_ERR, "can't connect to server");
    //clean up
    asl_free(message);
    return 0;
}
```

Notice that the same message is used twice, to log two different events. The ASL library sets the level and message text separately on each occasion, but reuses all the other values that have been configured for the message. In effect the aslmsg structure acts as a template for each log record.

The LoggerServerName key set on the message in this example is not a key that ASL has defined or that it uses itself, but it will store the key and value with the message just as it would any predefined key. These custom keys could be used by a log-viewing client to provide additional context for the messages it shows to the user.

The first parameter to asl_log(), which has not been used in any of these examples, is a *client* structure. Each client can be used only from a single thread at a time — the NULL value for a client causes the library to use a single, shared client for the whole process, with a lock to ensure there is no concurrent access from multiple threads. A multi-threaded application could create a different client in each thread to avoid blocking when using ASL — another solution could be to define a dispatch queue or operation queue used by all threads for posting log messages asynchronously.

Creating Additional Log Files

You may want your application to store its logs in a particular file, either to control the permissions and access rights for the log entries, or for the convenience of your users who won't need to search through the ASL database for events pertaining to your application.

Your application can programmatically add any open file descriptor to an ASL client, as demonstrated in Listing 7-3. Log messages sent to that ASL client are automatically written out to the file descriptor, in addition to being written to the ASL database. This forwarding mechanism gives you complete control over the external file, which could even be a network socket, pipe, or other descriptor. Clients created with the ASL_OPT_STDERR option automatically get the standard error descriptor added on creation. However, you have no control over the format of the message, which is fixed by the ASL library.

LISTING 7-3: Logging to a custom file [asl_file.c]

Available for download on Wrox.com

```
#include <asl.h>
#include <fcntl.h>
#include <stdio.h>
#include <stdlib.h>
#include <unistd.h>

int main (int argc, const char * argv[]) {
    aslclient client = asl_open("asl_file",
                                "com.example.logger",
                                0);
    int logFile = open("/tmp/asl_file.log", O_WRONLY | O_CREAT, 0600);
    if (logFile == -1) {
        asl_log(client, NULL, ASL_LEVEL_ERR, "can't open file: %m");
        exit(-1);
    }
    asl_add_log_file(client, logFile);
    asl_log(client, NULL, ASL_LEVEL_INFO, "logging to external file");
    //clean up
    asl_remove_log_file(client, logFile);
    close(logFile);
    asl_close(client);
    return 0;
}
```

The file /tmp/asl_file.log is created with the following content:

```
Fri Jan 15 14:43:39 jormungand.local asl_file[1126] <Info>: logging to external file
```

The only other method for directing ASL messages to external log files is to modify the configuration of ASL. It is best to leave that up to your users and administrators, if they want to do so; changing the configuration of an operating system service to suit a third-party application's needs is not recommended. The syslogd daemon is configured through two different files; /etc/syslog.conf and /etc/asl .conf. The syslog.conf file allows users to direct messages received by syslogd to various destinations based on their facility and log level, with the effect being similar to the redirection demonstrated in listing 7-3. By configuring asl.conf, users can filter messages into multiple databases according to complex filter predicates, with the messages being stored in the same raw format as the master ASL database. The predicates are described in the next section, "Searching the ASL Database."

Searching the ASL Database

Writing audit messages out to a log is only worthwhile if the messages can subsequently be read. Writing the messages to a system-wide logging facility is reliable and convenient, but does mean that the messages from your application are all in the same place as those from multiple operating system facilities and third-party applications. For a user to find the needle of useful information in the haystack of recorded messages, she must be able to filter the messages and look only at those that are interesting in the current situation.

Search queries in ASL are based on filtering of the values assigned to keys in the messages, so a query could require that the log level be greater than "error" and the facility equal to com.example.MyApp. In addition to binary comparisons and string prefix/suffix matching, ASL queries can employ Regular Expression matching of the value associated with any key. As the examples in this chapter have all sent messages using the com.example.logger facility, Listing 7-4 contains a program to find and display all messages in the database logged from that facility.

LISTING 7-4: Searching for messages in ASL [asl_filter.c]

Available for download on Wrox.com

```
#include <asl.h>
#include <stdio.h>

int main (int argc, const char * argv[]) {
    //create a new query
    aslmsg query = asl_new(ASL_TYPE_QUERY);
    //configure the search
    asl_set_query(query,
                  ASL_KEY_FACILITY,
                  "com.example.logger",
                  ASL_QUERY_OP_EQUAL);
    //the query will deposit results in a "response" object
    aslresponse response = asl_search(NULL, query);
    aslmsg foundMessage;
    //iterate over results in the query
    while (NULL != (foundMessage = aslresponse_next(response))) {
        const char *messageText = asl_get(foundMessage, ASL_KEY_MSG);
        const char *procName = asl_get(foundMessage, ASL_KEY_SENDER);
        const char *procID = asl_get(foundMessage, ASL_KEY_PID);
        printf("%s[%s]: %s\n", procName, procID, messageText);
    }
    //clean up
    aslresponse_free(response);
    asl_free(query);
    return 0;
}
```

Notice that because this code is responsible for handling the display of messages, the output format is much more flexible than the use of file redirection. The application could use any of the keys in a message, for example by preparing a table view with different font attributes based on the message severity.

All the values in the database are stored as strings. The library accepts a query option, ASL_QUERY_OP_NUMERIC, converting both the value and the comparison quantity to integers before performing the comparison. A tool that needed to search for messages only from system users with user identifiers below 501 would need to use that option:

```
    asl_set_query(query, ASL_KEY_UID, "501",
    ASL_QUERY_OP_LESS | ASL_QUERY_OP_NUMERIC);
```

ASL response objects do not update in real time. Once a query has been run, if new messages matching the search criteria are added to the database, they will not be detected by subsequent calls to aslresponse_next(). To search for new messages, the searching application must start a new query. To avoid having to reread all the messages that it has already seen, it can add a search on the ASL_KEY_TIME field (the time at which messages were sent), returning only those values newer than those of the last message it has already processed.

Access Control

As mentioned at the beginning of this chapter, the confidentiality of audit records can be important. The logs may contain important information about the computer's configuration or environment that could be useful to an attacker, or you may wish to avoid having the attacker know what actions are being recorded, as such information can help attackers cover their tracks. Some network security personnel operate sacrificial computers called *honeypots*, the purpose of which is to allow attackers to break in so that the techniques and tools used can be observed. If attackers could see that a computer was recording detailed information about their actions, they might conclude that the machine was a honeypot and break off their attacks before leaving any useful clues.

ASL provides a way to restrict read access to individual messages to particular users or groups. If a message has the ASL_KEY_READ_UID set to a numerical user ID, then only that user or root can read the message through the query API. Similarly, the ASL_KEY_READ_GID key restricts access to members of a particular group, though root will always be permitted to read restricted messages.

Applications that attach extra file descriptors to ASL clients using asl_add_log_file() are responsible for ensuring that the access rights on those files are appropriate. Messages with ASL_KEY_READ_UID or ASL_KEY_READ_GID will be sent to the configured files regardless of the files' permission settings.

By combining restricted access with a factored Authorization Services application, as described in the previous chapter, you could implement any conceivable access control mechanism. Consider an application that logs messages with a security clearance rating, like "unclassified," "classified," "secret," and "top secret." The viewer for those messages could be a factored application that has to acquire authorization for each clearance rating before it can show messages logged with that rating.

BASIC SECURITY MODULE

In the 1980s and 1990s, the U.S. National Computer Security Center published a "rainbow series" of books that described security features of a "trusted computing base" platform, and evaluation of those features. The evaluation criteria themselves, described in the "orange" book, were organized into divisions based on protection category, with higher divisions offering successively improved confidence in the protection of sensitive or classified data. A system with none of the outlined security measures is in division D, and is considered *minimally protected*. Division C describes requirements for discretionary access control and access auditing. Division B adds requirements for mandatory access control based on security classification meta-data. Finally, systems conforming to division A requirements are *verified protected,* with formal proofs that conformance to the trusted computing base requirements can be derived from the design of the product.

The NCSC rainbow series documentation is freely available on the Web, at `http://csrc.ncsl.nist.gov/publications/secpubs/rainbow/`. *The orange book evaluation criteria have been superseded by the Common Criteria evaluation scheme, which is discussed later in this section.*

UNIX systems of the era typically offered the discretionary access control portion of division C, but not the auditing facilities described in the "tan" that are necessary to obtain a complete division C evaluation. Conformance to these requirements was important at the time for vendors who were seeking to win expensive contracts with the U.S. government; Sun implemented the tan book requirements as an extension of its Solaris operating system called BSM, or Basic Security Module. The same library was implemented in the Mac OS X kernel, xnu, by McAfee (more famous as vendors of anti-virus software) and is now part of the TrustedBSD project which maintains it for both FreeBSD and Mac OS X. BSM projects for the Linux operating system kernel also exist.

The BSM facility in Mac OS X is enabled by default, though it is configured to record only a limited set of events related to authorization events or attempts, which could be useful in discovering privilege escalation attacks. BSM is integrated into the kernel, so any time one of the interesting events occurs it tests whether to record that event; attackers can work around it only by accessing the sensitive data from a different operating system. The records are stored in a compact binary format that is not easy to tamper with, unlike English-language log files. Logs, which are stored in the /var/audit folder, are automatically *rotated* (the current file is closed and moved, a new file opened, and old files deleted) periodically, as the BSM can generate a large amount of data when it is configured more aggressively. To view the audit records, a super-user uses the praudit command.

```
bash-3.2# praudit -ls /var/audit/current | grep Jan\ 18
header,59,11,AUE_audit_startup,0,Mon Jan 18 09:47:19 2010, + 208
msec,text,launchctl::Audit startup,return,success,0,trailer,59,
header,309,11,AUE_ssauthorize,0,Mon Jan 18 09:47:28 2010, + 808 msec,subject,-
1,root,wheel,root,wheel,50,100000,50,0.0.0.0,text,config.modify.com.apple.CoreRAID.admin
,text,client
/System/Library/PrivateFrameworks/CoreRAID.framework/Versions/A/Resources/CoreRAIDServer
,text,creator
/System/Library/PrivateFrameworks/CoreRAID.framework/Versions/A/Resources/CoreRAIDServer
,return,success,0,trailer,309,
[...more messages...]
header,200,11,AUE_ssauthorize,0,Mon Jan 18 09:48:32 2010, + 799 msec,subject,-
1,root,wheel,root,wheel,42,100000,42,0.0.0.0,text,system.login.done,text,client
/System/Library/CoreServices/loginwindow.app,text,creator
/System/Library/CoreServices/loginwindow.app,return,success,0,trailer,200,
header,213,11,AUE_ssauthorize,0,Mon Jan 18 09:48:49 2010, + 289
msec,subject,leeg,leeg,staff,leeg,staff,189,2419427,189,0.0.0.0,text,system.print.admin,
```

```
text,client /System/Library/Printers/Libraries/makequeuesagent,text,creator
/System/Library/Printers/Libraries/makequeuesagent,return,failure : Operation not
permitted,4294907291,trailer,213,
header,102,11,AUE_auth_user,0,Mon Jan 18 13:48:35 2010, + 237
msec,subject,root,root,wheel,root,wheel,920,0,0,0.0.0.0,text,Authentication for user
<leeg>,return,success,0,trailer,102,
```

Even in their formatted state, these messages are not particularly easy to interpret. Each record contains a header detailing the size of the record, the version of the record format, the event name, extra information about the event (unused in these examples), and the date. The subject then lists the user name or ID of the auditing user, the real user and group of the process that caused the event, and the effective user and group of the process, and identifies the audit session and terminal in use. There are text sections with additional information, and an indication of whether the operation succeeded (and if it didn't, why not). From the extract just shown, you can see that a makequeuesagent process running under my account attempted to get the Authorization Services right system.print.admin shortly after I logged in, and was unable to do so. Some time later I managed to get root access in a different session.

Audit sessions are created when users log in, and are inherited by any process the user creates. That makes it possible to track one person's behavior even if that user switches accounts using su or sudo, since the identifier for the audit session will not change.

The BSM audit facility is configured by files stored in /etc/security. Using these files, administrators can enable logging for events such as file accesses and new processes, even configuring different audit policies for different users. They can choose when logs should expire and be deleted, and whether the operating system allows processes to continue if it cannot write audit records or if it halts instead.

BSM's API allows applications to add their own tokens to the audit log. Listing 7-5 demonstrates this — an action that must be performed with super-user privileges (i.e., you must use sudo to run this tool).

Available for download on Wrox.com

LISTING 7-5: Recording audit events in BSM [bsm_write.c]

```
#include <errno.h>
#include <stdio.h>
#include <unistd.h>
#include <bsm/libbsm.h>
#include <bsm/audit_uevents.h>

int main (int argc, const char * argv[]) {
    // initialize the audit session state
    au_id_t auid = 0;
    int auditResult = getauid(&auid);
    if (auditResult != 0) {
```

```
        fprintf(stderr, "cannot get audit user identifier: %s\n",
                strerror(errno));
        return -1;
    }

    // authorize a user for a task...
    // ...
    // log the result
    auditResult = audit_submit(AUE_ssauthorize,
                               auid,
                               0, // status (error) of task
                               0, // return value from the task
                               "successfully authorized user");
    if (auditResult != 0) {
        fprintf(stderr, "cannot submit audit record: %s\n",
                strerror(errno));
        return -1;
    }
    //perform the task
    return 0;
}
```

On successful return from audit_submit(), a record is added to the BSM log, which praudit displays like this:

```
header,100,11,SecSrvr AuthEngine,0,Tue Jan 19 12:24:31 2010, + 71 msec
subject,leeg,root,wheel,root,wheel,916,916,50331650,0.0.0.0
text,successfully authorized user
return,success,0
trailer,100
```

Notice that even though the real and effective user IDs of the process were both root (as is required for submission of audit entries from a user application), the audit user shown in the record subject is leeg. I had run this example in a terminal session via the sudo command, and BSM correctly tracked that it was the leeg user who had logged in and had escalated to root.

Pay attention to the flow of control around audit records. If your application fails to log an event (perhaps because the auditing subsystem is unavailable, or the disk containing the logs is full), the user-friendly part of your being will want to let the user get on with the task at hand anyway. The security-conscious part will prefer to avoid completing the task, as security administrators and forensics staff will have no indication that the task ever took place. Whether it is appropriate to "fail open," allowing operations to proceed after the security mechanisms have failed, or "fail closed," denying access after security mechanisms have failed, depends on the environment and your application's security requirements. It may even be appropriate to leave configuration of this choice to the user: make sure the default option is appropriate for the majority of cases. Review your threat model and decide whether carrying on with actions that are not recorded in the logs is appropriate behavior. The decision you make should be consistent with the idea of "fail-safe" computing, introduced in Chapter 3.

COMMON CRITERIA

The security evaluation principles documented in the rainbow series, and discussed in this chapter, have since been superseded by an internationally used guide known as the Common Criteria for Information Technology Security Evaluation, often referred to simply as the Common Criteria. Like the rainbow book guides, the Common Criteria describe ways to evaluate whether information systems conform to security requirements, and rank those systems depending on the confidence with which the requirements are seen to be met. (The Common Criteria rankings are known as into *Evaluation Assurance Levels* or EALs.) The Common Criteria do not prescribe the security model itself, unlike the orange book with its specific requirements. Therefore a product submitted for Common Criteria evaluation contains two components: the *Target of Evaluation* (TOE) is the software, along with documentation about how it is to be installed and configured in the evaluation environment; the *Security Target* document describes the security countermeasures and expected protection afforded the TOE by those countermeasures.

There are seven EALs, with EAL1 offering least assurance (the TOE has been independently found to conform to its functional specification) and EAL7 the most (the TOE has been formally verified to be consistent with its security target), but as the security requirements are input for the evaluation process, it does not necessarily follow that an EAL4 product is more secure for any given task than an EAL3 product.

Mac OS X version 10.6.0 (though not updates — evaluation of any one version typically takes months and hundreds of thousands of dollars to complete) has been evaluated against an independent security target called the Controlled Access Protection Profile, which is relevant to any commercially available operating system. It was evaluated at EAL3, which means that the security requirements and countermeasures have been methodically tested. Apple produces a guide to installing and using OS X in a way that is consistent with the evaluated setup, available at `https://ssl.apple.com/support/security/commoncriteria/CommonCriteriaAdminGuide.pdf`, which includes more information about the configuration and use of BSM. The configuration and usage described in the Common Criteria Admin Guide may be useful information if your application is destined for strongly security-conscious environments, such as government departments handling classified information.

SUMMARY

Auditing involves collecting information about a system while it is in operation, so that users, administrators, and forensics officers can discover what happened to the system while it was in use. While this may seem less useful than concentrating on protective or prohibitive countermeasures, which stop attacks before they begin, it may actually be more efficient to provide auditing facilities, since the law of diminishing returns says that progressive attempts to reduce the likelihood of penetration will yield progressively fewer results. There may also be regulatory, legal, or policy requirements mandating the generation of audit records.

Many components of Mac OS X generate logs of interesting events, often associated with changes in privilege level, which could indicate a privilege-escalation attack. The majority of these components record information using Apple System Log, a system-wide log API that is also available to any third-party application on the system. The Apple System Log records log entries in a central database, and both application authors and users can configure additional log files in which to record interesting messages. Environments with strong data-protection requirements may require use of the Basic Security Module audit facility, which was designed to implement U.S. government and international requirements for operating system auditing. You should always try to use available standards rather than bespoke implementation to reflect the standards an organization might already have implemented for auditing.

8

Securing Network Connections

WHAT'S IN THIS CHAPTER?

- Authenticating users on remote services
- Reliance on data from distant sources
- Automatic service discovery
- Filtering network connections
- Protecting network traffic from eavesdroppers

Many of today's applications on both Mac and iPhone are not standalone, but rely on data available from a remote system on the network. The data may come from a peer system — another player in a multiplayer game, or another machine on the local network with which the application's data is synchronized. The relationship between the local app and the remote data source may be that of client and server, as when the application is designed to work with web services like social networking sites. Interacting with remote systems means providing a very easily accessible entry point to would-be attackers. The far end of a network connection could be under malicious control, as could ancillary services used to find and use that connection.

REMOTE AUTHENTICATION

When you're using remote services, it is almost always the case that the user accounts on the server are not the same as those on the Mac on which your application is running. The server is certainly not going to have shared accounts with an iPhone, which has no networked directory services. In Chapter 5 you discovered how the user's credentials for the distant server can be securely stored on the keychain, but now you need to get those credentials over the network. Different servers use different techniques for authenticating users on client computers, and each of these techniques has its own security requirements, benefits, and drawbacks.

HTTP Authentication

The HTTP protocol has a built-in capability for negotiating authentication. When a client requests a resource with limited access, the server responds with code 401 (unauthorized), along with a WWW-Authenticate header with more information about the authentication requirement. If you visit a protected resource in a web browser and see the standard "The server requires a password" dialog, the site-specific text presented in the dialog comes from that WWW-Authenticate header.

The Internet standards document for HTTP authentication is RFC 2617, which describes two methods for completing the authentication process. In both methods, the client must repeat its request, with an Authorization header containing a response to the WWW-Authenticate challenge. When using Basic mode, the client just sends the username and password in plain-text form in the header. Anyone who observes the network traffic during a Basic mode authentication can easily obtain the user's credentials. The alternative is Digest mode authentication, in which the client calculates a hash based on the credentials, the details of the request, and a "nonce" value sent by the server, and returns that. The "nonce" value is a number chosen by the server at random, that changes for each authentication request. The server is protected against replay attacks by this nonce value, as clients cannot provide the same hash in response to different authentication challenges. Using Digest mode lets you get around having to send the password unencrypted over the network.

Digest mode protects only against attackers "sniffing" the password in transit and replay attacks (capturing the authentication data and sending it again to the same server); it is not a complete security measure. An eavesdropper capable of observing the authentication traffic can just ignore it, and capture the protected resource when that gets sent to the client.

An attacker can introduce a proxy server between client and server that intercepts and forwards HTTP communications between the two systems. The proxy, seeing a digest authentication challenge from the server, rewrites it as a basic challenge to capture the user's password. It then uses the password to satisfy the digest request, and neither client nor server an detect any suspicious behavior. This attack is a member of the man-in-the-middle *class, so called because the proxy server has been inserted between the two legitimate parties.*

The only ways to avoid confidential information's being intercepted over an HTTP channel are either to arrange for the network to be inaccessible to third parties (which is not feasible on the Internet), or to encrypt the asset so that if it is recovered by an attacker, it cannot be deciphered.

In Cocoa and Cocoa Touch, the negotiation of which authentication scheme to use and generation of the appropriate response header is encapsulated in the URL-loading mechanism. NSURLConnection delegate objects receive a -connection:didReceiveAuthenticationChallenge: if the application needs to supply credentials to complete the download. Use of this delegate method is demonstrated in Listing 8-1.

Available for download on Wrox.com

LISTING 8-1: Using HTTP authentication from Cocoa [http_authAppDelegate.m]

```
- (void)connection: (NSURLConnection *)conn
didReceiveAuthenticationChallenge: (NSURLAuthenticationChallenge *)challenge {
    NSAssert(conn == connection, @"unknown URL connection");
    if ([challenge previousFailureCount] == 0) {
        // prompt the user for credentials
        [NSApp beginSheet: authSheet
           modalForWindow: window
            modalDelegate: self
           didEndSelector: @selector(sheetDidEnd:returnCode:contextInfo:)
              contextInfo: challenge];
    }
    else {
        //one failed attempt is a bit harsh, but in this case enough
        NSLog(@"user failed authentication for connection: %@",
              [challenge sender]);
        [connection cancel];
        self.connection = nil;
    }

}

- (void)sheetDidEnd: (NSWindow *)endedSheet
         returnCode: (NSInteger)returnCode
        contextInfo: (void *)info {
    NSURLAuthenticationChallenge *challenge = info;
    if (returnCode == NSOKButton) {
        //use the credentials we were given
        NSString *user = [userField stringValue];
        NSString *pass = [passwordField stringValue];
        NSURLCredential *cred = [[NSURLCredential alloc]
                                 initWithUser: user
                                 password: pass
                                 persistence: NSURLCredentialPersistenceNone];
        [[challenge sender] useCredential: cred
               forAuthenticationChallenge: challenge];
        [cred release];
    }
    else {
        //the user cancelled authentication
        [[challenge sender] cancelAuthenticationChallenge: challenge];
    }
}

- (void)takeCredentials:(id)sender {
    [NSApp endSheet: authSheet returnCode: NSOKButton];
}

- (void)cancelAuth:(id)sender {
    [NSApp endSheet: authSheet returnCode: NSCancelButton];
}
```

The application presents a sheet, as shown in Figure 8-1, allowing the user to enter a username and password for the web site. To demonstrate unsuccessful authentication results, the application allows only one try at entering a password: if you enter incorrect details it gives up on the loading attempt. Note that the URL-loading system in Cocoa includes a search for credentials on the keychain, so if you try to visit a URL for which you already have stored information it will ask to use that username and password before the method calling the sheet is displayed.

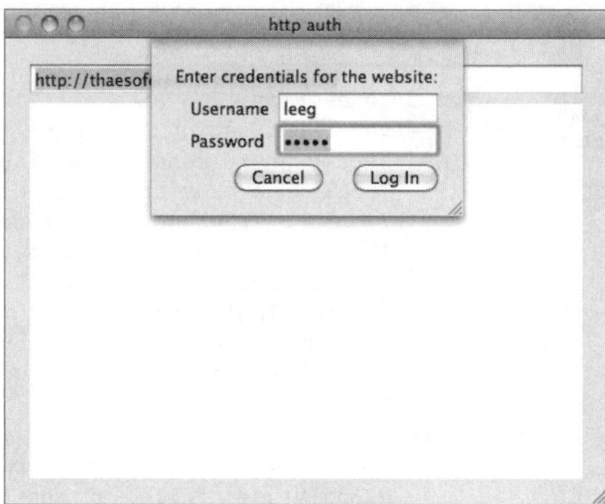

FIGURE 8-1: Prompting a user for a web site's password

The NSURLCredential class, which encapsulates the username and password to be passed to the web server, can also handle identity-based authentication using SecIdentityRef and SecCertificateRef objects, which were discussed in the section on Certificate, Key and Trust Services in Chapter 5. Using digital identities for authenticating users to servers is still uncommon — identifying the server through certificates is much more common, as this chapter's later section on SSL demonstrates. It has an advantage over password-based authentication in that the user does not need to have a separate password to remember for every different web site. If two servers trust the same identity, the user can offer that identity to each server. There is also a disadvantage: the user must keep the private key secret, but it must be available on every system for which the user wishes to log in to servers using that identity — so there must be some way to protect the private key in transit. One common way to transfer private keys is in PKCS#12 files, which are password-protected. Again, the security of the system is limited by users' abilities to remember distinct and complex passwords, although in this case the password is used only for disseminating the identity.

Other Authentication Methods for Web Services

Go to a web site like Twitter, Google, or the Apple Store and you won't be presented with a 401 HTTP status and a standard authentication dialog, as described earlier. Instead the web site will present an HTML form in which you can enter your log-in details, which are then sent to the server as part of an HTTP POST submission. The server maintains its own identification and authentication system, and keeps track of your log-in session itself. As a result of this custom user-identification mechanism, applications that consume web services often need to deal with authentication systems other than the WWW-Authenticate portion of the HTTP standard.

Kerberos

Kerberos was introduced in Chapter 2 as a ticket-based authentication system, providing both a single sign-on facility (the user authenticates once to get a ticket, then presents that ticket to log in to other services) and a mutual authentication facility (the user is confident of the server's identity when he gains a service ticket). Kerberos is popular in enterprise web applications, as network administrators can use the same KDC to issue tickets for desktop log-ins and web applications. A user who has gained a ticket-granting ticket when logging in to her desktop computer gets single sign-on access to the web applications.

The same GSSAPI functions discussed in Chapter 2 can be used to access Kerberized web services.

OpenID and OAuth

With the proliferation of different web sites and web services in use today, maintaining and remembering passwords for each is a mammoth undertaking for many users. Relying on Kerberos single sign-on across services run by disparate companies and organizations on the Internet is not a satisfactory solution, as it would rely on a shared global ticket-distribution service. A common solution adopted by many web service providers is federated log-in, in which a user can use an account on one web service as identification for numerous other services.

OpenID allows one web site to delegate authentication to another. Every user has a unique identifier, which is a URL identifying that user to the OpenID provider, for example `http://leeg.provider.example.com`. The user visits a *relying site* (one that uses OpenID for identification), and enters his or her OpenID URL. The relying site discovers the provider from the URL, and asks that site to verify the identity of the user. Verification can either be immediate, if the user has a session in progress with the provider site, or involve the provider site's challenging the user and requiring authentication. OpenID does not impose any requirements for the authentication step: passwords can be used, or a more stringent test of identity like biometric analysis. If the provider is satisfied with the user's identity, it redirects the user back to the relying site with a token confirming the user is as claimed.

To avoid spoofing attacks, developers of relying OpenID services and applications should consider carefully which providers they trust and the privilege given to users identified by provider sites. Because authentication has been delegated to the provider service, relying services cannot impose constraints such as password policies, which would be possible were authentication carried out locally.

OAuth takes the idea of federated log-in further, by allowing relying services and applications to share the account of the providing service without having access to the credentials of that service's users. As an illustration of the idea, consider Twitter. The main web site lets users upload short messages, but users want to share pictures and videos, so third-party services like Twitpic and Yfrog have appeared. Traditionally, there would be two ways for a user to post a picture using Twitpic and Twitter:

- Upload the picture to Twitpic. Copy a URL from Twitpic. Log in to Twitter, paste the URL into a tweet and send it.
- Upload the picture to Twitpic. Enter Twitter credentials into Twitpic, so it can log in on the user's behalf to post a tweet.

The first of these alternatives leads to an unsatisfactory experience, as the two services are disconnected even though the user is trying to use them together. The second choice suffers from a trust problem: the user must enter identifying details into a third-party website. A malicious Twitter application can harvest those credentials to gain unauthorized access to users' Twitter accounts — and potentially other accounts, if users recycle the same usernames and passwords elsewhere.

Using OAuth, users authenticate with the providing service (Twitter, in this case) and gain a token for interacting with the relying service (Twitpic). This token allows the relying service to interact with the provider on behalf of the user, without needing to collect the user's credentials or even identify the user for itself. The relationship among the three parties is demonstrated graphically in Figure 8-2.

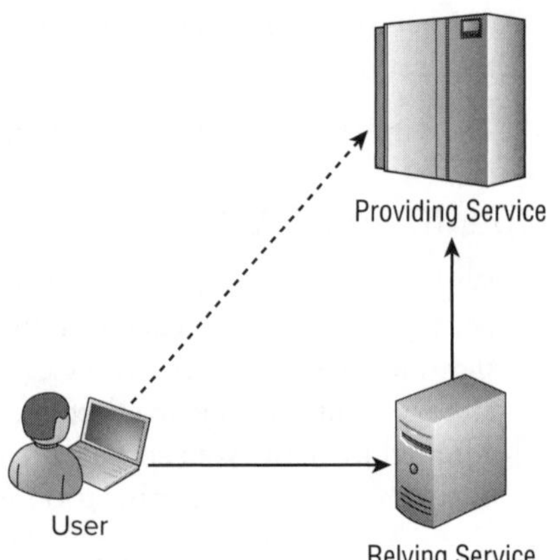

FIGURE 8-2: The three parties involved in an OAuth interaction

This interaction involves a collection of confidential items. The user's log-in credentials for the providing service should be known only to the user and the provider. The client (relying) service has a client secret, known only to itself and the provider, to authenticate the client to the provider, and a client key used for encrypting content transferred between the client and the provider. Finally, for each successfully authenticated session there is a session token identifying to the provider the instance of the identified user interacting with the known client. That session token must not be leaked to other clients or users.

Note that in desktop applications, the client secret and key will be distributed to all users, so the providing service cannot rely on their being unknown to malicious users. OAuth is then suitable for two distinct classes of interaction; one in which the client identity is not important and is performing tasks directly on behalf of a user, as a replacement for the provider service's web interface, and one in which the client service itself performs a useful task and the user works with it in conjunction with the providing service. These classes of operation are referred to as *two-legged* and *three-legged operation*, respectively.

On the Mac and iPhone, it is possible to use OAuth through Objective-C as a client application with a library called OAuthConsumer. OAuthConsumer provides an NSMutableURLRequest subclass that uses OAuth data in the background, once a session has been negotiated. Note that because of the requirements of three-legged authentication, the client and the user must both authenticate with the provider; this reduces the potential both for misuse by unknown users and for Trojan horse clients' taking advantage of the provider service.

The OAuthConsumer library is available from Google Code at `http://code.google.com/p/oauth/`. *Documentation on using OAuthConsumer can be found at* `http://code.google.com/p/oauthconsumer/wiki/UsingOAuthConsumer`.

While this book was being written Twitter announced an extension to OAuth with a better user experience for two-legged authentication, in which the relying service collects the credentials and passes them to the provider. Twitter has yet to provide documentation or a specification for this extension, however.

PRIVILEGE BOUNDARIES IN NETWORKED APPLICATIONS

The connection between an application or daemon and remote systems over the Internet clearly represents a privilege boundary, but rather than being between two users with different rights on the system, this boundary stands between all the assets of your application and a world of entirely unknown entities. Legitimate users, useful services, and attackers alike could all be on the remote end of a network connection. With this in mind, it is unreasonable to assume that all data received on such a connection is real information from a friendly source, and even that all data sent on such a connection will get exclusively to the legitimate intended recipient. As discussed in Chapter 1, there are many intermediaries between two computers communicating on the Internet, including service providers, domain name services, network operators, and network equipment manufacturers. Even when information does go to its intended destination, it can often be inspected by a snoop, especially on wireless networks.

While this book was being written, researchers were able to break two common encryption mechanisms used on GSM networks (see `http://www.nytimes.com/2009/12/29/technology/29hack.html` *and* `http://www.gearlog.com/2010/01/researchers_crack_3g_network_e.php` *for more information). The KASUMI mechanism is used on 3G networks to protect iPhone and iPad data, and once a worldwide communications standard like GSM depends on a particular encryption protocol it can take years and millions of dollars to replace, even if that protocol is found to contain flaws. Do not assume that when an iPhone is on a 3G network it is safe from snoopers.*

When designing your application's network communications scheme, always ask yourself whether any particular communication is absolutely necessary to the app's function. If it is not needed, leave it out. The Taligent software company had a maxim, "There is no code faster than no code," and a similar statement could be made with respect to network security: there is no communication safer than no communication.

For each remaining command or request to travel over the network, there are three assets to consider in the threat model: the data itself, the channel over which that data is sent, and the module or component that will interact with the data. One attacker might want to read all the information sent to your app, while another doesn't care about the content but notices that the socket receiving the data can be fed bad data to cause malicious behavior in the app.

Penetration testers have a technique called *fuzz testing*, or *fuzzing*, which is discussed in detail in Chapter 9. For now it is sufficient to know that fuzzing involves sending unexpected data over communications channels to observe the behavior of the receiving application. Attackers also use fuzzing to investigate the operation of a target app and search for vulnerabilities. If a particular command channel calls for a ten-byte command packet, attackers will try sending nine bytes, or eleven, or three megabytes, or ten bytes that don't match a known command. They will also try variations on the data, for example fuzzing with integers when only letters are expected. Your application should be ready for these cases and able to respond in a known and reliable fashion. Attackers might also try sending many times more legitimate commands than your application usually encounters in any time interval, in the hope that it cannot cope with the higher rate of transmission.

PING OF DEATH

One particularly insidious example of the misuse of a communications channel by means of bad data is the "ping of death," a vulnerability that affected DOS, Windows, Macintosh, Linux, and some UNIX operating systems in the mid-1990s. Ping packets (Internet Communications Messaging Protocol echo requests, or ICMP Type 8, Code 0 packets), were expected by many operating system networking stacks to be exactly 65,535 bytes long, the maximum length of a single Internet packet. However, by using the fragmentation and recombination features of the Internet protocol, attackers could send as much data as they wanted to a target computer, which would then attempt to reconstruct it all into a single large ping message.

The operating systems affected had a fixed buffer big enough for only one packet to hold ping messages, so the result of the recombination step was that all the extra data was written into unallocated memory. The networking capability of the operating systems was part of the kernel, so even in systems with memory-protection capabilities the effect was to overwrite any memory with data written by the attacker. Theoretically the target computers could have been taken over and made to run any code of the attacker's choosing, but the usual result was either a crash or a spontaneous reboot of the target.

The ultimate root cause of ping of death was a failure on the part of the protocol implementers to understand the results of an interaction between two features of a very complex protocol. Further information and sample code related to the vulnerability (now long obsolete) can be found at `http://insecure.org/sploits/ping-o-death.html`.

A common way to deal with potentially dangerous data coming from the network is to have a *sanitization* step. The goal of sanitization is to inspect data as it arrives, and rewrite or discard illegitimate data before passing it on to the real recipient. The class or module responsible for handling the data sees only legitimate — or at least acceptable — traffic. A firewall is a simple, configurable implementation of the sanitization pattern: administrators indicate that certain types of network packets are unacceptable, and the firewall discards them before they reach their destination. Discarding bad data is much more common than trying to rewrite it to make sense, as it can be hard to decipher what (if any) original meaning there was in a broken message. If an attacker was just trying to find a vulnerability in the app, then processing a message based on something similar to the attacker's fuzz attempt makes little sense.

An effective sanitization module must be like the gate in a city wall, in that it must be the only route in and out of the application. If attackers can avoid the border guards by crossing the border elsewhere, there is little value in employing the guards. Border guards can carry out their job in two different ways: by keeping out only people known to be attackers, or by only letting in visitors known to be trusted. Each data sanitization technique works in one of these two ways, too. You can either "blacklist" input known to be bad, or "whitelist" input known to be good. The whitelisting approach provides better protection, because the range of acceptable data is explicitly defined. However a blacklist can be more readily re-used in protecting different entry points.

A good example of the problems that result from not sanitizing network input comes in the form of the web browser. All major web browsers have suffered from vulnerabilities that can be triggered by visits to malicious web pages. Such pages often take advantage of the fact that browsers will try to render even the most broken HTML documents, because standards-compliant HTML is a relatively scarce commodity on the Web. For example, many browsers were recently discovered to parse HTML tags found after the declared end of the document (the </html> tag). As soon as an application starts working with nonconforming data, there is literally no way to predict what it will receive or how it should handle specific cases.

DOES 'BONJOUR' MEAN IT'S ADIEU TO NETWORK SECURITY?

Bonjour is Apple's marketing name for a collection of networking technologies built around zeroconf network creation (also known as the link-local Internet protocol or IPv4LL), multicast DNS (mDNS), and DNS-based service discovery (DNS-SD). These technologies combine to provide automatic network configuration for Macs, iPhones, and other systems and devices.

Consider a home network with a couple of computers, a smartphone, and a printer connected via a wireless link. In most homes, neither of the computers would be a server, and neither would there be an IT support expert to configure a server or the network structure. Devices use IPv4LL to automatically assign themselves Internet addresses in the range of 169.254.x.y, so that each computer and appliance on the network has a unique address and they can all communicate with each other. Each runs its own DNS server, including DNS-SD records describing the network services available on that computer. The DNS servers all respond to requests on a multicast address, so when one device wants to find a service it asks all the other devices on the network whether they provide that service. Those that do then respond, allowing the first device to find the service it needs. In this way the whole network structure is decentralized, but the different systems and appliances can still find each other.

As an example, imagine that the user on one of the computers on the home network needs to print a document. This user presses Command+P, bringing up the print dialog. The computer automatically makes an mDNS request for print services, which the printer receives and responds to. The computer discovers what the capabilities of the printer are and adds it to the print dialog, so the user chooses this printer and the computer sends it the document to print. The user has printed his document without needing to configure the printer, or tell the computer what model the printer is or its network location.

Networks can make use of parts of the Bonjour technology stack and still provide the same experience. Systems using the IPv6 protocol can automatically negotiate link-local connections without employing IPv4LL, and many routers include DHCP capabilities so that devices do not need to auto-negotiate IP addresses. Nonetheless, such systems can still make use of mDNS and service discovery to provide automatically discovered network services. Networks that are connected to the Internet typically have both multicast DNS and a configured DNS server to look up public domain names on the Internet, such as `www.wiley.com`. Mac OS X and iPhone OS both use the domain suffix `.local` to refer to Bonjour name service results, so `www.wiley.com` is a server on the Internet and `www.local` is on the local network.

In Cocoa, Bonjour service notification and discovery are encapsulated in the NSNetService and NSNetServiceBrowser classes. A server registers with Bonjour using NSNetService, which creates a record in the multicast DNS server for its computer. Clients use NSNetServiceBrowser to find instances of the server they are interested in. In Listing 8-2 a server is shown that simply reports to clients the hostname of its own computer.

LISTING 8-2: A network server registering for Bonjour service discovery [bonjour_server.m]

Available for download on Wrox.com

```
#import <Foundation/Foundation.h>
#import <unistd.h>

#define kPortNumber 1234

@interface GLServerNameVendor : NSObject <NSNetServiceDelegate> {
    NSSocketPort *socket;
    NSNetService *netService;
    NSFileHandle *fileHandle;
}

- (BOOL)publishService;
- (void)netServiceWillPublish: (NSNetService *)sender;
- (void)netServiceDidPublish: (NSNetService *)sender;
- (void)netService: (NSNetService *)sender didNotPublish: (NSDictionary *)error;
- (BOOL)startListening;
@end

@implementation GLServerNameVendor

- (BOOL)publishService {
    socket = [[NSSocketPort alloc] initWithTCPPort: kPortNumber];

    netService = [[NSNetService alloc] initWithDomain: @""
                                                 type: @"_hostname._tcp"
                                                 name: @""
                                                 port: kPortNumber];
    if (!netService) {
        NSLog(@"couldn't create a NSNetService object");
        return NO;
    }
    [netService setDelegate: self];
    [netService publish];
    return YES;
}

- (BOOL)startListening {
    int socketFD = [socket socket];
    if (socketFD < 0) {
        return NO;
    }
```

```
    fileHandle = [[NSFileHandle alloc]
                  initWithFileDescriptor: socketFD];
    [[NSNotificationCenter defaultCenter]
     addObserverForName: NSFileHandleConnectionAcceptedNotification
     object: fileHandle
     queue: nil
     usingBlock: ^(NSNotification *note) {
         NSFileHandle *connected = [[note userInfo]
                                    objectForKey:
NSFileHandleNotificationFileHandleItem];
         char hostname[256] = { 0 };
         gethostname(hostname, 256);
         NSData *hostnameBytes = [NSData dataWithBytes: hostname
                                                length: strlen(hostname)];
         [connected writeData: hostnameBytes];
         [connected closeFile];
         [fileHandle acceptConnectionInBackgroundAndNotify];
     }];
    [fileHandle acceptConnectionInBackgroundAndNotify];
    return YES;
}

#pragma mark NSNetService delegate methods
- (void)netServiceWillPublish: (NSNetService *)sender {
    NSLog(@"service will publish: %@", sender);
}
- (void)netServiceDidPublish: (NSNetService *)sender {
    NSLog(@"service did publish: %@", sender);
}
- (void)netService: (NSNetService *)sender didNotPublish: (NSDictionary *)error {
    NSLog(@"service failed to publish, error: %@", error);
}

- (void)dealloc {
    [netService release];
    [[NSNotificationCenter defaultCenter] removeObserver: self];
    [fileHandle release];
    [socket release];
    [super dealloc];
}
@end

int main (int argc, const char * argv[]) {
    NSAutoreleasePool * pool = [[NSAutoreleasePool alloc] init];

    GLServerNameVendor *vendor = [[GLServerNameVendor alloc] init];
    if (![vendor publishService]) {
        NSLog(@"couldn't register Bonjour service");
        [vendor release];
        return -1;
    }
    if (![vendor startListening]) {
        NSLog(@"couldn't listen for inbound connections");
        [vendor release];
        return -1;
```

continues

LISTING 8-2 *(continued)*

```
    }
    //now just run the run loop forever, to service requests
    [[NSRunLoop currentRunLoop] run];

    [vendor dealloc];
    [pool drain];
    return 0;
}
```

The net service object is given an empty domain, indicating that it should use the default domain. In principle there could be multiple Bonjour domains, but in practice most networks use just the default link-local domain. The type, "_hostname._tcp", is a made-up service name to distinguish this hostname-reporting server from web servers, print spoolers and other network services. Finally, the service is given an empty name. This causes Bonjour to choose a default name for the service, which is normally the same as the computer name. If you use a custom name, it should be suitable for displaying in a list of services to help a user choose among multiple services running on the same network.

Once the service is published, it appears in the multicast DNS records for the system on which it is running. You can inspect the registered services by sending the SIGINFO signal to the mDNSResponder process, which manages the Bonjour service-discovery records:

```
jormungand:~ leeg$ sudo killall -INFO mDNSResponder
Password:
jormungand:~ leeg$ sudo cat /var/log/system.log
[...lots of output snipped...]
Jan 29 22:35:55 jormungand mDNSResponder[17]:  40: DNSServiceRegister
jormungand._hostname._tcp.local. 1234/1234
[...lots more output...]
```

The _hostname._tcp service appears in the multicast DNS information, so the service has been successfully registered. Of course, if you know where the server is you do not need to use Bonjour to find it.

```
jormungand:~ leeg$ nc 127.0.0.1 1234
jormungand.local
```

Bonjour is useful when you do not know beforehand the location of any servers, and want your application to connect to servers on the local network. An NSNetServiceBrowser-using client such as that shown in Listing 8-3 will be able to find servers.

LISTING 8-3: A client uses NSNetServiceBrowser to find servers [bonjour_browser.m]

Available for download on Wrox.com

```
#import <Foundation/Foundation.h>

@interface GLServerNameBrowser : NSObject <NSNetServiceBrowserDelegate> {
    NSNetServiceBrowser *browser;
}

- (void)startBrowsing;
```

```
@end

@implementation GLServerNameBrowser

- (void)startBrowsing {
    browser = [[NSNetServiceBrowser alloc] init];
    [browser setDelegate: self];
    [browser searchForServicesOfType: @"_hostname._tcp"
                            inDomain: @""];
}

#pragma mark NSNetServiceBrowserDelegate methods
- (void)netServiceBrowserWillSearch:(NSNetServiceBrowser *)aNetServiceBrowser {
    NSLog(@"browser is beginning to search");
}

- (void)netServiceBrowserDidStopSearch:(NSNetServiceBrowser *)aNetServiceBrowser
{
    NSLog(@"browser has completed search");
}

- (void)netServiceBrowser:(NSNetServiceBrowser *)aNetServiceBrowser
           didNotSearch:(NSDictionary *)errorDict {
    NSLog(@"browser did not search, error: %@", errorDict);
}

- (void)netServiceBrowser:(NSNetServiceBrowser *)aNetServiceBrowser
          didFindService:(NSNetService *)aNetService
              moreComing:(BOOL)moreComing {
    NSLog(@"service found with name %@, other updates %@on the way",
          [aNetService name],
          moreComing ? @"" : @"not ");
}

- (void)netServiceBrowser:(NSNetServiceBrowser *)aNetServiceBrowser
        didRemoveService:(NSNetService *)aNetService
              moreComing:(BOOL)moreComing {
    NSLog(@"service removed with name %@, other updates %@on the way",
          [aNetService name],
          moreComing ? @"" : @"not ");
}

- (void)dealloc {
    [browser release];
    [super dealloc];
}

@end


int main(int argc, char **argv) {
    NSAutoreleasePool * pool = [[NSAutoreleasePool alloc] init];

    GLServerNameBrowser *browser = [[GLServerNameBrowser alloc] init];
```

continues

LISTING 8-3 *(continued)*

```
        [browser startBrowsing];

        // run forever to look for servers
        [[NSRunLoop currentRunLoop] run];

        [browser release];
        [pool drain];
        return 0;
    }
```

The following snippet shows the output of this browser when I ran it with the server already running on the same computer. Some minutes later I started the same server on a different computer and then terminated it, before finally killing the browser process.

```
jormungand:~ leeg$ ./bonjour_browser
2010-01-29 23:39:47.135 bonjour_browser[1330:903] browser is beginning to search
2010-01-29 23:39:47.138 bonjour_browser[1330:903] service found with name
jormungand, other updates not on the way
2010-01-29 23:43:56.064 bonjour_browser[1330:903] service found with name heimdall,
other updates not on the way
2010-01-29 23:44:04.165 bonjour_browser[1330:903] service removed with name
heimdall, other updates not on the way
^C
```

You can see that, confusingly, the browser reports that there are no more results coming with each update, even though it continues to notice subsequent changes to the state. What the NSNetServiceBrowser object is actually reporting is whether it has other updates ready to report when the delegate message is sent. If the browser finds 10 servers at once, it will send 10 delegate messages sequentially. If the services are populating some UI like a table view, it would be visually jarring for the table view to update 10 times in rapid succession. The browser reports that there are still updates coming with the first nine servers but not the 10th, so that a controller can wait and coalesce the view updates. NSNetServiceBrowser continues to notice changes in the background and reports when they come in.

So Bonjour and NSNetService make it easy for computers to find services on their networks and take advantage of them. But do they perhaps make it too easy? Couldn't an attacker place a device on the network that responds to mDNS requests, directing client computers and phones to malicious servers?

Whether an attacker could truly achieve that depends on the level of access the attacker has to the network. A cabled network in a physically restricted environment is a different proposition from an open wireless access point in a café, with different risks associated. However, a single compromised host in the network could be repurposed for attacks (which is an increasingly common use of malware) — it is therefore better to assume in the security model that the local network is simply not trustworthy, building in explicit validation of identity for hosts or services you need to work with. Once a device is connected to a network it is free to observe and respond to mDNS traffic as it chooses, so it can insert itself into the list of servers available to clients on the same network. Even if the user knows there should be only one shared music library on the network instead of two, identifying which is the correct one could be beyond the user's technical capability.

A neat solution to this problem has been borrowed by many applications from the world of Bluetooth Personal Area Networks, where choosing which device to "pair" with has long been an issue. To examine its use in the Bonjour context, take a look at the Apple Remote application, which allows an iPhone or iPod to control iTunes running on a Mac or PC. If iTunes allowed any iPhone to control the playback, a miscreant on the same network as a legitimate user could spoil the user's music enjoyment. To mitigate that threat, the Remote application must be paired with the iTunes library. However, if this process is too complicated, then the benefits of Bonjour as a zero-configuration network service will be lost.

To pair, the user first puts the iPhone into "add library" mode. This presents the user with a four-digit passcode, shown in Figure 8-3. The iPhone is advertising a service, which iTunes on the computer discovers and displays in the source list. Selecting the device in the source list prompts the user of the computer to enter the passcode displayed on the phone's screen, shown in Figure 8-4.

FIGURE 8-3: Displaying a pairing passcode on the iPhone

In order to pair the two devices, the same person must be able to see the iPhone display and control the computer. The iPhone also tells the user its name, to further reduce the chance for confusion. Notice that the pairing could have been done the other way around, with a passcode shown on the computer and entered on the phone. That is an easier process to subvert, because it requires viewing the computer's screen and controlling the phone — if an attacker is using his or her own phone and the monitor is easy to view, those conditions can be met by the attacker. To the user the two processes are roughly equivalent, so the one that's harder to misuse is preferred.

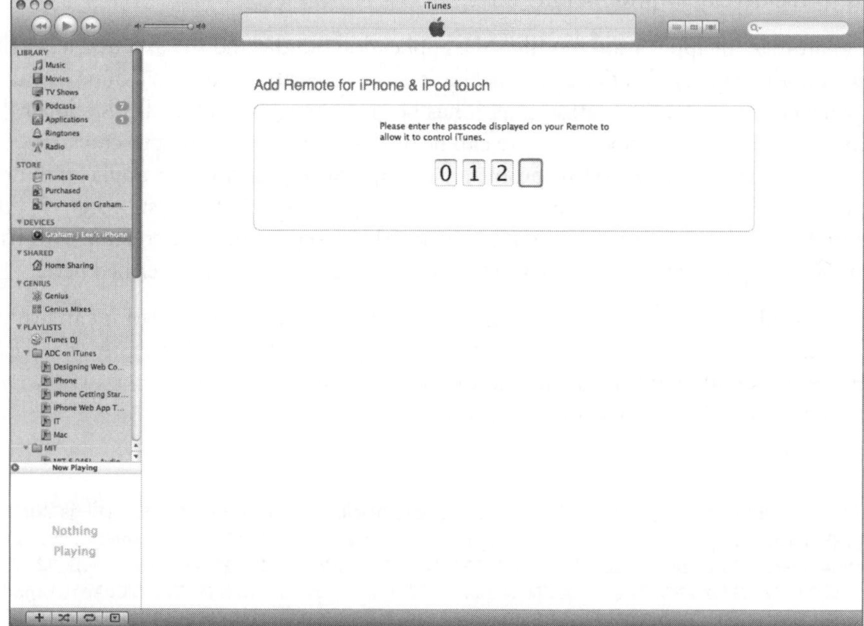

FIGURE 8-4: Entering the passcode in iTunes

WORKING WITH THE FIREWALL

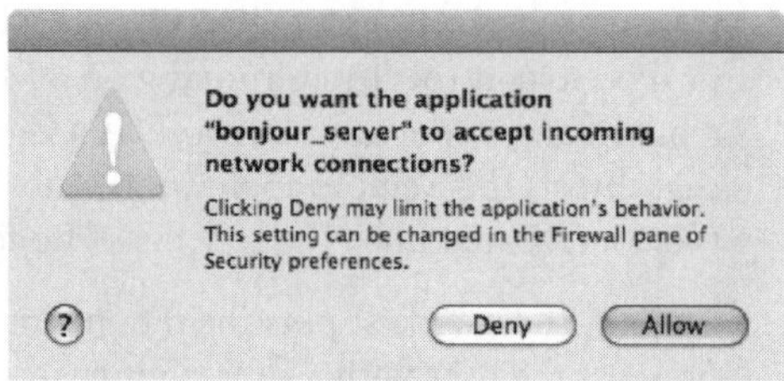

FIGURE 8-5: Firewall notification in Mac OS X

If you compiled and ran the Bonjour server in Listing 8-2 on version 10.5 or later of Mac OS X, and have the firewall configured, you would have been presented with a message similar to the one in Figure 8-5.

This alert comes from the application firewall. Rather than limiting which packets get processed by the computer, as traditional firewalls do, the application firewall restricts which applications are permitted to listen on network sockets. Any packet sent to the machine will be received but only approved applications can accept and work with network connections. Policy based on applications is arguably much more user-friendly. Many users wouldn't understand the implications of a given IP's using a protocol and random port, but they can decide if Skype.app should be allowed.

Application Firewall Behavior

The application firewall identifies different processes using their code signature identities, which were introduced in Chapter 4. If an application does not have an identity, then the firewall will sign it itself to create an ad hoc identity. When the user downloads a new (unsigned) version of the application, Mac OS X creates a new ad hoc identity. The operating system cannot tell from the two identities that the two applications are different versions of the same product, so any firewall configuration applicable to the first version is not relevant to the second. In short, applications without a developer-provided identity will prompt the user for firewall exemptions with every update, while applications signed by the developer prompt only once.

Attaching a code signature to an application modifies the application bundle and the executable, as the signature is embedded in the app. Applications that include custom integrity validation can be confused by ad hoc signing, which changes the application after it has been deployed (i.e., after the developer has finished with the app). Use of an ad hoc signature can be interpreted as an attempt to crack the application. While the long-term solution to this problem is to sign the application, the application firewall configuration file (`/Library/Preferences/com.apple.alf.plist`) includes a list of *sign exceptions* — conditions under which the firewall avoids causing an ad hoc signature to be created. This list identifies a selection of third-party applications that have experienced the problem described here.

The format of the com.apple.alf.plist file is not documented by Apple, but inspection of it can lead to an understanding of how the firewall operates. A top-level configuration key, "allowsignedenabled," defines whether applications with valid signatures should be permitted to listen on the network. Each application is identified with a dictionary similar to this one:

```
<dict>
      <key>alias</key>
      <data>PD94bWwgdmVyc2lvbj0iMS4wIiBlbmNvZGluZz0iVVRGLTgiPz4KPCFET0NUWVBFIHBsaXN0IFBV
QkxJQyAiLS8vQXBwbGUvL0RURCBQTElTVCAxLjAvL0VOIiAiaHR0cDovL3d3dy5hcHBsZS5jb20vRFREcy9Qcm9w
ZXJ0eUxpc3QtMS4wLmR0ZCI+CjxwbGlzdCB2ZXJzaW9uPSIxLjAiPgo8ZGF0YT4KQUFBQUFBR2VBQU1BQVF4Tl1X
TnBiblJ2YzJnZ1NFUUFBQUFBQUFBQUFBQUFBQUFBQUFERTJQWU1TQ3NBQUFFZnVmNFhSR1ZzYVdOcApiM1Z6SUV4
cFluSmhjbmtnTWk1aGNIQUFBQUFBQUFBQUFBQUFBQUFBQUFBQUFBQUFBQUFBQUFBQUFBQUFBQUFBQUFBQUFB
```

```
QUFBCkFVWmdWOGN2bFM4QUFBQUFBQUFBQVAvLy8vOEFBQWtnQUFBQUFBQUFBQUFBQUFBQUFBQUFERUZ3Y0d4cFky
RjBhVzl1Y3dBUUFBZ0EKQU1UWTUvd0FBQUFSQUFnQUFNY3ZsUzhBQUFBQkFBd0JIN24rQUFMcHBRQUF1WXdBQWdB
OFRXRmphVzUwYjNOb01FaEVPbFZ6WlhKegpPbXhsWldjNlFYQndiR2xqWVhScGIyNXpPa1JsYkdsamFXOTFjeUJN
YVdKeVl5SjVJRE11WVhCd0FBNEFNQUFYQUVRQVpRQnNBR2tBCll3QnBBRzhBZFFCCekFDQUFUQUJwQUdJQWNnQmhB
SElBZVFBZ0FESUFMZ0JoQUhBQWNBQVBBQm9BREFCTkFHRUFZd0JwQUc0QWRBQnYKQUhNQWFBQWdBRWdBUkFBU0FD
OVZjM1lZ5Y3k5c1pXVm5MMEZ3Y0d4cFkyRjBhVzl1Y3k5RVpXeHBZZMmx2ZFhNZ1RHbGljbUZ5ZVNBeQpMbUZ3Y0FB
QUV3QUJMd0QvL3dBQQo8L2RhdGE+CjwvcGxpc3Q+Cg==</data>
       <key>bundleid</key>
       <string>com.delicious-monster.library2</string>
       <key>reqdata</key>
       <data>+t4MAAAAAFgAAAABAAAABgAAAAIAAAAeY29tLmRlbGljaW91cy1tb25zdGVyLmxpYnJhcnkyAAAA
AAAE/////wAAABTEP+bjkYZegFsD6mwQge9dR/5a0w==</data>
       <key>state</key>
       <integer>0</integer>
</dict>
```


An alias is a filesystem record that can track files even if they are moved — see “Aliases and Bookmarks” in Chapter 3. The dictionary also contains the application’s bundle identifier, and a code-signing requirement (a condition the code’s identity must satisfy to accept that the firewall is looking at the correct application) in binary form. The *state* key indicates whether the application is permitted to listen on the network: a value of 0 means that it has permission, 2 means that it is denied. Other values for the state cannot be configured through the user interface.

There is no API for modifying the firewall rules; all changes to the configuration have to be made by the user either in System Preferences or in response to a dialog such as the one in Figure 8-5.

ipfw

Before the application firewall was introduced in Leopard, Mac OS X relied on the ipfw kernel packet filter, from the FreeBSD project. The newer releases of OS X also include the ipfw filter, though the System Preferences firewall GUI does not permit users to configure it. A command-line configuration interface and an API both exist.

Ipfw (like its close relation, ip6fw, which controls access to Ipv6 networks) does not identify applications connecting to the network. It maintains a list of rules specifying what should happen to packets that are sent or received on particular ports. The rules are numbered from 1 to 65535, and whenever a packet appears at a network interface the rules are evaluated in order. Multiple rules can have the same number, in which case they are evaluated in order of insertion. The first rule to match the properties of the packet defines what happens to that packet, so that low-numbered rules should be more specific and high-numbered rules more general. The last rule, number 65535, is hard-coded on Mac OS X to allow any packet. Because Mac OS X has another firewall module, Apple makes light use of ipfw. The entire default configuration on Snow Leopard is the default allow rule. If *stealth mode* is enabled in the Security section of System Preferences, the following rule is added:

```
deny log icmp from any to me in icmptypes 8
```

That rule says that packets using the ICMP protocol, that are of ICMP message type 8, with any source address and an address on this computer (“me”) as the destination, , should be denied and that a message should be recorded in the log when this happens. Message type 8 is the echo request message (i.e., ping), so this rule drops ping requests destined for the computer on which the firewall is running.

The super-user inspects and changes the configuration of ipfw through a command-line tool, also called ipfw. This tool uses the same API, based on socket options, that is available to third-party developers for viewing and modifying the configuration. To read details of the ipfw configuration, create a raw IP socket and use getsockopt(). Similarly, the setsockopt() call can be used to change the configuration. In each case, a structure of type ip_fw, detailed in Listing 8-4, holds each rule.

LISTING 8-4: The ipfw rule structure (from /usr/include/netinet/ip_fw2.h)

```
struct ip_fw {
    u_int32_t version;          /* The API version.
                                 * Always use IP_FW_CURRENT_API_VERSION */
    void *context;              /* Context pointer; unique for each rule */
    struct ip_fw *next;         /* linked list of rules */
    struct ip_fw *next_rule;       /* next rule if this rule has a 'skipto' */
    u_int16_t act_ofs;          /* offset to the action (allow/deny) */
    u_int16_t cmd_len;          /* size of the instruction structure */
    u_int16_t rulenum;          /* rule number (1..65535) */
    u_int8_t set;               /* rule set (0..31) */
    u_int32_t set_masks[2];     /* masks for working with sets */
    u_int8_t _pad;              /* padding (unused) */
    u_int64_t pcnt;             /* Number of matching packets seen */
    u_int64_t bcnt;             /* Number of matching bytes seen */
    u_int32_t timestamp;        /* Time the last matching packet was seen */
    u_int32_t reserved_1;       /* reserved: always set to 0 */
    u_int32_t reserved_2;       /* reserved: always set to 0 */
    ipfw_insn cmd[1];           /* start of the command structure(s) */
};
```

The final field in this structure is a variable-length storage for instruction structures. Every instruction contains an operation code, indicating what the instruction means. The template instruction structure provides space for a single uint16 argument, but some arguments require more space than that, so not all instructions are the same size. When working with ipfw rules in code, you must be careful to calculate pointer offsets correctly to avoid crashing your application or configuring it in an unexpected way. It is rare to need to deal with ipfw on systems newer than 10.5, though administrators on some heterogeneous networks may still use it to provide consistent firewall rules across multiple platforms.

NETWORK CONFIGURATION WITH SYSTEMCONFIGURATION

When an application communicates with network services, having an accurate view of the network is important. Should the application fail to notice a change in its environment, it could stop talking to the computer at the remote end of the connection (an availability risk) or even start sending to and receiving from a different machine (affecting the integrity and confidentiality of the network traffic).

Mac OS X's networking features are based on UNIX's connection capabilities, which were designed at a time when computers were installed in a single location and connected to a relatively static network. The original Macintosh, in the speech it made with a synthesized voice at its 1984 introduction, (`http://www.youtube.com/watch?v=G0FtgZNOD44`) said, "Never trust a computer you can't lift," but you can trust it on one thing: it isn't likely to move very far." Therefore UNIX's network software was designed to work with unchanging environments — a computer always had the same address, as would all the other computers it needed to communicate with. Furthermore, as all the other computers were run by military or academic establishments, the other machines out there could be trusted.

The environment of a modern Mac is entirely different from this scenario. During one day, a MacBook laptop could be used on a home wireless network to check the morning news, then connected to a 3G network during the commute into the office, and plugged into the corporate ethernet during the day. When the user goes out for a cup of coffee, the laptop is used on a different wireless network. With each of these environments, the network configuration is different, the neighboring computers change, and the amount of control the computer's owner has over the network varies. Mac OS X handles these changes with little to no effort on the part of the user. In addition to DHCP and Bonjour for dynamic configuration and service discovery, the operating system watches for changes to the network environment and updates its view of the world accordingly. It also allows users to maintain preset lists of location-based network settings, and choose different settings when they move between locations.

Access to these capabilities is provided by the SystemConfiguration framework, which is also responsible for maintaining the network configuration state. Many applications that offer a network-based feature can present different user interfaces depending on whether the feature can currently be used, indicating the availability to the user. The availability of a network connection can also have security implications; if a remote auditing facility cannot be used the application may have to run in a degraded mode, store up audit records locally, or even refuse to operate until the facility becomes available once more.

SystemConfiguration provides an interface for determining the "reachability" of a remote system, defined as the computer's ability to emit an Internet packet destined for that system. Note that this is not a foolproof test of whether a connection could be made, as the other computer might be offline, or an intermediate device could signal a problem with the network. A reachability test is still useful as a first-order test of whether to use the application's network features. The code in Listing 8-5 determines whether the securemacprogramming.com server is reachable and changes the user interface of its application to reflect that state.

LISTING 8-5: Determining a remote computer's reachability [reachabilityAppDelegate.m]

Available for download on Wrox.com

```
- (void)updateReachabilityUI {
    SCNetworkReachabilityRef reachable =
    SCNetworkReachabilityCreateWithName(NULL, "securemacprogramming.com");
    SCNetworkReachabilityFlags flags;
    BOOL validFlags = SCNetworkReachabilityGetFlags(reachable,
                                                    &flags);
    if (!validFlags) {
        [reachabilityLabel setStringValue:
         @"securemacprogramming.com status unknown"];
    }
    else {
        if (flags & kSCNetworkReachabilityFlagsReachable) {
            [reachabilityLabel setStringValue:
```

continues

LISTING 8-5 *(continued)*

```
            @"securemacprogramming.com is reachable"];
        }
        else {
            [reachabilityLabel setStringValue:
             @"securemacprogramming.com is unreachable"];
        }
    }
    CFRelease(reachable);
}
```

Checking whether a host is reachable once does not provide a good user experience or an accurate impression of the network status. To be useful through the life of an application, its reachability information needs to remain up-to-date. Reachability objects provide a run loop source so that they can emit callbacks when the reachability of a host changes. In Listing 8-6, the run loop source is used to provide up-to-date reachability reports.

Available for download on Wrox.com

LISTING 8-6: Live updates of a host's network reachability [reachabilityAppDelegate.m]

```
#pragma mark callback function
void reachabilityCallback(SCNetworkReachabilityRef target,
                          SCNetworkReachabilityFlags flags,
                          void *info) {
    // just call back into the delegate object
    [[NSApp delegate] updateUIWithReachabilityFlags: flags];
}
- (void)applicationDidFinishLaunching:(NSNotification *)aNotification {
    [self startWatchingReachability];
}
- (void)updateUIWithReachabilityFlags: (SCNetworkReachabilityFlags)flags {
    if (flags & kSCNetworkReachabilityFlagsReachable) {
        [reachabilityLabel setStringValue:
         @"securemacprogramming.com is reachable"];
    }
    else {
        [reachabilityLabel setStringValue:
         @"securemacprogramming.com is unreachable"];
    }
}

- (void)startWatchingReachability {
    smpReachability =
    SCNetworkReachabilityCreateWithName(NULL, "securemacprogramming.com");
    if (!SCNetworkReachabilitySetCallback(smpReachability,
                                          reachabilityCallback,
                                          NULL)) {
        NSLog(@"didn't set reachability callback");
        return;
    }
```

```
    if (!SCNetworkReachabilityScheduleWithRunLoop(smpReachability,
                                                  [[NSRunLoop currentRunLoop]
                                                   getCFRunLoop],
                                                  kCFRunLoopDefaultMode)) {
        NSLog(@"didn't schedule reachability callback in run loop");
    }
}

- (void)dealloc {
    SCNetworkReachabilityUnscheduleFromRunLoop(smpReachability,
                                               [[NSRunLoop currentRunLoop]
                                                getCFRunLoop],
                                               kCFRunLoopDefaultMode);
    CFRelease(smpReachability);
    [super dealloc];
}
```

Applications with lower-level requirements like network-configuration utilities need to be able to monitor the configuration of the network interfaces. SystemConfiguration exposes that information in two forms, both of which resemble dictionary objects with the usual key-value semantics. The first is the persistent store, which represents the network settings configured by users and administrators through the System Preferences application or the scutil tool. The second is the dynamic store, reflecting the current state of the active network configuration on the Mac. The dynamic store is usually related to the persistent store, as the configuration is dependent on one of the location definitions in the persistent store, but the dynamic store may have more information if some of the network settings are delegated to automatic discovery services like DHCP. As with the network reachability API, the dynamic store allows applications to schedule run loop sources and receive callbacks when the configuration changes.

TAKING ADVANTAGE OF SSL

One of the most likely risks associated with network communication has, for a very long time, been *snooping* or interception of network traffic. On early ethernet networks, all the packets were distributed on the same wire (the eponymous "ether") and so could be viewed by any of the computers on the network. This was still true in the days of hub-based network topologies, when the hardware redistributed every packet to every network interface. For a short time switches were employed, which were usually capable of routing a packet only to its destination interface. Nowadays switches are still common in large, high-traffic installations, but the "final hop" of a network is commonly based on wireless communication. Wireless network traffic is again undirected, with the result that anyone with a receiver within the transmission distance of the base station can read any transmitted data.

Ordinarily a "gentlemen's agreement" exists among interfaces on a network, to prevent any of them from reading traffic bound for another interface. Each packet is addressed to a specific interface, identified by its Media Access Code (MAC address). When a system reads a packet whose destination does not correspond to its MAC address, it disregards the packet. That agreement can easily be ignored. Interfaces can be put into *promiscuous mode*, when they stop checking the destination MAC and pass every packet received on to the operating system.

The U.K. Government Code and Cipher School, famous for breaking the Enigma and Lorenz ciphers employed by the Axis forces during World War II, could only get its work done because of the Axis powers' adoption of wireless technology. In the 1940s, Germany built the world's (then) most powerful radio transmitter, "Goliath," at Kalbe an der Milde in Saxony-Anhalt. Goliath was so powerful that its transmissions could be received worldwide, permitting listening stations in the UK to intercept encrypted Nazi communications which were then forwarded to the GC&CS's codebreakers, working in Bletchley Park.

Thanks to the recent declassification of some relevant documentation, the story of Bletchley Park, including the birth of modern computing and modern cryptanalysis, is becoming available to the public. The Bletchley Park site itself has been turned into a tourist attraction, and is well worth a visit. A great reference for the history of the site and the GC&CS is Colossus: Bletchley Park's Greatest Secret *by Paul Gannon, Atlantic Books, 2007.*

Most wireless networks support a form of encryption, based on either the Wi-Fi Protected Access (WPA) standard or the older, deprecated Wired-Equivalent Protection (WEP) standard. In common scenarios both encryption systems rely on a shared key known to the access point and to users of the network, so can protect data from interception only by attackers who have not joined the network. Attackers on the same network (a common scenario in offices and public access points) are able to use promiscuous mode and read all the network traffic.

The WEP standard has long been deprecated as a wireless encryption mechanism. Modern attack techniques can successfully recover the shared key in only a few minutes on standard home computer hardware.

About SSL

It is not possible to rely on the connection between the two computers being safe from eavesdropping. If the data sent over the network by your application is confidential, you will need to arrange for the data to be protected. This is where SSL (Secure Sockets Layer) comes in. SSL allows two computers to negotiate an end-to-end encrypted transport over standard networks, which may or may not themselves provide encryption. Once the SSL encryption is established, data leaving either computer is encrypted and never appears in plain form on the network, being decipherable only at the remote end of the connection. In addition to providing confidentiality, SSL also protects the integrity of transmitted data, stopping man-in-the-middle attackers from submitting packets claiming to be part of the data transfer.

SSL offers certificate-based authentication of the communicating parties. Usually only the server is authenticated (this is the case when you visit an https:// URL in a web browser), but SSL also supports mutual authentication in which the two participating systems exchange certificates and validate each others' identity. Whether one or both parties are authenticated, this all takes place during an establishing phase (often called a *handshake*) in which the parties also agree on which cryptographic algorithms to use during communication.

SSL was originally created by Netscape, now part of AOL. The latest version of the SSL specification is version 3, but the Internet Engineering Task Force has taken stewardship of the specification and renamed it Transport Layer Security (TLS), though SSL is still the most commonly used name for the technology. Current versions of the IETF standards documents relating to TLS and its extensions are available from the IETF web site, at `http://www.ietf.org/dyn/wg/charter/tls-charter.html`.

The client system, which initiated the connection, encrypts a random number using the server's public key and an asymmetric algorithm. The server decrypts this random number with its private key, and both parties use the same number to derive a session key with which the confidential content is symmetrically encrypted. Now the handshake is over and the encrypted channel established. The reason for using the asymmetric encryption to exchange a session key rather than encrypting all data asymmetrically is pragmatic: protecting a given number of bytes with similar confidence using asymmetric techniques is much more expensive (in terms of computer resources used) than using symmetric algorithms.

Note that because of the establishment of end-to-end encryption, SSL is incompatible with proxy servers that operate at higher levels in the network protocol "stack," including HTTP proxies. Different networks treat SSL-protected traffic in different ways if the traffic must traverse a proxy. In many cases the traffic is forwarded with no interruption. Be aware that some networks may be configured to drop all SSL-encrypted traffic or interpose a proxy as a man-in-the-middle eavesdropper, if the security policy rates content inspection as more important than privacy. If your application is to be deployed to such a network, you will need to agree with your customers on an appropriate balance between your application's security requirements and the existing site policies.

Using SSL

The URL-handling classes in Foundation contain automatic support for HTTPS, the HTTP protocol delivered over an SSL connection. Most HTTPS servers do not require the client to be authenticated, so the authentication step is one-sided. To use NSURLConnection or NSURLDownload with an HTTPS server, simply use an NSURLRequest object whose URL has the https:// scheme.

You can encapsulate any network protocol in a secure tunnel by using the Secure Transport API. Secure Transport, part of the Security framework, is a wrapper for the cross-platform OpenSSL library. OpenSSL implements the SSL protocol as defined in the relevant IETF standards documents. Both clients and servers implemented with Secure Transport are capable of interoperating with network peers based on other operating systems.

To support SSL in a network communications protocol, you first establish a connection using ordinary sockets or Foundation networking API. Once the network connection is made, pass it to an SSL session context object, along with callbacks to be used for sending and receiving data over the channel. On the server side you must set a certificate for the session context, so that the client can authenticate its connection to the server. This step is unnecessary on the client side, but available to provide mutual authentication. In Listing 8-7, the server used in Listing 8-2 to demonstrate Bonjour service discovery is given encrypted communication using Secure Transport.

Available for download on Wrox.com

LISTING 8-7: SSL-enabled version of the hostname service [ssl_server.m]

```
#import <Foundation/Foundation.h>
#import <Security/Security.h>
#import <unistd.h>

#define kPortNumber 1234

@interface GLServerNameVendor : NSObject <NSNetServiceDelegate> {
    NSSocketPort *socket;
    NSNetService *netService;
    NSFileHandle *fileHandle;
}

- (BOOL)publishService;
- (void)netServiceWillPublish: (NSNetService *)sender;
- (void)netServiceDidPublish: (NSNetService *)sender;
- (void)netService: (NSNetService *)sender didNotPublish: (NSDictionary *)error;
- (BOOL)startListening;
@end

OSStatus sslServerRead(SSLConnectionRef connection,
                       void *data,
                       size_t *dataLength) {
    NSFileHandle *handle = (NSFileHandle *)connection;
    NSData *readData = [handle readDataOfLength: *dataLength];
    *dataLength = [readData length];
    memcpy(data, [readData bytes], *dataLength);
    return noErr;
}

OSStatus sslServerWrite(SSLConnectionRef connection,
                        void *data,
                        size_t *dataLength) {
    NSFileHandle *handle = (NSFileHandle *)connection;
    NSData *writeData = [NSData dataWithBytes: data length: *dataLength];
    [handle writeData: writeData];
    return noErr;
}

@implementation GLServerNameVendor

- (BOOL)publishService {
    socket = [[NSSocketPort alloc] initWithTCPPort: kPortNumber];

    //use a new service name, to distinguish this server from unencrypted ones
```

```
    netService = [[NSNetService alloc] initWithDomain: @""
                                              type: @"_shostname._tcp"
                                              name: @""
                                              port: kPortNumber];
    if (!netService) {
        NSLog(@"couldn't create a NSNetService object");
        return NO;
    }
    [netService setDelegate: self];
    [netService publish];
    return YES;
}

- (BOOL)startListening {
    int socketFD = [socket socket];
    if (socketFD < 0) {
        return NO;
    }
    fileHandle = [[NSFileHandle alloc]
                  initWithFileDescriptor: socketFD];
    [[NSNotificationCenter defaultCenter]
     addObserverForName: NSFileHandleConnectionAcceptedNotification
     object: fileHandle
     queue: nil
     usingBlock: ^(NSNotification *note) {
         NSFileHandle *connected = [[note userInfo]
                                    objectForKey:
NSFileHandleNotificationFileHandleItem];
         // negotiate the SSL connection
         SSLContextRef sslContext;
         OSStatus sslResult = SSLNewContext(YES, &sslContext);
         if (noErr != sslResult) {
             NSLog(@"unable to create an SSL context");
             return;
         }
         SSLSetIOFuncs(sslContext, sslServerRead, sslServerWrite);
         SSLSetConnection(sslContext, (SSLConnectionRef)connected);
         // set the SSL identity, in this case the system default identity
         SecIdentityRef identity;
         sslResult = SecIdentityCopySystemIdentity(kSecIdentityDomainDefault,
                                                   &identity,
                                                   NULL);
         if (noErr != sslResult) {
             NSLog(@"cannot obtain system default identity");
             return;
         }
         CFArrayRef certs = CFArrayCreate(kCFAllocatorDefault,
                                          (const void **)&identity,
                                          1,
                                          &kCFTypeArrayCallBacks);
         sslResult = SSLSetCertificate(sslContext, certs);
         CFRelease(certs);
         if (noErr != sslResult) {
             NSLog(@"unable to set the ssl context's identity");
```

continues

LISTING 8-7 *(continued)*

```
                return;
            }
            // establish the secure tunnel
            sslResult = SSLHandshake(sslContext);
            if (noErr != sslResult) {
                NSLog(@"unable to establish an SSL channel");
                return;
            }
            char hostname[256] = { 0 };
            gethostname(hostname, 256);
            // send the data through the SSL tunnel
            SSLWrite(sslContext, hostname, strlen(hostname), NULL);
            SSLClose(sslContext);
            [connected closeFile];
            CFRelease(sslContext);
            [fileHandle acceptConnectionInBackgroundAndNotify];
        }];
    [fileHandle acceptConnectionInBackgroundAndNotify];
    return YES;
}

#pragma mark NSNetService delegate methods
- (void)netServiceWillPublish: (NSNetService *)sender {
    NSLog(@"service will publish: %@", sender);
}
- (void)netServiceDidPublish: (NSNetService *)sender {
    NSLog(@"service did publish: %@", sender);
}
- (void)netService: (NSNetService *)sender didNotPublish: (NSDictionary *)error {
    NSLog(@"service failed to publish, error: %@", error);
}

- (void)dealloc {
    [netService release];
    [[NSNotificationCenter defaultCenter] removeObserver: self];
    [fileHandle release];
    [socket release];
    [super dealloc];
}
@end

int main (int argc, const char * argv[]) {
    NSAutoreleasePool * pool = [[NSAutoreleasePool alloc] init];

    GLServerNameVendor *vendor = [[GLServerNameVendor alloc] init];
    if (![vendor publishService]) {
        NSLog(@"couldn't register Bonjour service");
        [vendor release];
        return -1;
    }
    if (![vendor startListening]) {
        NSLog(@"couldn't listen for inbound connections");
```

```
        [vendor release];
        return -1;
    }
    //now just run the run loop forever, to service requests
    [[NSRunLoop currentRunLoop] run];

    [vendor dealloc];
    [pool drain];
    return 0;
}
```

Besides the definition of the callback functions, all the SSL behavior is localized to the code managing the connection to the client. The callbacks use Cocoa NSFileHandle objects, but this is not required: the connection pointers are untyped, so anything that can identify the connection to the callback code could be used, such as an NSNumber containing the file descriptor. In this example the computer's default identity was used, but in real-world applications you will probably want to allow administrators to configure which certificate is used on any connection.

While it is still possible to use the telnet or nc commands to connect to the server in Listing 8-7, such clients are not capable of negotiating the SSL handshake. A dedicated client should instead be used, such as that in Listing 8-8, which connects to the server on the local host. The command-line openssl tool can also be useful in debugging SSL-based network code.

LISTING 8-8: Client for connecting to the SSL-enabled hostname service [ssl_browser.m]

Available for download on Wrox.com

```
#import <Foundation/Foundation.h>
#import <Security/Security.h>
#import <sys/socket.h>
#import <netinet/in.h>
#import <arpa/inet.h>

#define kPortNumber 1234

@interface GLSSLServerNameClient : NSObject {
}
- (void)useService;
@end

OSStatus sslServerRead(SSLConnectionRef connection,
                       void *data,
                       size_t *dataLength) {
    NSFileHandle *handle = (NSFileHandle *)connection;
    NSData *readData = [handle readDataOfLength: *dataLength];
    *dataLength = [readData length];
    memcpy(data, [readData bytes], *dataLength);
    return noErr;
}

OSStatus sslServerWrite(SSLConnectionRef connection,
                        void *data,
                        size_t *dataLength) {
```

continues

LISTING 8-8 *(continued)*

```
    NSFileHandle *handle = (NSFileHandle *)connection;
    NSData *writeData = [NSData dataWithBytes: data length: *dataLength];
    [handle writeData: writeData];
    return noErr;
}

@implementation GLSSLServerNameClient

- (void)useService {
    int socketFD = socket(AF_INET, SOCK_STREAM, 0);
    if (socketFD == -1) {
        NSLog(@"couldn't create socket");
        return;
    }
    struct sockaddr_in address;
    address.sin_family = AF_INET;
    address.sin_port = htons(kPortNumber);
    address.sin_addr.s_addr = inet_addr("127.0.0.1");
    if (connect(socketFD,
                (struct sockaddr *)&address,
                sizeof(address)) == -1) {
        NSLog(@"couldn't connect");
        return;
    }
    NSFileHandle *handle = [[NSFileHandle alloc]
                            initWithFileDescriptor: socketFD];
    // now set up the SSL context, similar to the server-side code
    SSLContextRef sslContext;
    OSStatus sslResult = SSLNewContext(NO, &sslContext);
    if (noErr != sslResult) {
        NSLog(@"unable to create an SSL context");
        return;
    }
    sslResult = SSLSetIOFuncs(sslContext,
                              sslServerRead,
                              sslServerWrite);
    if (noErr != sslResult) {
        NSLog(@"cannot set I/O callbacks");
        return;
    }
    sslResult = SSLSetConnection(sslContext, handle);
    if (noErr != sslResult) {
        NSLog(@"cannot set the filehandle as the connection");
        return;
    }
    //now establish the tunnel
    sslResult = SSLHandshake(sslContext);
    if (noErr != sslResult) {
        NSLog(@"couldn't complete the SSL handshake");
        return;
    }
    char hostname[256] = { 0 };
    size_t actuallyRead;
```

```
        SSLRead(sslContext, hostname, 256, &actuallyRead);
        SSLClose(sslContext);
        NSLog(@"server gave its hostname as %s", hostname);
        [handle closeFile];
        [handle release];
        CFRelease(sslContext);
    }

    @end

    int main(int argc, char **argv) {
        NSAutoreleasePool * pool = [[NSAutoreleasePool alloc] init];
        GLSSLServerNameClient *client = [[GLSSLServerNameClient alloc] init];
        [client useService];
        [client release];
        [pool drain];
        return 0;
    }
```

The client-side code for handling the SSL connection is very similar to that used on the server, but because this service uses one-sided authentication the client does not need to add a certificate to the SSL context. Notice that if you are using test certificates to authenticate your SSL connections in a development or staging environment, you may need to make the SSL library less strict in negotiating the handshake. The Secure Transport API documentation describes how to disable expiry date checking and trust evaluation in an SSL context.

SUMMARY

Using services available over a network is an important part of many applications, but opens the application up to a new world of potential attackers. Applications dealing with network data must not assume that the entity in charge of the remote end of a connection can be trusted, and should treat all connections as possible attacks.

A common tactic for handling network data is the use of a form of gatekeeper, which inspects the information on a network connection and cleans or destroys malformed data before it can be handled by the application. Mac OS X includes two different firewall systems that fill this gatekeeper role, and applications can use the pattern too to inspect the data at the level of that application's semantics.

In order to make networking easy for home users, Mac OS X and iPhone OS both provide Bonjour, a technology that enables the creation of ad hoc networks and the automatic discovery of network services. Bonjour may seem counterproductive for securing network services, but there are ways to ensure that your application is talking to an expected peer.

Even if an application and server have authenticated their connection, and are talking to the correct remote hosts, it is still possible for an eavesdropper located on the network between those hosts to intercept the traffic and insert data that appears to be part of the legitimate stream. The SSL encryption layer offers both confidentiality and integrity protection to network communication, and the Secure Transport library implements an object-oriented API for SSL. A layered approach to security proportional to data security requirements should be deployed, validating the data and protecting the transport independently.

Writing Secure Application Code

WHAT'S IN THIS CHAPTER?

- Potential security pitfalls in Objective-C
- Common vulnerabilities in C language code
- Techniques for finding bugs, including security issues

Even the best-designed application can be vulnerable if it is not coded defensively. This chapter will not give you an exhaustive list of issues to look out for; that's a topic that can (and does!) fill several books. You will find out about the more important problems, and why they can lead to vulnerabilities. You will also discover how to detect these problems before they get into the products your customers use.

SECURE OBJECTIVE-C CODING

The Objective-C language used in Cocoa development was designed at a company called Stepstone, at roughly the same time that AT&T was developing C++. Both Objective-C and C++ are extensions to the C language, adding object-oriented features, but the two languages take very different approaches. Where C++ relies on decisions made by the compiler to statically resolve classes and methods, Objective-C has a dynamic nature inspired by the Smalltalk language, and leaves those decisions until runtime.

Since Apple taking stewardship of the language by acquiring NeXT Software in 1997, Apple has added many new features and designed a new runtime library for use in 64-bit Mac applications and on the iPhone. The language itself has largely remained unchanged. There are some simple patterns to bear in mind when writing Objective-C code to avoid some security pitfalls, many of which have existed since the early days of the language.

This section also includes "lightning tours" of the main Cocoa and Cocoa Touch frameworks, telling you about the security highs and lows.

Object Instance Variable Privacy

The important fact about instance variable (or ivar) privacy is that there isn't much of it on the older Objective-C runtime, used on the 32-bit Mac architectures. That confidential data is kept in a private instance variable doesn't mean that it isn't readable from elsewhere in the code, and high-integrity data in a private ivar can still be written.

Objective-C provides four distinct levels of visibility declaration for ivars. These document which code should be able to access the instance variables directly (i.e., bypassing any accessor methods, or lack thereof). The four visibility directives are as follows:

- @private ivars are visible only to the class in which they are declared.
- @protected (the default visibility) ivars are visible to the class that declares them and to any subclass of that class.
- @package behaves in different ways depending on the context. In 32-bit Mac OS X processes it is synonymous with @public. On the iPhone and in 64-bit Mac OS X processes, ivars with @package visibility are visible to any code in the same framework or library as the declaring class, and invisible outside of that scope.
- @public ivars are visible everywhere.

The problem with relying on this distinction is that it can be worked around. Listing 9-1 demonstrates a class AnObject with a private instance variable, x. The property declaration of x provides a public interface for *reading* x, but not for *setting* it. That doesn't stop the code in main() from changing the value. The code in Listing 9-1 will compile with a warning for ppc or i386 Mac architectures and run as expected, but will cause a compiler error for x86_64 or the iPhone. On the 32-bit Mac runtime, @private is only a recommendation to the authors of code using the class that declares private ivars: it is not actually enforced.

LISTING 9-1: Directly accessing private ivars [ivarprivacy.c]

Available for download on Wrox.com

```
#import <Foundation/Foundation.h>

@interface AnObject : NSObject {
    @private
    int x;
}
@property (readonly) int x;
@end

@implementation AnObject

@synthesize x;

- (id)init {
    self = [super init];
    if (self) {
        x = 3;
    }
```

```
    return self;
}

@end

int main (int argc, const char * argv[]) {
    NSAutoreleasePool * pool = [[NSAutoreleasePool alloc] init];

    AnObject *myObject = [[AnObject alloc] init];
        /*if AnObject's x ivar is truly private, this won't work - main() is
outside
     *the implementation of the AnObject class.
     */
    myObject->x = 5;
    int xNow = myObject.x;
    NSLog(@"myObject->x = %d", xNow);
    [myObject release];
    [pool drain];
    return 0;
}
```

Even in the newer architectures, instance variables that should be invisible because of the scope declaration can be accessed by default in any code. External code interacts with these instance variables by using Key-Value Coding (KVC), the indirect property-accessing mechanism used by Cocoa Scripting and other parts of the Cocoa framework. In KVC, the calling code sends the target object a "key," which is the name of the property that the calling code wants to get or set. The object then looks up and accesses the property itself, which of course means that it has access to ivars with any visibility declaration, including @private variables. If the key matches the name of an instance variable, then KVC will return or modify the value of that variable. Listing 9-2 demonstrates this in code that works in either of the Objective-C runtimes.

LISTING 9-2: Accessing private ivars through KVC [kvcprivacy.m]

Available for download on Wrox.com

```
#import <Foundation/Foundation.h>

@interface AnObject : NSObject {
    @private
    int x;
}
@property (readonly) int x;
@end

@implementation AnObject

@synthesize x;

- (id)init {
    self = [super init];
    if (self) {
        x = 3;
    }
```

continues

LISTING 9-2 *(continued)*

```
    return self;
}

@end

int main (int argc, const char * argv[]) {
    NSAutoreleasePool * pool = [[NSAutoreleasePool alloc] init];

    AnObject *myObject = [[AnObject alloc] init];
        [myObject setValue: [NSNumber numberWithInt: 7] forKey: @"x"];
    int xNow = myObject.x;
    NSLog(@"myObject->x = %d", xNow);
    [myObject release];
    [pool drain];
    return 0;
}
```

It is possible to restrict the capabilities of KVC and stop remote objects from using it to access restricted instance variables. Properties accessed by KVC are resolved at runtime by one of two methods, -valueForKey: and -setValue:forKey:. These will look for instance variables with the same name as the key (or the same name prepended with an underscore, such as _myIvar) only if the class returns YES for +accessInstanceVariablesDirectly, which is the default return value. By overriding this method, as shown in Listing 9-3, a class can protect its instance variables from KVC access. This means that *none* of its ivars can be used through KVC; therefore the class will need to provide accessors or property declarations for variables that are part of its public interface. If code using the class tries to access a key that would otherwise cause direct ivar access, the object will now behave as if the key does not exist. This results in the object's calling -[self valueForUndefinedKey:], which raises an exception if that method is not overridden.

LISTING 9-3: Hiding instance variables from KVC [kvcivarhiding.m]

Available for download on Wrox.com

```
#import <Foundation/Foundation.h>

@interface AnObject : NSObject {
    @private
    int x;
}
@property (readonly) int x;
@end

@implementation AnObject

@synthesize x;

- (id)init {
    self = [super init];
    if (self) {
        x = 3;
    }
```

```
    return self;
}

+ (BOOL)accessInstanceVariablesDirectly { return NO; }

@end

int main (int argc, const char * argv[]) {
    NSAutoreleasePool * pool = [[NSAutoreleasePool alloc] init];

    AnObject *myObject = [[AnObject alloc] init];
        [myObject setValue: [NSNumber numberWithInt: 7] forKey: @"x"];
    int xNow = myObject.x;
    NSLog(@"myObject->x = %d", xNow);
    [myObject release];
    [pool drain];
    return 0;
}
```

While this method closes the door to access via KVC, the story is still not completely over. If your application can load code in bundles (not a concern for iPhone applications, which don't support dynamic code loading), malicious code could just add a category to your class to expose its private instance variables.

Instance and Class Method Privacy

If the story for hiding instance variables was somewhat disheartening, then trying to hide a class's methods is positively demoralizing. In Objective-C, an object's methods are invoked via a *message sending* action. The calling code sends a message to the object, which is represented by the Objective-C runtime library as a *selector*. The definition of each class in the runtime maps selectors onto *implementations*, which are the actual functions the object will execute. Class and instance methods are both treated in this way by the runtime library.

Any method defined on a class will be compiled as an implementation with a corresponding entry in the selector table for the class. There is no way to restrict the availability of any method selector, so you can invoke any method on a class by sending a message from any other code in the application, and if the object is vended over Distributed Objects then the methods can be invoked from other processes too. This includes methods that are not defined in the public header, such as those in class continuations. Listing 9-4 demonstrates how a "private" method can be called without even a compiler warning. Tools such as class-dump (`http://www.codethecode.com/projects/class-dump/`) and F-Script (`http://www.fscript.org`) can be used to find the undocumented methods on a class by people who may wish to experiment with them, including attackers.

Available for download on Wrox.com

LISTING 9-4: Calling an undocumented method [privatemethod.m]

```
#import <Foundation/Foundation.h>

@interface GLPrivateMethods : NSObject {
}
```

continues

LISTING 9-4 *(continued)*

```
// don't declare any methods here
@end


int main (int argc, const char * argv[]) {
    NSAutoreleasePool * pool = [[NSAutoreleasePool alloc] init];

    GLPrivateMethods *myObject = [[GLPrivateMethods alloc] init];
    [myObject performSelector: @selector(secretMessage)];
    [myObject release];

    [pool drain];
    return 0;
}

@interface GLPrivateMethods ()
// the main() function can't see this declaration
- (void)secretMessage;

@end

@implementation GLPrivateMethods

- (void)secretMessage { NSLog(@"You found me!"); }

@end
```

This problem with outside code's being able to call any methods on a class or object should actually be thought of as two separate problems, which must be dealt with in different ways. The first problem is that of a method that should be called only when the object is in a particular state. This sort of method often occurs in an object with some complicated setup process, or one that is responsible for managing a task that takes a long time, like a download. If the method is called out of sequence or before the object is set up correctly, there could be unexpected behavior such as accessing of uninitialized memory. You can use an object-oriented technique known as the State pattern to change the implementation of the method at runtime depending on the state of the object.

The State pattern was originally described by Erich Gamma, Richard Helm, Ralph Johnson and John Vlissides (the "Gang of Four") in Design Patterns: Elements of Reusable Object-Oriented Software *(Addison Wesley, 1995). Their version of the pattern calls for the state-dependent parts of a class to be implemented in separate classes, instances of which are swapped into an ivar of the main class as the state changes. The following example uses the method-swizzling capabilities of Objective-C, enabling you to avoid the complexity of multiple classes. You lose some flexibility in this approach, as all instances of the class are always in the same state.*

The State pattern does not stop other code from calling the method, but renders the method "safe" at times when the object's state makes it unsuitable for the real implementation of the method to be invoked. Listings 9-5 through 9-7 demonstrate a version of the State pattern using Objective-C's method-swizzling functions. Listing 9-5 is the interface for the class with stateful behavior.

Available for download on Wrox.com

LISTING 9-5: Statefully hiding a method: object header [GLStatefulObject.h]

```
#import <Cocoa/Cocoa.h>

@interface GLStatefulObject : NSObject {

}
// this important work must be done before using the object.
+ (void)setUp;
// this should only be done after setting the object up.
- (void)doWork;
@end
```

The GLStatefulObject is implemented in Listing 9-6. The class's +setUp method is where the state is changed by the swapping of the implementation of the -doWork method.

Available for download on Wrox.com

LISTING 9-6: Statefully hiding a method: object implementation [GLStatefulObject.m]

```
#import "GLStatefulObject.h"
#import <objc/runtime.h>

@implementation GLStatefulObject

// this is the real work, which will be swapped in when the setup is done
static void GLStatefulObject_realDoWork(id self, SEL _cmd) {
    NSLog(@"really doing the work");
}

// this is the dummy implementation which can be swapped out when ready
- (void)doWork {
    // don't do anything here, it would be dangerous
    @throw [NSException exceptionWithName: NSInternalInconsistencyException
                                   reason: @"object used before being set up"
                                 userInfo: nil];
}

+ (void)setUp {
    // some complicated setup work...
    // now that's done, swap the real work implementation in
    class_replaceMethod([GLStatefulObject class],
                        @selector(doWork),
                        (IMP)GLStatefulObject_realDoWork,
                        "v@:");
}
@end
```

The effects of using the class, with both out-of-sequence and in-sequence method calls, are demonstrated by Listing 9-7.

LISTING 9-7: Statefully hiding a method: using the object [methodstate.m]

Available for download on Wrox.com

```
#import <Foundation/Foundation.h>
#import "GLStatefulObject.h"

int main (int argc, const char * argv[]) {
    NSAutoreleasePool * pool = [[NSAutoreleasePool alloc] init];
    GLStatefulObject *myObject = [[GLStatefulObject alloc] init];

    //try using the object without setting it up
    @try {
        [myObject doWork];
    }
    @catch (NSException * e) {
        NSLog(@"oops: %@", [e reason]);
    }
        [[myObject class] setUp];
    @try {
        [myObject doWork];
    }
    @catch (NSException * e) {
        //this won't happen this time
        NSLog(@"oops: %@", [e reason]);
    }

    [myObject release];
    [pool drain];
    return 0;
}
```

The class hides its dangerous method from the outside world by declaring it as a function that is not connected to the Objective-C runtime until after the class has been set up. The function has static linkage, so it can be accessed only from within the GLStatefulObject implementation file. The class_replaceMethod() function swaps the safe implementation for the real one in the +setUp method. Notice that the real implementation is defined as a function, GLStatefulObject_realDoWork(), rather than as a method. Declaring it as a function avoids the compiler's automatically adding it to the class's selector table. Because the function is inside the class @implementation section, it still has access to instance variables of the class. The two parameters that are implicit in definitions of Objective-C methods, self and _cmd, must be explicitly included in the function prototype.

The second form of the problem in which it is necessary to hide a method from external code occurs when a method should never be used outside the class that defines it. An example in which this problem arises is that of a method that calculates a confidential secret, such as an encryption key. The method can be hidden by being converted into a function with static linkage, as seen in the previous example and in Listing 9-6. Rather than dynamically adding it to the class's method list using class_replaceMethod or a different mechanism, you should always call it as a regular function. By passing the calling object as an argument to the function, you can still call methods on the object and access its instance variables. However, because the function has static linkage it cannot be used from outside the class implementation.

Loadable Bundles

A common approach to providing extensibility in an application is to permit developers to create "plug-ins," loadable code bundles that are dynamically added to the application to add custom behavior. By gaining access to the internals of the application, the bundle author has a very simple interface to extend or modify the application's workflow as desired.

Unfortunately this very flexibility leads to significant security concerns associated with the provision of a bundle mechanism. The loadable bundles execute inside the parent application's process, and have the capability to modify the state or behavior of the whole application. This provides malware authors with a great opportunity: the ability to hide their malicious payload inside a legitimate application so that audit records and requests for services such as authentication to acquire privileges appear to come from a known and trusted app.

INPUT MANAGERS

A particularly infamous example of the misuse of loadable bundles is that of the Input Manager. Since the earliest days of Mac OS X, the AppKit allowed Input Managers to augment the text input system, so that users could write in languages or methods not natively supported by AppKit. As the interface for Input Managers was a loadable bundle that got loaded into every Cocoa application, this mechanism was appropriated by authors of "haxies" — bundles that modified or extended applications that did not provide a native extension interface.

Occasionally a haxie implemented as an Input Manager would introduce some instability into its target application, or even in an unrelated application, as they are injected into any Cocoa app, leading to denial-of-service problems in the host application. Users would, understandably, complain to the application's developer that it was crashing, when the problem in fact was related to the haxie bundle, usually provided by some other developer.

With recent versions of Mac OS X, Apple has restricted the situations in which Input Managers will be injected into Cocoa applications, including by removing the interface completely from 64-bit apps. This has failed to deter the haxie developers, who are now using AppleScript scripting additions to load their bundles into target apps.

In Cocoa applications (both graphical apps and Foundation tools), plug-in bundles are typically represented as instances of the NSBundle class. Bundles contain Objective-C code, including one class that is designated the *main class*. The application loading the bundle initializes an instance of the main class and uses that to access the additional functionality present in the bundle.

Bundles can also include *categories*, partial implementations of classes that augment existing classes in the application or frameworks. Loading categories can be dangerous, as they have the ability to add undesirable behavior to a class, such as publicizing confidential data. Categories can also replace existing methods on classes, causing an application to execute unexpected behavior even when performing a usual workflow. Once your application has loaded a bundle, you can no longer place any confidence in the threat model of the app; it could be doing something completely different from your intentions.

Categories are automatically loaded and registered by the Objective-C runtime, but the application still needs to call the augmented methods before they will be executed. A bundle can, however, even run its (potentially) malicious payload if your application loads but never uses the bundle. Any class or category can declare a class method called +load, which will be executed as soon as the object containing the method (be it the main executable, a framework, or a bundle) is loaded into the process. Therefore any decision about whether to use a particular bundle must be made *before* the bundle is loaded into the application.

Bundles can be signed with the identity of their developer, which can then be checked via the code signature API available in Snow Leopard and newer versions of Mac OS X. One method to safely work with a loadable bundle interface then is to adopt a strategy similar to Apple's method for dealing with iPhone apps. You test third-party bundles against your app, and when you are satisfied that they do not cause any harm sign them with your own identity. Your application then only loads bundles that are signed with your identity. This gives you a great amount of control over the bundles loaded by your app, but puts all the burden of testing the bundles (potentially in many different combinations) on you. The code signature API is explored in the next chapter, on securely deploying code.

A different approach is taken by modern web browsers. Most browsers provide a plug-in interface to render content that the browsers do not natively understand, such as Flash and Silverlight. However, most denial-of-service problems in browsers are the result of bugs in the plug-ins crashing the browser process, and other vulnerabilities in the plug-ins can give attackers access to the whole browser. Chrome and recent versions of Safari break the browser up into multiple sandboxed processes, such that problems in any one process have a minimal effect on the rest of the browser. Safari now runs each plug-in as its own process so that problems in the plug-in are limited to its host process, and cannot affect the general operation of the browser. By using the Distributed Objects API discussed in Chapter 4, you could provide a bundle interface that is expressed in the same way as if it were being hosted by your app, but that is actually running in its own process with limited access to your application's internal structure and resources.

Types of Returned Objects

There are numerous APIs in both Cocoa and Cocoa Touch that have a return type of id, meaning that they can return any kind of Objective-C object. Examples include Foundation's -[NSArray objectAtIndex:] and +[UIButton buttonWithType:] in the UIKit. You will probably write your own methods that return id, or use third-party library and framework code that does so.

If you have an object of type id, what can you do with it? The fact is, it can be hard to know. If you are comfortable that you control the source of the object, then perhaps you are confident that the id is actually a member of a specific class in the context in which you're using it, but there are many times when that will not be the case. If you are restoring objects from an archive or property list, the content could have been modified by an external agent including an attacker. The risk of modification is greater if the content is being retrieved from a remote site, or passed from a process with different privileges than those in which you are handling the objects. In these cases, the objects you get back may not be as you expect.

Handling an object as if it is of a different class than is really the case is almost certain to result in a denial of service, as you will sooner or later send it a message to which it doesn't respond. The default behavior of an object receiving an unknown message is to send itself -doesNotRespondToSelector:, which will raise an exception, usually aborting the application.

When dealing with objects restored from an untrustworthy source, you should verify that you can do what you require with the object before proceeding. The Objective-C runtime has powerful introspective capabilities, so any object can report on its capabilities in a number of ways. You can check that an object is an instance of a particular class:

```
id someObject = [anArray objectAtIndex: idx];
if ([someObject isKindOfClass: [NSArray class]]) {
    // good, an array was expected, and that is what we got
}
```

The -isKindOfClass: method returns YES if an object is an instance of the specified class or any subclass of that class. A related method, -isMemberOfClass:, returns YES only if the object is an instance of the particular class you pass it. In object-oriented design, the point of a subclass is that it is a specialized version of its parent. Its instances should be treated as members of the parent class, so -isMemberOfClass: is usually too specific to be useful.

A particular case in which the distinction between the two methods is important is in dealing with class clusters, *such as the collection classes in Foundation (NSArray, NSDictionary, and NSSet). A class cluster is defined through an abstract parent class, with a number of subclasses that implement the parent's interface. There are thus no objects that will, for example, return YES to -isMemberOfClass: [NSArray class], because NSArray is just the abstract interface and is never instantiated.*

You can also test whether an object conforms to a particular *protocol*. A protocol is an abstract declaration of a list of properties and methods. The properties and methods declared in a protocol can be required or optional; by declaring conformance to a protocol a class declares that it implements all the required methods and properties.

If you need some objects you handle to implement certain methods but are not concerned with which classes the objects are members of, you can create a protocol to declare the methods and have the classes that implement the methods declare conformance to the protocol. You can then test at runtime whether the objects conform to the protocol:

```
id someObject = [anArray objectAtIndex: idx];
if ([someObject conformsToProtocol: @protocol(MyProtocol)]) {
    // all the required methods in MyProtocol can be used
}
```

Protocols are instances of a class called Protocol, so the @protocol() directive is replaced by the correct Protocol object when the code is compiled.

Protocols can also be used for static type checking, if you declare an object variable with a protocol in its type:

```
id <MyProtocol> anObject;
```

The compiler now knows that the variable is supposed to conform to the protocol. When you build the application, you will receive warnings if the variable is sent messages that are not part of the protocol. Methods like -retain, -release, -conformsToProtocol:, and so on are part of the NSObject protocol, so you will often want to declare the variable as conforming to NSObject too:

```
id <MyProtocol, NSObject> anObject;
```

For the optional methods in a protocol, or for simple checks of an object to see if you can send it a single message, you can test whether the object responds to a particular selector. You do this by sending the -respondsToSelector: message:

```
id someObject = [anArray objectAtIndex: idx];
if ([someObject respondsToSelector:
@selector(replaceObjectAtIndex:withObject:)]); {
    // the object can be sent the -replaceObjectAtIndex:withObject: message
}
```

Notice that the selector is constructed using the @selector() directive, using all the parts of the method name including the colons but excluding the argument names.

Objective-C Exception Handling

A common cause of denial of service in a Mac or iPhone application is for an exception to be raised that is not handled by the application. Uncaught exceptions are passed through to the global exception handler, which by default aborts the application.

The Cocoa frameworks typically use exceptions to signal error conditions that are likely to be the programmer's fault, such as trying to use KVC to access a nonexistent key, or asking an array for an object beyond the end of the array. A notable exception, if you will excuse the pun, to this rule is Distributed Objects that raise exceptions when the connection to the remote object goes away or times out. Such "exceptional" conditions can become more common if you are dealing with externally supplied data without being defensive about the way in which you handle it.

Consult the documentation for the APIs you are using, including those for third-party frameworks and libraries if applicable. The documentation should indicate under what conditions the APIs will throw exceptions: is it really impossible for those conditions to be met in your application? If you believe that the code will never throw the exception, you could document this belief using an assertion macro to make it easier in development to spot conditions under which the assumption is broken. If not, then you need to be prepared to deal with the exception.

Exceptions in Objective-C can actually be instances of any object, although it is conventional to use instances of NSException or a subclass. NSException can carry information about the reason for the exception and supporting information to describe to the code dealing with the exception why it occurred. The class used in Listing 9-6, to limit the effects of calling a method out of sequence, uses an exception to signal that the method has been used inappropriately. The exception is raised with the Objective-C @throw keyword. The NSException class also provides an instance method, -raise, which has the same result.

Listing 9-7, given earlier, shows how this exception is dealt with in the calling code. The API call that could potentially throw an exception is wrapped in a @try block, which is followed by a @catch block. This pairing of @try and @catch indicates that an exception could occur in the code contained inside the @try block, and that if it does the program flow should jump to the @catch block, where the exception is handled. In this case the @catch block simply logs the reason for the exception and continues; whether or not an exception is raised the program will continue through the rest of the function. A variant on this style of exception handling adds a third block with the @finally keyword: the @finally block will execute either after the @try block finishes or, if an exception is raised, after the @catch block has dealt with it. You can also arrange for there to be multiple @catch blocks dealing with different types of exception by specifying different classes in the parameter to the @catch keyword, with the most specific type (e.g., a custom NSException subclass) going closest to the @try block, and the most general (usually id, indicating that the block can handle any exception object) going last.

It is usually a good idea to handle an exception in the most specific way possible, as close to the point where it is generated as you can. By handling any exception specifically you are better able to identify what exactly went wrong, and what steps can be taken to recover from it. If a complicated workflow or use case could throw five different exceptions and you handle them all in one @catch block, then you have a hard time picking apart exactly what went wrong and dealing with the problem, especially if the same exception could be thrown at multiple points in the workflow.

With this in mind it is often not useful to change the behavior of the global exception handler, although you can do so using the NSSetUncaughtExceptionHandler() function. The default operation of the uncaught exception handler is to abort the application, leaving a crash log, which is a reasonable step to take when all you know is that somewhere in the application it got itself into an inconsistent state, and wasn't able to deal with the problem where it occurred.

Lightning Tour: Foundation

The Foundation framework is used in all Cocoa and Cocoa Touch applications. It contains classes for managing data like strings, dates, and numbers, for managing collections, and for making network connections, among other features. The classes in Foundation are used as the basis for data models in the AppKit for Mac applications, and the UIKit for iPhone apps.

Security problems can occur during conversion between Foundation objects and more primitive C types, particularly strings or buffers. Both the deprecated NSString factory method +stringWithCString: and its supported replacement +stringWithCString:encoding: are unaware of the length of the buffer being passed as the C string, so either could read off the end of the buffer if it is not terminated by a NUL character.

NSData can create data objects that use the buffer they were passed in the argument as their data, using the various ...BytesNoCopy: methods. As the data objects will be managed either by reference counting (the -retain/-release/-autorelease messages) or the garbage collector, but the buffer is managed directly via the C malloc()/free() functions, it is possible for the life cycle of the object and its content to get out of sync. The objects can optionally free the buffers themselves if they are deallocated, and if you are not using the buffer for anything else it is a good idea to let the objects manage that. If the object and buffer do not match up, the consequences range from a crash to the manipulation of arbitrary data, if the memory at the buffer location gets reused.

Buffer overruns can arise from use of the collection classes. Each of the collections (NSSet, NSArray, and NSDictionary) has an initializer that takes a list of objects, exemplified by +[NSArray arrayWithObjects:]. The list of objects passed as the argument is of variable length, and the method expects the end of the list to be signified by the nil object. If you do not pass nil as the last item in the list, these initializers will carry on reading through the process's stack. Writing to memory outside an allocated buffer is also possible, with the -[NSArray getObjects:] method. This method writes a C-style array of the object pointers into a buffer specified in its argument, but cannot check the length of the buffer before doing so. If the buffer has space for fewer than -[NSArray count] objects, it will overflow.

Using NSFileHandle to write data out to disk is potentially subject to a race condition. The class enables you to create a file handle for writing with the factory method +fileHandleForWritingAtPath:, but will return an object only if there is already a file at that path. That forces you to create and open the file as two distinct steps, which gives an attacker the opportunity to replace your newly created file with some other file that your application will overwrite when it stores its own data. If you need to create a new file for writing temporary data, follow the recommendation later in this chapter in the section on tmpnam() and mktemp(), "Secure C Coding." You can then create an NSFileHandle from the file descriptor you get using -initWithFileDescriptor:.

Lightning Tour: AppKit

The AppKit (short for Application Kit, the name of the framework in the NeXTSTEP operating system which predated OS X) contains controller and view objects to be used in Cocoa applications. In addition to menus, windows, buttons, and text fields, AppKit has classes for managing multiple documents, handling events, and the internal plumbing of a Cocoa app.

One class that immediately stands out in an assessment of the security situation of AppKit is the NSSecureTextField. This class is a specialized subclass of NSTextField, designed to be used for password entry. It is "secure" in that it provides greater confidentiality than a regular text field; however, this confidentiality is still limited. The text is hidden from the user interface, as the characters are replaced by bullets in the control. Users cannot cut or copy text from a secure text field, nor can they drag the text from the control to a different text field. As far as the users are concerned, secure text fields can only be written to, not read from. The special subclass makes it harder for an attacker to turn a secure text field into a regular text field than if the two were different configurations of the same class. This raises the bar for a "blended threat" combining a code change in the UI with a shoulder-surfing attack.

From the application's perspective, the secure text field is very similar to regular text fields. The text is still stored as a plain old NSString inside the code, so the model is no more confidential than a regular text field. You must still analyze the requirements for storing and processing a string separately, even when it is presented to the user in a secure text field. The string's confidentiality is protected in the view layer by the secure text field, but if it is unencrypted on disk or in memory then it remains vulnerable to other attacks.

Cocoa Scripting is an implementation of AppleScript support, the basis for which is provided by AppKit. Adding AppleScript to an application is equivalent to providing an extra user interface; there are now more ways for users to interact with the app. Any actions exposed via the scripting interface should be analyzed in the same way as those available in the GUI, as a potential source of vulnerabilities. Users may download scripts from web sites and run them without inspecting them, so if the script can damage important assets there should be a way for the users to undo the changes.

AppKit adds extra entry points to an application process. It interacts with the window server to draw views, accept events from user interaction, and discover when it has become active or the user has used its Dock icon. It also adds default handlers for accepting some Apple Events (the inter-process communication mechanism that is the basis for AppleScript control), and as previously mentioned will automatically load code contained in Input Manager or Scripting Addition bundles. Because of this you should use AppKit only where it is strictly required, otherwise these entry points can play a part in threats across a larger portion of your app than is strictly required. If your application is composed of multiple processes, then factoring all the user interface into a single AppKit process limits the extent to which these entry points permit access to the assets in the system. It also makes it easier for users to understand how to use your application, as there is a single GUI app for them to deal with.

Lightning Tour: UIKit

The basis for graphical applications on the iPhone, UIKit is different from the other frameworks discussed here for numerous reasons. It is the only framework that was created from scratch in this century, although the developers clearly took a lot of inspiration from AppKit. UIKit was, then, designed for modern systems and takes into account the security concerns of the modern age. Because of the lack of support for background processes on the phone, it is also mandatory for an iPhone app to use the UIKit (even if it does so via some third-party UI library).

While there is no AppleScript equivalent on the iPhone, applications can still interact with each other by opening URLs that have been registered as belonging to a different app. As an example, URLs that use the mailto: scheme will cause the built-in Mail application to open. Your application could, in principle, do anything in response to a request to open a URL with its custom scheme. It would be both surprising and potentially damaging if it were possible to automatically delete part of your app's data from a different app by opening a URL.

SECURE C CODING

Like UNIX, the C language was designed long before many of the security risks in modern operating systems were understood. The main reason the risks were not discovered until later is that a number of the vulnerabilities arise from the design of the C language and its library itself. These issues exist in Objective-C programs too, so you should be aware of them and code defensively in Cocoa applications.

Buffer Overflows

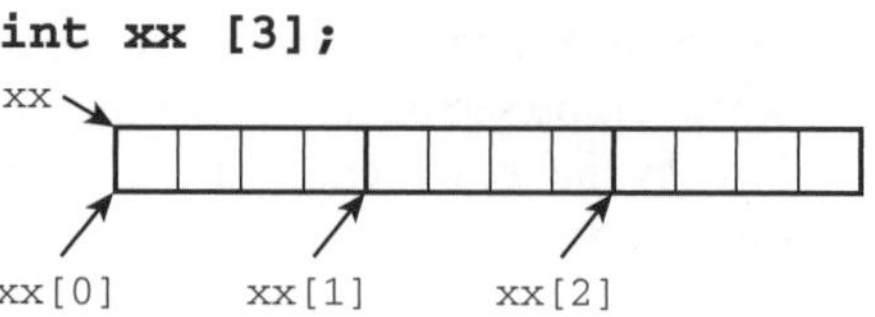

FIGURE 9-1: A C array's memory layout

Buffer overflows are among the most common root causes for documented vulnerabilities. Because vulnerability advisories frequently cite buffer overflows as a cause of serious or critical bugs, the words "buffer overflow" engender a sense of hysteria in press and public alike — including customers and potential customers. The basis for the flaw is the way in which the C language deals with arrays and pointers, and the operating system's handling of memory allocation to processes. A C array (as distinct from the Objective-C class, NSArray) is just a pointer to an area of memory that has space allocated for the members of an array. Figure 9-1 shows the memory layout of an array, xx, which contains three integers.

There are two ways to access the elements in xx. The first, as shown in the figure, is to use C's index notation so the third element would be written xx[2]. The alternative is to use the array variable as a pointer to the start of the array, add an offset to the pointer, and dereference the result. With this notation, the third element of xx would be found via *(xx+2). The same forms can be used for working with memory that has been dynamically allocated by a program using malloc() or a related function. The problem that C introduced is that there is no checking in either of these cases that the index used is within the space reserved for the array. It would be possible to use constructs like xx[37] or *(xx+126) without the C library's noticing anything amiss (the compiler could, in many circumstances, notice the problem, but usually doesn't). A buffer overflow, then, occurs when code that reads or writes a given memory area (the buffer) carries on past the end of the reserved space without stopping, i.e., the index overflows the range of the array or buffer.

But what would the program find at these locations? It is likely that each points to a valid location in the virtual address space of the application, i.e., that the resulting address can actually be used by the program. What it contains depends on a number of factors, but it could be some other data or even part of the application's code or its runtime environment. Modifying any of these could have disastrous consequences for the application. A common misuse of this ability to write anywhere in the process space is to change the process's *call stack*, the area of memory that records where the application will jump to after it has returned from the current function. In this way, attackers can cause the application to jump into library functions or even their own code. The term "arbitrary code execution" is often used to describe this consequence, because it really does permit the attacker to run any instructions of his own choosing. This could have disastrous consequences. The attacker would typically install a "back door" — a secret entry point allowing the attacker continued access to the computer — but could even enable the iSight camera and take photos of your user.

Attackers can exploit buffer overflows anywhere they can provide the app with data. Any of the application's entry points is a potential source of buffer overflow attacks. Frequently they are associated with text input (because a string in C is just an array of characters, with a NUL ('\0') character marking the end) although buffer overflow vulnerabilities have also been discovered in other data-handling code, including image and video processing libraries. Anywhere your application receives data from an external source, consider whether you really trust the data to be well-formed and legitimate (and if so, why you trust it). Be prepared for too much data to be sent to the entry point, and use one of these alternatives to cope with the flood:

- **Truncate the data:** This means that you're probably still handling malformed data, even though the chance of buffer overflow has been mitigated.
- **Grow the buffer:** A buffer allocated with malloc() can be resized with realloc(). If you do this, be careful not to let an attacker indefinitely send data to cause a denial of service.
- **Break the request into manageable chunks:** If you really do expect input of any size to be offered to your application (perhaps your app allows users to download files that could be many gigabytes long), this is a safe way to handle the input.
- **Ignore the oversize data:** If there is a reasonable upper limit to the length of legitimate input, ignoring anything longer than that can be appropriate, although if the maximum permissible length you choose is too short you could end up frustrating users.

Listing 9-8 shows a short program that is vulnerable to a buffer overflow attack.

LISTING 9-8: Buffer overrun vulnerability [bufferoverrun.c]

Available for download on Wrox.com

```
#include <stdio.h>
#include <string.h>

int main (int argc, const char * argv[]) {
    char argument[16];
    strcpy(argument, argv[1]);
    printf("you said: %s\n", argument);
    return 0;
}
```

For short input, the program behaves as expected:

```
mabinogi:~ leeg$ ./Buffer\ Overrun 'hello computer'
you said: hello computer
```

If the input in the first argument is much longer than the 16-character space allotted, the behavior becomes somewhat different:

```
mabinogi:~ leeg$ ./Buffer\ Overrun
'AAAAAAAAAAAAAAAAAAAAAAAAAAAAAAAAAAAAAAAAAAAAAAAAAAA'
you said: AAAAAAAAAAAAAAAAAAAAAAAAAAAAAAAAAAAAAAAAAAAAAAAAAAA
Segmentation fault
```

The crash log Mac OS X wrote to ~/Library/Logs/CrashReporter/ shows what happened here:

```
Process:         Buffer Overrun [289]
Path:            ./Buffer Overrun
Identifier:      Buffer Overrun
Version:         ??? (???)
Code Type:       PPC (Native)
Parent Process:  bash [262]
```

```
Date/Time:        2009-09-16 11:49:35.828 +0100
OS Version:       Mac OS X 10.5.8 (9L30)
Report Version:   6
Anonymous UUID:   7C8F3B72-329E-496C-807C-403087B49DB0

Exception Type:   EXC_BAD_ACCESS (SIGSEGV)
Exception Codes:  KERN_INVALID_ADDRESS at 0x0000000041414140
Crashed Thread:   0

Thread 0 Crashed:
0   ???                                   0x41414140 0 + 1094795584

Thread 0 crashed with PPC Thread State 32:
  srr0: 0x41414140  srr1: 0x4000d030    dar: 0x00800000 dsisr: 0x40000000
    r0: 0x41414141    r1: 0xbffff920     r2: 0x00000000    r3: 0x00000000
    r4: 0x00000000    r5: 0x0000003f     r6: 0x0000000a    r7: 0x0000003f
    r8: 0x00000889    r9: 0x00000889    r10: 0x00000010   r11: 0x82000022
   r12: 0x00000000   r13: 0x00000000    r14: 0x00000000   r15: 0x00000000
   r16: 0x00000000   r17: 0x00000000    r18: 0x00000000   r19: 0x00000000
   r20: 0x00000000   r21: 0x00000000    r22: 0x00000000   r23: 0x00000000
   r24: 0x00000000   r25: 0x00000000    r26: 0xbffff980   r27: 0x0000000c
   r28: 0x00000000   r29: 0x00000000    r30: 0x41414141   r31: 0x41414141
    cr: 0x24000042   xer: 0x00000006     lr: 0x41414141   ctr: 0x927a1ec0
vrsave: 0x00000000
```

The process tried to jump to address 0x41414140, because the call stack contained the number 0x41414141, but instructions on PowerPC must start on word (four-byte) boundaries. That caused the process to crash. If you convert the number 0x41 into an ASCII character you will find that it is the character A; the call stack told the computer to go to the address AAAA. That's because it was overwritten in this buffer overflow attack (referred to as "smashing the stack"); the attacker can control where the program goes after it has handled the malicious input, just by writing his or her choice of return address into the input. By setting the return address to the start of a system call or library function, the attacker can cause the program to perform a system action such as executing a different program, in what is called a *return-to-system* or *return-to-libc* attack. If the attacker can exploit enough space in memory with the buffer overflow attack, then he can insert his own code (commonly called "shellcode," since one goal is to start a login shell on the target computer) into the overwritten space and cause the program to jump into that code. It's hard for the attacker to know exactly what address the shellcode will start at. Shellcode typically begins with a "NOP sled," a series of no-operation instructions that the CPU skips through when executing the malicious code. The NOP instruction on Intel CPUs is 0x90 and on PowerPC CPUs is 0x60000000 — crash reports with return address values of 0x60000000 or 0x90909090 could be indicative of attempts to exploit a buffer overflow by inserting shellcode containing a NOP sled.

It was the strcpy() function that overflowed the argument buffer; this function does not know the size of either the source data or the destination buffer, so it carries on copying data until it sees a NUL character. Because the attacker passed a very long string to the function, strcpy() did not stop until it was beyond the end of the destination buffer and overwriting other, inappropriate areas of the process's memory space. In the next section you will find out about safer replacement functions to use instead of strcpy(), although in this case it is possible to secure the example program and still use strcpy().

ADDRESS SPACE LAYOUT RANDOMIZATION

This particular buffer overflow technique can be used on both the 32-bit Mac OS X architectures, ppc and i386, as well as the iPhone arm architecture. The x86_64 architecture of 64-bit Intel processes has some checks and features to stop arbitrary code execution as a result of buffer overflows; however, it replaces the code execution with process termination, so even on this architecture a buffer overflow will lead to a denial of service. There is no architecture on which it is appropriate to avoid checking for and mitigating buffer overflows.

On both the iPhone and Mac OS X since version 10.5, a feature called Address Space Layout Randomization (ASLR) exists, in theory making it harder to exploit buffer overflow vulnerabilities. When dynamic libraries, including the Cocoa frameworks and the fundamental libSystem library, are linked into a process, the address in the process's memory space where the library code starts should be randomized, so that an attacker cannot know *a priori* the interesting addresses to write onto the return stack. The entry point for each function is not the same on each computer, so the attacker cannot run a buffer overflow on his or her own computer to find an address of a function to jump to on the victim's. Notice that ASLR does not stop an attacker from inserting custom code that contains a NOP sled; it merely reduces the likelihood of return-to-system attacks succeeding. Enabling ASLR for your own library and application code is discussed in "Automated Hardening Measures," later in this chapter.

In Apple's implementation of ASLR, the dynamic linker function entry points are always the same. The dynamic linker library, /usr/lib/dyld, provides functions for attaching loadable code modules to processes, as well as stubs for some of the system library functions. Attackers can use return-to-system attacks to find out addresses in the dyld module, to link their own code to the target process, or to jump into particular libSystem functions.

In fact there is a second overflow condition in Listing 9-8; if you run the program without any arguments then argv will contain one element, but the program still tries to read the second element in the array. Exploiting this overflow vulnerability leads to a crash. Listing 9-9 demonstrates code that is resilient to both of these buffer overflows. The program will exit with an error condition if the argv array is not long enough, and handles an argument of any size by dynamically allocating sufficient memory.

It is usually not a good idea to carry on using the strcpy() function; however, in this situation, accepting any length of argument is safe because the kernel limits the size of the argument list that will ever be passed to the process. This means it is possible to be confident that the process's arguments will be of a reasonable size and will be terminated by the important NUL character. This confidence comes rarely, so replacements for strcpy() are recommended in the next section, on insecure functions.

LISTING 9-9: Safe buffer handling [safebuffer.c]

Available for download on Wrox.com

```
#include <stdio.h>
#include <string.h>
#include <stdlib.h>
#include <sysexits.h>

int main (int argc, const char * argv[]) {
    if (argc < 2) {
        // not enough arguments to continue
        return EX_USAGE;
    }
    char *argument = malloc(strlen(argv[1]) + 1);
    if (argument == NULL) {
        // no memory to copy the string into
        return EX_OSERR;
    }
    strcpy(argument, argv[1]);
    printf("you said: %s\n", argument);
    free(argument);
    return 0;
}
```

Insecure Functions

Some of the features of the C standard library of functions are hard to use without introducing vulnerabilities into your code. Others are just plain dangerous. This section introduces you to some of the nastier problems lurking in standard C as well as ways to deal with them. There are lists of banned functions and APIs published online by various security teams, including this comprehensive catalogue from Microsoft's SDL: `http://msdn.microsoft.com/en-us/library/bb288454.aspx`.

strcpy()

In the previous section you saw that strcpy() made it very easy to introduce buffer overflow vulnerabilities into your application. We fixed the vulnerable code by checking the input and changing the amount of memory allocated, but still used the strcpy() function. In fact it is almost never safe to use strcpy() in real code; the example relied on contrived circumstances in which the argv[] array is prepared by the kernel. For general data from unknown or untrusted sources, it is impossible to rely on strcpy() to avoid buffer overflows.

The attempt to address this problem in the standard library is the strncpy() function, which behaves like strcpy() but takes an additional argument: the maximum number of bytes to copy. If strncpy copies the maximum number of bytes without finding the end of the source string (the NUL character), it will stop, truncating the input to fit within the specified length. This still leaves the possibility that the destination buffer is not NUL-terminated, and that attempts to read it as a string would run off the end of the buffer. Use of strncpy() that takes the destination buffer termination into account is demonstrated in listing 9-10.

LISTING 9-10: Safe use of strncpy [safestrncpy.c]

Available for download on Wrox.com

```
void safe_strncpy_usage(char *source) {
    char destination[BUFSIZ];
    strncpy(destination, source, BUFSIZ);
    // no matter how many bytes were copied by strncpy(), guarantee that the
    // the destination string is null-terminated
    destination[BUFSIZ - 1] = '\0';
    // ...
}
```

There is also a nonstandard function, strlcpy(), available on both Mac OS X and the iPhone OS, as well as some other BSD-based UNIX systems. strlcpy() always leaves the destination buffer terminated with a NUL character, so you do not need to remember to add the NUL yourself. Listing 9-11 performs the same task as Listing 9-10, this time using the strlcpy() function.

LISTING 9-11: Safe use of strlcpy()

Available for download on Wrox.com

```
void safe_strlcpy_usage(char *source) {
    char destination[BUFSIZ];
    strlcpy(destination, source, BUFSIZ);
    //...
}
```

printf() and Friends

The most common problem with the printf() family of functions, including Foundation's -[NSString stringWithFormat:] and related methods, is ensuring that the number and type of arguments provided to the function match the format string specified as the first argument. An attacker can take advantage of a line like

```
printf(inputString);
```

by providing as input a string containing format specifiers such as %x %x %x %x. Because there is no list of arguments to the preceding printf() invocation, the function will just print whatever is on the stack, which could be valuable internal state information such as the addresses of calling functions. The little-used %n specifier writes the number of characters printed so far onto a variable given by an address on the stack, so an attacker can even use printf to modify your data or application.

Both of these problems belong to a class of vulnerabilities called format string vulnerabilities. Handling string input seems as though it should be a straightforward affair, but despite the age and well-publicized nature of string format vulnerabilities, there are still applications around that suffer from these problems. I had to fix one myself in an application I worked on in 2009. The Common Vulnerabilities and Exposures database (CVE) contains reports of format string bugs going back to 2000, and the general vulnerability category was mentioned in CVE's "unforgivable vulnerabilities" list in 2007: `http://cve.mitre.org/docs/docs-2007/unforgivable.pdf`.

Never print a string directly with printf (or sprintf, fprintf, or fellow functions); instead always format the string like this:

```
printf("%s", inputString);
```

Now if an attacker includes format specifiers in his or her input, the effect will be harmless.

The C compiler has an optional warning flag, -Wformat-security, that will tell you if your code uses a non-literal string as the format argument to a printf()-family function. The -Wformat-security flag is not implied by -Wall, so enable it manually in the Other Warning Flags field of the Xcode build configuration. Warnings presented by -Wformat-security should be treated as serious problems in your application, as they represent chances for attackers to crash or subvert the app.

The worst offender in the string-formatting family is sprintf(). It formats its arguments into a string specified by a pointer you pass to it, but like strcpy() it doesn't check the length of the string it writes to that location. Because the length depends on the values of the arguments and the way in which they get formatted, it is not easy to predict the length of the resultant string when preparing the call to sprintf(). The result is the dreaded buffer overflow, as demonstrated in Listing 9-12.

LISTING 9-12: Unsafe use of sprintf [sprintfbreakage.c]

Available for download on Wrox.com

```
#include <stdio.h>

#define SPRINTF_BUFFER 5

void broken_sprintf(char *source)
{
    char destination[SPRINTF_BUFFER];
    sprintf(destination, "%s", source);
    printf("destination contains \"%s\"\n", destination);
}

int main (int argc, const char * argv[]) {
    broken_sprintf("AAAAAAAAAAAAAAAAAAAAAAAAAAAAAAAAAAAAAAAAAAAAAAAAAAAAAA");
    return 0;
}
```

There are two possible ways around using sprintf() and its uncertain treatment of the output buffer. The first is to use the snprintf() function, which takes as one of its arguments the size of the output buffer. If the formatted string would be too long for the buffer, snprintf() will truncate and null-terminate the output, ensuring that it fits in the given space and is a well-formed string. The second is to use asprintf(), which allocates the memory itself to store the formatted output. The string returned by asprintf() is, assuming there is enough memory, guaranteed to be well formed and not to be truncated. Listing 9-13 shows how the preceding code could be fixed with the use of asprintf().

You will notice that there are numerous security issues associated with C strings and the library functions that act on them. All these problems arise from the design of C strings as byte arrays with a terminating character — there is no reliable way to find out how long a string is without reading it to the end.

The "managed" string types available to Cocoa and Cocoa Touch — NSString and CFStringRef — behave differently. Each of these string objects contains its length as a separate property from the list of characters in the string. Working with these types is therefore much safer, as functions and methods can find out how much memory is taken up by the string without having to trust the data itself. Use these types wherever you can in preference to C strings.

Available for download on Wrox.com

LISTING 9-13: Safe use of asprintf() [safeasprintf.c]

```
#include <stdio.h>

void safe_asprintf(char *source)
{
    char *destination = NULL;
    asprintf(&destination, "%s", source);
    if (NULL != destination) {
        printf("destination contains \"%s\"\n", destination);
        //asprintf used malloc() to create the output buffer
        free(destination);
    }
    else {
        //handle the error...
    }
}

int main (int argc, const char * argv[]) {
    safe_asprintf("AAAAAAAAAAAAAAAAAAAAAAAAAAAAAAAAAAAAAAAAAAAAAAAAAAAAAA");
    return 0;
}
```

tmpnam() and mktemp()

Applications frequently need to create temporary files to store data, if their working set would be too big to fit in memory. Even this practice can be subverted by an attacker to perform malicious acts.

The key concern in the security of temporary files is that of *atomicity*. An application needs to find a unique name for its temporary file and create a file with that name. If the application can perform both of these steps in one go (*atomically*), then all is good: the application now has a handle on a new file that it can use for its temporary data. If the two tasks must be performed separately (*nonatomically*), there is a chance for an attacker to create a file with the target name after the application has decided it does not exist but before it opens that file. Successful exploitation of this vulnerability causes the application to overwrite any file chosen by the attacker if the application has write privilege on the victim file. An attacker could for example make modifications to a password file to allow access, or overwrite critical files required to boot the system. The implications of such an attack can be significant for purely destructive purposes, or worse still for modification and subversion.

The attack does not need to be a deliberate attempt — if two copies of the program are running (which can even occur with GUI applications since the advent of Fast User Switching in OS X 10.3), they could both choose to use the same name for their temporary file if they check the availability at roughly the same time. Even two different threads in the same application could trip each other up in this way. Because the behavior of the kernel's task scheduler is strongly dependent on the state of the whole system, it is impossible to guarantee that the nonatomic approach to creating files will not be subverted.

The problem of nonatomic temporary file creation is a specific version of a generic class of problems — not all of which are vulnerabilities — called race conditions. *A race condition occurs anywhere that the behavior of a program depends on the sequence in which particular events occur. The program must race to perform its own work before the environment changes; if it loses the race, the program's behavior will not be as expected. In the case of tmpnam() and related functions, the application has identified an unused file name, and must race to create the file before the name gets used.*

It is not possible to use either the tmpnam() or mktemp() function in a way that avoids the race condition, referred to as a *TOCTOU* (time-of-checking/time-of-use) vulnerability. Each of these functions takes a file name template and returns a file name, based on the template, that was unused at the time the function was called (the time of checking). The program uses the returned file name to create its temporary file. However, there is no guarantee that the file name is still unused when the program actually creates it (i.e., at the time of use). Listing 9-14 demonstrates unsafe use of the mktemp() function.

Available for download on Wrox.com

LISTING 9-14: Unsafe use of mktemp [unsafemktemp.c]

```
#include <stdio.h>
#include <stdlib.h>
#include <string.h>
#include <fcntl.h>

int main (int argc, const char * argv[]) {
    char *template = "/tmp/myTempFile.XXXX";
    char *tmpFile = malloc(strlen(template) + 1);
    strlcpy(tmpFile, template, strlen(template) + 1);
    if (mktemp(tmpFile) != NULL) { // time of check
        /* this is where the race condition occurs. The app has to hope that
         * tmpFile is still unused before the next line, but there's no way to
         * be sure about that.
         */
```

```
        int fd = open(tmpFile, O_CREAT | O_RDWR | O_TRUNC, 0600); //time of use
        //... do something with the temporary file
    }
    return 0;
}
```

You can avoid the TOCTOU vulnerability by finding an atomic way to create a uniquely named file on the filesystem. The mkstemp() function achieves this by both performing the same substitution on the file name template as mktemp(), and opening the file before it returns. There is no longer a gap between checking and use, so the temporary file cannot be abused as just described. Use of mkstemp() is demonstrated in Listing 9-15.

LISTING 9-15: Safe use of mkstemp() [safemkstemp.c]

Available for download on Wrox.com

```
#include <stdio.h>
#include <stdlib.h>
#include <string.h>

int main (int argc, const char * argv[]) {
    char *template = "/tmp/myTempFile.XXXX";
    char *tmpFile = malloc(strlen(template) + 1);
    strlcpy(tmpFile, template, strlen(template) + 1);
    int fd = mkstemp(tmpFile);
    if (fd != -1) {
        //... do something with the temporary file
    }
    return 0;
}
```

On the iPhone, the /tmp folder used in the examples of mktemp() and mkstemp() usage is not available and it may not be appropriate for use on Macs because it is available to every user on the system. On both systems the Foundation library provides a function, NSTemporaryDirectory(), that returns a path to a folder that can be used for temporary files.

On the iPhone OS, the NSTemporaryDirectory() path is in the application's sandboxed area on the filesystem (at Application/*tmp) and is therefore accessible only to your application. No other application on the phone can even discover the contents of the temporary folder. Note that files created in the temporary folder for an app are not backed up when the phone is synced with iTunes.*

On Mac OS X, NSTemporaryDirectory() returns a path to a folder that is unique for the current login session. This folder is readable and writable only by the current user. The possibility of other code's subverting your use of this temporary directory is therefore limited to code running as the current user or root.

Removing Dangerous Functions

Knowing that some functions should not be used is part of the battle, but how can you be sure that you have removed every last invocation from your project? Only one use of strcpy() is sufficient to allow an attacker in, and then the effort you spent removing all the others is immaterial. It would be best to ensure that there are no remaining uses of insecure functions, and that they cannot be reintroduced by developers who do not know your conventions (or by you a few months down the line).

There are a couple of tools at your disposal to find and eradicate unsafe functions in your code. The Xcode tools include a refactoring utility called tops, which can perform syntax-aware substitutions on C and Objective-C code. The following one-line tops script inserts a compiler error anywhere the strcpy() function is used:

```
replace strcpy with same error "Do not use strcpy() to copy strings"
```

When you run a tops script, it performs in-place substitution — in other words it will modify your original source file. Make sure that before running tops on any important code you have a backup or have checked the code into your version control system.

The tops program can be used to perform some more complicated substitutions. The next script replaces invocations of strcpy() with strlcpy(). It also adds a warning to indicate that the replacement should be inspected. You should always check up on the result of automatic refactoring tools to ensure you are not swapping one bug or vulnerability for another. In particular, this script works well for stack-based character arrays, but not for dynamically-allocated strings on the heap (see if you can spot why). Listing 9-16 shows the result of running this script on the program in Listing 9-8, which previously contained a buffer overrun vulnerability.

```
replace "strcpy(<dest>, <src>)" with "strlcpy(<dest>, <src>, sizeof(<dest>))"
warning "tops replaced use of strcpy here; check the result and remove this
warning"
```

Available for download on Wrox.com

LISTING 9-16: Using tops to sanitize strcpy() usage [cleanedbytops.c]

```
#include <stdio.h>
#include <string.h>

int main (int argc, const char * argv[]) {
    char argument[16];
#warning tops replaced use of strcpy here; check the result and remove this warning
    strlcpy(argument, argv[1], sizeof(argument));
    printf("you said: %s\n", argument);
    return 0;
}
```

In the example substitution in Listing 9-16, the use of strlcpy() proposed by tops is safe, so the warning it has inserted can just be removed. Had the argument been a pointer to a memory region prepared by malloc(), then the length argument to strlcpy() inserted by tops would need fixing up to represent the true size of the buffer.

Once you have used tops to discover and remove all uses of unsafe functions and methods in your code, you also need to ensure that such functions do not creep back into your project later. Both the GCC and LLVM compilers allow you to "poison" symbols so that they will not accept code that tries to use those symbols. Listing 9-17 shows the same program from Listing 9-8, this time with the strcpy() function poisoned. When you try to compile this code, you will see one of the following errors from the compiler:

```
mabinogi:~ leeg$ gcc poisonstrcpy.c
poisonstrcpy.c:8:2: error: attempt to use poisoned "strcpy"
mabinogi:~ leeg$ clang poisonstrcpy.c
poisonstrcpy.c:8:2: error: attempt to use a poisoned identifier
        strcpy(argument, argv[1]);
        ^
1 diagnostic generated.
```

Available for download on Wrox.com

LISTING 9-17: Poisoning the strcpy() function [poisonstrcpy.c]

```
#include <stdio.h>
#include <string.h>

#pragma GCC poison strcpy

int main (int argc, const char * argv[]) {
    char argument[16];
    strcpy(argument, argv[1]);
    printf("you said: %s\n", argument);
    return 0;
}
```

Any insecure symbols must be poisoned after *standard header files and framework header files are included in your source files. These header files contain lots of references to insecure functions (including their declarations), and the compiler will report errors if you include a system header file after poisoning a function or method it declares.*

The poison pragma can also be used to poison Objective-C methods. You cannot write colons in a poison directive, so to poison the -stringWithCString: method you must write the following:

```
#pragma GCC poison stringWithCString
```

Where to Find Out More

This chapter so far has given you an introduction to the security implications of parts of the Objective-C and C languages and APIs. A complete guide to vulnerability mitigation in C development would take up an entire book, so this chapter can show you only some of the issues and how to identify and solve them. There are more comprehensive resources available, none targeting Mac or iPhone development specifically but all offering a more thorough listing of implementation vulnerabilities in C-language code.

CERT (Computer Emergency Response Team) is a department of the Software Engineering Institute at Carnegie-Mellon University that discovers and shares information about cybersecurity incidents. CERT publishes a coding standard for C programmers that contains hundreds of rules to follow in writing secure C code. Each rule is justified, and the vulnerability it mitigates is ranked in terms of likelihood and impact. The CERT standard offers examples of vulnerable and conforming code to illustrate the application of each rule. The standard is published by Addison-Wesley as *The CERT C Secure Coding Standard.*

The book *Writing Secure Code, 2nd Edition* by Michael Howard and David LeBlanc, published by Microsoft Press, focuses on Windows and .NET issues but contains lots of information about general C and C++ security concerns.

CODE REVIEWS AND OTHER BUG-FINDING TECHNIQUES

It's rare that anyone writes perfect, bug-free code the first time. Sometimes bugs are introduced as the result of one too many late nights as you try to meet the next project deadline. On other occasions, the subtle interaction of distinct modules and APIs can lead to conditions that aren't obvious when you're writing the code. You must also take into account that new vulnerabilities and attacks are always being discovered, so code thought secure today might be unsatisfactory tomorrow. As you've seen throughout this chapter, code defects can lead to security problems in your app, so it's worth taking steps to hunt out and eradicate the bugs. The information in this section is about bug-hunting in general, not security defects specifically, but of course vulnerabilities are a particular variety of bug.

Code Reviews

As the name suggests, a code review involves reading through the code to check for bugs. The concept was first described by Michael Fagan based on a study at IBM in 1976 [M.E. Fagan, "Design and Code Inspections to Reduce Errors in Program Development," 1976, *IBM Systems Journal*, Vol. 15, No 3, pp. 182–211], where "software inspections" were a heavyweight process involving a large number of participants. The reviewers would gather in a meeting room, armed with printouts of the source code or a projector showing the code, as well as other documents, including a specification of the software, have a long discussion, and log all the bugs found in the meeting. The author would then go back and fix the code, after which it would be prepared for review.

While this process does discover bugs that then get addressed before the software ships, it's still a very expensive way to find those bugs. Each of the developers must spend a few hours in total on the inspection, both in the actual meeting and in preparation while they all familiarize themselves with the code and the requirements. Fagan reported that the technique worked for inspections of up to 250 lines of code: imagine the time required to review a 15,000-line iPhone application! Development teams engaged in this review process often found developers spending 20% of their time (one day per working week) waiting for people to get together in a code review. Once they managed to organize the review, as many as two-thirds of the bugs discovered at one company were considered to be "trivial," with no effect on the software's behavior. Trivial defects include changes to the names of variables and functions, and requests to add comments to code.

Thankfully, code reviews do not need to be this costly. Just giving your code to someone else to examine, test, and ask questions about can reveal problems, or identify situations you haven't already considered and need to deal with in the application.

While you could review your own code, there is a good chance that you would not find many more problems than the ones you initially dealt with while writing the code. People have a tendency to consider or easily spot some problems while failing to identify others, or not appreciating their importance. This is very much the case when you're trying to criticize your own work, having already poured a lot of effort and creativity into writing it. Somebody else reviewing your code can bring fresh eyes, and will spot a new set of problems while overlooking others.

If you are an independent developer with no coworkers, your immediate question is likely to be "Who is the other reviewer?" You could consider "buddying up" with another micro-ISV developer, whose apps don't compete with your own. That way you both get the benefits of peer code review, as well as a chance to swap tips and learn from each other. And an Internet search will reveal a range of companies offering professional code review services.

The review should focus on discovering situations that the code you have written does not account for, or assumptions you have made that may not be valid. You can easily write your assumptions in the code by using assertion macros like NSAssert():

```
- (IBAction)addSomething: (id)sender {
    NSAssert([sender isKindOfClass: [NSButton class]], @"This only gets
called by clicking a button");
    // …
}
```

An assertion is an executable way of saying "I believe that this condition is always true," so in this snippet the author is claiming that the sender parameter will only ever be an NSButton instance (or subclass). In Xcode's default build configurations, assertions will cause exceptions (which usually lead to the application's termination) in Debug mode, but are disabled in Release mode. Documenting your assumptions like this makes it easy for the reviewer to know what to check for. Is there a way this method can be called without the sender's being a button object? If not, then your assumption is incorrect and you need to handle the other cases that are discovered. Other common places in which assertions can be useful include methods where you assume objects used by the method will have been initialized, and code that works on collections like sets or arrays and expects a minimum number of objects in the collection to work on. As assertions are statements of facts you hold to be inalienable, in each case consider whether you really mean to assert the condition or should handle the alternative case instead. Sometimes preparing for the code review helps you to find your own bugs just as readily as the review itself; understanding and questioning the assumptions made in your code is a fine example of this.

What specific issues to search for in code reviews depends on a number of factors; the type of code you are writing, the interactions between that code and the API, and the kinds of bugs you most frequently find in your code. One of the recommendations in Chapter 1 about creating threat models was to identify while designing your app vulnerabilities that could arise in the implementation, and to document these in the design or in code comments. The code review gives you a great opportunity to go back to these notes and ensure that you have dealt with the potential issues. If your threat model identifies particular classes or modules as being at risk from attack, concentrate more effort in the review on those classes and modules. Be especially thorough when inspecting code that interacts with critical assets. The various issues you wish to search for can be incorporated into a code checklist, described in the next section.

One company I worked at used both frequent code reviews and a special security-focused review as part of each software project. In the security review, developers would meet with security experts and explain what threats they had considered and how the design and implementation of the product mitigated any vulnerabilities. The code would be walked through by the developers to help the people from outside the project see how (or if) the vulnerabilities were addressed. We typically did this twice during a project: once when the design was roughly known but not yet implemented, and again before the software was "code complete" (i.e., before beta testing began). In each case this came up with a few problems we hadn't considered or had failed to address properly, which we then fixed as part of the regular bug-fixing work.

The most important consideration when conducting a code review is to leave egos at the door; the reviewers are not trying to show how many mistakes you make in your code, or how much better they are at programming. They are trying to help you build better software. Each bug or vulnerability discovered in review is one that does not need to be fixed with an update after you have already shipped, and one that your customers do not need to worry about. Your responsibility as the author of the code is not to defend the code you have written; instead you should be looking for opportunities to incorporate the feedback from the reviewer, and learn about the problems in your code so that you do not include the same bugs the next time.

Adding code reviews to your development workflow means adding more collaborators to the project, so there are more readers who must try to understand the code. In addition to yourself, your past self, and your future self, you are now also working with your reviewer. Interestingly, although object-oriented programming undoubtedly makes it easy to model problems in software and design applications to solve those problems, researchers have found that object-oriented code can be harder to review. [Alastair Dunsmore, Marc Roper, Murray Wood, "Object-Oriented

Inspection in the Face of Delocalisation," *Software Engineering, International Conference on*, pp. 467, 22nd International Conference on Software Engineering (ICSE '00), 2000.] The reason is referred to as *delocalization*; the code to perform any task in the app is spread across multiple methods and classes in many different files, making it harder for a reviewer to both find and keep track of all the information he needs to understand the code under review.

Unfortunately some of the nicer features of the dynamic Objective-C runtime can lend themselves to the creation of delocalized code in which the behavior is hard to understand from a read-through of the source. A good example is message forwarding, where one object sends messages it doesn't handle to an instance of another class. A *proxy object* is an object that forwards messages it does not respond to itself to an instance of a different class. While this capability is undoubtedly powerful, a reviewer coming to such code from scratch will see the proxy object being messaged — for instance she might see

```
NSInteger count = [proxy count];
```

and look for a method called -(NSInteger)count; on the proxy class. When he does not find it, he might just think that the object doesn't respond to that message — unless he happens to check the -forwardInvocation: implementation. Even when he does, he has to then discover where the target object is defined, and decide what state it's in at the time that this -count message is forwarded. You can already see that the number of different places the reviewer has to visit just to work out the result of this message is large, and so the chance for bugs and vulnerabilities to go missed increases.

The class interface for a proxy object is shown in Listing 9-18: notice that it does not declare any of the methods it can respond to via its delegate object; indeed these are not even known before the program runs.

LISTING 9-18: [GLProxy.h]

Available for download on Wrox.com

```
#import <Foundation/Foundation.h>

@interface GLProxy : NSObject {
    id delegate;
}

@property (nonatomic, retain) id delegate;

@end
```

The GLProxy class is implemented in Listing 9-19. A reviewer armed with this listing could still not determine which messages the class responds to at run time, because that information is hidden in the (context-dependent) delegate variable.

LISTING 9-19: [GLProxy.m]

Available for download on Wrox.com

```
#import "GLProxy.h"

@implementation GLProxy
```

continues

LISTING 9-19 *(continued)*

```
@synthesize delegate;

- (NSMethodSignature *)methodSignatureForSelector: (SEL) aSelector {
    if ([[self class] instancesRespondToSelector: aSelector]) {
       return [[self class] instanceMethodSignatureForSelector: aSelector];
    }
    return [delegate methodSignatureForSelector: aSelector];
}

- (void)forwardInvocation: (NSInvocation *)anInv {
    [anInv invokeWithTarget: delegate];
}

- (void)dealloc {
    [delegate release];
    [super dealloc];
}

@end
```

Finally, Listing 9-20 shows how the class defined earlier could be used in an application. Because this example is necessarily brief, it is not too hard to see that the -count message will be sent to the array object. Imagine the same proxy class being used in a more complicated app. What information would you need to decide what any message sent to a proxy object would result in? How easy would it be to find that information?

LISTING 9-20: [ProxyObject.m]

Available for download on Wrox.com

```
#import <Foundation/Foundation.h>
#import "GLProxy.h"

int main (int argc, const char * argv[]) {
    NSAutoreleasePool * pool = [[NSAutoreleasePool alloc] init];

    NSArray *strings = [NSArray arrayWithObjects: @"Hello",
                         @"World!",
                         nil];
    GLProxy *proxy = [[[GLProxy alloc] init] autorelease];
    proxy.delegate = strings;
    NSInteger count = [proxy count];
    NSLog(@"There are %d objects", count);
    [pool drain];
    return 0;
}
```

You should record the results of any code review. Any bugs discovered should be noted: if you use an issue-tracking system like Lighthouse or Bugzilla, raise a bug report for each of the problems identified. If the bugs are security vulnerabilities, determine their DREAD classifications and prioritize fixing the vulnerabilities appropriately. Add the vulnerabilities back into the threat model so that you remember to look for similar vulnerabilities in future development. Doing so also helps ensure you don't inadvertently reintroduce the bug in later maintenance work — you don't want to have to explain to your customers how you "unfixed" a known vulnerability.

Code Checklists

You'll probably find after a couple of code reviews that very similar issues are being reported in each case; perhaps you often forget to escape dangerous characters in SQL strings, or frequently get retain counts incorrect. It would be great to deal with these common problems quickly (or even eradicate them altogether), so that you can focus on discovering more esoteric or complex bugs in the review.

Look for the common patterns in your review results, and create a list of frequent pitfalls. Combine this list with the important implementation notes from your threat model to create a checklist of important issues to avoid in your code. This checklist will be useful in two situations. While you are writing your app, you can refer to it to try to avoid having the problems arise in the first place. You can also give the checklist to whoever reviews your code as a guide to the issues to look for in a first pass through the code.

The checklist should not be an exhaustive style guide, because then going through it will be such a chore for both you and the reviewer that it is likely you will skip parts or not go into much depth. Instead, concentrate on the five or so most frequently found bugs and important vulnerabilities, and spend a good deal of effort on ensuring they are avoided in your code. Hopefully it will not take the reviewer long to go through the issues on the checklist, because you already dealt with them when you were coding. Remember that the later a problem is fixed, the more expensive the fix will be to implement — the goal of code review is to catch bugs early. By capturing important issues in the review checklist, you reinforce these issues in the minds of the developers and reviewers, reducing the cost of producing a good product. The following table lists example entries in a code review checklist:

- **Data handling:** Unsafe NSString methods -cString: and -stringWithCString: should not be used.
- **Dealing with errors:** Ensure the "NSError **" parameter is never NULL.
- **Cleaning up:** KVO and NSNotification registrations must not outlive the registered object.
- **Avoiding unexpected behavior:** Instance variables must be initialized before they are used by methods.
- **Memory management:** Verify retain/release usage.

Having a style guide makes a lot of sense where code is frequently shared between multiple developers, typically if you are working on an application with other members of a team. By coding to the style guide you ensure that the code written by all of your team is consistent, and that when any developer reviews another's code she can concentrate on the behavior and meaning of the code instead of trying to interpret an unfamiliar layout or idiosyncratic style.

Entries on code checklists can be single sentences, each of which describes the problem for which the reviewer should be looking. The description should be as specific as you can make it without missing important problems that need addressing. As an example, if you frequently over-release objects in non-garbage-collected code, add that to the checklist; however, if you also return objects without autoreleasing them it is more appropriate to have the reviewer verify the reference-counted memory management in general.

As with any of the documentation produced in software development, your code review checklist is useful only if it is being kept up to date. As you use the checklist to ensure that you have handled a particular problem before getting the code reviewed, you will find that you introduce that problem into your software less frequently. Other problems will become more important, and you should add these to the checklist in preference to older, less common issues. In this way both you and your reviewer will be sure to spend your time addressing bugs and vulnerabilities that have a chance of otherwise lying hidden in your code.

Static Analysis

In version 3.2 of Xcode, Apple introduced a static analysis tool based on the clang language parser, which is part of the LLVM compiler project. Static analysis involves inspecting the behavior of a program that has been converted into an intermediate state between the Objective-C source and the final machine code. The static analyzer investigates the relationships between all the operations in a source file, rather than inspecting each line individually as the warning-generating feature of the compiler does. It can thus explore every code path in a function or method and discover bugs, including vulnerabilities, that might otherwise be easy to miss. You can think of the analyzer as an automated checklist runner for your code.

The static analyzer is also available in source form from the clang website, `http://clang-analyzer.llvm.org`*. The project includes a standalone analysis tool called scan-build that can be used to analyze C or Objective-C projects, including those built with earlier versions of Xcode or other build systems like make. At the time of writing, the clang parser, and as a result the static analyzer, does not support C++ or Objective-C++.*

To run the analyzer on your Xcode project, choose "Build and Analyze" from the Build menu. There are some techniques to silence any false positives (analysis messages about correct code) you might encounter:

- For messages about potential NULL pointer dereferences of arguments to a function or method that will never be NULL, add the nonnull attribute to the method declaration.
- In other situations in which the analyzer reports problems that will not exist because the preconditions will not be met, use an assertion macro such as NSAssert() to indicate this to the analyzer.

Adding your own rules to the static analyzer's checklist is not an easy task, as the rules are expressed in C++ code inside the analyzer. You must edit the source for the analyzer tool to add your custom rule, then recompile the analyzer. Even if you do this there is then no way to make Xcode use your customized static analyzer, so you need to run it from the command line.

Unit Testing

Writing unit tests serves multiple purposes. While you are developing new functionality, writing tests helps to understand what the various conditions and requirements on the new code are and to ensure that you have handled them. When you are revisiting old code to add new capabilities or to fix bugs, the existing unit tests will act as documentation to help explain how the code works; they will also act as a bellwether to help you avoid introducing regression bugs. Finally, when you're reviewing another developer's code, unit tests will help you to understand the conditions and scenarios the author considered while writing the code.

Unit testing provides a way to verify the behavior of parts of the code in your app at various levels of granularity down to individual methods, by running those parts of the code in isolation and making a number of assertions regarding the results. Unlike assertion macros in the code itself, which document invariant conditions in the code, the unit test framework hosts the code under test so the test cases can explore the behavior of the code with different preconditions and parameters, discovering whether the outcome in each case meets your expectations. If your expectations are not met, the test framework will record an error when you run your tests. Designing unit tests and testable code is beyond the scope of this book, but is covered well in *Test-Driven Development* by Kent Beck (Addison-Wesley, 2002).

From a security perspective, unit tests provide a way to ensure that some of the threats in your application's threat model are not realized as vulnerabilities. By testing that buffers are the correct size, that user input is validated or handled as required, and that logic errors do not exist in the application, you improve your confidence in the safety of your code.

The Xcode Tools come with a test framework called OCUnit that lets you write unit tests as Objective-C methods, grouped into classes each of which tests a particular aspect of your application. OCUnit automatically discovers the test classes and methods using the Objective-C runtime's introspection capabilities. The tests can be built either as a standalone target that runs in a dedicated process called octest, or as a bundle that is loaded into your app before the tests are run. In the latter case the tests can validate aspects of the app like the connections in Interface Builder, and can also run on a real iPhone or iPod Touch, which is not true for standalone test targets.

Automated Hardening Measures

The compiler has a number of features that can add protection against common vulnerabilities in C code. You have already seen the poison compiler pragma to forbid use of unsafe functions in application code. This section describes other ways in which the compiler can help to defeat the attackers. Most of these countermeasures protect against buffer overruns and stack smashing attacks, so why should you implement more than one of them?

The answer lies in the concept of *defense in depth* — the idea that multiple countermeasures can increase the protection of the application against an important attack or class of attacks. Castles with moats still have thick ramparts with places for archers to stand, even though both of these are countermeasures against attacking armies. The point of having multiple defenses is that if any of them fails, the assets are still protected. So it is with these stack-smashing countermeasures: should any one of the defenses fail, your app can still be protected from the attack.

_FORTIFY_SOURCE Preprocessor Macro

Compiling your application in GCC with the _FORTIFY_SOURCE macro set enabled checks that functions that potentially could be the source of buffer overflows are being used safely. The value of _FORTIFY_SOURCE should be either 1 or 2: setting it to 2 enables stricter checking but with the slight risk of false positives (i.e., "safe" programs failing the tests).

The _FORTIFY_SOURCE macro is not supported by the llvm-gcc or llvm-clang compilers provided with Xcode 3.2. To take advantage of the additional checks performed when you enable _FORTIFY_SOURCE, you must compile with the GCC compiler.

Tests are performed on code compiled with the _FORTIFY_SOURCE macro set in two passes. While compiling, the compiler will detect uses of the unsafe functions where the size of the buffer is already known to be incorrect, and will emit a warning. For cases in which the outcome cannot be determined at compile time, the compiler will insert calls to checking functions that evaluate the safety of the call while the program is running. If the runtime check determines that the function would not be safe to call with the arguments supplied, it will abort the process. This is preferable to executing arbitrary code supplied by the attacker, but it would still be better to avoid buffer overflows completely so that your application always behaves as intended. Listing 9-21 demonstrates some of the different tests that will be performed when _FORTIFY_SOURCE is set.

The result of a compile-time failure in a test enabled by _FORTIFY_SOURCE is always a warning, not an error. When the application that caused the warning is run, it will always abort when it reaches the line that caused the warning. It is therefore imperative to address all warnings that arise as a result of _FORTIFY_SOURCE tests.

Available for download on Wrox.com

LISTING 9-21: The outcomes of _FORTIFY_SOURCE tests [fortifysource.c]

```
#include <stdio.h>
#include <string.h>

int main (int argc, const char * argv[]) {
    char buffer[16];
```

```
    //this use of strcpy() will pass the compile-time test, and no run-time test
    //will be inserted. It is straightforward to detect that the source data is
    //shorter than the buffer to which it will be copied.
    strcpy(buffer, "hello");
        //this use of strcpy() fails the compile-time test, so the compiler will
    //emit a warning that the call always overflows. It can be seen that the
    //source data is too long to be copied into the 16-character buffer.
    strcpy(buffer, "This sentence is much too long for you.");
        //the compiler cannot tell whether this call will result in a buffer
    //overflow, because the size of the argument cannot be determined until the
    //code is run. Therefore the run-time check will be enabled for this call.
    strcpy(buffer, argv[1]);

 return 0;
}
```

If an application crashes as the result of failing a runtime _FORTIFY_SOURCE test, the backtrace in the crash report will show where in the application the failing test was:

```
Process:         a.out [4361]
Path:            /Users/leeg/Documents/Security Book/Buffer Overrun/a.out
Identifier:      a.out
Version:         ??? (???)
Code Type:       X86-64 (Native)
Parent Process:  bash [2195]

Date/Time:       2009-09-22 16:59:11.980 +0100
OS Version:      Mac OS X 10.6.1 (10B504)
Report Version:  6

Exception Type:  EXC_CRASH (SIGABRT)
Exception Codes: 0x0000000000000000, 0x0000000000000000
Crashed Thread:  0  Dispatch queue: com.apple.main-thread

Application Specific Information:
__abort() called

Thread 0 Crashed:  Dispatch queue: com.apple.main-thread
0   libSystem.B.dylib              0x00007fff82fb5ff6 __kill + 10
1   libSystem.B.dylib              0x00007fff83057013 __abort + 103
2   libSystem.B.dylib              0x00007fff8304b857 mach_msg_receive + 0
3   libSystem.B.dylib              0x00007fff82fa4f21 __strcpy_chk + 47
4   a.out                          0x0000000100000ea9 main + 73
(fortifysource.c:20)
5   a.out                          0x0000000100000e58 start + 52
```

To enable this protection in your application, you must define the _FORTIFY_SOURCE macro. Right-click the project icon in the Groups & Files list in the Xcode window for your application's project, and choose Get Info in the pop-up menu. Now choose the Build tab to set the build configuration. Find the Preprocessor Macros build setting, and add this line to it:

```
_FORTIFY_SOURCE=2
```

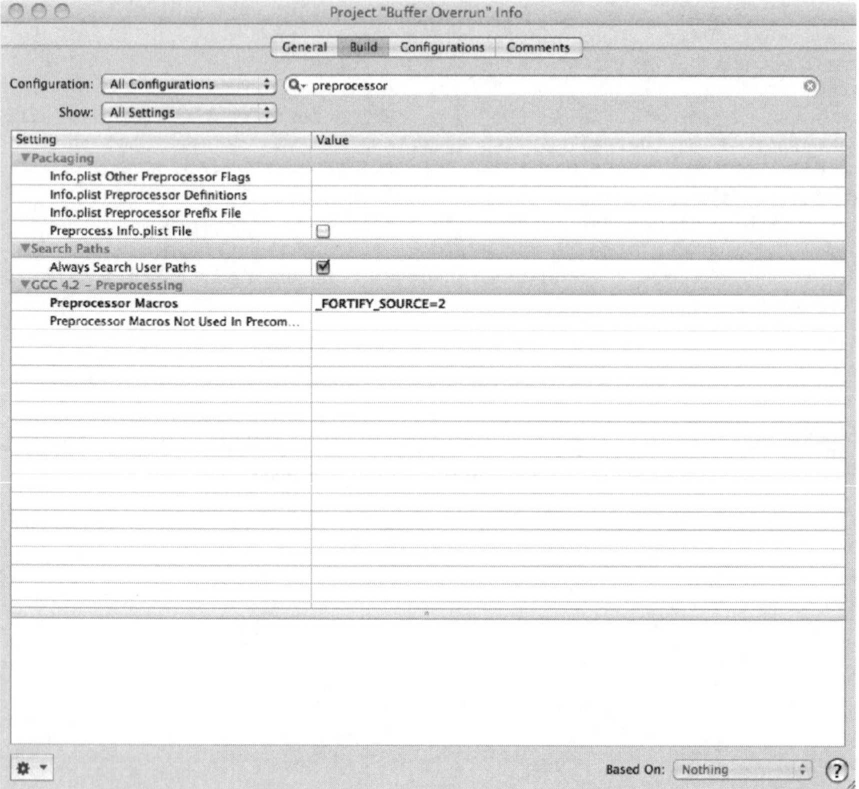

FIGURE 9-2: Enabling buffer overrun checking in Xcode

Stack-Smashing Protection

Buffer overflow attacks that lead to stack-smashing or that can corrupt function pointer variables are particularly dangerous, as they allow the attacker to run code of her choosing from the context of the vulnerable application, with all the privileges afforded to that application. The GCC compiler has a stack-smashing protection (SSP) feature that mitigates these vulnerabilities in two different ways:

- By sorting the layout of variables in memory so that buffers that could potentially be overflowed come after pointers and other variables, so that these variables are unlikely to be overwritten.
- By protecting the stack through use of a *canary* guard.

A stack canary is shown in Figure 9-3. The canary is set up on entry to a function by the writing of some random data below the stack. When the function is completed, the value of the canary is compared with the value that was initially written. If the canary has changed, a buffer overflow vulnerability has been exploited to overwrite the stack, and the program is terminated to avoid potentially executing the attacker's code. This is another example of fail-safe design: it is better to quit the application than to continue, unsure of whether the application is still behaving as intended.

You enable SSP in the compiler by specifying the -fstack-protector-all flag in the Other Compiler Flags Xcode build setting. The related flag -fstack-protector enables SSP only for functions with particular properties, such as those that use large character buffers.

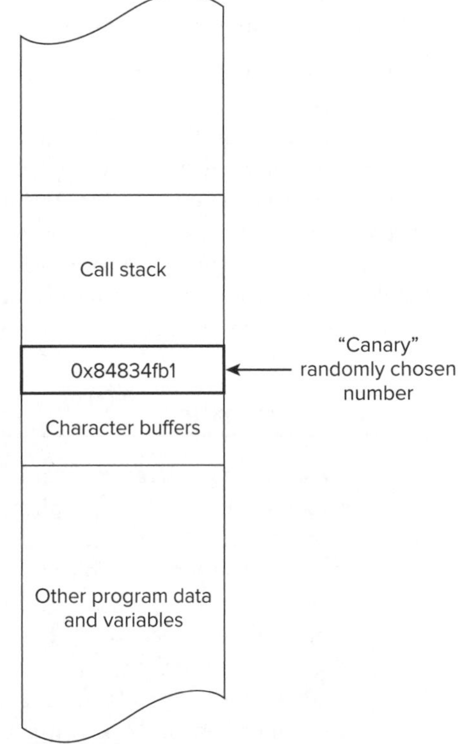

FIGURE 9-3: A canary protecting a process's stack

Address-Space Layout Randomization

As previously discussed, Mac OS X includes an implementation of ASLR that randomizes the entry points of functions in most of the system libraries (though not those of the dynamic linker, dyld). The benefit of doing this is in thwarting return-to-system attacks by ensuring that the attacker does not know where to get the application to jump to.

The linker can randomize the link address of your application and framework or library code too, to make it harder to target your application's code in return-to-system attacks. Taking advantage of ASLR in your own code requires that it be compiled as Position-Independent Executable code (PIE). This is opt-in, because there is a small performance cost associated with the extra indirection that occurs every time a jump or branch occurs in position-independent code.

Is this performance cost something to worry about? You can't answer that question until you've measured the performance of your application. Use developer tools like Instruments and Shark to decide where to focus your optimization efforts, rather than dismissing "slow" code without understanding just how slow it is. Remember that a decision between a security enhancement and a performance enhancement is trading off risk for speed or responsiveness; consider where the balance would be for your users.

When your code is compiled as PIE, the linker is free to choose an address at which to load the code into a process, and can randomly change that address. You enable position-independent executable compilation for your code by passing the -pie flag to the linker, set in the Other Linker Flags build configuration setting in Xcode.

Addressing Security Defects

If an audit for insecure functions or other implementation-level vulnerabilities demonstrates a security problem in your application, use the DREAD classification to work out how important that vulnerability is. You can then treat it in the same way as a design-level vulnerability, addressing the most important issues first.

Sometimes you will get reports of a bug that represents a potential vulnerability, but that you do not identify as such. It would be useful to know when such bugs are vulnerabilities, to help reassess the threat model of your software, and to try to identify related vulnerabilities. Apple produces a tool called CrashWrangler, available at the Apple Developer Connection web site at `http://connect.apple.com`, which helps you find out whether crashing bugs are potentially exploitable or not. You run your crashing test case in CrashWrangler's harness, which traps the exception that occurs just before the crash and inspects the application process to determine whether the bug that led to the crash could have been exploitable. CrashWrangler can also analyze a collection of crash reports to determine whether any of them are duplicates, and contains a script to aid in performing *fuzz testing.*

FUZZ TESTING

Fuzz testing is a strategy used in security testing, both by legitimate testers and attackers, to see how an application deals with different forms of input at one of its entry points. By submitting lots of different inputs at the entry point, testers can discover whether the application is resilient to unexpected data. The data can be subtly different from legitimate input: for instance, if the format includes a header that specifies the length of the payload, the fuzzed data may have a length that is slightly different than that declared in the header. Alternatively, the fuzzed data could be entirely random. Fuzz testing looks for the application to be able to handle the malformed data gracefully, without crashing or other unexpected behavior. If you do not fuzz test your entry points, an attacker will do it for you — and will take advantage of the results.

If you have some automated testing process such as unit tests, you should try to develop a test that demonstrates the vulnerability as a test failure and, more importantly, is passed when the vulnerability is fixed. As well as helping you see when you have fixed the bug, this will add the assurance that the problem cannot be reintroduced as a regression in later development.

It may be the case that you have used the same pattern that led to the discovered vulnerability elsewhere in your code. Make sure you check related and similar methods for the same problem, getting a code reviewer to help you where you can. If this vulnerability is very important or frequently occurs in your app, add it to your review checklist.

Vulnerabilities you discover while the application is still in development can be dealt with — market pressures notwithstanding — at your leisure, as long as they are addressed by the time you ship. If your app is already in the field and the vulnerability exists in the released version, your customers are exposed to the vulnerable version, and therefore to the possibility of attack through the vulnerability. You must consider deploying a security update to your customers. Secure software deployment is the subject of the next chapter.

SUMMARY

Vulnerabilities do not arise only from design problems; there are also security matters to take into consideration while writing application code. Certain features of the C and Objective-C languages are particularly likely to lead to vulnerabilities, and care should be taken when using them.

The C library was not designed with security in mind. The way the library functions handle arrays — and strings in particular — results in a common exploitable flaw called buffer overflow. It is often possible to get an application to write past the end of a memory buffer and into sensitive memory, even controlling the code that will be run by the app. Certain functions cannot be used in a way that prevents buffer overflows, and replacement functions should always be used instead.

Other functions in the C library, which deal with naming temporary files to be used by the application, result in a race condition, which can be exploited by an attacker to cause the application to overwrite files. These functions too should be avoided, as safe alternatives exist.

There are tools to automate the discovery and replacement of insecure functions in your application code. Tools also exist to detect some kinds of bugs and defend your application against buffer overflows. You can also have your code reviewed by a peer developer: both the review of the code and preparing for the review will lead you to question your assumptions, uncovering bugs, including potential vulnerabilities.

10

Deploying Software Securely

WHAT'S IN THIS CHAPTER?

- How to explain security requirements
- Proving that your application came from you
- Packaging your application
- Handling security issues in the field

A comprehensive threat model helps you identify the risks to which your customers are exposed. By designing your application with those risks in mind, you can act to mitigate them, but only once your customers have the application and are able to use it. Software must be installed, deployed, and used appropriately for the threat model to remain valid and the security countermeasures to be effective.

WRITING SECURITY DOCUMENTATION

In creating your threat model you may have found some risks that cannot be mitigated in code — the connection to a remote service is at risk if the user sets a poor password, and the password is chosen outside your app. The risk cannot be ignored, and yet because the application cannot take care of the problem automatically, the user's attention must be drawn to it. Manuals are notorious for not being read (nor even downloaded, in these post-boxed-software days), so the user guide may not be the most appropriate place to record security requirements. Many users expect to download and launch an application, then discover how to use it while they begin working with the app. The only text they ever see might be on your product marketing page or the iTunes app store.

As always, knowing your customers could change your perception. In enterprise environments, software is likely to be evaluated and the documentation carefully pored over before software is deployed in the live environment. In fact, the manual may be read before the software is even purchased.

In fact the view of users as completely eschewing any form of written documentation is overly simplistic. User experience experts say that a user will indeed RTFM (read the fine manual), but the extent to which he or she is willing to look for a solution depends on the value this user perceives will come from completing the task at hand. If a user cannot complete a casual task like registering for a game, that user will find a different game. If the user cannot complete a project on which a bonus depends, the user will go to greater lengths to find out how to proceed. For documentation to have most relevance to the user, it should be located nearest the user's work — in the application.

In-Application Security Documentation

To understand how good security documentation can help a user, it is informative to turn to a case study. The Keychain Access dialog for creating a new keychain item and Password Assistant (Figures 10-1 and 10-2) are useful examples.

FIGURE 10-1: New keychain item dialog

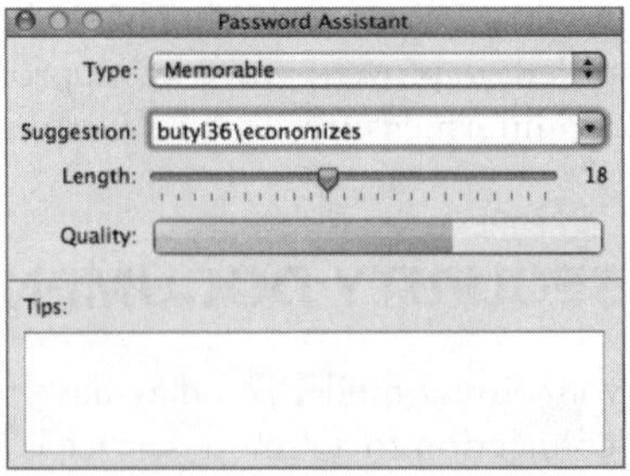

FIGURE 10-2: Mac OS X Password Assistant

The dialog shown in Figure 10-1 updates a "password strength" field, giving the user feedback on the password he or she wants to use. By clicking the words "Password Strength" or the key icon, the user can bring up the Password Assistant, which offers suggested passwords based on criteria for length and type of content. The Tips field in the Password Assistant displays messages such as "Mix upper case, lower case, punctuation, and numbers."

The Password Assistant is a private part of the Security framework: Relying on private classes in your own applications is a recipe for trouble. That said, a guide to using the Password Assistant in custom applications is available at `http://www.cocoadev.com/index.pl?PasswordAssistant`.

The threat being addressed here is evident (to people writing or reading a book on constructing and responding to threat models — more on that later): the confidentiality of any assets protected by the keychain item is limited by the strength of the user's password. An attacker attempting to discover the password will find it easier if the password is weak. The operating system cannot force the user to choose a particular password, so the best way to mitigate the threat is to inform the user of the issue.

The feedback presented to the user in these dialogs is useful because it is succinct, and appropriate to the task at hand. The user is engaged in selecting a password for a keychain item, so security documentation *related to password selection* is presented. Information on anything else, regardless of its quality, would be irrelevant and either frustrating or confusing to the user.

The relevance of the information is enhanced by *real-time updating*. As the user types the password, the quality-feedback bar is updated to reflect the strength of the password. The user can see how changes to the password affect the strength, and make a final choice accordingly. This mode is entirely distinct from the all-too-common pattern of validation after entry. Some applications (names shall not be provided, but web applications are frequent offenders) accept any information the user enters, then either ask for confirmation or simply reject it as unacceptable. If you know something is wrong, do not wait to tell the user after he has finished his work — that's just irritating.

Asking for confirmation is not a good approach either; readers interpret the question "Are you sure you want to [fact-filled explanation]?" as "Would you like me to stop bugging you now?" Usability studies have shown that users recognize important features of a UI quickly and (subconsciously) ignore the rest; in the case of a confirmation dialog the Yes button is quickly discovered. In fact, having provided the relevant information up front, the new keychain item dialog does not seek confirmation at all.

The quality-feedback bar takes advantage of *progressive disclosure* to remain unobtrusive, while providing the user with as much information as desired. As the user enters the password, the quality bar in the keychain item sheet is the only feedback about the strength of the password. By allowing the user to drill down into the assistant to find the tips and suggestion field, the operating system developers avoided overloading the user with all the information at once, while still ensuring it is available.

There is a major problem with both the new keychain item dialog and the Password Assistant — while they both explain the solution to the user, neither attempts to address the *problem* to which the solution is relevant. A user with no understanding of the risks associated with poor passwords will wonder why the operating system is saying the password is low quality, especially if it is one that has served for years on other web sites.

Your threat model includes descriptions of the users and their likely technical skills: use this to advise you about the level of knowledge and expertise you can assume when presenting risks and security information in the UI or documentation. If in doubt, conduct some usability testing to investigate the impact of a security message or change to the workflow designed to accommodate a security requirement. *A/B testing* is considered good practice in the user-experience world — give each user one of two different versions of the application, for example two different versions of the wording in a security message. Each user should be instructed to perform the same task, without being led through that task. Investigate whether the message has any impact on the user's ability to perform the task, or on the user's understanding of the security issues.

Security Documentation in the Manual

The printed or downloadable documentation for a software product is a good place to document more complicated security matters: deployment requirements and appropriate security maintenance procedures. Remember that users are not going to have the manual open all the time they use your application, so the documentation is not the best place to describe day-to-day security issues (though that certainly shouldn't preclude its appearance there). If it makes sense to document security issues within the application's UI, as described in the previous section, do so. A user who is told that you aren't responsible for a loss because "the problem was documented on page 412 of the manual" is not a happy user. If you are embarrassed to draw the user's attention to a security risk in the application UI, the best course of action is to address the risk in development, so the user need never know it was present.

Your threat model already describes the risks associated with the application and its use, so refer to the threat model while writing your application's documentation. In particular, make sure that the manual describes the risks that are present and why the steps you are recommending in the documentation are appropriate to mitigate those risks. Users do not enjoy being told that a task must be carried out without understanding why; they bought computers to do work on them, not to follow your setup instructions. Explain the conditions under which the risk you are describing is an actual threat, the severity and likelihood of the threat, the damage that the threat can cause, and the reasons your instructions address it.

If you find that the documentation says all *users should follow a particular procedure, remove that section from the manual and make the procedure automatic, either as part of the installation process, or the application's initial startup procedure. The application should be secure in its default configuration for the majority of users, or users will lose confidence in the application.*

The security instructions associated with mitigating a risk should describe precisely the steps to take. Developers sometimes assume that the things they find obvious or trivial must be equally clear to everybody else, though this is not necessarily the case. You may want to engage a technical author to write the documentation if you find writing the steps difficult. Technical authors will undoubtedly ask a lot of questions about the application and its operation, and this may get frustrating, but each question the author asks relates to something that the application does not make clear — the outcome of a particular action, or the meaning of some data in the UI. You may be surprised to find how much of your application's behavior is not obvious to people who did not develop it.

It is a good idea to make the security portions of the documentation easy to find, so that a user or administrator referring to the manual is unlikely to miss them. Just as information in the UI should appear near to where the user performs the appropriate action, security details in the manual should appear near the documentation of the task to which they are relevant. That usually means you should refer to the security matter within the documentation for a particular task. Consider adding a section heading for security to the table of contents, and a specific discussion of the application's security that references the other appropriate sections of the documentation — this way even casual readers can see that there are security issues to be considered, and may go on to read the appropriate documentation.

If you are writing software for particularly security-conscious customers, you may be able to deliver the security documentation as a separate artifact and still be confident that it will get read. This is particularly true if your software will be used in scenarios where legal or policy compliance is relevant to its operation, such as in government departments and publicly traded companies.

IDENTIFY YOURSELF WITH CODE SIGNING

Code signing has been brought up previously, as a method of identifying your application to its plug-ins (see Chapter 4), Keychain Services (Chapter 5) and the application firewall (Chapter 8). Signing your application does not merely allow the *application* to be identified, it also makes the identity of the application *provider* — that's you — known. A user can find out who delivered the application he or she is about to install.

The signing process (in Xcode, or at the command line via the code-sign tool) embeds the *certificate* associated with the signing identity in the signature attached to the signed application, along with any certificates needed to validate the identity of the signer. If you use a certificate issued by a commercial certificate authority (CA), your application's signature will include your certificate and the certificate of the CA. This allows the recipient of the application (i.e., your customer) to see who is backing up the claim that you delivered the application, and to decide whether to trust that assertion.

The value of this identification comes from the tamper-resistant nature of code signatures. If either the signature or the application is modified, any attempt to verify the identity of the code will fail. Consider a third-party software vendor, Malicious Monster, that wants to distribute a modified version of your application. Whether it develops a new application from scratch to mimic yours or takes a copy of your application and alters it, what it comes up with is *not* your application. The signature you added to your shipping application fails to identify the Malicious Monster version of the app as your app — after all, it isn't your app. Malicious Monster could sign the app itself, replacing your signature with its own (valid for its identity), distribute an unsigned application, or leave your (now broken) signature intact. In none of these scenarios can the application be passed off as yours, provided that the user has verified that the identity used to sign the application both is yours and is valid. Unfortunately, as you shall soon find, Mac OS X does not make such validation simple.

The scenario described in the preceding paragraph is valid only if you keep your signing identity's private key a secret. An attacker with access to your private key is able to pass off his or her own applications as your work. Only people building your applications need to use your private key.

This issue of private key secrecy sometimes causes confusion for developers working on open-source projects, which can be built from source code by anyone. The developers are concerned that if people grabbing the source code and rolling their own versions of the project cannot sign the built product, it will behave differently from the precompiled version on the project website.

That's actually exactly the point of code signing. If someone is able to distribute a version of your app that looks as if it comes from you, but is buggy or malicious, it will reflect badly on you. The maintainers of an open-source project cannot guarantee that a build of the application made by a third party behaves identically to one they produced. Therefore they should not *allow the third party to sign a build on their behalf. The project's code-signing identity should be restricted to use on the project's build computers, and used solely for signing official project releases.*

Unfortunately, while the code-signing system is capable of reporting the identity of an application's originator in a way that is very hard to spoof, the user interface for this capability is notable in its absence. If an application's identity changes so that it is no longer identifiable as the app a user originally had, then firewall and keychain access dialogs normally suppressed by a valid signature will become visible again. Relying on the user to question the source of an application when these dialogs appear, rather to click the "please let me get on with my work" button, is not possible. If the signature is actually broken the application will not work with those components of the OS at all. But a user cannot tell if a legitimate version of the app has been replaced by an illegitimate one, if the original version was illegitimate and the new app is valid, or even if each is from a different illegitimate source. There is no user interface that a non-technical user could be expected to work with that displays the identity of an application on disk.

Using some of the techniques discussed in earlier chapters of this book, you can provide your own such interface. The code-sign command line tool can extract the certificate chain from an application signature, and Certificate, Key and Trust Services can be used to display the certificates in a way that allows users to inspect the identities and associated trust settings. In Listing 10-1, an application retrieves the leaf-signing certificate from an application of the user's choice, and prepares a SFCertificateView to display details of that certificate to the user.

LISTING 10-1: Displaying code-signing information graphically [Signature_ViewerAppDelegate.m]

Available for download on Wrox.com

```
- (IBAction)chooseApp: (id)sender {
    NSOpenPanel *openPanel = [NSOpenPanel openPanel];
    [openPanel setCanChooseFiles: YES];
    [openPanel setCanChooseDirectories: NO];
    [openPanel setAllowsMultipleSelection: NO];
    [openPanel setTitle: @"Choose an application"];
```

```
    [openPanel setAllowedFileTypes: [NSArray arrayWithObject: @"app"]];
    [openPanel beginSheetModalForWindow: window
                      completionHandler: ^(NSInteger result) {
                          if (result == NSOKButton) {
                              NSURL *appURL = [[openPanel URLs] lastObject];
                              NSString *appPath = [appURL path];
                              [appName setStringValue: appPath];
                              NSImage *icon = [[NSWorkspace sharedWorkspace]
                                                 iconForFile: appPath];
                              [appIcon setImage: icon];
                              NSArray *codeSignArgs = [NSArray
                                                         arrayWithObjects:
                                                         @"-d",
                                @"--extract-certificates=/tmp/app-certs",
                                                         appPath,
                                                         nil];
                              NSTask *codesign = [NSTask
                                                     launchedTaskWithLaunchPath:
                                                     @"/usr/bin/codesign"
                                                     arguments: codeSignArgs];
                              [codesign waitUntilExit];
                              if (0 == [codesign terminationStatus]) {
                                  NSData *certData = [NSData
                                                        dataWithContentsOfFile:
                                                        @"/tmp/app-certs0"];
                                  SecCertificateRef cert =
                                  SecCertificateCreateWithData(NULL,
                                                               certData);
                                  /* even if the cert is NULL, display it. The
                                   * cert view class shows an appropriate
                                   * placeholder view.
                                   */
                                  [certView setCertificate: cert];
                                  [certView setNeedsDisplay: YES];
                              }
                              else {
                                  NSLog(@"object isn't well-signed");
                                  [certView setCertificate: NULL];
                                  [certView setNeedsDisplay: YES];
                              }

                          }
                      }];
}
```

The application displays a view very similar to that of Keychain Access, displaying details of the signing identity and its trust status on the Mac. Figure 10-3 shows what this looks like for Apple's Address Book application.

This view makes it very simple to identify the entity that delivered an application. In Figure 10-4, Address Book's code-signing identity is again displayed, but in this case it is a "Trojan" version of Address Book that I have signed with a different identity.

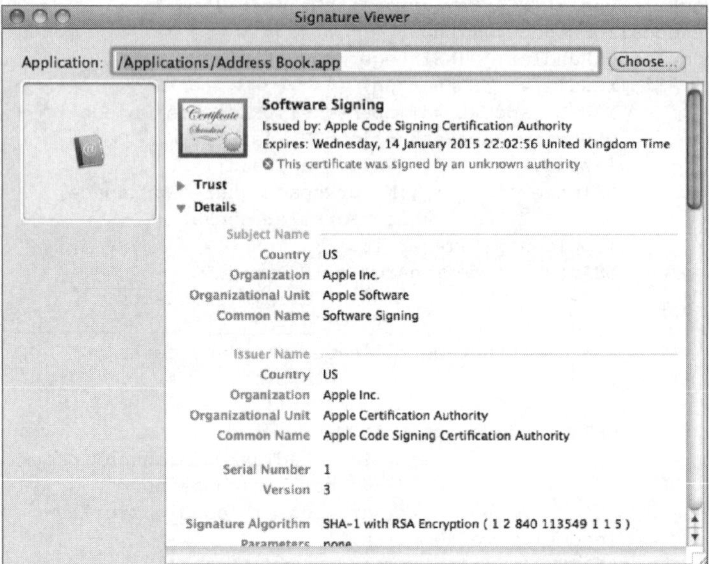

FIGURE 10-3: Viewing the certificate with which Address Book was signed

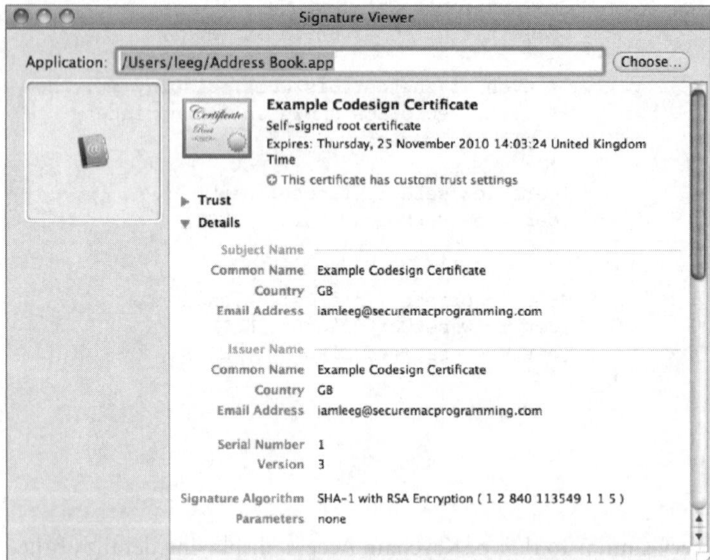

FIGURE 10-4: Address Book identity when re-signed by a different developer

In this example the identities are obviously different, since the subject's name, country, and e-mail address are not the same in both certificates. However, even if an attacker were to spoof these details, the certificate fingerprints (hash codes derived from the public key) are included in the certificate details, and it would be very difficult indeed to duplicate those.

GIVING YOUR CODE TO YOUR USERS

An application should be deployed in a state in which it is ready to use; in particular any protection its assets require in operation should already be in place when its user launches the app for the first time. The deployment or installation process used depends on both the security requirements and the user's environment. Of course on the iPhone there are only two supported deployment techniques — the app store and enterprise deployment. There are more ways to get an application onto a Mac.

Disk Images and Drag-Installs

Because applications are bundles rather than single files, users cannot download an application directly from a web site or FTP server. The simplest solution for most home users is to compress the application in a zip file or disk image, and upload that file to a web server. The user downloads the archive, and depending on the browser configuration may need to open the file or the browser may extract the application automatically. The user can run the application directly from the downloads folder or disk image, but will often move the app into the /Applications folder. This is why the process is called a *drag-install*: the user drags the application from wherever it downloaded to a chosen location.

This deployment style works well for applications with very simple deployment requirements. If your app does not have components running as different users, and no resources must be shared by multiple users, then a drag-install will be easy to implement and easy for users to work with.

The hdiutil tool in Mac OS X is capable of "Internet-enabling" disk images, which are perfect for this type of installation process. Internet-enabling an image turns on extra processing of the image in web browsers. When a user downloads an Internet-enabled disk image, he or she will see your license agreement (if you provided one), and after the user accepts it the operating system extracts the application to the user's downloads folder and moves the disk image file to the trash automatically. To the user, it seems as if there is really just a single application file to download. Safari automatically processes Internet-enabled disk images, but third-party browsers might not, in which case the user will have to go through the same procedure as required after downloading any other disk image file.

To produce an Internet-enabled disk image for your product, create a .dmg file containing the application using Disk Utility or hdiutil. Then run this command:

```
hdiutil internet-enable image-file
```

where *`image-file`* is the name of your disk image.

If your application is going to be distributed with any kind of drag-install scheme, be aware that the user may choose *not* to drag it from the downloads folder, or may put it in a folder other than /Applications. A non-admin user doesn't have permission to write to the /Applications folder, and so may put the app in ~/Applications or another location. Don't rely on knowing what the path to your application on the filesystem is; instead, if you need to find it, get the path to the application's bundle folder using `[[NSBundle mainBundle] bundlePath]`.

Installer Packages and PackageMaker

If the security requirements of deploying your software cannot be met with a drag-install, an installer package is a good choice. Installer packages are useful when your application needs files installed under the ownership of different users, or with custom access controls. The installer offers powerful flexibility for performing custom operations at many steps of the install process, so providing installer packages is also appropriate when deployment of your application or some of its components depends on the configuration of the destination computer. If you need to set up a file with setuid or setgid file-system permissions, an installer package is really the best option. Mac OS X ignores ownership-setting flags on removable media and strips them when copying files, and when a user performs a drag-install the product is owned by that user, losing any original ownership information.

Installing software from a package is more complicated for most users than a drag-install. The packages are installed through the Installer GUI (or the "installer" command-line tool), and there are multiple steps during which the user is asked to make choices or confirm operations, unlike with the very straightforward process of moving an app from the downloads folder to its destination. The process can also be less flexible than a drag-install, with files being deployed to locations specified in the package instead of locations of the user's choice.

For certain customers, though, the installer is a very easy means of deploying software. On sites, such as those of schools and offices, with many computers, administrators use Apple Remote Desktop, which can distribute installer packages to multiple computers on the network simultaneously. Packages can even be added to custom operating system install images that are deployed over the network with NetInstall (part of Mac OS X Server), so that their payloads become part of the standard operating system environment on that network.

When a package is installed on a Mac, it leaves a "receipt" in /var/db/receipts with a "bill of materials," indicating the files that were installed, along with their ownership and permissions settings. This allows later inspection and correction of the installed files, done in Disk Utility's Verify Permissions action. The receipt information does not make uninstalling packages easy. There is no reference-count for files, so an uninstaller cannot tell whether deleting a package's file will affect any other packages, without reading in all the other receipts.

Installer packages are created with the PackageMaker application. PackageMaker supports different package formats compatible with different versions of Mac OS X: all the supported formats can be installed on both Leopard and Snow Leopard. The earlier formats are all bundles (directories with content distributed across multiple files), while 10.5 and above also support a "flat" format, which is a single file, easy to distribute via web servers.

When you launch PackageMaker, you are first asked for the name of your organization (use the reverse-DNS naming convention, as in Figure 10-5) and for the minimum version of Mac OS X the package should target.

To add the payload to the installer package, simply drag the content into the pane on the left side of the package document window. Installed content can be grouped into "choices," so that when a user performs a custom install he can decide which components to deploy. Each option should be named and given a description to help the user understand what it provides (Figure 10-6).

The overall package, and each choice inside the package, can be assigned a set of requirements. In addition to using a selection of canned requirements (Figure 10-7), you can base your requirement on custom Javascript or shell script code. When the requirements for an installation choice are not met, the default action is to disable that choice and remove the ability for the user to enable it. When a package requirement is not met, the package will not be installed.

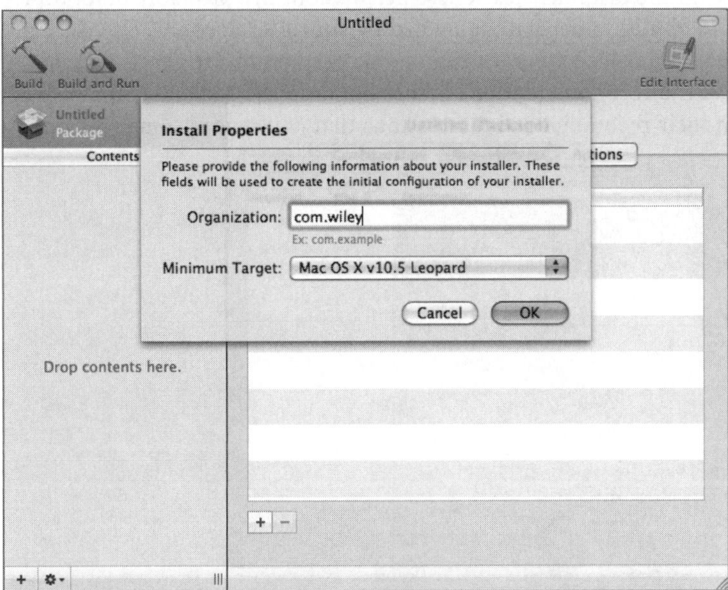

FIGURE 10-5: The first step in creating an installer package

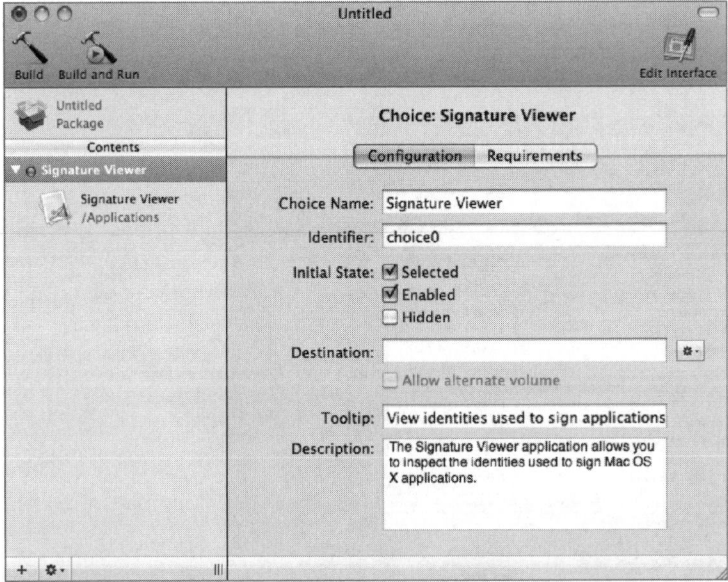

FIGURE 10-6: Configuring a single choice in a package

The owner, group, and permissions for every file in a package can be individually configured (Figure 10-8). Filesystem access control lists cannot be set inside the installer package, but can be applied in a post-install action. When you add files to an installer package, the permissions that are initially set are those that were on the original files. These permissions are probably inappropriate: an application in your Xcode build folder will be owned by your user account. Use the Apply Recommendations button to have PackageMaker set reasonable permissions for each file, but remember to review and correct the recommendations before building the package. Some versions of PackageMaker have bugs in their recommended permissions that can render some files unusable once the package is installed.

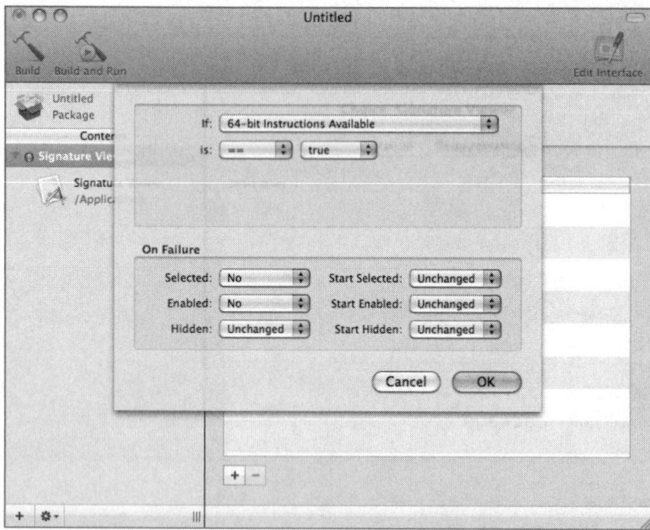

FIGURE 10-7: Configuring installation requirements

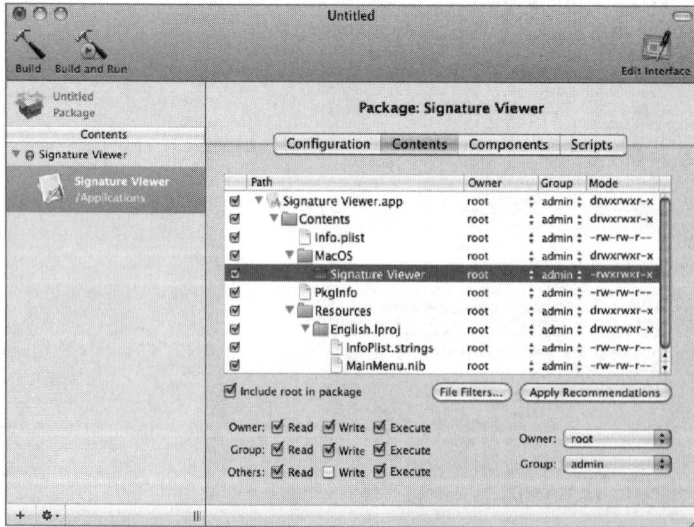

FIGURE 10-8: Setting permissions for installed files

The top-level package configuration allows you to provide a name, a description, and requirements for the whole package. Importantly from a security perspective, you can also choose an identity with which to *sign* the package, as shown in Figure 10-9. A package signature works in a very similar way to a code signature, with one important (and welcome) distinction: the certificate is shown in the Installer user interface when the package is installed (Figure 10-10), so the user can verify the identity of the package distributor.

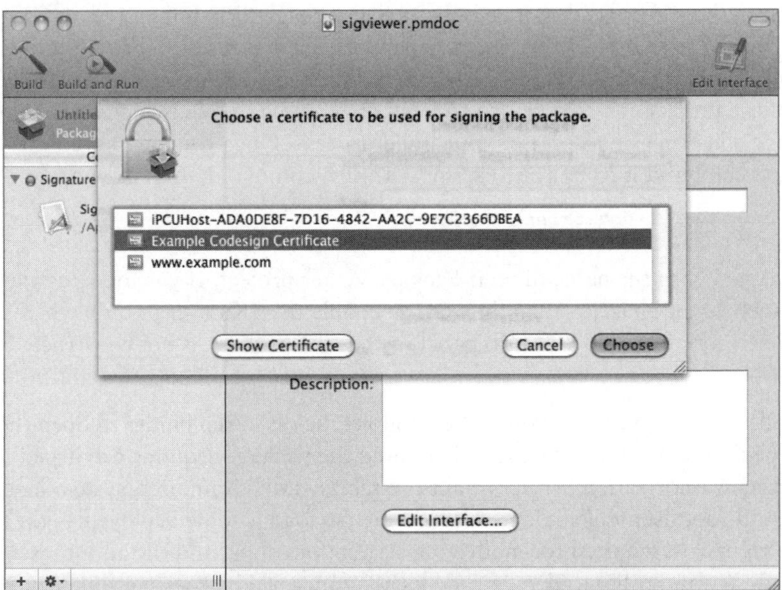

FIGURE 10-9: Choosing an identity with which to sign the package

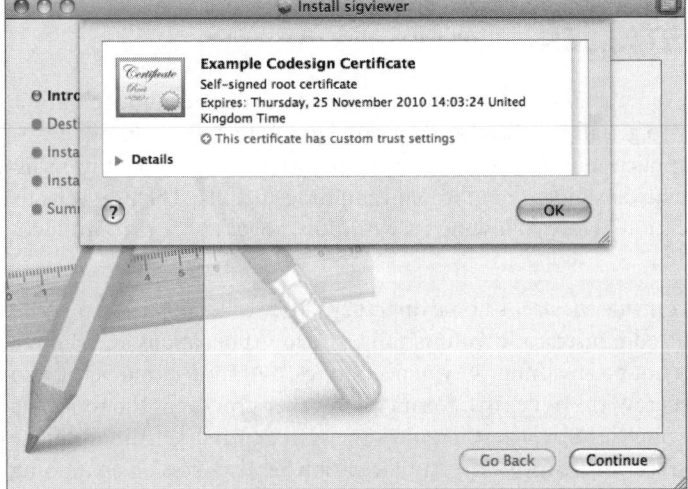

FIGURE 10-10: and verifying the identity in Installer.app

As with signed applications, a signed package is sealed, and cannot be modified without the signature's becoming invalid. Users installing your signed packages can be confident that the package is the same one you intended to give out, and that you are the package author. The choice of whether to *trust* you, once your identity is known, is always left to the user.

By clicking Build you can create the package designed in PackageMaker and test it in the Installer. PackageMaker automatically chooses the most appropriate package format based on the requirements of the package project. Simple projects can be built as flat package files, but more complicated projects (especially those that include other packages as dependencies) will result in *distribution packages* or metapackages: bundles that act as packages and themselves contain or reference other packages. The building of the project can also be driven from the command line, which is useful for automating the package construction as part of your build process. Once you have saved the PackageMaker project, you can build it from a shell script with this command:

```
`xcrun -find packagemaker` --doc filename.pmdoc
```

— where `filename` is replaced with the name of your PackageMaker project. If you are running this as part of an Xcode shell script phase, you might want to enable the "Run script only when installing" option in the shell script phase's Get Info panel so that the package is not constructed with every build.

Once users have downloaded your installer package, they double-click it in the Finder to open the Installer application and begin the installer process. If installing the package requires privileged access, Installer.app requests Authorization Services rights system.install.admin.user, system.install.root.admin or system.install.root.user, depending on where the payload is to be deployed — the root.user and root.admin rights are required for modifying system locations, and the admin.user right for /Applications, /Library and other folders in the "local" domain. The PackageMaker project lets you specify whether the user must log out, restart, or shut down the computer after installation: Installer.app guides the user through fulfilling this requirement.

ROLLING YOUR OWN INSTALLER

The most important fact about custom installers in this book is this: I do not recommend building your own installer. It's a good way to get all the disadvantages of Apple's Installer without any of the advantages. Custom installer applications do not integrate well with the deployment tools used by systems administrators, and are always more complicated than drag-installs. The user effectively needs to deploy the installer application before following its workflow to get at the real product, and then must remove the installer.

To reliably deploy files to locations outside the user's home directory, an installer application needs to acquire appropriate privileges (while administrator accounts can write to /Applications and /Library, the user running the installer might not be an admin, so you need to test). Authorization Services provides a function, AuthorizationExecuteWithPrivileges(), to run an installer process as the root user. A successful call to AuthorizationExecuteWithPrivileges() requires the system.privilege.admin right, and on completion the installer process receives a copy of the Authorization Services session containing that right. The installer should make sure before doing its work that it really did acquire that right, by receiving an external form of the authorization reference (this was covered in Chapter 6: see the section "Factored Applications with Authorization Services"). The application and helper can communicate with each other, to the standard input and output of the installer tool.

AuthorizationExecuteWithPrivileges() will run any command with any arguments based on its input. It is therefore a good target for abuse by an attacker, who can use it to get full super-user access to the system if he or she can modify its input. You should either strongly protect the strings used as arguments to AuthorizationExecuteWithPrivileges(), or follow the advice given at the beginning of this section and avoid writing a custom installer application.

An application that launches a privileged installer is listed in Listing 10-2.

LISTING 10-2: Calling a privileged installer tool [Custom_InstallerAppDelegate.m]

Available for download on Wrox.com

```
- (IBAction)startInstall: (id)sender {
    NSString *helperPath = [[NSBundle mainBundle]
                            pathForAuxiliaryExecutable: @"installhelper"];
    if (nil == helperPath) {
        NSLog(@"no helper tool found");
        return;
    }
    AuthorizationRef auth;
    OSStatus authResult = AuthorizationCreate(NULL,
                                              kAuthorizationEmptyEnvironment,
                                              kAuthorizationFlagDefaults,
                                              &auth);
    if (authResult != noErr) {
        NSLog(@"cannot create auth ref");
        return;
    }
    AuthorizationItem item = { 0 };
    item.name = kAuthorizationRightExecute;
    AuthorizationRights requested, *granted;
    requested.count = 1;
    requested.items = &item;
    authResult = AuthorizationCopyRights(auth,
                                         &requested,
                                         kAuthorizationEmptyEnvironment,
                                         kAuthorizationFlagDefaults |
                                         kAuthorizationFlagExtendRights |
                                         kAuthorizationFlagInteractionAllowed |
                                         kAuthorizationFlagPreAuthorize,
                                         &granted);
    if (authResult != noErr || granted->count != 1) {
        NSLog(@"couldn't pre-authorize to run the installer");
        return;
    }
    AuthorizationFreeItemSet(granted);
```

continues

LISTING 10-2 *(continued)*

```
        authResult = AuthorizationExecuteWithPrivileges(auth,
                                                        [helperPath
                                                         fileSystemRepresentation],
                                                        kAuthorizationFlagDefaults,
                                                        NULL,
                                                        NULL);
        if (noErr != authResult) {
            NSLog(@"couldn't launch helper");
            return;
        }
        // do whatever is needed to watch/inform the installation process.
        AuthorizationFree(auth,
                          kAuthorizationFlagDefaults);
    }
```

DEPLOYING PRIVILEGED HELPERS WITHOUT INSTALLERS

Developers targeting Snow Leopard can install privileged helper tools from inside their applications, without needing a separate installer workflow. The user thus gets the advantage of a simple drag-install deployment, while the application can still make use of a helper process running as the super-user.

The application must "bless" its helpers using the System Management framework. The process of blessing indicates to the operating system which helper tool is associated with which application. The application/helper pair is identified through code-signing identities on both executables, so a helper can be called only by its "owning" application and the application can bless only its own helpers — mitigating the problem with AuthorizationExecuteWithPrivileges() whereby any program can be launched with elevated privileges. The helper can be blessed only if the user can acquire the authorization necessary to modify the system launchd domain, as that is where the helper will be registered.

For the application and helper to identify each other, each must have a code-signing *requirement* it can use to test the identity of other code. The application carries the code-signing requirement for its helper in its Info.plist file, in a dictionary called SMPrivilegedExecutables. The helper also carries the requirement for its application in its Info.plist file, in an array called SMAuthorizedClients. Because the helper is a standalone tool and not a bundle, it cannot use an Info.plist file. Instead the Mac OS X link editor, ld, allows you to embed an Info.plist file into the executable itself. This must also be done for the launchd.plist job specification, which will be extracted and written to the file-system when the job is successfully blessed. In the build settings for the helper, add the following to Other Linker Flags:

```
-sectcreate __TEXT __info_plist $(SRCROOT)/helper-info.plist
-sectcreate __TEXT __launchd_plist $(SRCROOT)/helper-launchd.plist
```

The files helper-info.plist and helper-launchd.plist contain the contents of the Info.plist and launchd .plist dictionaries that will be embedded into the tool. The helper-info.plist file should look similar to Listing 10-3, though note that the bundle identifier and certificate hash should be appropriate for *your* client application and signing identity. Sign an application, then use `codesign -d -rDesktop/requirements.txt Application.app` to find the designated requirement for an app you have signed, where *`Application.app`* is the path to the app. The file requirements.txt on your desktop will include the designated requirement, which contains the certificate hash. The special filename "–" can be used to output the requirements to the Terminal.

LISTING 10-3: Embedded info.plist for a launchd helper [helper-info.plist]

Available for download on Wrox.com

```
<?xml version="1.0" encoding="UTF-8"?>
<!DOCTYPE plist PUBLIC "-//Apple//DTD PLIST 1.0//EN"
"http://www.apple.com/DTDs/PropertyList-1.0.dtd">
<plist version="1.0">
<dict>
        <key>CFBundleIdentifier</key>
        <string>com.example.blesshelper</string>
        <key>CFBundleName</key>
        <string>blesshelper</string>
        <key>SMAuthorizedClients</key>
        <array>
                <string>identifier &quot;com.example.With-My-Blessing&quot; and
certificate
leaf = H&quot;b0482aff7d83c2b6c1b2973135d1bfbbd8b2589f&quot;</string>
        </array>
</dict>
</plist>
```

The embedded launchd.plist just needs to include a unique label, which can be the same as the CFBundleIdentifier in Info.plist. It should also contain any information relevant to the helper's launch conditions so that launchd knows when to initiate the helper — starting launchd jobs was covered in Chapter 4. The arguments to the helper tool will be overwritten when the job is blessed, so do not expect to be able to configure the tool's command line arguments. The helper must be able to get all the information it needs from the environment, or by communicating with its client application.

The Info.plist for the application will look like Listing 10-4. Notice that because I have signed both the application and the helper with the same certificate, the hash value is the same in both this plist and the helper-info.plist files. However, the fact that the requirements call for different identifiers means that the requirements cannot both be satisfied by one of the signed code entities.

LISTING 10-4: Info.plist for an application carrying a privileged helper [With My Blessing-Info.plist]

Available for download on Wrox.com

```
<?xml version="1.0" encoding="UTF-8"?>
<!DOCTYPE plist PUBLIC "-//Apple//DTD PLIST 1.0//EN"
"http://www.apple.com/DTDs/PropertyList-1.0.dtd">
<plist version="1.0">
<dict>
        <key>SMPrivilegedExecutables</key>
        <dict>
               <key>com.example.blesshelper</key>
               <string>identifier &quot;com.example.blesshelper&quot;
```

continues

LISTING 10-4 *(continued)*

```
                    and certificate leaf
= H&quot;b0482aff7d83c2b6c1b2973135d1bfbbd8b2589f&quot;</string>
        </dict>
        <key>CFBundleDevelopmentRegion</key>
        <string>English</string>
        <key>CFBundleExecutable</key>
        <string>${EXECUTABLE_NAME}</string>
        <key>CFBundleIconFile</key>
        <string></string>
        <key>CFBundleIdentifier</key>
        <string>com.example.${PRODUCT_NAME:rfc1034identifier}</string>
        <key>CFBundleInfoDictionaryVersion</key>
        <string>6.0</string>
        <key>CFBundleName</key>
        <string>${PRODUCT_NAME}</string>
        <key>CFBundlePackageType</key>
        <string>APPL</string>
        <key>CFBundleSignature</key>
        <string>????</string>
        <key>CFBundleShortVersionString</key>
        <string>1.0</string>
        <key>LSMinimumSystemVersion</key>
        <string>${MACOSX_DEPLOYMENT_TARGET}</string>
        <key>CFBundleVersion</key>
        <string>1</string>
        <key>NSMainNibFile</key>
        <string>MainMenu</string>
        <key>NSPrincipalClass</key>
        <string>NSApplication</string>
</dict>
</plist>
```

With this infrastructure in place, the application is able to bless its helper and get it installed by launchd. Blessing must be done before the application's first attempt to use the helper, so in Listing 10-5 the application startup code tests whether the helper has already been installed, and blesses it if it hasn't been. Blessing the helper tool requires an Authorization Services privilege, so if the application depends on the helper to a great extent it will not be useful until the helper has been blessed.

Available for download on Wrox.com

LISTING 10-5: Blessing a privileged helper [With_My_BlessingAppDelegate.m]

```
- (void)applicationDidFinishLaunching:(NSNotification *)aNotification {
    NSString *jobLabel = @"com.example.blessHelper";
    NSDictionary *jobDict = SMJobCopyDictionary(kSMDomainSystemLaunchd,
                                                    jobLabel);
    if (jobDict) {
        //nothing to do
        [jobDict release];
        return;
```

```
    }
    // the job must be blessed
    AuthorizationRef auth;
    OSStatus authResult = AuthorizationCreate(NULL,
                                              NULL,
                                              kAuthorizationFlagDefaults,
                                              &auth);
    if (noErr != authResult) {
        NSLog(@"error creating auth ref");
        return;
    }
    AuthorizationItem item = { 0 };
    item.name = kSMRightBlessPrivilegedHelper;
    item.valueLength = 0;
    item.value = NULL;
    item.flags = 0;
    AuthorizationRights requestedRights;
    requestedRights.count = 1;
    requestedRights.items = &item;
    // gain the right to install the helper
    authResult = AuthorizationCopyRights(auth,
                                         &requestedRights,
                                         kAuthorizationEmptyEnvironment,
                                         kAuthorizationFlagDefaults |
                                         kAuthorizationFlagExtendRights |
                                         kAuthorizationFlagInteractionAllowed,
                                         NULL);
    if (noErr != authResult) {
        NSLog(@"unable to acquire right to bless the helper");
        AuthorizationFree(auth, kAuthorizationFlagDefaults);
        return;
    }

    // now bless the helper
    NSError *error = nil;
    BOOL blessed = SMJobBless(kSMDomainSystemLaunchd,
                              jobLabel,
                              auth,
                              &error);
    AuthorizationFree(auth, kAuthorizationFlagDefaults);
    if (!blessed) {
        NSLog(@"failed to bless the helper");
        [NSApp presentError: error];
        return;
    }
    NSLog(@"successfully blessed the job");
}
```

Once the job has been blessed, an operating system component called launchdadd copies the helper tool into /Library/PrivilegedHelperTools, so that the application can be relocated without launchd's losing the helper. The helper's launchd.plist is extracted from the executable and written out to /Library/LaunchDaemons, and the job is loaded into the system launchd domain from that moment and on every subsequent reboot of the computer.

RESPONDING TO SECURITY PROBLEMS

No matter how diligent you are, there's always the possibility that a vulnerability will be discovered in your application. A threat you decided was not of a high enough priority to address might actually turn out to be targeted by an attacker after all. A security researcher, eager to get his first post to the Bugtraq mailing list, could decide to publicize a vulnerability you thought unlikely to be uncovered. None of this should be surprising — the goal of the risk analysis and mitigation techniques presented here has always been to expend a reasonable effort to *reduce* the risk of attack, not obliterate the chance of attack at all costs. Anyway, for whatever reason, you now have a vulnerable application in the wild, and your customers have it, too.

Handling Security Bug Reports

Once a vulnerability has been discovered in your application, you need to manage a reaction to that vulnerability. Of course it must be fixed, but that is only part of the process. You must communicate with the reporter and your customers to ensure that the risks are well understood, and update your view of the risks facing your application.

Many security vulnerabilities are initially discovered by security researchers, who have established expectations regarding the handling of their discoveries. An ethical researcher will contact you to describe the bug, expecting you to acknowledge this contribution to your application's security. Such acknowledgment comes in the form of permission for the researcher to publish details of the vulnerability on his or her web site and on mailing lists like Bugtraq, once you have issued a fix. The researcher will also expect to be credited for the discovery in the release notes for your update.

It is both good form and a good idea to accept these conditions, establishing with the researcher a timeline over which you will issue an update and he or she can publish the research. Allowing security researchers to receive the credit they deserve for improving your application obviously assists them a great deal, but it also increases their desire to work with you in the future. Researchers who feel they are not receiving appropriate recognition have been known to forgo privately contacting developers, instead publicizing security defects before the bugs have been addressed.

No matter who discovered the bug, it is now time to address it and work on a fix. Based on the DREAD classification (from Chapter 1, remembering now that the "Discoverability" is moot, since the vulnerability is discovered), you can derive an idea of the issue's severity, and use that estimation to triage the defect and prioritize fixing it. Consider whether the issue as reported represents the entire extent of the problem: could a buffer overflow reported in a particular text field be part of an endemic problem with handing strings? You're going to have to release a security update anyway, so it makes sense to make the most efficient use of the resources you spend on the update. If you fail to address an issue closely related to the discovered bug, you can be sure it will be found quickly and you will need to issue another update.

Go back to your threat model, and try to identify threats similar to that realized by the reported vulnerability. Might these threats be more likely now that a related vulnerability has been discovered? Was the impact as bad as you expected, or worse? By asking these questions and updating your threat model accordingly, you stand a better chance of having an up-to-date view of the real threats your application faces and a good idea of which to deal with next.

Providing Software Updates

The easier it is for your users to download and deploy updated versions of your application, the more likely they are to be running the most up-to-date version you supply. If updating is entirely automatic you can be fairly confident that security updates will be rapidly applied, with customers downloading the updates as a matter of course. Many of the security exploits that have affected Microsoft's Windows have targeted vulnerabilities *that were already patched*, on computers where the patch had not yet been applied. Malware authors actually reverse-engineer the patch to find the vulnerability it addresses, and use that knowledge in creating their malicious code. This points to a need to reduce or close the window between discovering a vulnerability and the time when your customers are all using a patched release of your software.

Writing your own updating mechanism is not a good strategy, unless you have very particular requirements that render any of the existing update frameworks unacceptable. The security requirements surrounding reliable downloading and installation of software updates mean a lot of risks to address, ultimately meaning you will spend plenty of time developing code that has nothing to do with your application's use cases.

The main risk associated with automatic updating involves the availability of the "payload" — i.e., your application. If the update process fails during the deployment of an update, then the application might be left in an unusable state, its identity with respect to code signing might be broken, or the application might disappear from its installed location completely. You can fix any other bug by shipping an updated version, but if your update mechanism itself fails, users will be left with an old, and buggy, version of your application.

The other significant risk is the possibility of an attacker's injecting different software into the update process, effectively replacing your application with a Trojan horse. As the application would appear to come from you as a legitimate update, users would not necessarily question the authenticity of such a malicious update.

A very common solution to the problem of delivering simple, reliable software updates to Mac OS X applications is to use the Sparkle framework. Sparkle is an open-source project, available from `http://sparkle.andymatuschak.org/`. Adopting Sparkle in a Cocoa application requires no code changes; just add the framework to your project and instantiate a SUUpdater object in Interface Builder (Figure 10-11).

The Sparkle updater retrieves information about available updates from an RSS feed called an *appcast*. Entries in an appcast are normal RSS articles, with an enclosure element providing a link to the application download. When Sparkle retrieves an article with a newer version of the application than its own, it asks the user whether to install the updated version. If the user agrees, Sparkle manages the download and installation of the newer version.

Both your appcast feed and your download files should be distributed through an SSL connection (i.e., over the https protocol) so that Sparkle can verify the authenticity of the update files. Sparkle offers additional integrity protection in the form of update signatures, based on an asymmetric key pair. A "man in the middle" attacker can intercept SSL communications and replace the appcast feed and the update files, but the attacker cannot generate correct update signatures. You can use the generate_keys.rb script included in the Sparkle distribution to create a DSA key pair:

```
heimdall:Sparkle 1.5b6 leeg$ ruby Extras/Signing\ Tools/generate_keys.rb
Generating DSA parameters, 2048 bit long prime
This could take some time
[...]
Generating DSA key, 2048 bits
read DSA key
writing DSA key

Generated private and public keys: dsa_priv.pem and dsa_pub.pem.

BACK UP YOUR PRIVATE KEY AND KEEP IT SAFE!

If you lose it, your users will be unable to upgrade!
```

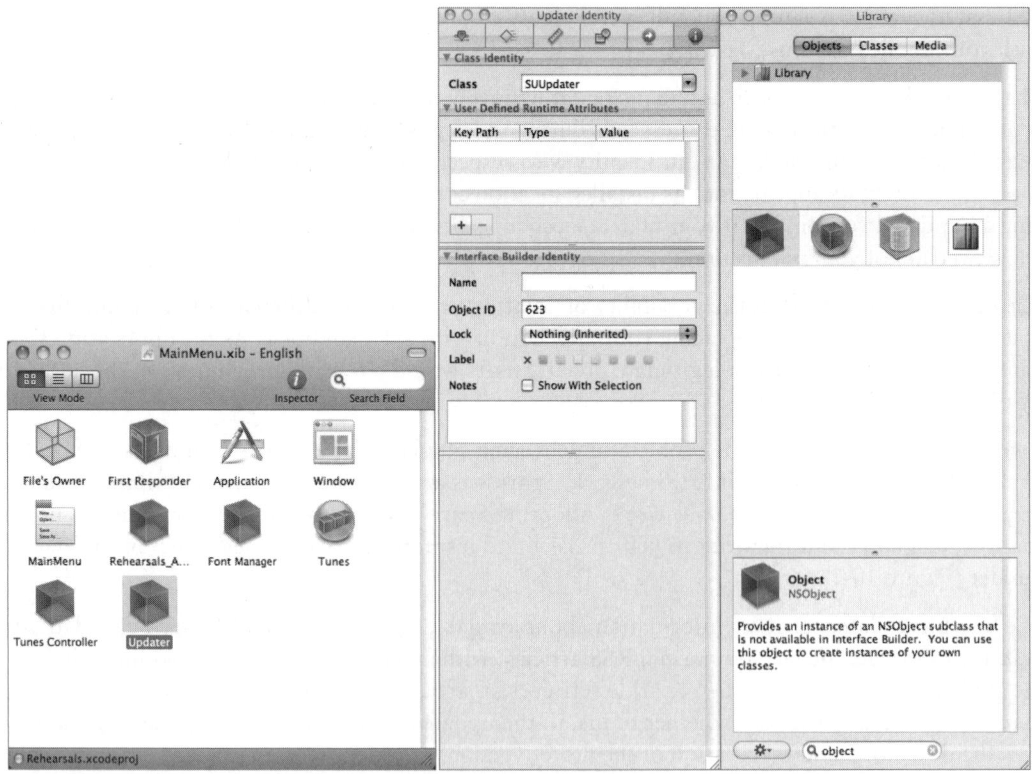

FIGURE 10-11: Integrating Sparkle with a Cocoa application

The private key must be kept secret, and needs to be made available only to the computer from which you publish updates to the download web server. The public key needs to be bundled in your application, as that is the information Sparkle needs to verify the legitimacy of downloaded updates. Once you have generated a private key you use the sign_update.rb script to generate a signature:

```
heimdall:Sparkle 1.5b6 leeg$ ruby Extras/Signing\ Tools/sign_update.rb \
SigViewer-
1.0.1.zip
dsa_priv.pem
MC0CFHaOZ+LOrYuwa8IpP6V8jrcaygM3AhUA4o8kRX5mOLRj0GfHY8rZEj446M4=
```

The line of output is the signature, derived from the content of the update and your private key. You should add that line to a special property in the enclosure field of the appcast article for the update, called sparkle:dsaSignature. When Sparkle downloads the update, it verifies the signature using the public key, to determine that you really did generate the downloaded software.

Be specific in documenting the security content of your product updates. Users do not need enough detail to be able to exploit the vulnerabilities themselves, but they will appreciate being given the opportunity to understand the risks involved for themselves when evaluating the update. Remember that even when you're using Sparkle, updating is not a fully automatic process and takes users away from using your application for their work: the least you can do is explain why this is necessary. Users who understand that there is a real risk associated with using the earlier version of your software are more likely to update, so don't be shy about publicizing the security content. Being seen as proactive about addressing security issues is good PR, and outweighs any benefit that might be gained from burying the problems.

SUMMARY

Developing a nice complete threat model and using it to mitigate risks in your application development is fine, but you then need to get the product into your customers' hands. Ideally the application should be in a secure and usable state directly after deployment, so that most users can just launch and use it without needing to concern themselves over security. If there are reasons for users to take additional steps to improve or obtain security in the application, make sure the processes and reasons are clearly documented as close to the workflow as you can manage.

Despite your best efforts in preparing a secure application, the possibility of a vulnerability's being discovered is still real. You can be prepared for this eventuality by having a strategy for liaising with security researchers and customers about the severity of reported vulnerabilities, and a process for deploying patched versions of your product.

Automatic software update systems come with their own risks, and take time to implement correctly. This is time you are not spending on improving your application; find a well-trusted framework like Sparkle and use that, if it meets your security requirements.

11

Kernel Extensions

WHAT'S IN THIS CHAPTER?

- The kernel's security environment
- Vetoing filesystem access

Writing kernel extensions, or KEXTs, is a very different matter from building user applications. Your kernel extension code receives an unmatched level of access to the operating system's facilities, and a corresponding elevated level of care must be taken to stop that access from being abused.

Apple's kernel programming guide tells you to keep out of the kernel. This is a good warning, and I want to reinforce it here. Only ship a kernel extension if your product cannot be implemented without it. The restrictions and requirements on kernel code are entirely unlike those on a user application, and there are many pitfalls that can lead to systems becoming unresponsive with no chance for users to save their data.

For some scenarios in which you might consider developing a KEXT, there are alternatives that allow you to avoid it. If you want to implement a new filesystem, use the MacFUSE library, available at `http://code.google.com/p/macfuse/`. *MacFUSE implements a small, well-tested virtual filesystem KEXT that calls out to user-level applications to read and write data. You write an application that interacts with your filesystem and responds to callbacks from the KEXT — avoiding the need for you to deal directly with kernel development.*

If you need to write a device driver, consider using the user-level library provided by Apple, IOKit.framework, to stay out of the kernel. For many USB and FireWire devices, IOKit.framework is the best option for writing stable device drivers.

THE KERNEL ENVIRONMENT

The conditions that exist inside the kernel are more similar to those encountered by a Mac OS 9 application than to those encountered by a user-level application on Mac OS X. Many of the protections that separate Cocoa applications from each other and from system processes do not exist for kernel extensions, meaning that you have to be much more defensive in your development practices. While it is rare to encounter a malicious KEXT (though the kernel would certainly be a good place for a *root kit* — code that hides malware from the user — to dwell), poorly programmed KEXTs are likely to interfere with each other or the correct operation of the kernel. Any such interference is very likely to lead to a loss of stability or availability of the entire operating system: the dreaded *kernel panic*.

The main problem you will encounter in developing your KEXT is a lack of *memory protection*. At the user level, each application has its own memory allocation, which is reserved by the kernel and inaccessible to other processes. Any application is responsible for any reading or writing in its allocated memory, and while that doesn't entirely preclude memory access problems, it does reduce the attack surface to issues introduced by the process owning the memory. In contrast, any code running in the kernel's memory space (the code in Apple's kernel, xnu, itself, and all loaded KEXTs) has the same permission to all memory. A buffer overflow in your KEXT could end up writing into memory in another KEXT or the kernel, causing a change in behavior, a kernel panic, or even execution of code introduced by an attacker. Code running in the kernel has unfettered access to the computer's resources, with even more permission than the root user. If your KEXT permits attackers to introduce their own programs to the kernel, you really do give up the keys to the kingdom.

To mitigate the risk of buffer overflow in your KEXT code, review the techniques presented in Chapter 9 and ensure that you are applying each wherever it is appropriate to do so. Where possible, implement the KEXT's functionality as a reusable library that can be loaded into both the kernel and user-level environments. Doing so means that you can test the behavior with the many user-level debugging tools available, including Instruments and the guarded malloc library.

Memory must be used sparingly in the kernel, as well as correctly. Because all the kernel extensions share the same address space, your KEXT code is vying for the same memory as all the network filters, device drivers, and other KEXTs on the computer, in addition to memory used by the main kernel code to track processes, threads, and even memory allocations. Some of the more important data in the kernel and its extensions is stored in *wired* memory, which cannot be paged out to disk and so remains permanently in RAM. The more wired memory used, the less RAM available for other tasks, including user-level processes, which leads to an overall reduction in system performance. Once the kernel runs out of memory in its address space, or finds all the RAM allocated to wired memory, there is nothing left for it to do except panic and stop execution.

You need to consider carefully your use of other resources, not just memory. While the kernel is implemented as a multi-threaded, re-entrant environment, meaning that multiple processes can all simultaneously be executing kernel or KEXT code, many of the functions and resources are protected by locks to ensure that no two processes are accessing any one of them concurrently. Your KEXT can cause a *deadlock* — a stalemate condition in which the process cannot continue — by incorrect acquisition of in-kernel locks. Because you cannot predict which other KEXTs will be in use on any Mac and which locks those KEXTs require to perform their own processing, there is no easy way to avoid these deadlock conditions. The only robust solution is to avoid taking locks at all, which might not be feasible. Try to avoid requiring multiple simultaneous locks, as the chance of deadlock rises exponentially with the number of locks in use.

A particular deadlock problem that occurs in KEXT code and doesn't require an interaction with any third-party software is the *kernel upcall deadlock*. Consider a KEXT that, like MacFUSE, communicates with a user-level process to do its work. The KEXT has a critical section, which is protected by a lock. When the KEXT receives a request, it takes the lock before calling out to the user-level process. That process then makes a system call that ends up entering the KEXT code again — only this request cannot continue because the lock cannot be taken. As the KEXT is now stalled waiting for the lock, the *original* request cannot be completed, and all subsequent requests stall too.

You can avoid kernel upcall deadlocks by avoiding the use of locks completely. If that is not possible, consider treating your user-level process specially, allowing it to use a code path in the KEXT that bypasses the critical section. If that is not possible, then implement a get-out handler, a special piece of watchdog code that allows the KEXT to escape the deadlock by canceling pending requests or exiting the critical section without completing the KEXT's work.

The watchdog handler described here is an implementation of a security pattern called "in emergency, break glass." In this pattern, the usual mode of operation of an application is suspended to allow a special situation to be handled. A hospital emergency room provides a good example of this pattern in use. Most of the time an emergency room has a waiting room where patient details are recorded, and a small number of triage nurses are tasked with prioritizing the cases that come in based on the severity of symptoms and danger presented to the patient. If the emergency room is deluged with patients, the staff switches to a disaster-handling mode in which patient details are not taken and triage is limited to a quick visual inspection.

The code executed inside the kernel is not subjected to many of the access controls used to protect resources from unauthorized use by user-level applications. In particular, all the computer's memory and files are accessible to kernel code. A mistake in kernel code could accidentally allow a user to have read or write access to an asset that this user is not permitted to use, or conversely deny access to a permitted resource. The easiest way to mitigate this problem is to avoid it, not providing users access to resources from the kernel space. There are situations in which kernel-level access to assets must be provided. Rather than replacing the existing access controls, you should aim to augment those controls. Do not give a final answer to access control questions inside your KEXT, but choose simply whether to deny access to the resource. If your KEXT does not expressly forbid access to the asset, allow the operating system to fall through to its default access controls. In this way you have reduced the number of potential problems from two to one: false rejection of legitimate access.

FILESYSTEM ACCESS AUTHORIZATION WITH KAUTH

Kauth (kernel authorization) is a KEXT API for providing custom access limitations to kernel objects. Kauth provides access controls for signaling or tracing processes, but is most commonly used for filesystem objects. A kauth KEXT indicates one of three access permissions for any test it is asked to perform: allow, deny, or defer. A defer result indicates that the current KEXT has no opinion about whether access should be granted or denied. If multiple kauth KEXTs are loaded, their tests are carried out in turn when access to a file or folder is requested. A deny response from any one of the tests leads to the requested access being forbidden. If, across all the interrogated KEXTs and the kernel's default access controls, there was at least one allow response and no deny responses (i.e., all other KEXTs responded defer), access is granted.

The kauth interface is entirely generic, so you can use it for implementing access controls to your own kernel-level objects defined in a kernel extension. You need to arrange for the extension to call the kauth_authorize_action() function before every attempt to use one of your objects.

Kauth is implemented as a callback mechanism, requiring any interested KEXT to register a function that will be called for every attempt to access a file. The function can use any information available to choose whether to limit access. Because user-level processes don't get to read the file until after your KEXT callback has returned, you can even rewrite the contents if the file needs sanitizing. This ability to modify files in the kernel gives you the ability to change files beyond the user's permission, so as with granting access it is important not to make changes that the system administrator would not have authorized.

Introduction to the VFS

As you saw in Chapter 3, there are plenty of different filesystems used on Mac OS X. If kauth modules had to support each of these individually, they would never get released; there are always additional third-party filesystems that you have not yet come across and would need to integrate into the KEXT. Inside the kernel, filesystems are abstracted into a common view called the Virtual Filesystem (VFS), and kauth KEXTs can work with this abstraction.

In the VFS, each volume or mounted device is represented by a virtual filesystem (lowercase vfs). The actual format of each vfs is unimportant, as filesystem drivers on the Mac expose APIs that convert vfs requests into appropriate actions on each filesystem. Every file, folder, link, or special file on the filesystem is represented by a virtual node (vnode), the VFS layer's equivalent of a file descriptor. As with vfs operations, filesystem drivers expose vnode functions that convert common processes into filesystem-specific implementations. Kernel APIs that work with filesystems, files, and folders — including the system call interfaces that can be used from user-level applications — see the universal, abstract VFS interface instead of implementation details about all the different supported filesystems.

Every attempt to access a file or folder in an application leads to an attempt to perform one or more VFS operations. Some operations are certain to create multiple requests. Reading from an HFS+

compressed file, for example, requires reading the extended attributes (to discover the compression scheme) and the data stream (to extract the compressed content) — these are separate actions on the file's vnode. Applying kauth filtering to operations in the file operation scope already results in a fast stream of requests: listening in the VFS operation scope is like connecting to a fire hose. However the file operation scope (which contains notification of system call events like open, close, and unlink) is not suitable for access control — it provides notification of interesting events only after they happen. Operations in the VFS scope must wait for all kauth callbacks to complete before the kernel can decide whether the operations are allowed — a lengthy callback function can lead to very poor performance across the whole operating system.

Vetoing Filesystem Operations

This section explains Listing 11-1, which is a kauth kernel extension to filter access to the filesystem. In particular, it denies the right for a process to open a file with the string DARN in its path (a nod to the Politically Correct Filesystem sample code distributed by Apple with the Rhapsody operating system, back in the late 1990s). The filter does not stop the root user from accessing any file, to avoid breaking operating system services.

LISTING 11-1: Vetoing filesystem operations in the kernel [pcfsfilter.c]

Available for download on Wrox.com

```
static int politicallyCorrectListener(kauth_cred_t credential,
                                      void * context,
                                      kauth_action_t action,
                                      uintptr_t arg0, //VFS context
                                      uintptr_t arg1, //vnode
                                      uintptr_t arg2, //parent folder vnode
                                      uintptr_t arg3  //on-return error
                                      ) {
    if (action & KAUTH_VNODE_READ_DATA) {
        vnode_t vn = (vnode_t)arg1;
        if (vn == NULL) {
            return KAUTH_RESULT_DEFER;
        }
        char fileName[MAXPATHLEN] = {0};
        int fileNameLength, getPathResult;
        getPathResult = vn_getpath(vn,
                                   fileName,
                                   &fileNameLength);

        if (getPathResult != 0 || fileName[0] == '\0') {
            return KAUTH_RESULT_DEFER;
        }
        char *rudeFile = strnstr(fileName, "DARN", strlen(fileName));
        if (rudeFile == NULL) {
            // not found
            return KAUTH_RESULT_DEFER;
        }
        else {
            printf("found a rudely-named file: %s\n", fileName);
            // always allow root user
```

continues

LISTING 11-1 *(continued)*

```
            uid_t callingUid = kauth_cred_getuid(credential);
            if (0 == callingUid) {
                return KAUTH_RESULT_DEFER;
            }
            else {
                int *error = (int *)arg3;
                *error = EACCES;
                return KAUTH_RESULT_DENY;
            }
        }
    }
    else {
        //uninterested in these operations
        return KAUTH_RESULT_DEFER;
    }

}

static kauth_listener_t listener;

kern_return_t pcfsfilter_start (kmod_info_t * ki, void * d) {
    listener = kauth_listen_scope(KAUTH_SCOPE_VNODE,
                                  politicallyCorrectListener,
                                  NULL);
    if (listener != NULL) {
        printf("installed kauth handler\n");
        return KERN_SUCCESS;
    }
    else {
        printf("error installing kauth callback\n");
        return KERN_FAILURE;
    }
}

kern_return_t pcfsfilter_stop (kmod_info_t * ki, void * d) {
    if (listener) {
        printf("removing kauth callback\n");
        kauth_unlisten_scope(listener);
    }
    return KERN_SUCCESS;
}
```

The functions `pcfsfilter_start` and `pcfsfilter_stop` are responsible for installing and removing the kauth callback, respectively. The callback is executed in the thread of a process making a system call, so there may be callbacks "in flight" at the time the listener is removed. The preceding filter is fast and doesn't rely on external state, so any callbacks in progress when the listener is removed will quickly finish without problems. More complicated filters need to ensure that all in-flight callbacks have finished using shared resources before the KEXT's stop function cleans up those resources.

The main work of the filter is in the kauth callback, `politicallyCorrectListener`. It checks whether the operation being attempted is the read operation, and makes an access control decision only if it is. The action parameter to a VFS-scope callback is a bitfield, as a single operation could cause multiple VFS actions. If the action does need to be filtered, the callback recovers the path of the file represented by the vnode and tests it for appropriate content.

SUMMARY

Developing custom software for the Mac OS X kernel is very different from developing OS X applications, and the risks associated differ accordingly. It is possible for a KEXT developer to circumvent access controls, modify kernel data, or bring the entire operating system to a standstill with buggy or insecure code. Wherever possible, developers should stay away from the kernel, though there are some tasks that can be performed only within a KEXT.

The kernel provides an access control framework called kernel authorization, or kauth. Kauth allows developers to discover and react to a variety of events on the operating system, though it is most frequently used for providing custom access control to the filesystem. Access control must be implemented at the VFS level — VFS is a virtual filesystem that abstracts all the details of the various real filesystems in use on Mac OS X.

12

Conclusion and Further Reading

WHAT'S IN THIS CHAPTER?

- Where to go now
- Bibliography and other reading material

You have now seen one approach to reasoning about security and how to model the threats faced by your users. You've also had a tour through the operating system features that Apple provides to implement the security controls or countermeasures required by your Mac or iPhone application. You've seen how to avoid introducing vulnerabilities in the way you use the Objective-C language, and how to get your secure application into the hands of your customers. We've covered a lot of ground, but not all of it will be relevant to your application. Use those parts that directly relate to the use cases in your app, and leave the rest for future reference.

The one aspect of Cocoa application security that is relevant to every single application on the platform — including those you have not yet shipped — is the threat model. You cannot apply appropriate security countermeasures if you have not considered the goals and concerns of your users, or the motivations and techniques that attackers will employ. The threat modeling process described in Chapter 1 is just one possible technique. Its principal benefit is that it's a methodical approach based on industry practice: the references given in "Further Reading" offer a wealth of information about similar techniques. I have found that this process has worked for me on a number of projects, but if you decide it's not for you, don't worry. As long as you find a way to systematically and comprehensively discover the security requirements for your application, you can apply the techniques in this book to deliver a risk-free app your customers can use with confidence.

Of course, if you do find a better approach than the threat-modeling technique presented in this book, I'd love to hear about it. Industry practices only improve if we all act together as a community, sharing those things that work, and discussing why some things don't work. Send any suggestions to `iamleeg@securemacprogramming.com`.

In Chapter 1 I described the nonsensical "ultimate security system": a computer encased in concrete and sunk to the bottom of the ocean. I hope that this book has shown you that a secure application can be a beautiful, accessible, and easy-to- use application. Apple gives you standard, friendly interfaces for working with identities (Chapter 2) and certificates (Chapter 5), which makes it easy for you to provide security management interfaces in a way users will understand. In fact an application that's easier to use will be a *safer* application, as it will support users' aims and reduce the risk that they will make mistakes.

As public awareness of information security issues increases, the demand for secure applications will also rise. Armed with an understanding of Cocoa's security features, you will be well-placed to meet this demand.

FURTHER READING

Advanced Mac OS X Programming, Mark Dalrymple and Aaron Hillegass, Big Nerd Ranch, 2006. A book on the OS X APIs that picks up where the introductory textbooks leave off, covering directory services, authorization, networking and IPC techniques.

The CERT C Secure Coding Standard, Robert C. Seacord, Addison Wesley, 2009. A very comprehensive set of recommendations and prohibitions to follow in developing with the C language. A nice feature of the secure coding standard is that it provides at-a-glance risk assessment for each of the rules presented, so you can choose the level of compliance you want to achieve.

Foundations of Mac OS X Leopard Security, Charles S. Edge Jr., William Barker, and Zack Smith, Apress, 2008. A guide for users interested in applying security countermeasures to Mac OS X and Mac OS X Server, Foundations is a comprehensive overview of the security capabilities in Mac OS X.

Introduction to Cryptography, 2nd edition, Hans Delfs and Helmut Knebl, Springer, 2007. A mathematically intensive description of the common cryptography functions and protocols in use today.

iPhone Forensics, Jonathan Zdziarski, O'Reilly Media, 2008. An excellent and succinct summary of the security features of iPhone OS and the limitations of those features.

Mac OS X Internals, Amit Singh, Addison Wesley, 2007. The undisputed bible for people who need to understand the innards of Mac OS X, particularly the XNU kernel. Written for OS X version 10.4 (Tiger) on PowerPC systems, this book remains useful.

Managing Information Security Risks: The OCTAVE Approach, Christopher Alberts and Audrey Dorofee, Pearson Education, 2003. The Operationally Critical Threat, Asset and Vulnerability Evaluation technique describes an approach to risk analysis very similar to that presented in Chapter 1 of this book, but is applied to entire businesses instead of software products.

OS X Exploits and Defense, Paul Baccas (ed.), Kevin Finisterre, Larry H., David Harley, and Gary Porteous, Syngress, 2008. A book about using Mac OS X for "black hat" purposes, including wardriving and vulnerability detection. A good summary of the third-party security tools available on the Mac, unfortunately presented with a bias toward antisocial applications.

Practical Unix & Internet Security, 3rd edition, Simson Garfinkel, Gene Spafford, and Alan Schwartz, O'Reilly Media, 2003. A good overview of UNIX security concerns from the point of view of systems and network administrators. It's a bit dated now, but it's good to see what the risks are for a computer in a corporate network.

Security and Usability: Designing Secure Systems That People Can Use, Lorrie Faith Cranor and Simson Garfinkel (eds.), O'Reilly Media, 2005. A collection of essays and computer science papers exploring the human factors relevant to information security. The final chapter, "Why Johnny Can't Encrypt," is an absolute classic, discussing a "usable" GUI that still provides a poor user experience because the security requirements are too complicated for users to understand.

Security Patterns: Integrating Security and Systems Engineering, Markus Schumacher, Eduardo Fernandez-Buglioni, Duane Hybertson, Frank Buschmann, and Peter Sommerlad, John Wiley & Sons, 2006. A collection of reusable patterns applicable to a range of security-engineering disciplines from requirements engineering to vulnerability triaging. A lot of the design- and architecture-level patterns presented can be implemented to mitigate the risks described in this book.

Threat Modeling, Frank Swiderski and Window Snyder, Microsoft Press, 2004. A good introduction to the concepts of risk analysis, threat modeling, and vulnerability classification. The threat-modeling workflow presented by Swiderski and Snyder is very time-consuming, but very comprehensive.

Writing Secure Code, 2nd edition, Michael Howard and David LeBlanc, Microsoft Press, 2003. Covers many code-level vulnerabilities as well as testing, review, and documentation procedures useful for finding and understanding security problems in code. While the book mainly focuses on Windows, a lot of the content is applicable to any application code.

INDEX

A

E

N

Q

R

S

T

U

V

W